CHINA IN THE GLOBAL ECONOMY

ENVIRONMENTAL TAXES

Recent Developments
in China and OECD Countries

ORGANISATION FOR ECONOMIC CO-OPERATION AND DEVELOPMENT

ORGANISATION FOR ECONOMIC CO-OPERATION AND DEVELOPMENT

Pursuant to Article 1 of the Convention signed in Paris on 14th December 1960, and which came into force on 30th September 1961, the Organisation for Economic Co-operation and Development (OECD) shall promote policies designed:

- to achieve the highest sustainable economic growth and employment and a rising standard of living in Member countries, while maintaining financial stability, and thus to contribute to the development of the world economy;
- to contribute to sound economic expansion in Member as well as non-member countries in the process of economic development; and
- to contribute to the expansion of world trade on a multilateral, non-discriminatory basis in accordance with international obligations.

The original Member countries of the OECD are Austria, Belgium, Canada, Denmark, France, Germany, Greece, Iceland, Ireland, Italy, Luxembourg, the Netherlands, Norway, Portugal, Spain, Sweden, Switzerland, Turkey, the United Kingdom and the United States. The following countries became Members subsequently through accession at the dates indicated hereafter: Japan (28th April 1964), Finland (28th January 1969), Australia (7th June 1971), New Zealand (29th May 1973), Mexico (18th May 1994), the Czech Republic (21st December 1995), Hungary (7th May 1996), Poland (22nd November 1996) and Korea (12th December 1996). The Commission of the European Communities takes part in the work of the OECD (Article 13 of the OECD Convention).

OECD CENTRE FOR CO-OPERATION WITH NON-MEMBERS

The OECD Centre for Co-operation with Non-Members (CCNM) was established in January 1998 when the OECD's Centre for Co-operation with the Economies in Transition (CCET) was merged with the Liaison and Co-ordination Unit (LCU). The CCNM, in combining the functions of these two entities, serves as the focal point for the development and pursuit of co-operation between the OECD and non-member economies.

The CCNM manages thematic and country programmes. The thematic programmes, which are multi-country in focus, are linked to the core generic work areas of the Organisation (such as trade and investment, taxation, labour market and social policies, environment). The Emerging Market Economy Forum (EMEF) and the Transition Economy Programme (TEP) provide the framework for activities under the thematic programmes. The EMEF is a flexible forum in which non-members are invited to participate depending on the theme under discussion. The TEP is focused exclusively on transition economies. Regional/Country programmes, providing more focused dialogue and assistance, are now in place for the Baltic countries, Brazil, Bulgaria, China, Romania, Russia, the Slovak Republic (a candidate for accession to the OECD), and Slovenia.

FOREWORD

There is growing interest and emerging experience in applying environmental taxes in both China and OECD countries. This is driven by several factors. From an environmental policy perspective, the search for more efficient and cost-effective approaches for implementing domestic environmental policies has intensified. From a fiscal policy perspective, there have been growing pressures to reduce rates of personal and corporate rates of income tax and to offset this by broadening the tax base. This provides opportunities to introduce new environmental taxes within the broader context of "green" tax reform, which aims to integrate environmental considerations into the design of tax systems. Such reform is likely to focus on three complementary approaches: removing or reforming environmentally-damaging

subsidies and tax measures, restructuring existing taxes and introducing new environmental taxes.

A review of the evolving experience in applying environmental taxes in China and OECD countries was the focus of a workshop held at the OECD on 5-6 October, 1998. Particular emphasis was given to examining trends in the use of environmental taxes in the two groups of countries and the institutional and political contexts that influence their implementation; identifying the key policy challenges and opportunities in reforming environmentally-damaging subsidies, drawing on lessons from the energy and agriculture sectors; and reviewing experience in the design and implementation of environmental taxes in the energy and transport sectors.

This publication presents the papers from the workshop, the second on environmental policy issues organised within the framework of the OECD's Programme of Dialogue and Co-operation with China[1]. The views expressed are those of the individual authors and do not necessarily represent the views of the OECD, its Member countries or of the institutions to which the authors are affiliated. The volume is published on the responsibility of the Secretary-General of the OECD.

---

[1] The proceedings of the first workshop are published as OECD, 1997: *Applying Market-Based Instruments to Environmental Policies in China and OECD Countries*. OECD. Paris.

TABLE OF CONTENTS

PART 3: DESIGNING AND IMPLEMENTING ENVIRONMENTAL TAXES IN THE ENERGY AND ROAD TRANSPORT SECTORS

RAPPORTEURS' REPORT

Ma Zhong
Institute of Environmental Economics
Renmin University, China

and

Alberto Majocchi
Department of Public and Territorial Economics
University of Pavia, Italy

Part 1:   Overview of Trends in OECD Countries and China

Key Issues

In many OECD countries there has been a trend towards reductions in taxes on personal income and profits and increases in consumption taxes and social security contributions.   These shifts have provided an opportunity for governments to introduce environmentally-related taxes within the broader context of "greening" tax systems.   In 1995, environmentally-related taxes accounted for between 3.8% and 11.2% of total tax revenue in 17 OECD countries, with an average of 7%, while direct taxes accounted for 35% of the total, consumption taxes for 32% and social security contributions for 25%.   As a percentage of GDP, environmentally-related taxes vary between 1% and 4.5%.

China undertook a major reform of its tax system in 1994, resulting in a policy framework that is more consistent with the needs of market-based economy.   Since the country adopted its "open door" policy to foreign investment and increased trade linkages in 1978 tax revenue has grown rapidly, the main source being income tax paid by industry and business.   Six environmentally-related taxes have been introduced within China's tax system: a natural resource tax, a consumption tax, an urban construction and maintenance tax, a vehicle use tax, a fixed asset investment direction adjustment tax and a land use tax.

The main issue regarding the establishment of environmental taxes is their consistency with the objectives and principles of fiscal policy.   The same principles on which modern tax systems are based - equity, neutrality, transparency, sustainable revenue generation, flexibility and administrative efficiency - should apply also to the design and implementation of environmental taxes.

Overview of the Themes

In his paper *Environmental Taxes in OECD Countries: An Overview*, Jean-Philippe Barde reviews recent developments and notes that environmental taxes are potentially an effective way to simultaneously protect the environment and improve economic efficiency.   He suggests that it is possible to achieve positive economic structural adjustments that promote greater efficiency by internalising costs, by eliminating subsidies and taxes that have adverse economic and environmental impacts and by introducing appropriate tax shifts. From a social point of view, reducing taxes on labour and employment seems particularly desirable in countries where unemployment is high and widespread.

The achievement of a "double dividend"[1] through fiscal reforms is not a "free lunch", however. The design of efficient environmental polices should draw upon a combination of economic, regulatory and voluntary instruments. Environmental taxes are not a panacea. In some cases public health concerns will require a ban on hazardous substances and products; in other cases the administrative costs of implementing environmental taxes may outweigh their benefits.

Green tax reform should involve three complementary policies: eliminating tax distortions, restructuring existing taxes and introducing new environmental taxes. While the primary objective of taxation systems is often to obtain maximum revenue with minimum distortions and impact on behaviour patterns, and thereby achieve fiscal neutrality, green tax reform is generally implemented in a context of a constant tax burden in which new environmental taxes tend to offset reductions in existing taxes.

Susan Himes and Flip de Kam note in their paper *Environmentally-Related Taxes : A Tax Policy Perspective* that three specific concerns are frequently raised concerning the introduction of environmental taxes:

- the stability of the revenue. Apart from taxes on energy and transport the principal goal of environmental taxes is not to raise large amounts of revenue. In addition, a reduction in the tax base related to environmentally-harmful products or activities is a desirable outcome of this kind of taxation. Concerns have therefore been raised about the sustainability of revenues from environmental taxes;

- adverse distributional effects. Regressive effects may be countered by compensating lower income groups through reductions in assessable personal income tax;

- competitiveness and economic growth. To date, environmental taxes do not appear to have had a negative impact on competitiveness, either at the sectoral level or for OECD economies as a whole.

In general, but particularly for an emerging market economy like China, the design of environmental taxes should be guided primarily by practical considerations of simplicity, uniformity and transparency. Environmental taxes work best where the taxpayer is easily identifiable, the number of taxpayers is relatively limited and the pollution is easy to quantify. If there are many polluters, instead of measuring waste emissions governments could adopt a second best approach of taxing an input or other activity that is associated with the polluting activity. As more information about pollution costs becomes available, it should become progressively easier to set the tax rate at the appropriate level.

In their paper *Taxation and the Environment in China: Practice and Perspectives* Jinnan Wang et al. describe the current situation and possible future developments concerning environmental taxes in China. China has established a tax system that is beginning to approximate that of OECD countries.

---

[1]   Much debate has focused on the so-called employment-environment double dividend. This refers to the potential for addressing unemployment by offsetting reductions in taxes on labour (including employers' social security contributions) by the introduction of new environmental taxes on, *inter alia*, energy and waste disposal through landfilling.

Within this system the six environmentally-related taxes identified in the previous section account for about 8% of national tax revenue.

China introduced a nation-wide pollution levy system in 1981. It has played a positive role in promoting air and water pollution control and in environmental capacity building, but it needs a radical reform. In particular:

- a re-definition of the rate schedules upon which pollution charges are set, shifting from a focus on charging for discharges that exceed national and local standards to charging for all discharges;

- changing the revenue distribution system so that all the money collected is channelled to the Ministry of Finance. A specific budget appropriation could be established to fund investments in environmental protection;

- adopting a loan system and charging market interest rates for all projects.

The greening of China's tax system should focus on the natural resource tax, the consumption tax, the urban maintenance and construction tax and the vehicle use tax. The scope of the reform should be to include as many environmental costs as possible within the relevant tax categories and to reflect this in the tax rates. Preferential tax rates could be established for investments in environmental protection.

Key Messages from the Discussion

Several issues emerged from the discussion. First, there is a large gap between theory and practice in implementing environmental taxes. This is reflected, for example, in uncertainties about the environmental effects of environmental taxes. These effects depend on the tax structure and aspects related to country's differing economic structures. In particular, environmental effectiveness has been impaired by granting various exemptions, applying reduced rates and recycling payments for competitiveness reasons to sectors affected by the tax.

Second, the impact on competitiveness. There is a widespread fear that environmental taxes could impact negatively the international competitiveness of firms or sectors. A clear distinction should be drawn between short- and long-term effects of environmental taxes. It is also important to consider the use of the revenue collected. If the revenue is used to reduce the rates of distortionary taxes or to promote investments that are able to improve the economic effectiveness of the firms, environmental taxes and green tax reform more generally could help improve the overall competitiveness of the economy in the long run.

Third, distributional effects. It is important to verify that the introduction of environmental taxes does not have unacceptable impacts on low-income families. Where such impacts occur, a case by case analysis is required before any compensation measures are introduced.

Fourth, the stability of the revenue stream. In some cases there could be a trade-off between environmental effectiveness and ensuring revenue sustainability. For example, an improvement in environmental conditions could result in a decrease in the amount of revenue raised through a tax linked to emissions of polluting substances.

There was consensus that further progress in green tax reform is urgently needed given the crisis that progressive income taxation is facing everywhere. This implies a shift from taxing income and savings to taxing the consumption of goods and natural resources. This could have not only positive environmental effects but also enhance economic efficiency.

The notion of a "double dividend" for employment and the environment, even if controversial on theoretical grounds, could be an important pillar in promoting fiscal reform From a practical perspective, this implies that the environmental effects of fiscal reform should be taken into account from the outset. At the same time the introduction of environmental taxes should be supported by a reduction in distortionary taxes. In this manner general welfare could be raised and negative distributional impacts avoided.

Green tax reform should promote an efficient use of the revenue raised by environmental taxes, reduce labour costs in the sectors concerned and improve economic competitiveness. Shifting the burden of taxation away from labour and towards the use of natural resources may be the optimal approach to achieve the objectives of environmental effectiveness and economic efficiency.

The issue of revenue stability should not be overemphasised. In the long run if environmental taxes raise less revenue than projected the need for public expenditure will be reduced given the improvement of environmental conditions.

Environmental taxes should be administratively simple, i.e. easy to assess and with low collection costs. This requirement is particularly important in China which faces serious constraints on the administrative capacity at national and sub-national levels of government to collect tax revenue. More specifically, given that existing environmentally-related taxes account only for about 8% of China's overall tax revenue consideration needs to be given to the prioritisation of the tax collection effort.

Part 2: Reforming Environmentally-Damaging Subsidies

Key Issues

In general, the reform or removal of environmentally-damaging subsidies can have several potential benefits: increase economic efficiency, reduce government budget expenditure and improve environmental quality. However, the environmental impacts of subsidies may vary, depending on site- and country-specific circumstances, economic output, existing environmental policies and tax regime, and the assimilative capacity of the affected environment. Careful analysis of the subsidy's purpose, design and implementation and impacts on the environment is necessary.

In OECD countries, agriculture and energy are the two major sectors that receive subsidies from governments. In China a larger number of sectors presently receive direct or indirect subsidies from the government. Both China and OECD countries need to identify those sectors where subsidy reform or removal is most urgent from an environmental point of view.

Several approaches exist to reform or remove progressively environmentally-damaging subsidies. Key issues concern the need to address distributional and competitive impacts, building stakeholder support for reform and designing strategies that are appropriate for different sectors and for different economic structures.

10

Overview of the Themes

In their paper *Subsidy Policy and the Environment in China*, Chazhong Ge et al. note that subsidy policy in China is the result of price distortions in a planned economy. During the period of transition to a market economy, these price distortions are being gradually removed. Prices for water, energy and fertilisers are being progressively liberalised so that market signals are playing a larger role. The authors state that China is now eliminating some subsidy policies in an effort to reduce national government expenditure. Further efforts are needed to address the pricing of those resources which remain set by the state. In the view of the authors, when China's policy-makers develop subsidy policies they are only concerned with the economic and social aspects. They suggest that environmental considerations also need to be taken into account.

In *Gains from Reducing Coal Support, With Particular Reference to the UK Experience*, Jan Pieters takes the coal industry in the UK as a case study to examine the effects of re-orienting economic support away from production towards other, less environmentally-damaging objectives. Pieters argues that although it is impossible to quantify precisely the effect of support removal, important beneficial effects have been obtained. These include improvements in environmental quality, enhanced transparency in institutional arrangements and the creation of new markets.

Alexander Golub and Elena Strukova's paper focuses on the *Reform of Subsidies to the Energy Sector: The Experience of Russia*. They conclude that in the long run subsidy elimination could have positive economic and environmental impacts and help promote structural change in the economy. In particular, it could create incentives for sustainable development in the energy and related sectors. They also note that subsidy elimination might have different impacts in different sectors and regions of Russia. In general, the impacts are positive but in some regions subsidy elimination could encourage rapid economic growth and a concomitant rise in pollution. In this scenario, subsidy elimination should be complemented by a robust environmental policy framework that is well enforced by regulatory and other policy instruments.

In his paper *Reforming Agricultural Policies and the Environment: The Experience in OECD Countries*, Wilfrid Legg suggests that the "baseline" to assess environmental performance in agriculture has often been distorted over a long time period by significant levels of support in many countries. By reducing the level of support from commodity and input-linked policies, and associated trade measures, the reform of agricultural policies should improve resource use efficiency, reduce inappropriate farming practices on environmentally sensitive land and limit the excessive use of chemicals. These outcomes would directly benefit the environment. It is not clear, however, what environmental "services" the market would deliver if support to agriculture were removed.

Key Messages from the Discussion

The papers were particularly helpful in summarising the history of subsidy polices in the energy, agriculture and other sectors in China and OECD countries. Reforming subsidy policies could yield multiple benefits. In terms of environmental effects, it would mitigate environmental pollution, improve environmental quality and promote the wider use of cleaner, more resource efficient technologies. Such reform could also increase the transparency of policies and improve institutional and economic efficiency.

China's experience shows that during the early phase of transition from a planned to a market economy subsidy policies could help in addressing price distortions and in balancing the demand and supply of goods and services. Care is needed, however, to ensure that such policies do not themselves create new or exacerbate existing distortions. As the economic reform process in China deepens and broadens to encompass a wider range of sectors, a comprehensive review and reform of subsidy policies is becoming urgent.

Particular concerns in China about the reform of environmentally-related subsidies relate to the need to balance national economic development goals, social stability and distributional equity. The redefinition of property rights is also an important factor related to the reform of subsidy policies. For example, an increasing number of small- and medium sized state-owned enterprises are being privatised or corporatised and urban residents are being encouraged to purchase their government-subsidised apartments. These measures should contribute to both reducing the volume and rationalising the structure of existing subsidies.

It is difficult to state a general conclusion about the reform or elimination of subsidies. There are many types of subsidies with various objectives. In addition, there are hidden subsidies and policy measures which indirectly provide economic support. A case-by-case analysis is required that takes account of the specific economic, environmental, social and political context in which the subsidy operates.

The two following factors should be considered in an analysis of the implications of subsidy reform or elimination:

−   the need to avoid sudden price increases through a drop in the level of subsidies, with negative distributional effects; and

−   the impact on competitiveness following any price increase associated with the decrease in the level of subsidies.

These factors could be addressed by a gradual implementation of the subsidy reduction policy and by complementary measures targeted on supporting efficiency improvements, with due regard to distributional equity and competitiveness concerns.

Part 3:   Designing and Implementing Environmental Taxes in the Energy and Road Transport Sectors

Key Issues

Simplicity and efficiency have been the main concerns in designing and implementing environmental taxes. As the number of pollutants subject to taxation increases, the administrative costs also rise and the calculation of effective tax rates becomes more complicated. To ensure that environmental taxes are transparent, acceptable and environmentally effective, it is important that the tax base is directly related to the externality targeted.

There is a trade-off between the objectives of abating pollution and raising revenue. The key issue is how to establish a tax rate that provides an incentive for polluters to change their behaviour and which will also generate a sustainable source of revenue. There is a potential conflict of interest between the environmental and taxation authorities, the former being more concerned with the environmental effectiveness of the tax while the latter is more interested in the amount of revenue raised. This raises the issue of how to establish coherent policy goals that meet short- and longer-term objectives.

The use of the revenue raised by environmental taxes is a further issue. In particular, the choice between earmarking the revenue or providing it to the general budget. Earmarking can be a source of public funds for environmental investments but it raises various problems with regard to economic efficiency, programme lifespan, responsiveness to evolving public policy priorities and the risk of institutional and interest group capture. In this context, earmarking should be considered with great caution. There may be a case for earmarking as a transitory approach in economies in transition but, in general, revenue raised through environmental taxes should be channelled to the general budget.

In terms of pollution abatement cost, taxes are more transparent than command and control policies. There are concerns, however, that environmental taxes may have a negative impact on the competitiveness of industry both domestically and internationally. To address this concern some governments have introduced exemptions or rebates to affected industries as well as establishing mechanisms to recycle the revenue to contributors.

Overview of the Themes

In their paper *SO_2 Charge and Tax Policies in China: Experiment and Reform*, Dong Cao et al. indicate that China has accumulated valuable experience in designing and implementing SO_2 charges to address problems of increased acid rain deposition and SO_2 emissions. A reform of the SO_2 charge is underway, based on the results of a trial programme begun in 1993. The authors recommend that the charge rate for SO_2 emissions should be increased gradually until it is four times its existing rate (i.e. eventually reaching 200 yuan/per ton). With this charge rate, 6.67 billion yuan per annum could be raised in the two acid rain control zones defined by the government, providing substantial funding for SO_2 control measures. The longer-term goal is to introduce an SO_2 tax in China, an idea that has attracted much interest among the relevant government ministries. This tax could be included within the existing natural resource tax and consumption tax. The tax rate should be linked to the sulphur content of coal, providing an incentive to reduce the extraction and consumption of high sulphur coal.

In his paper *Energy Taxes: The Danish Model*, Hans Larsen describes the Danish system of taxes on energy. These comprise three elements:

- energy taxes on oil, coal, gas and electricity, where an attempt has been made to balance the rate for the different fuels according to their energy content;

- a CO_2 tax on energy, where the rate for the different fuels is balanced according to the amount of CO_2 emitted during combustion;

- an SO_2 tax on energy, where the rate depends on the sulphur content of the fuels or the net amount of SO_2 emitted during combustion.

The Danish government has strongly promoted the use of voluntary agreements between the authorities and individual companies as a means of enhancing energy efficiency. These agreements are well suited to the most energy-intensive companies. The Danish Energy Agency can enter into agreements with the following types of companies:

- those with particularly energy-intensive processes;

–   those utilising light manufacturing processes where the tax burden amounts to more than 3 percent of the company's sales minus the company's purchases, but at least to 10 percent of the company's sales.

At the same time as the decision was made to introduce CO_2 and SO_2 taxes, it was decided that the revenue raised should be returned to contributors in the form of investment subsidies for energy savings. A pool has also been set aside to support smaller companies and the agriculture sector. Some of the revenue is also recycled by reducing employers' labour market supplementary pension payment and their labour market contribution. This reduction will be increased in the period 1996-2000, whilst the investment subsidies for energy savings will be gradually phased out.

Gustav Teir in his paper *(Environmental) Energy Taxes: The Experience of Finland* recalls that environmental energy taxation was introduced in Finland in 1990, when taxes based on the carbon content of fuels were adopted to supplement conventional fuel taxes. From 1990 to 1992 environmental energy taxes were levied solely on primary energy sources containing carbon, i.e. coal, natural gas, fuel oils and milled peat. This tax consisted of a basic rate and an additional rate. The basic rate was assessed on oil products; the additional tax was an environmental tax linked partly to the carbon content of fuels. Compared with other fuels, however, the additional taxes on gasoline and diesel oil were significantly higher than their carbon content justified.

In 1993 the tax rate was almost doubled and a new electricity tax based on energy content was adopted, shifting the emphasis in taxation from emissions to energy content. At the same time, an additional tax was imposed on liquid fuels used in transport based on criteria wider than just carbon content. A CO_2 tax was introduced in 1994 as a combined CO_2/energy tax. Seventy-five per cent of the tax was determined on the basis of the carbon content and the remaining 25% according to the energy content.

Until 1997 Finland was the only country that did not grant reductions in energy taxation to industry. Compared with other Nordic countries the energy taxation of industry was much higher, which provoked concern among Finnish industry about the economic impact on their operations vis-à-vis their foreign competitors. Energy intensive industries in Finland now receive a partial refund of their energy taxes. In addition, provisions for exemptions and reductions in the Finnish tax system are both smaller in number and magnitude than in other European countries.

The paper by Stephen Perkins on *Environmental Taxation of Transport* reports the results of an investigation by the European Conference of Ministers of Transport (ECMT) into the external costs of transport. The rates of existing road freight charges in four different European countries are examined (France, Germany, the Netherlands, Switzerland), showing that excise duties on diesel are the largest source of revenue in these countries. In evaluating the impact on the transport sector of changes to the tax rate, it is misleading to examine transport charges in isolation from taxes on labour and capital. The difference in net taxation between the countries examined is roughly double when transport charges only are considered. This reduces to 25% when taxes on labour and capital are included in the analysis. More significantly, the ranking of countries from low to high rates of taxation changes dramatically. The real impact of increases in fuel taxes on the marginal costs of road haulage is therefore less than might be expected and the profitability of the road haulage industry in these countries is more sensitive to rates of taxation on labour than to changes in the rate of diesel excise duty.

The experiences presented vary widely. China has been focusing on controlling emissions from coal burning because coal is its dominant energy source. Policy priorities in OECD countries are different since their energy sources are more diverse.

OECD countries have accumulated more experience than China in the design and implementation of environmental taxes in the energy and transport sectors. China is still in the process of reforming its general tax system so that it more closely matches that established in market economies. However the goals of this reform in the short-, medium- and long term have been identified and agreed among the relevant government ministries. The expectation is that China's tax system will in the near future include a stronger environmental dimension. In particular, provision within the natural resource tax and consumption tax for an SO_2 tax linked to the sulphur content is a possibility.

The present SO_2 charge in China is a fine on industries or firms for non-compliance with national standards. The charge rate is too low to provide an effective incentive to modify the behaviour of polluters and a large share of the revenue is recycled back to polluting firms to fund investments for pollution control. The charge should be transformed ultimately into a tax, set at an appropriate rate to stimulate modification of polluters' behaviour, and the revenue used to fund, *inter alia*, investments in environmental protection nation-wide.

Effective internalisation policies in the transport sector should be based on a mix of regulatory and pricing instruments. Existing regulations could be better enforced, tightened progressively and combined with incentives designed to encourage achievement of stricter standards. Existing charges and taxes should be differentiated to link them more closely to external costs. Higher use-charges for transport may be appropriate in many cases and the role of policy instruments such as electronic km-charges and road pricing should be further examined. Preliminary estimates suggest that transport costs might increase on average by 15-30% in Europe as a result of full internalisation of externalities in this sector.

Environmental externalities are closely linked to fuel use. This suggests that in the short term fuel taxes could represent the main fiscal approach to internalisation in view of their simplicity and relatively low cost of application. The distance driven, which corresponds in part to fuel consumption, is a factor in NO_x, CO, VOC, benzene and particulate emissions. It seems appropriate therefore to include an element in fuel charges for the internalisation of their residual costs, while differentiation of fixed charges - purchase taxes or annual vehicle or road fees - should be used as a complement to reflect differences in specific emissions according to vehicle type, installation of a catalytic converter, etc. In the field of regulations, fuel quality standards and vehicle emissions standards constitute the main policy tools to reduce air pollution from road transport.

Urban road pricing could be used to internalise air pollution externalities. Cities might also be given the flexibility to set emissions standards that are stricter than the national standards. Another option is allowing cleaner-fuelled vehicles only into the city centre. Seeking to eliminate subsidies to public transport would probably be counter-productive. In regulating public transport systems, the public service functions required of railways, bus services, etc. must be identified and paid for by the state under a contractual arrangement that makes clear the services purchased and the funds to be paid.

In China a first step in developing an environmentally efficient tax system in the transport sector is to ensure a closer coverage of infrastructure costs through charging. Efficient pricing implies that long-term marginal social costs should be charged for users of fully utilised or congested infrastructure. When capacity is far from fully utilised and capacity costs are zero, only short-term marginal costs should be charged. Since one-half of infrastructure costs can be considered fixed and not dependent on road use, a combination of use-charges and fixed charges could ensure both economic efficiency and a fair allocation of costs.

Conclusions

It is timely for China and OECD countries to investigate further the role of environmental taxes and green tax reform. Environmental issues are emerging as one of the top priorities on China's political agenda and there is a huge demand for financing environmental investments. China is also reforming its general taxation system, which provides an opportunity to integrate environmental considerations from the outset.

The Chinese government has expressed its strong concerns about the potential impact on economic development (especially production and consumption choices and competitiveness) if China introduces environmental taxes. The distributional implications of environmental taxes is also an important consideration in a context where maintaining social stability is a high priority. The lessons and experiences of OECD countries could play a useful role in showing to the Chinese authorities what could be the actual benefits and costs of a wider adoption of environmental taxes and the implications of such taxes for sustainable development. This also underlines the need for both groups to understand better the specific policy and institutional contexts that influence the design and implementation of environmental taxes.

To deepen the analysis and dialogue on the role of environmental taxes it might be useful to undertake some in-depth case studies. These might focus on an existing programme (e.g. the pollution levy programme in China; implementation of environmental taxes in an OECD country) or focus on an urgent policy issue (e.g. control of SO_2 emissions in the energy sector).

This collaboration would be mutually beneficial. On the one hand, the analysis would assist Chinese policy-makers in designing more effective environmental policies and support efforts to integrate environmental considerations into sectoral policies. On the other hand, OECD countries would understand better the scale and diversity of environmental challenges that China is addressing and the commitment of the Chinese government to undertake domestic actions that contribute to solving global and regional problems, such as climate change and acid rain deposition.

PART 1:

OVERVIEW OF TRENDS IN
OECD COUNTRIES AND CHINA

ENVIRONMENTAL TAXES IN OECD COUNTRIES:
AN OVERVIEW

H23
Q28

Jean-Philippe Barde[1]
Environment Directorate, OECD

While the use of economic instruments to protect the environment (such as taxes, charges or tradable permits) has spread considerably in OECD countries, it may be said that the emphasis placed by some countries on environmental taxes, especially as part of new "green" tax reforms, reflects the latest generation of economic instruments. This tendency is due to many factors [Barde (1992, 1997), OECD (1994)], particularly the need to improve the effectiveness of policies based to a great extent on rigid and cumbersome regulations, which are costly both for the public authorities and for the regulated sectors, and which are difficult and sometimes impossible to implement. It has also appeared that "integrating" environmental policies effectively with sectoral policies (such as energy, transport or agriculture) is the best way of making such policies more effective [OECD (1996a)]. In this context, fiscal instruments provide an ideal means of injecting appropriate signals into the market, of eliminating or reducing structural distortions (such as unsuitable energy and transport tariffs) and of internalising externalities, while at the same time improving the efficiency of existing measures. The end result is a real structural readjustment of economies.

Other factors which account for the tendency include the need for more tax revenues to finance the general government budget, as well as specific environmental funds or programmes, and the search for "alternatives" or complements to traditional regulations, as part of the move towards "regulatory reforms" or "deregulation" which currently prevails in most industrialised countries [OECD (1997a)].

1.0   Environmental Taxes and Fiscal Reform

Most countries, and OECD countries in particular, urgently need to introduce more flexibility and efficiency in their economic structures. This implies, *inter alia*, adjusting tax systems in order to reduce distortions and increase market flexibility, and making environmental policies more effective. Most OECD countries have undertaken significant tax reforms since the end of the 1980s, chiefly in two ways: first by reducing tax rates in the higher income tax brackets (which fell on average by ten points between 1986 and 1995) and lowering corporate tax (down 8.5 points over the same period); secondly, by broadening the tax base, especially for indirect taxes (VAT and consumption taxes)[2]. This thorough

---

[1]   The views expressed are those of the author and do not necessarily reflect the views of the OECD or its Member countries.

[2]   However the share of income taxes in total tax revenue decreased only slightly because of the broadening of the base of these taxes.

overhaul of tax systems has provided an excellent opportunity to introduce an environmental dimension in taxation, a policy which is now referred to as "green tax reform" or "greening tax systems".

This greening of taxation may consist of three complementary policies: eliminating tax distortions, restructuring existing taxes, and introducing new environmental taxes, or "ecotaxes".

1.1 EliminatingTax Distortions

Many fiscal measures can either directly or indirectly produce adverse effects for the environment. One such measure is *direct subsidies*. For example, *farming subsidies* (estimated at 297 billion dollars a year in OECD countries in 1996, or 1.3 per cent of GDP) are one of the causes of overfarming of land, excessive use of fertilisers and pesticides, dry soil conditions and other problems [OECD (1996b)]. Similarly, irrigation water is often charged below its real price, which leads to wastage (in the United States, irrigation water is subsidised to the extent of 75 per cent). In the area of *energy*, subsidies on coal, the most polluting fuel, still came to 7 billion dollars in 1996 in six OECD countries, which admittedly was lower than the 16.5 billion dollars for 1989. It is estimated that subsidies to industry amounted to 49.3 billion dollars in 1993; when subsidies encourage the use of certain raw materials and greater energy consumption, there can be negative fallout in terms of recycling and waste.

Table 1: Changes in support levels in some countries

Support for :	1986-1988[a]	1989	1991	1993	1995	1996	Remarks
Agriculture							
Total transfers	279	264	332	337	333	297	US$ billion
	253	239	269	287	255	234	ECU billion
Total transfers as % of GDP	2.2	1.8	2.0	1.9	1.5	1.3	
PSE %[b]	45	37	42	42	40	36	
Coal output	13.2	16.4	10.3	8.0	8.1	6.7p	Total PSE[b] in Germany, UK, Spain, Belgium and Japan (US$ billion)
Industry[c]		39.0	54.2	49.3			Declared net public expenditure in OECD countries (US$ billion)

p - preliminary

[a] 1987 for coal output statistics.

[b] Production subsidy equivalent: measure of the value of monetary transfers to producers, determined by policies in any given year, including transfers from both consumers and taxpayers.
PSE % is total gross PSE expressed as a percentage of output value.

[c] Support for industry overlaps other estimates, such as support for energy.

Source: OECD (1998).

A second category of distortion arises from tax measures (tax variations or exemptions). For instance, *coal*, the most polluting fuel, is also the least taxed; in OECD countries in 1995, the average coal tax per barrel of oil equivalent was 0.3 dollars in 1995, compared with 22 dollars for oil (IEA). The *transport* sector, a major source of pollution and other harmful effects, is affected by many distortions (see Box 1). For instance, the virtually systematic undertaxing of diesel oil in many countries has led to a constant increase in the number of diesel vehicles, which are more polluting and noisy, and to undue development of road transport of goods. In countries of the European Union, the proportion of diesel fuel comes to between 30 and 61 per cent (except for Finland, where it is only 16 per cent) [EUROSTAT (1996)]. Figure 1 clearly shows that the proportion of diesel vehicles rises in countries where the tax differential is highest. In France, diesel vehicles accounted for 47 per cent of the market in 1994.

There are many more examples of that kind. It is clear that the "greening" of taxation has to start with a systematic inventory and a correction of fiscal measures (subsidies and taxes) which are harmful for the environment. This tidying up should be done before any thought is given to introducing ecotaxes. The OECD report on *Improving the Environment Through Reducing Subsidies* [OECD (1998)], presented at the ministerial-level OECD Council meeting in April 1998, concluded:

"If an environmentally detrimental activity is subsidised, the method which consists in creating a price differential in favour of other solutions less harmful to the environment, by subsidising less detrimental activities, is only second best. It is preferable to remove all support for the environmentally detrimental activities and to internalise any external costs they may entail." (p. 41).

Figure 1: Diesel Vehicles as % of New Registrations
(Selected EU Countries)

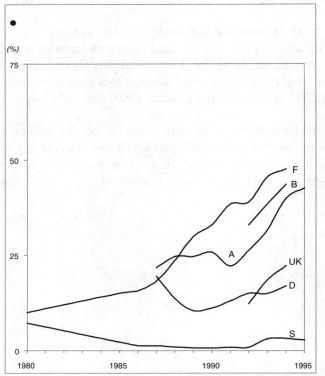

Source: EUROSTAT(1996a)

Box 1: Environmentally Detrimental Tax Measures
in the Area of Transport

Parking space	Free (or reduced-cost) parking space provided by employers is often not included as taxable income (benefit in kind).
Company cars	The use of company cars for commuting is not considered a taxable benefit in some countries.
Deductibility of commuting expenses	The costs of commuting may be deductible from taxable income and in many countries no distinction is made between the use of public transport and private cars.
Refund of commuting costs	Commuting costs (by private car or public transport) are reimbursable on a non-taxable basis in a number of OECD countries, which allows employers to reimburse employees using private cars (according to the distance from home to work) free of income tax.
Under-taxation of diesel oil	In the European Union, diesel oil is always taxed less than lead-free petrol (except in the United Kingdom).
Tax exemption of aviation fuel	Encourages growth of air transport.
No VAT on airline tickets	Same effect.

Source: OECD, EUROSTAT

1.2   Restructuring Existing Taxes

Many existing taxes could be changed so as to benefit the environment. It is a question of adjusting relative prices by increasing taxes on the most polluting products and activities. Since energy is one of the main sources both of pollution and of tax revenue, an "environmental" restructuring of prices and taxes is essential. The possibilities are to restructure existing energy taxes and/or to introduce new environmental taxes. For instance, in most OECD countries, taxes on fuel account for over 50 per cent of the pump price (Figure 2). This leaves plenty of scope for restructuring taxes on the basis of environmental parameters, such as carbon or sulphur content, as the Nordic countries and the Netherlands have done. For instance, the introduction of a new CO_2 tax in Denmark, Norway and Sweden, was accompanied by a decrease in existing energy taxes, in particular on industry[3].

The environmental impact of such measures will depend both on the total tax burden on taxed fuels and on the availability of substitute products. Thus most OECD countries have introduced a tax

---

[3]   This restructuring of energy taxes was done with different modalities according to countries. For instance, in Norway, the decrease in energy taxes took place a few years after the introduction of the CO_2 tax.

differential between leaded and unleaded petrol. This has led to a marked fall in the proportion of leaded petrol (less than 25 per cent of the market in Germany and the Netherlands) and in some cases to its disappearance from the market (Austria, Denmark, Finland, Norway and Sweden). In 16 countries, car sales taxes and/or annual car taxes have been adjusted in such a way as to stimulate the use of less polluting vehicles. Since 1994, Sweden has applied different taxes to two types of unleaded petrol, according to their sulphur, benzine and phosphorous content. This has been leading to a gradual reduction in the use of the most polluting petrol.

Figure 2: Fuel Prices and Taxes in OECD Countries in US$ (1997)

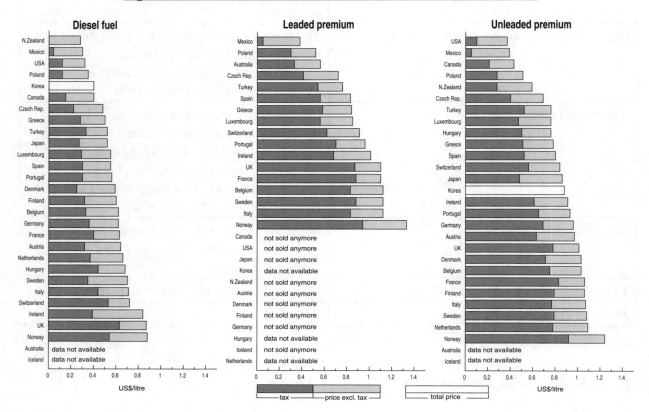

In fact, many studies show that while fuel taxes generally cover or more than cover infrastructure costs, they are not enough to internalise the external costs of road transport (Table 2). According to ECMT estimates, in order to cover external costs, fuel taxes should on average be increased as follows: car petrol, +0.83 ECU; car diesel, +1.04 ECU; truck diesel, +0.74 ECU (ECMT, 1998).

Table 2: Revenues Generated by Road Usage as a Percentage of Road-Related Expenditure, including and excluding External Costs, in France, Japan and the United States in 1991

	France - urban areas (billion FF)	France - rural areas (billion FF)	Japan (billion Yen)	United States (billion US dollar)
Revenues	57.0	100.2	9 530	62 747
Expenditure	44.2	61.2	11 665	78 260
Balance	+12.8	+39	-2 135	-15 513
Revenues as percentage of expenditure	*127 %*	*164 %*	*82 %*	*80 %*
External costs[a]	56 to 92.7	33.8 to 48.2	2 742	117 800 to 371 700[b]
Balance - external costs	-43.2 to -79.9	- 9.2 to +5.2	-4 877	-356 187 to -102 287
Revenues as percentage of expenditure + external costs	*42 % to 57 %*	*92 % to 105 %*	*66 %*	*14 % to 32 %*

(a) In all three studies, external costs include costs related to the following factors:
  France: local and regional pollution; greenhouse effects; congestion; accidents; noise.
  Japan: pollution; greenhouse effects; accidents; noise; disappearance of natural areas.
  United States: effects of air pollution on human health, materials and crops; climatic changes; congestion; accidents; noise; vibrations.
(b) These external cost estimates do *not* include non-taxable parking space for employees, which represents an estimated total cost of US$ 19 billion.

Source: OECD (1998), Part II.

1.3   Introducing New Environmental Taxes

The most obvious and widespread practice is to introduce new taxes whose prime purpose is to protect the environment. These may be taxes on *emissions* (for instance on atmospheric pollutants or water pollution) or taxes on *products*. The latter are more frequent. Since the beginning of the decade, many ecotaxes have been introduced on products ranging from packaging to fertilisers, pesticides, batteries, chemical substances (solvents), lubricants, tyres, razors and disposable cameras.

2.0   Revenues from Environmental Taxes

2.1   Evaluating Ecotax Revenues

The OECD, EUROSTAT and IEA have developed a joint statistical framework for data on ecotaxes, defined as any tax likely to produce a beneficial impact on the environment, regardless of its initial objective. Thus energy taxes, which have a purely fiscal purpose, are considered to be ecotaxes because of their beneficial environmental impact. What matters most is the tax base and the *price signal*, so that it would really be preferable to refer in such cases to "environmentally-related" taxes.

On that basis, preliminary results for 17 countries (Figure 3) indicate that "environmentally-related" taxes account for between 3.8 and 11.2 per cent of total tax revenue, depending on the countries concerned, or 7 per cent on average. As a percentage of GDP, these taxes vary between 1 and 4.5 per cent.

Practically all the revenues (Figure 4) arise from taxes on petrol and diesel fuel (2/3 of revenues), transport and electricity. Very few taxes are levied on heavy fuels used by heavy industry. Next come revenues from vehicle taxes. The proportion accounted for by other ecotaxes (such as pesticides, detergents, etc.) is negligible. Another feature is that industry is relatively little affected, owing to various exemptions.

Figure 3: Revenues from environmentally-related taxes in per cent of total tax revenue and GDP (1995)

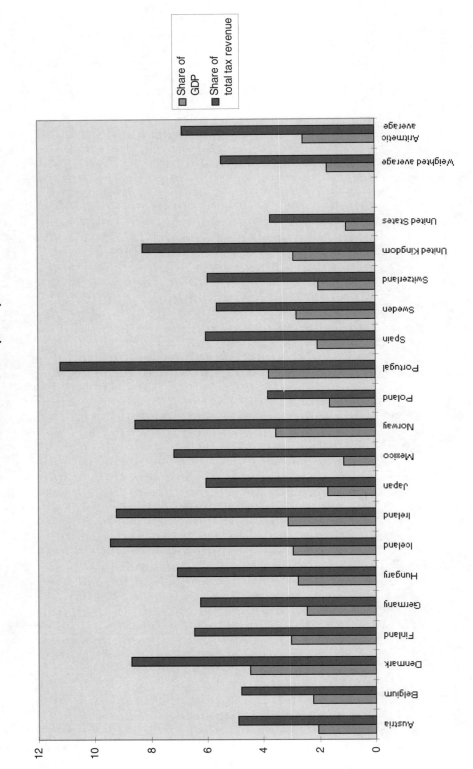

28

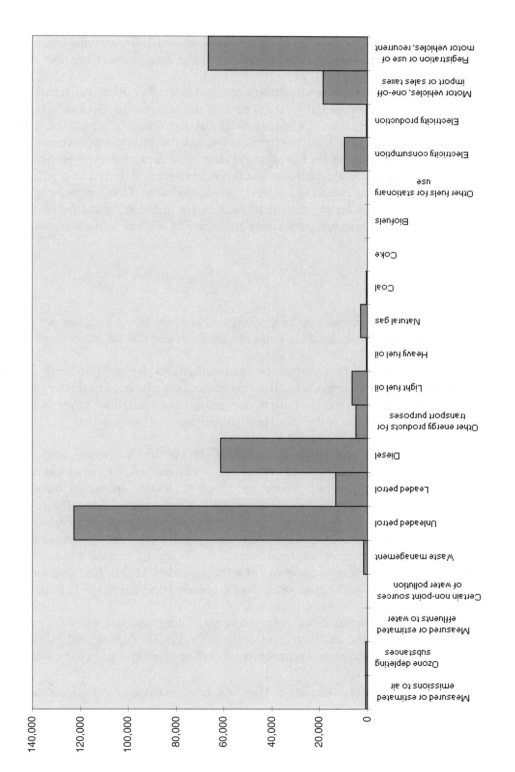

Figure 4: Revenues from environmentally-related taxes in 1995 (million US dollars)

29

2.2   The Sustainability of Revenue

From a fiscal point of view, a "good" tax is one that produces maximum revenue with efficiency, stability and simplicity. In the case of ecotaxes, this configuration may turn out to be complex or even paradoxical. The tax rate has to be sufficiently high to have an incentive effect[4]. However, the more the incentive works, the more pollution will diminish and therefore the less tax revenue will be collected. For instance, taxes on polluting fuel oils in Sweden have led to their virtual disappearance from the market. Again in Sweden, the revenue obtained from the sulphur tax has fallen rapidly owing to the environmental success of the tax: before the tax was introduced, annual revenue was estimated at 0.5 - 0.7 billion Swedish kronor. Between 1991, when the tax was introduced, and 1997, revenue fell from 0.3 to under 0.2 billion Swedish kronor. For the same reason, leaded petrol has disappeared altogether in several countries.

In other words, there is a contradiction, at least once rigidities and reaction times have been allowed for, between the environmental effectiveness of the tax and its fiscal effectiveness, leading to a potential conflict between the ministries of finance and the environment. In practice, however, the conflict between effectiveness and revenue is not so clear cut. In order to ensure that revenue is sustainable, there will be a tendency to tax products with low demand elasticity, such as energy products. Moreover, when ecotaxes produce long-term or gradual effects, the fall in revenue is deferred or gradual, which allows for appropriate tax adjustments and smoothing of revenue in good time. One last point is that the stability of the tax base is never guaranteed for any tax, as illustrated, for instance, by the fall in revenue from labour taxes and the difficulties affecting social security financing as a result of rising unemployment in many countries.

2.3   The Use of Revenues

How should ecotax revenues be used? This is a key question which has not only fiscal, but also environmental implications. There are three main categories where the use of ecotaxes is concerned.

a)   The first way such tax revenue can be used consists in paying it in to the general government budget, in accordance with fiscal orthodoxy. The revenue can then be used to reduce public sector deficits, to increase public expenditure or, the tax burden remaining equal, to reduce other distortionary taxes (see in section 4.3 the approach known as the "double dividend").

b)   Secondly, the tax revenue can be *allocated* to specific purposes, some of which may be environmental, especially by setting up funds or mechanisms for reallocating the revenue to environmental protection programmes. There are many examples in waste management and water management (through the financing of public equipment or the payment of depollution subsidies). In most cases, this category concerns *charges* rather than taxes, i.e. requited payments (see Box 1). The amounts involved are far from negligible: in France, over the period 1992-1996, water charges (pollution and levies) came to an annual average of 8 billion French francs (or 1.6 billion dollars); in the Netherlands, revenue from water pollution charges came to 1.9 billion guilders (1.2 billion dollars). Strictly speaking, taxes may also be allocated, as in the case where fuel taxes are allocated to road building.

Allocation entails serious drawbacks, however. Fixing the use of a tax revenue *in advance*, without evaluating its economic or even environmental rationale *beforehand*, may lead to economic wastage. This situation may prevent an optimisation of public expenditure. In the case, for instance, of the

---

[4]   Considering that we are in a "second best" universe, below the ideal of a "Pigovian" tax.

considerable revenue generated by energy and transport taxes, allocation may prove dangerous and may introduce rigidities. For instance, allocating taxes to road infrastructures may lead to over investment in that sector. Programmes may last longer than their optimal period as a result of habits, administrative slowness, situation returns or other "acquired rights". If the allocation of a certain proportion of public revenue creates a precedent, the public authorities may over time find themselves unable to redefine priorities.

Nevertheless, allocating revenues does have its advantages. *The political acceptability* of taxes and charges will be enhanced because of transparency of use, clearly dedicated to the popular cause of environmental protection. Similarly, payers feel, rightly or wrongly, that the revenue from such taxes or charges is in some way returned to them in the form of subsidies or public investments.

3.0 The Effectiveness of Ecotaxes

While the theoretical advantages (especially the static and dynamic efficiency) of ecotaxes are well known, few data are available. There are several reasons for this. In the first place, experience is often too recent to allow for an objective evaluation. Secondly, there is a shortage of data and practice when it comes to policy evaluation. Everything, or practically everything, still remains to be invented, particularly a methodology and technical and institutional mechanisms for collecting and analysing data. The problem of evaluating ecotaxes is particularly complex insofar as they are generally applied simultaneously with other instruments (such as regulations), which makes it difficult to isolate the impact of a tax. Some countries, however, have started to evaluate their ecotaxes. The results indicate that they are definitely environmentally effective, even though there are still not sufficient data to gauge the economic efficiency of the taxes (cost reduction). Some of the data have been collected in an OECD study [OECD (1997b and c)][5].

For example, the Swedish sulphur tax (introduced in 1991) led to a fall in the sulphur content of oil-based fuels of more than 50 per cent *beyond the legal standards*. The sulphur content of light oils has now fallen below 0.076 per cent (i.e. less than half the legal limit of 0.2 per cent). The tax also stimulated emission abatement measures in combustion plants. It is estimated that yearly emissions of sulphur dioxide [SO_2] have been reduced by around 19 000 tonnes by virtue of the tax [Swedish Environmental Protection Agency (1997)]. Also in Sweden, a tax differentiation was introduced in 1991 on *diesel fuels* in order to stimulate the use of less polluting fuel oils. From 1992 to 1996, the proportion of "clean" diesel sold in Sweden rose from 1 to 85 per cent, which led to a reduction of more than 75 per cent on average in the sulphur emissions of diesel-driven vehicles.

In Norway, carbon dioxide taxes introduced in 1991 lowered CO_2 emissions of some stationary combustion plants by some 21 per cent, whereas in other sectors the fall was less. It is estimated that CO_2 emissions produced by mobile household combustion devices fell by 2 to 3 per cent as a consequence of the CO_2 tax [Larsen and Nesbakken (1996)]. It is also estimated that CO_2 emissions per unit of oil produced by the Norwegian oil sector fell by 1.5 per cent due to measures taken by the industry in response to the CO_2 tax [ECON (1994)]. The Swedish CO_2 tax led to a reduction in emissions of 5 million tonnes in 1994, or 9 per cent of total emissions [Swedish Environmental Protection Agency (1997)].

The tax differentiation between *leaded and unleaded petrol*, combined with a series of measures such as regulations making it compulsory for service stations to offer unleaded petrol and introducing new emission standards for motor vehicles, based on such requirements as catalytic converters, led to a heavy

---

[5] See also Barde and Smith (1997).

31

fall in consumption and in the share of leaded petrol, which was actually withdrawn from sale in Denmark, Austria, Finland, Norway and Sweden. The fiscal incentive greatly speeded up the process, despite slow penetration of new vehicles equipped with catalytic converters.

In Denmark, the tax on non-hazardous waste had the effect of doubling the cost of waste dumping and increased the cost of incineration by 70 per cent. Between 1987 and 1993, household waste fell by 16 per cent, construction waste by 64 per cent and "miscellaneous" waste by 22 per cent. Industrial waste, however, increased by 8 per cent. Recycling also increased considerably: +77 per cent for paper and cardboard, +50 per cent for glass [Andersen (1998)].

In the United States, about 3 400 local communities in 37 States apply taxes on household waste, which are calculated according to the volumes discharged. The result was a significant reduction in the volume of discarded waste and a significant increase in recycling [Anderson *et al.* (1997)].

Not all taxes have been successful, however. The effects of ecotaxes in Belgium (on disposable razors, etc.) were hardly noticeable. Similarly, the Swedish tax on pesticides, which was too low, produced no incentive effect [Swedish Environmental Protection Agency (1997)].

4.0   Implementing Green Tax Reforms

4.1   Base, Rate and Revenue: The "Tragic Triangle"

In fiscal terms, a "good" tax is one that produces maximum revenue with efficiency, stability and simplicity. In the case of ecotaxes, however, this configuration can be complex and even paradoxical.

In the first place the tax base has to be simple and stable. In the case of emission taxes, the measure may be complex, for instance when pollution arises from a combination of substances, such as organic materials, particles or heavy metals, in the case of water discharge. It may also be difficult and costly to measure the quantities emitted. A compromise will therefore have to be found between complex tax bases and excessive simplification, which would not reflect the real pollution situation. This problem of the "linkage" between pollution and the tax paid is crucial. The looser the link, the weaker the incentive effect of the tax[6]. But complicated arrangements will make it difficult to implement the tax and will encourage tax evasion. The tax base therefore has to be explicit and simple. It is generally easier to determine the tax base in the case of product taxes (e.g. the sulphur content of a fuel).

The tax *rate* must be sufficiently high to have an incentive effect[7]. However, the more effective the incentive is, the more pollution will be reduced and hence the less tax will be collected. In Sweden, for instance, taxes on polluting fuel oil caused it virtually to disappear from the market and the revenue from the sulphur tax has fallen rapidly as a result of the environmental success of the tax (see above, section 2.2).

These contradictions between the environmental effectiveness and the fiscal efficiency of the tax may be illustrated by the "tragic triangle" (Figure 5).

---

[6]   Notwithstanding the incentive effect related to the tax *rate*.

[7]   Considering the fact that we are dealing with a "second best" universe, below the ideal of a "Pigovian" tax.

Figure 5: The Tragic Triangle of Ecotaxes

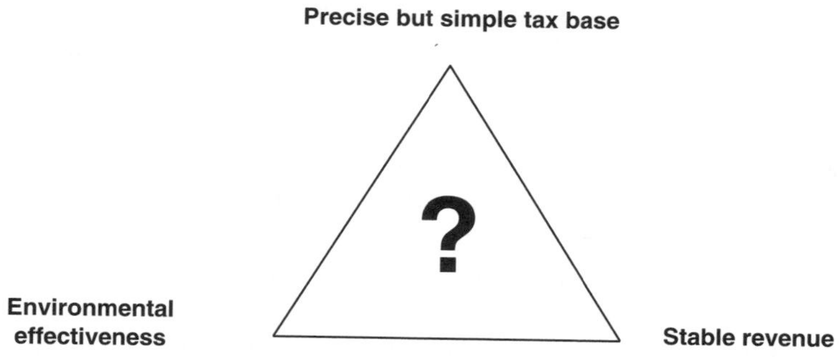

Precise but simple tax base

?

Environmental
effectiveness

Stable revenue

4.2   What Tax Neutrality?

It is clear that any "green" tax reform entails many aspects, ranging from the in-depth reform of existing taxation to the introduction of new taxes. This means that the objective pursued by the reforms is not only environmental. Many other benefits may be obtained, in fiscal terms (a better return), in economic terms (greater efficiency by internalising externalities and eliminating distortions), and in terms of employment (lower unemployment thanks to a lowering of labour taxes financed by new ecotaxes — see below).

This approach is opposed to the dogma of "fiscal neutrality", whereby the sole objective of taxation systems is to obtain maximum revenue with minimum distortion and minimum impact on behaviour patterns. Some tax experts view mixed objectives with suspicion and are often opposed to the use of taxation for other than strictly fiscal purposes. Yet there are very few taxes which either accidentally or deliberately do not exert some influence on behaviour or on economic structures. In some countries, many tax measures cover related objectives (e.g. in France the cost of heat insulation for housing is tax deductible as a means of encouraging energy savings). Environment is a case in point, and many taxes are observed to produce negative effects in this respect. Similarly, a growing number of ecotaxes are deliberately aimed at altering behaviour patterns.

But while ecotaxes, by definition, are not fiscally neutral, green fiscal reforms are generally implemented in a context of a *constant tax burden*, in the sense that new ecotaxes tend to offset reductions in existing taxes. In fact, a constant tax burden is an essential condition of the *acceptability* of ecotaxes. Industry in particular is strongly opposed to ecotaxes on the grounds of a possible loss of competitiveness (see below). Similarly, consumers may fear that ecotaxes might lead to price increases; it is then essential to show clearly that other taxes are being reduced to ensure the political acceptability of green tax reforms.

Finland was the first country to introduce a carbon tax in 1990, followed by a progressive greening of the tax system. While the carbon tax started in 1990 at a fairly modest level of FIM 24.5 per ton of carbon, the rate has been steadily increased since, to reach FIM 374 in 1998. This evolution has been accompanied by a number of significant changes. First, the carbon tax was significantly restructured in 1996. The tax had been initially applied to fossil fuels used in both heat and power production, and in transport. As from (January) 1997, the new carbon tax applies to heating and transport fuels. As for electricity, however, the tax was moved from fuels to the end product, i.e. kWh of electricity (paid only at 54 per cent by industry, - 61 per cent in 1998- while no tax exemptions were initially granted to industry). Second, the greening of the tax system is being pursued by measures such as the exemption of rail transports from the electricity tax (1998) and the implementation of a new waste landfill tax in (September) 1996. Third, this increase in green taxes is compensated by a reduction of the tax wedge on labour (decreased income tax and social insurance contributions) with the explicit objective to reduce unemployment.

In Sweden, the 1991 tax reform was based on a significant reduction in income tax, which was largely offset by a series of new ecotaxes, especially on carbon, sulphur and nitrogen oxides, by a restructuring of energy taxation and by a broadening of the VAT tax base. The net effect was a 6 per cent redistribution of GDP, including about 1 per cent related to ecotaxes.

Denmark has also been engaging in a general reform of its tax system, over the period 1994-1998 with a continuing evolution of energy-related taxes till 2002[8]. The main objectives of the reform are the reduction of marginal tax rates in all income brackets; the elimination of a series of loopholes in the tax law; and a gradual transfer of tax revenue from income and labour to pollution and scarce environmental resources [Danish Ministry of Finance (1995)]. Since 1996, the authorities have introduced new ecotaxes on industry's use of energy (on CO_2 and SO_2), rising gradually until 2000. The revenue produced by these taxes is reverted entirely to industry in the form of investment aids for energy saving and reduced employers' social security contributions.

The Netherlands provide an interesting example of a progressive transformation of earmarked charges into fiscal taxes. Between 1971 and 1998, the Dutch system of environmental taxes and charges gradually evolved from being essentially a means of financing environmental protection programmes to consisting of a series of unallocated ecotaxes. Until 1988, about 7 specific environmental charges (on water, air, waste, noise, soil and chemical waste) were levied to finance specific environmental protection measures. These charges were yielding limited revenue, and were complex to implement. Therefore the 1988 "General Environmental Provision Act" replaced all these charges by one single "general fuel charge". Between 1988 and 1998 this earmarked charge was replaced by a series of taxes (on fuels, waste, groundwater, uranium and small energy users). The new "energy regulating tax" on small energy consumers (households, small businesses, office blocks, etc.), introduced in 1996, is expected to yield 2.1 billion guilders in 1998. The revenue is to revert to households in the form of reduced income tax and to employers in the form of reduced social security contributions [Vermeend and Van der Vaart, 1998].

Switzerland has introduced two new ecotaxes: from 1 July 1998, on extra light heating oils, and from 1 January 1999, on volatile organic compounds (VOCs). The revenue is to be fully returned to households in the form of reduced compulsory sickness insurance premiums. A general green tax reform is being considered for 2001.

4.3   Is There a "Double Dividend"?

As was explained earlier, a double benefit may arise from fiscal reforms: firstly, in terms of a more efficient economy, rid of distortional taxation; secondly, in terms of more effective environmental protection. According to Bovenberg and Mooij (1994), this concept of a "double dividend" may have three meanings: in one sense, the double dividend arises from greater economic efficiency due to the ecotax, compared with direct controls (the static efficiency concept of taxes); in a second sense, the double

---

[8]   See Larsen, Hans: "Energy Taxes - The Danish Model" in this volume.

dividend is related to the notion of a "no-regrets policy", based on the supplementary environmental benefits obtained by a carbon-energy tax beyond the targeted gains and objectives (e.g. through greater energy efficiency, less road transport congestion, less emissions of other air pollutants produced by fossil energy combustion); in the third sense, the double dividend relates to efficiency gains obtained with an ecotax, which both internalises external costs and replaces existing distortional taxes. In this third case, the really burning question at present is whether this type of fiscal reform could extend to the drive against unemployment by financing a reduction in labour taxes (including employers' social security contributions) with new ecotaxes, especially on energy (CO_2 tax). This question of a double environment-employment dividend has generated prolific literature and lively controversy, which is far from over. There may be three main questions which are worth mentioning at this stage.

1. *Can lower labour taxes favour employment?* There are many factors involved, such as the flexibility of the labour market and the mobility of capital. Most models (though not all) seem to indicate some potential for employment creation by reducing the so-called "tax wedge" on labour (i.e. the burden of employers' social security contributions and income taxes) in low income categories in countries where this tax burden is high. Majocchi (1996) has shown that the results of many models converge to indicate that a carbon-energy tax would yield some double employment-environment dividend. The employment effect, however, would be limited (a rise in employment of the order of 2 per cent).

2. *Will ecotaxes be high enough to finance a significant fall in the tax wedge on employment?* The more the employers' social security contributions are reduced, the greater the effect will be on employment. New taxes are needed, therefore, to produce sufficient income to offset the drop in contributions. In the case of the introduction of an energy ecotax, which is also intended to reduce polluting emissions, the "double dividend" possibility should be considered in both a short-term and a long-term perspective. In the short term, one essential variable is the price elasticity of the demand for energy and energy-intensive goods. In the event of high elasticity, the ecotax will cause a strong drop in demand, and will therefore have a favourable effect on the environment, but it will produce relatively low revenue, which will perhaps be insufficient to offset a significant fall in employers' social security contributions. Low elasticity will have the reverse effect: high tax revenue, but weak environmental effect (see also section 2.2). This means there is, if not an actual contradiction, at least some conflict between the two objectives of employment and environmental protection. In any event, it is worth maintaining a dynamic view and management of the process.

3. In the longer term, technological innovations may lead to greater energy efficiency and therefore to lower tax revenue. A simulation by OECD's GREEN model of the revenue trend of the old projected community tax on carbon and energy (10 dollars a barrel, or 40 dollars per tonne of carbon) shows a long-term decreasing tax return [OECD (1995)], which may not yield sufficient revenue to offset the fall in social security contributions. In any event, taxes on carbon are few and far between and revenue derived from them still fairly limited, owing to low rates and exemptions. Apart from *existing* taxes on energy and transport, the *new ecotaxes* on products such as pesticides or batteries yield negligible revenue (see section 2.1), which is unlikely to finance a significant reduction in the tax burden on labour.

Nevertheless, there is bound to be a *potential* double dividend, even though it may be limited. One then has the feeling that this is a typical case of "no regrets policy", in the sense that the ecotax, which is anyway good for the environment, might in addition be good for employment. There is also a "political dividend" to the extent that the potential effect on employment may help the political legitimacy of the ecotax. This is not to be underestimated, considering the vociferous opposition by industry to any form of ecotax, especially in the energy sector. In fact, some countries have in one way or another already bet on the double dividend effect, or are considering doing so (Box 3). How effective these mechanisms really are, however, still remains to be seen.

Box 3: The Double Employment-Environment Dividend - Current Practice	
Countries	**Tax shift**
Belgium	The revenue of a "special levy on energy" (introduced in 1993) is paid into a special fund to finance social security expenditures.
Denmark	New or increased environment-related taxes will increase revenues by DKr 12.2 billion by 1998, with a simultaneous lowering of income tax. Since 1996, part of the revenue of the newly increased CO, tax on industry has been allocated to reducing employers' social security contributions.
Finland	Starting in 1997, lower taxes on income and labour (Fmk 5 600 million in cuts in 1997), offset in part by new ecotaxes (e.g. a landfill tax, Fmk 300 million per year) and energy taxation.
Netherlands	A large part of the revenue of the new "regulatory tax on energy" goes towards reducing employers' social security contributions. The current fiscal reform should accentuate this tax shift.
Switzerland	Revenue from new ecotaxes on VOCs and extra-light heating fuels will be redistributed to households in the form of reduced compulsory sickness insurance contributions (1999).
Sweden	A tax reform in 1991 resulted in a SKr 15 billion tax shift to environment-related taxes, leading to a reduction *inter alia* in marginal income tax rates. A reduction in employers' social security contributions is being considered.
United Kingdom	Revenue from a landfill tax introduced in October 1996 (£450 million/annum) is to be used to reduce employers' social security contributions by 0.2 percentage points.

Source: OECD (1997e) and update.

5.0   Distributional Implications of Environmental Taxes

Are ecotaxes socially regressive? This question is increasingly being asked and has become a preliminary to the introduction of any such tax. In so far as many ecotaxes apply to mass consumption products, such as motor-driven vehicles and energy, they can have a substantial effect on low-income households. The distributional effects of ecotaxes, especially those on energy, may be observed in three ways [Smith (1998)]:

1.   There will be a *direct* distributional impact related to the structure of household energy expenditure (on heating and transport) for different income brackets. The bigger the proportion of low-income household expenditure devoted to energy, the more regressive will be the impact of the tax.

2.   *Indirect* distributional effects will emanate from the taxation of production inputs. The more the processes are energy intensive, the greater will be the incidence of a tax on the goods produced.

Of course, the more the products fall into the prime necessity category, the more regressive the tax will be.

3.   Lastly, the distributional impact will be related to the *incidence* of the tax. An energy tax may affect end consumers, but it may also affect energy producers or production factors (e.g. through a fall in wages or lower return on capital). At the same time, part of the tax may be borne by energy consuming countries, and another part by energy exporting countries, according to the elasticities of supply and demand.

A distinction needs to be drawn, however, between relatively low ecotaxes on products such as detergents, fertilisers, batteries and pesticides, and large-scale and fiscally heavier ecotaxes, such as those on energy. In the first case there is no observable distributional impact, while in the second case, some studies indicate a risk of regressivity.

For example, an analysis of possible distributional effects of the carbon-energy tax in the United Kingdom, initially proposed by the European Commission, shows that the impact of this tax would be distinctly more marked on poorer households. While a tax of 10 dollars a barrel (i.e. $88 per tonne of carbon) would reduce total household energy consumption by 6.5 per cent, the reduction would be 10 per cent for the poorest 20 per cent of households [Pearson and Smith (1991)]. The figures vary considerably from country to country [Pearson (1992)]. In most cases (Figure 6), ecotaxes seem to be mildly regressive [Scott (1992)]. To be effective, however, an ecotax on energy should be much higher: according to the OECD GREEN model, a tax of $215 on average per tonne of carbon ($308 for OECD countries) would be needed to stabilise CO_2 emissions at their 1990 level by the year 2000.

Figure 6: Income Distribution Impacts of a Carbon Tax in Six European Countries

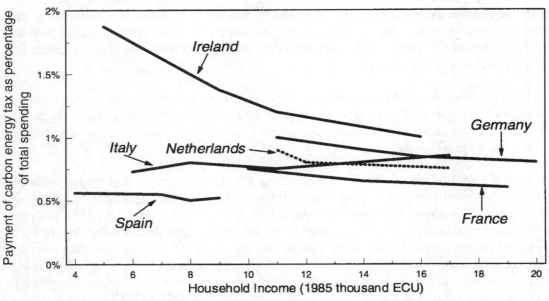

Source: Pearson and Smith (1991).

In its 1997 report, the Swedish Green Tax Commission estimated that doubling the CO_2 tax (from a 1997 rate of 0.37 to 0.74 Kronor per kg of CO_2) would have a fairly marked regressive impact; in order to maintain the same consumption level, the lowest incomes would need to receive compensation of 1.24 per cent of their consumption expenditure, and the highest revenues only 0.78 per cent. A Danish study (1996) of the distributional impact of taxes on water, electricity and petrol also found a regressive effect.

As far as *developing countries* are concerned, a World Bank study, reported by the IPCC (1995), shows mixed findings based on a study by Shah and Larsen (1992) on the impact of a carbon tax in Pakistan [see also OECD (1995b)]. According to hypotheses, this tax would have a mildly regressive or even progressive impact (Table 3). The surprising hypothesis that the impact in developing countries would be mildly regressive is related to two opposite effects: on the one hand, high carbon tax revenues would lead to a lowering of income tax, thus in effect (partly) substituting a regressive tax for one which is by nature progressive; on the other hand, tax evasion and the incidence of urban taxes on rural workers would make the income tax less progressive in practice. All in all, the impact of a carbon tax could be proportional to the income level, or even progressive.

Table 3: Institutional Effects on Carbon Tax Incidence in Developing Countries

Institutional Considerations	Implications for tax shifting	Tax Incidence with Respect to		
		Income	Expenditure	Lifetime Income
(a) Foreign ownership and control	Borne by foreign treasury through foreign tax credits	Nil	Nil	Nil
(b) Full market power Perfectly inelastic demand or perfectly elastic supply	Full forward shifting (100% on final consumption)	Regressive (pro-rich)	Less regressive	Less regressive
(c) Price controls and legal pass-forward of the tax disallowed Completely inelastic supply	Zero forward shifting (100% on capital income) Reduced rents	Progressive (pro-poor)	Progressive	Progressive
Import quotas and rationed foreign exchange	No effect on prices (100% on capital income)			
(d) An intermediate case of (a) and (b) above	Partial forward shifting (31% on capital income, 69% to final consumption)	Proportional	Progressive	Progressive

Source: Shah and Larsen (1992), as reported in IPCC (1995), Chapter 11, p. 67.

If an ecotax is manifestly regressive, it is possible to consider corrective measures, such as *lump sum compensation*, calculated on the basis of average tax payments per household. In this case, compensation would have a progressive incidence on the assumption that the poorest households on average pay less tax than the richest households. The new Swiss taxes on VOCs and light heating oil are refunded to households.

Another approach consists in *reducing other taxes*, such as labour and income taxes (see section 4.3). The net distributional implication of this approach is not clear, considering that the poorest households pay the least income tax, unlike wealthy households, who will benefit most from any lowering of income tax. According to Smith (1998), this form of compensation may even prove to be strongly regressive.

Another approach, known as "mitigation", consists in reducing ecotax rates for low-income categories. If such an approach is at all feasible, however, the outcome would be to weaken the desired environmental impact of the ecotax.

To sum up, there is no simple or uniform answer to the problem of the distributional impact of ecotaxes, which needs to be analysed on a case-by-case basis. In any event, vigilance is called for, especially if ecotaxes are to become more popular.

6.0 Environmental Taxes and Competitiveness

6.1 A Snag?

The main obstacle to implementing new ecotaxes is the possible loss of international competitiveness. Countries tend to adopt a wait-and-see attitude: who will go first? How can sectors exposed to international competition be protected? Is there a need for international harmonisation in this area and if so how should one go about it? Industry is strongly opposed to environmental taxes on the grounds that they can cause a significant loss of international competitiveness. The greater the "visibility" of ecotaxes compared with other environmental policy instruments, the more outright the opposition will be, insofar as they are a direct levy which is additional to the costs of other antipollution measures. Another problem, which may turn into an explicit threat, is the "relocation" of activities to countries which are less fussy about environmental protection or to other "pollution havens". Like the "double dividend", this question is the subject of heated debate.

The concept of "competitiveness" can be apprehended in different ways. It is important, for instance, to differentiate between the competitiveness of individual companies and sectors of the economy and of the economy of a country. Similarly, competitiveness may have a national or an international dimension (Box 4).

Box 4: The Concept of Competitiveness

It is important to distinguish clearly between the competitiveness of individual companies and sectors of the economy and that of the whole economy in general. Competitiveness will have a different meaning at each level. A *company* or *sector* is competitive if it is able to compete in international markets, with a satisfactory rate of return. For *a country as a whole*, the concept of competitiveness is more complex: at the economy-wide level, correcting for market failures provides an improvement in the overall economic outcome, and what represents increased costs for one firm or industry may lead to reduced costs for others. One should also distinguish between a shorter and a longer time perspective. In the shorter run, exchange rate levels will be of importance. In the longer run, the country's ability to sustain a satisfactory wage level should also be taken into consideration. So also should its balance of payments and its ability to use its resources efficiently (including its labour resources). One definition of competitiveness, from the International Institute for Management Development (IIMD), is "the ability of a country to create added value and thus increase national wealth by managing assets and processes, attractiveness and aggressiveness, globality and proximity, and by integrating these relationships into an economic and social model" [IIMD (1996)]. When evaluating a particular policy, the effects on the economy are in general more important that the effects on certain individual sectors.

Source: OECD (1997c).

6.2 Some Available Data

Currently available studies and data show no significant impact of environmental taxes on international trade. Jaffe *et al.* (1995) examined over 100 studies on the potential effect of environmental regulations (and therefore not only taxes) on the competitiveness of American industry. They concluded that: "Overall, there is relatively little evidence to support the hypothesis that environmental regulations have had a large adverse effect on competitiveness, however that elusive term is defined". This conclusion is based on a number of arguments: 1) generally speaking, environmental protection costs are relatively modest and in any case too low to affect competitiveness; 2) environmental constraints in OECD countries are comparable (which is not necessarily the case in other regions of the world); in most cases, whenever environmental constraints are less restrictive in a given country, outside investors tend to apply stricter standards than those of the host country.

Several other studies tend to agree. [Adams (1997)] concludes: "In general terms, the point of view whereby there is a conflict between competitiveness and environmental protection must be rejected". The OECD study on *Economic Globalisation and the Environment* [OECD (1997d)] reaches the same conclusion.

6.3   The Case of Carbon Taxes

However, this rather reassuring view that environmental policies have negligible effects on international trade and competitiveness is only provisional: first, as mentioned earlier, heavy and export industries are generally totally or partially exempted from carbon and energy taxes (see also Figure 4). Furthermore, this view is based on fairly limited data and reflects a situation where these policies have perhaps not yet crossed a certain intensity threshold. This could change, for instance, if drastic measures are taken against the greenhouse effect. In the specific case of taxes, one may wonder how competitiveness would be affected if carbon taxes were introduced at the sort of levels required to attain the objectives of the Convention on Climate Change, and more specifically, those of the Kyoto Protocol.

A number of economic models (such as the OECD GREEN model) have evaluated the impact in terms of effects on growth and "leakage" (i.e. the increase of CO_2 emissions in countries not applying any tax) of different carbon tax scenarios. The type of impact varies considerably according to the various hypotheses, particularly with regard to the use of tax revenue [see OECD (1995)]. However, these models do not really offer any way of evaluating impact in terms of competitiveness.

A study by Baron and ECON-Energy (1997) tries to determine the potential impact of a carbon tax using a statistical survey of industrial structures, of energy (and carbon) intensity and of the structure of international trade of OECD countries or groups of countries. They have found first of all that there are clear differences in terms of energy intensity and carbon intensity between different OECD regions; in particular, the higher the energy intensity, the higher the carbon intensity tends to be, with the highest values being observed in Australia, Canada and the United States (Figure 7).

Figure 7: Energy and Carbon Intensities[3] in Total Industry, Selected OECD Countries

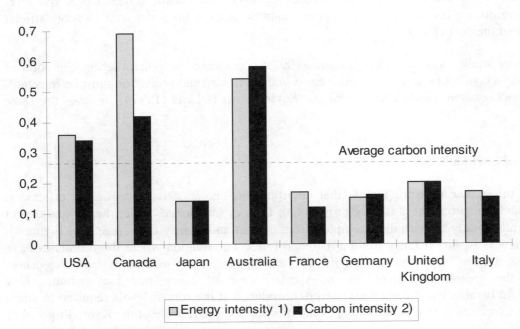

1)   Kilogram oil equivalents per US$ value added
2)   Kilogram of carbon per US$ value added
N.B.:   Carbon intensities are from direct use of fossil fuels (incl. feedstock) in industry, but not process emissions from use of coke in aluminium production. Carbon intensity includes derived carbon emissions in electricity generation.
Source: IEA/OECD, 1992 data.

The greater the carbon intensity of an industrial sector, the more pronounced will be the impact of a carbon tax on competitiveness. There are other structural factors which need to be taken into account, however, such as the place of industries on the world market and the structure of trade in different countries or regions. In the OECD area, the proportion of energy intensive industries amounts to 20 to 25 per cent of GDP. It has also been observed that the proportion of exports by energy intensive industries of OECD countries varies considerably according to the regions or countries: while only 15 per cent of the exports of energy intensive industries of OECD/Europe countries go to countries other than Annex I[9], the proportion is greater than 30 per cent for North America and almost 70 per cent for OECD/Pacific countries; the discrepancy is similar for imports. Table 4 gives an idea of the trade structure of energy intensive products (iron and steel, non-ferrous metals, pulp and paper, chemical products); it may be seen that these products account for only a relatively modest proportion of total trade (between 3.2 and 7.5 per cent of exports and between 1 and 3.7 per cent of imports).

---

[9]   Annex I Parties to the United Nations Framework Convention on Climate Change (FCCC) are the industrialised countries (OECD Member countries plus nine non-OECD countries at the time of the agreement in 1992).

Table 4: Trade in Energy-Intensive Products for Major OECD Regions (1994)

Region	OECD Europe	OECD North America	OECD Pacific
1. Exports of energy-intensive products* to non-Annex I over total exports	3.2%	4.9%	7.5%
2. Imports of energy-intensive products* from non-Annex I over total imports	1.0%	1.8%	3.7%
3. Share of exports (imports) of energy intensive products* to (from) Annex I	80.7% (88.9%)	66.6% (79.1%)	33.3% (67.2%)
4. Net exports of energy intensive products* to non-Annex I (Billion)	US$ 39.8	US$ 16.0	US$ 21.3
5. Net exports of energy intensive products* to other regions (Billion)	US$ 53.0	US$ 2.7	US$ 8.0
6. Contribution of trade to GDP (Imports + Exports) / GDP	27.3 %	13.4 %	9.8 %

* "Energy intensive products" are: iron and steel, non-ferrous metals, paper and pulp, and chemical products.
Source: Baron et ECON-Energy (1997)

Baron and ECON-Energy have calculated the cost increases from a tax of 100 dollars/tonne of carbon on energy intensive industries. The results indicate a cost increase varying between 1.2 and 5.2 per cent according to countries, with further variations according to sectors (Table 5).

Table 5: Selected OECD Countries Cost Increases[1] from a Tax of 100 USD/ton Carbon as Percent of Production Value

	Total energy-intensive industries	Iron and steel	Non-Ferrous metals	Chemical	Pulp and paper
USA	2.8 (2.5)	2.3	3.1	2.8 (2.2)	3.2
Canada	4.1 (3,3)	6.2	3.7	4.1 (2,3)	5.0
Japan	1.2 (1,0)	2.0	0.7	1.0 (0,6)	0.6
Australia	5.2 (5,0)	5.8	11.4	1.7 (1,4)	2.6
France	1.4 (1,1)	2.4	1.4	1.3 (0,8)	0.6
Germany	1.6 (1,4)	2.6	1.2	1.4 (1,1)	1.0
United Kingdom	1.6 (1,3)	3.6	1.9	1.2 (0,8)	1.2
Italy	1.4 (1,2)	2.0	1.1	1.3 (0,9)	0.7
Belgium	2.3 (2,1)	7.3	0.8	1.6 (1,2)	0.6

1) The figures also include carbon emissions through electricity generation and from process emissions in aluminium production.
Numbers in parentheses indicate cost increases when the tax is applied only to fossil fuels used for energy purposes, i.e. not-sequestered in the final products.

Source: OECD/IEA data, sectoral energy data: Energy Information Agency (1994), ECON-Energy calculations, see Appendix II.

It appears that cost increases are generally low (under 2 per cent), except for Australia and Canada, which are more carbon intensive. In fact, the weaker the energy (and carbon) intensity is, the weaker the impact of a carbon tax will be on competitiveness; its impact would therefore probably be limited in the European Union and in Japan. On the other hand, more marked effects might be expected in other countries, such as Australia and Canada in the OECD area, as well as in developing and transition countries. It should be noted that this is a *static* form of analysis, which does not take account of the tax implications for the economy as a whole and its effects on prices in general.

6.4   Policy Aspects

In any event, the threat or fear of loss of competitiveness remains one of the main obstacles to the introduction of environmental taxes, particularly on carbon and energy. Few countries at present apply carbon taxes, and those that do tend to take other measures to protect sectors exposed to international competition.

Exemptions or reduced rates are the first type of protective measure. For instance, Sweden initially gave industry a 75 per cent rebate on the carbon tax (and total exemption in the case of the energy tax); the rebate was then reduced to 50 per cent in July 1997. In Denmark, a 50 per cent rebate on the CO_2 tax was granted to industry for the period 1993-1995. Other such examples could be mentioned. A certain "precautionary principle" therefore has to be applied, especially in the most innovating and from the point of view of green tax reforms the most advanced countries, although the risk then arises of reducing the incentive effect of the tax.

Another approach is to apply the tax *conditionally*. In Switzerland, for instance, the CO_2 bill provides for a "subsidiary tax" on carbon if industry fails to attain emission abatement objectives (down 10 per cent by 2010, compared with the 1990 level).

One can simply exclude the main industries from the application of the tax: in the Netherlands the new regulatory tax on energy applies exclusively to households and small businesses.

Lastly, certain forms of *recycling* of the tax can mitigate its effect on payers. In Denmark, for example, CO_2 and SO_2 taxes are fully redistributed to industry in the form of subsidies for energy saving investments and lower employers' social security contributions.

The impact of ecotaxes depends not only on a number of economic factors, but also on *how* the taxes are implemented. Thus the potential impact on competitiveness can be attenuated and even avoided altogether if taxes are announced in advance, implemented in consultation with the parties concerned, and gradually increased, according to a planned schedule and possibly subject to negotiation, until they reach the desired rates. While the carbon tax has sometimes been compared with an oil price "shock", and while the desired effect in both cases is an increase in the price of fossil fuels, the two cases should be seen as entirely different (see Box 5).

Box 5: Comparison of Ecotax and Oil Price Shock

Oil price shock	Ecotax
Sudden	Announced
Unilateral	Negotiated
Once-only price increase	Gradual tax increase
Sharp price increase	Moderate rate
No specific modalities	Flexible arrangements according to circumstances
No compensation	Tax shifts and other redistributional measures (if necessary)
Global	National (with the possibility of international harmonisation)

Lastly, the impact on competitiveness of an ecotax (especially on energy) will also depend on the following factors:

- From a general point of view, the tax is only a form of transfer between economic agents: there may be winners and losers, but overall the transfer is neutral.

- An economically efficient tax should reduce and ideally minimise the total cost of combating pollution ("static efficiency" of taxes). Ecotaxes should therefore produce a competitive advantage, at least in the longer term, even if there may be some short-term adjustment costs.

In any case, any environmental policy is bound to affect costs to some degree, for instance through pollution standards, technical standards or regulations. There is no need to single out ecotaxes in particular.

Can countries act independently? A consumption tax affecting imports and not exports (in the event of border adjustments) does not give rise to any real problem of competitiveness or any risk of relocation. On the other hand, any tax affecting the productive sector can encourage relocation in energy intensive sectors. It all depends on the mobility of capital. According to the European Commission (1993), the risk of capital mobility is greater in a small open economy than in a large "relatively closed" grouping such as the European Union. That would already entail concerted action among many countries. However, a consumption tax with border tax adjustment should be a way of minimising the risk of trade distortion. Moreover, the lower labour costs resulting from the reduction in employers' social security contributions (in the event of a "double dividend") should offer some competitive advantages, especially in labour intensive sectors.

In any event, the question of competitiveness remains central to the debate on ecotaxes and the most advanced countries in this area are proceeding very carefully. There is no doubt that any form of harmonisation or concerted action on an international level would facilitate the introduction of green tax reforms. The "conditionality clause" attached to the initial proposal (now abandoned) for a European carbon/energy tax did stipulate that such a tax could only be adopted if similar measures were applied by the other trading partners. It seems reasonable to believe that there will be no large-scale green tax reforms without some form of international co-ordination.

It is worth keeping a watch on developments. It is really up to the European Union and WTO to spell out the rules of the game. In 1997, for instance, the European Commission submitted a

"Communication on environmental taxes and charges in the single market" and, also in 1997, a draft Directive on the taxation of all energy products, with minimum rates and a regular increase between 1998 and 2002.

7.0   Environmental Taxes After Kyoto?

The first economic instrument considered as a means of combating greenhouse gases, and particularly CO_2, was taxes. Some pilot countries have in fact already introduced carbon taxes. Proposals had also been made, however, for an *international carbon tax*; one example of this was the proposal for a European carbon-energy tax, which was eventually rejected. The idea of an international tax on carbon now appears to have been abandoned and the instrument favoured by the Kyoto Protocol to the United Nations Convention on Climate Change (December 1997) is one or more systems of tradable permits. But this does not mean to say that taxes would have no role to play; quite on the contrary, for a number of reasons.

In the first place, the Kyoto Protocol itself recommends that Annex I parties "…implement and/or further elaborate policies and measures, in accordance with its national circumstances, such as … a progressive reduction or phasing out of market imperfections, fiscal incentives, taxes and duty exemptions and subsidies in all greenhouse gas emitting sectors, that run counter to the objectives of the Convention, and apply market instruments".[10]

In fact, in order to fulfil its Kyoto commitments, each country is expected to introduce domestically the most efficient instruments it can for combating greenhouse gases. And taxes rank very high among such instruments. For example, a country might well choose to achieve its abatement objectives through taxes, while proceeding to trade *international* permits, either selling them or acquiring them in addition to the abatements obtained through the domestic tax system [Hourcade (1998)].

It is by no means sure, however, that tradable permits are an effective way of combating all emissions, especially those of mobile sources (transportation), which account for about a quarter of CO_2 emissions and are undergoing substantial, uncontrolled growth in OECD countries. Insofar as domestic tradable permit systems are introduced, it is possible to imagine that the two systems might coexist, in the form of tradable permits for fixed sources and taxes for mobile or diffuse sources.

There may also be the possibility from a taxation point of view of a follow-on solution based on *auctioned* tradable permits (in other words not allocated free of charge). The revenue obtained from permit sales could be redistributed in the form of reduced distortional taxes, such as labour taxes; in this way, a "double dividend" policy could use both ecotaxes and the sale of permits.

Systems *combining* ecotaxes and trading permits, that is, both a price approach and a quantity approach, still remain to be tested.

In any event, in a longer term perspective, it is likely that ecotaxes will play an increasing role and will become more diversified in the effort to combat greenhouse gases.

---

[10]   Article 2 §1(a)(v).

8.0   Conclusions

Ecotaxes are a potentially effective way of protecting the environment and at the same time enhancing economic efficiency. This is increasingly shown by the experience of OECD countries. The effectiveness of ecotaxes should be judged not only from a (primarily) environmental point of view, but also from fiscal, economic and social aspects.

From an environmental point of view, the prime objective of an ecotax must clearly be to protect the environment.

From a fiscal point of view, a "green" fiscal reform should provide an opportunity to eliminate tax distortions and to modernise taxation systems.

From an economic point of view, it should be possible by internalising costs, by eliminating subsidies and taxes which are harmful to the environment and to the economy and by introducing appropriate tax shifts, to achieve real structural adjustments of economies and thereby greater efficiency.

From a social point of view, reducing taxes on labour and employment is a desirable objective, particularly in the many countries where unemployment is rife.

Nevertheless, ecotaxes should not be seen as a panacea. Environmental policies include a whole range of instruments (such as regulations, standards, voluntary agreements, tradable permits, etc.). The right place for ecotaxes is most likely to be found in "mixed" systems combining a selection of these instruments.

Furthermore, ecotaxes are neither applicable nor even desirable universally. In some cases, involving toxic products for instance, it is preferable to ban than to tax. In other cases, ecotaxes may be difficult to apply because the situation is too complex (see the "tragic triangle").

While ecotaxes are an effective, flexible instrument for protecting the environment, they are not universally applicable and need to be considered within a general environmental, economic, social and international context.

Finally, it is likely, in the light of the Kyoto Protocol on Climate Change, that ecotaxes will play an increasingly important role as a means of combating greenhouse gas emissions.

REFERENCES

Adams, J. (1997): "Environmental Policy and Competitiveness in a Global Economy: Conceptual Issues and a Review of the Empirical Evidence", in OECD, *Globalisation and Environment: Preliminary Perspectives*, OECD, Paris.

Andersen, M.S. (1998): "Assessing the Effectiveness of Denmark's Waste Tax, *Environment*, May 1998.

Anderson, R.C., Lohof, A.Q., Carlin, A. (1997): "The United States Experience with Economic Incentives in Pollution Control Policy", Environmental Law Institute and U.S. EPA, Washington DC.

Barde, J.Ph. (1992): *Economie et politique de l'environnement*, Presses Universitaires de France, Paris.

Barde, J.Ph. (1997): "Economic Instruments for Environmental Protection: Experience in OECD countries" in OECD (1997): *Applying market-based instruments to environmental policies in China and OECD countries*, OECD, Paris.

Barde, J.Ph. and Smith, St. (1997): "Do Economic Instruments Help the Environment?" *The OECD Observer*, No. 204, March.

Baron, R. and ECON-Energy (1997): "Competitiveness Issues Related to Carbon/Energy Taxation", Working Paper No. 14, prepared for the Annex I Expert Group, IEA/OECD.

Bovenberg, L. and de Mooij, R. (1994): "Environmental Levies and Distortionary Taxation", *American Economic Review*, Vol. 84, No. 4, September.

ECMT (1998): *Efficient Transport for Europe*, ECMT, Paris.

European Commission (1993): "Taxation, Employment and Environment: Fiscal Reform for Reducing Unemployment", DSG II document, 3 December, Brussels.

ECON (1994): report 326/94, Oslo.

EUROSTAT (1996a): "Road Transport and the Environment: Energy and Fiscal Aspects", *Statistics in Focus*, 1996.2.

EUROSTAT (1996b): "Structures of the Taxation Systems in the European Union", Office for Official Publications of the European Communities.

Hourcade, J.C. (1998): "Les écotaxes et le Protocole de Kyoto" *La jaune et la rouge*, April 1998, Paris.

International Energy Agency, *Energy Prices and Taxes*, IEA, Paris.

IIMD (1996): The World Competitiveness Yearbook, International Institute for Management Development, Lausanne.

IPCC [Intergovernmental Panel on Climate Change](1995): Working Group 3 Draft assessment report, Washington D.C., January.

Jaffe, A., Peterson, S.R., Portney, P.R., Stavins, R.N. (1995): "Environmental Regulation and the Competitiveness of US Manufacturing: What Does the Evidence Tell Us?", *Journal of Economic Literature*, Vol. XXXIII, March.

Larsen, B.M. and Nesbakken, R. (1997): Norwegian Emissions of CO_2 1987-1994. A Study of Some Effects of the CO_2 Tax", *Environmental and Resource Economics*, in course of publication.

Majocchi, A. (1996): "Green Fiscal Reform and Employment: a Survey", *Environmental and Resource Economics*, Vol. 8, No. 4, December.

Michaelis, L. (1996): "The Environmental Implications of Energy and Transport Subsidies", in OECD (1996b).

Danish Ministry of Finance (1995): *Energy Taxes on Industry in Denmark*.

OECD (1994): *Managing the Environment: the Role of Economic Instruments*, OECD, Paris.

OECD (1995a): *Global Warming: Economic Dimensions and Policy Responses*, OECD, Paris.

OECD (1995b): *Climate Change, Economic Instruments and Income Distribution*, OECD, Paris.

OECD (1996a): *Integrating Environment and Economy: Progress in the 1990s*, OECD, Paris.

OECD (1996b): *Subsidies and Environment: Exploring the Linkages*, OECD, Paris.

OECD (1996c): *Implementation Strategies for Environmental Taxes*, OECD, Paris.

OECD (1997a): *Reforming Environmental Regulation in OECD Countries*, OECD, Paris.

OECD (1997b): *Evaluating Economic Instruments for Environmental Policy*, OECD, Paris.

OECD (1997c): *Environmental Taxes and Green Tax Reform*, OECD, Paris.

OECD (1997d): *Economic Globalization and the Environment*, OECD, Paris.

OECD (1998): *Improving the environment through reducing subsidies*, Parts I and II, OECD, Paris.

Pearson, M. and Smith, St. (1991): "The European Carbon Tax: an Assessment of the European Commission Proposal", Institute for Fiscal Studies, London.

Pearson, M. (1992): "Equity Issues and Carbon Taxes", in *Climate Change: Designing a Practical Tax System*, OECD, Paris, 1992.

Scott, S. (1992): "Theoretical Considerations and Estimates of the Effects on Households", in J. FitzGerald and D. McCoy (eds), *The Economic Effects of Carbon Taxes*, Policy Research Series, Paper No. 14, The Economic and Social Research Institute, Dublin.

Shah, A. and Larsen, B. (1992): "Carbon Taxes, the Greenhouse Effect, and Developing Countries", Background paper No. 6, prepared for the *Report on development in the world*, 1992, World Bank, Washington D.C.

Smith, St. (1998): "Distributional Incidence of Environmental Taxes on Energy and Carbon: a Review of Policy Issues", presented at the colloquy of the Ministry of the Environment and Regional Planning, "Green Tax Reform and Economic Instruments for International Cooperation: the Post-Kyoto Context", Toulouse, 13 May 1998.

Swedish Environmental Protection Agency (1997): *Environmental Taxes in Sweden*, Stockholm.

Vermeend, Willem and van der Vaart, Jacob (1998): *Greening Taxes: The Dutch Model*, Kluwer, Deventer.

ENVIRONMENTALLY-RELATED TAXES: A TAX POLICY PERSPECTIVE

Susan Himes and Flip de Kam[1]
Directorate for Financial, Fiscal and Enterprise Affairs, OECD

1.0   Introduction

Among OECD countries the use of so-called 'economic instruments' to foster environmental policy goals has increased over the last 5-10 years. Instruments are labelled as 'economic' if their objective is to induce changes in the behaviour of economic agents by changing relative prices, compelling those agents to take into account the estimated costs and benefits of alternative actions open to them. Such economic instruments include various charges/taxes, subsidies, tax incentives, tradable permits and deposit-refund systems, respectively. In the OECD area, environmentally-related taxes are prominent among these economic instruments. Yet, despite their growing use, and although recent experiences suggest that environmentally-related taxes have been effective in a number of cases, there has until now been no strong move in OECD countries towards comprehensive 'green' tax reforms. In their environmental policies, OECD countries continue to rely very much on direct regulation.

As a result, the role of 'ecotaxes' is limited indeed. By the mid 1990s, including taxes on energy and transport, their share in the tax mix amounted to about 7 per cent. This unweighted average is based on data for about half of all OECD countries (Barde 1998, p.12). Excluding taxes on energy and transport, which are not primarily designed to improve the environmental behaviour of consumers and producers and have a history which outdates the interest of policymakers in environmental issues, the share of ecotaxes is far less than 1 per cent of total tax revenues. This is even the case in Sweden, a country that has pioneered the use of environmental taxes (SEPA 1997, p.124).

A report recently released by OECD (1997a) identifies a number of obstacles which are seen as hindering a wider and more consistent use of environmentally-related taxes:

1)   Uncertainty as to precise environmental outcomes

2)   Uncertainty as to economic and budgetary implications

3)   Concerns about international competitiveness

4)   Concerns about distributional impacts

5)   Lack of co-operation between tax and environmental authorities

---

[1]   The views expressed here are those of the authors and do not necessarily reflect the views of the OECD or its Member countries.

6) Strong opposition by certain interest groups.

The OECD concludes that these concerns can be addressed in a number of ways (see below).

2.0   Specific position of China

The goal of the present workshop is to explore perspectives for an expanded role of environmentally-related taxes in the Chinese tax system. Apart from the obstacles already mentioned, China might face specific problems, which relate to the present stage and dynamics of its economic development and the capability of its tax administration to collect the revenues needed to finance essential state activities. Given their limited role, even in tax structures of high-income OECD countries, one cannot but wonder about the cost-effectiveness of introducing environmentally-related taxes in low- and middle-income countries where available administrative resources could probably be more efficiently employed to effectively collect major revenue-raisers such as broad taxes on income and consumption. This paper tries to contribute to the cost-benefit analysis involved, taking into account some country-specific considerations. This approach seems to be in line with the OECD (1997a, p.8) position, which boils down to the conclusion that opportunities for and the usefulness of 'green' tax reforms will depend on the particular tax under consideration and upon the economic and environmental conditions prevailing in individual countries.

3.0   Why Countries May Adopt Environmentally-Related Taxes

Integrating environmental concerns into the design of tax systems may be attractive for various reasons:

1) Taxes can offer a way of achieving environmental policy goals at lower cost than command and control instruments ('static efficiency')

2) Taxes can also provide a continuous incentive for pollution abatement and technical innovation ('dynamic efficiency')

3) Revenues from environmentally-related taxes may be earmarked to secure public funding of government programmes aimed at improving the environment

4) Similarly, revenues from newly introduced environmentally-related taxes may be used to reduce distortionary taxes, notably on income from labour and capital, in order to reap both environmental and economic benefits.

The well-known efficiency arguments will not be repeated here (see Baumol and Oates, 1988; OECD, 1997b). Earmarking of revenue from environmental charges (e.g. waste and water effluent charges) is used successfully in many countries. Charges are compulsory requited payments, i.e. a service is provided more or less in proportion of the payment. Taxes are compulsory, unrequited payments to general government: benefits provided by government are not normally in proportion to tax payments. Earmarking the revenue of environmental taxes should be considered with great caution. However, the OECD (1997a, p.9) recognises that earmarking may be appropriate as a transitory approach, for instance in economies in transition.

Some, especially in Europe where high taxes on wages and high rates of unemployment persist, have advocated to 'swap' taxes on labour for environmentally-related taxes to reduce labour costs and thus achieve higher levels of employment. This policy stance, its proponents conjecture, would produce a 'double dividend' in terms of both improved environmental protection and lower unemployment. The evidence regarding the existence of a double dividend is so far mixed. Ligthart (1998) reviews the recent literature and concludes (p.28) that a positive employment effect may materialise if the burden of environmental taxes can be shifted to agents outside the labour market, such as owners of capital, households consuming out of transfer income (unemployed, pensioners), and foreign countries -- through adjustments of the terms of trade.

For China realising a double dividend is unlikely to be a major policy goal as both labour costs and taxes on wages are low as compared to OECD countries. A better use of the revenues would be to limit the role of distortionary taxes or provide for specific budget appropriations, e.g. for environmental protection.

4.0   Concerns about Environmentally-Related Taxes

In relation to the introduction of environmentally-related taxes three specific concerns are frequently raised:

1) Stability of revenues (risk of 'base drain')

2) Adverse distributional effects

3) Competitiveness and economic growth.

We have already flagged the limited import of environmentally-related taxes in terms of revenue. Apart from taxes on energy use and the transport sector, the primary goal of environmental taxes is not to raise substantial amounts of revenue, in part as a consequence of the policy constraints identified in the Introduction to this paper. Moreover, a reduction of tax bases related to environmentally-harmful products or activities is a desirable outcome of the introduction of environmentally-related taxes. Therefore, understandable concerns have been raised regarding the sustainability of 'ecotax' revenues. However, there are limitations on the substitution possibilities between products. Whereas an extremely high tax on ozone-damaging chloro fluor carbons (CFCs) might drive this product from markets, the bulk of the revenue is (presently) produced by taxes on energy products and transport activities that will remain in effective demand - albeit perhaps somewhat reduced - thus providing sustained streams of revenue.

Environmentally-related taxes which apply to basic commodities, such as energy, will in many cases have regressive effects (OECD 1997a, p. 39-40). Such regressive effects may be countered by compensating lower income groups involved, notably through reductions of the personal income tax. This in fact is the strategy outlined in a policy document recently released by the Dutch government (Ministry of Finance 1997). As part of a major tax reform to be implemented in the year 2001, energy taxes will be raised substantially in the Netherlands, while simultaneously the income tax will be cut. The table below shows the distributional effects at several representative levels of income.

53

Tax reform and purchasing power (% change)

Income	increase VAT	increase env. taxes	reduce income tax	combined effect
legal minimum wage	- 1.1	- 1.6	+ 2.8	0.1
average production worker	- 1.0	- 1.3	+ 3.8	1.4
2 x average production worker	- 1.1	- 0.8	+ 2.5	0.6

Source: Ministry of Finance (1997, p. 94-95)

Current environmental policies in OECD countries do not seem to have had a significant impact on the competitiveness of either individual sectors or of economies as a whole (OECD 1997a, p.46). One reason may be that some countries (e.g. Sweden, the Netherlands) exempt export-oriented energy-guzzling industries such as refineries, chemicals, steel and aluminium from higher energy taxes. This policy stance is clearly motivated by competitiveness concerns, which seem justified in the light of various simulation studies carried out by the Dutch Bureau for Policy Analysis (CPB 1997, p.10). Exemptions of export oriented industries from eco-taxes, however, could defeat the environmental objective of the tax.

To the extent that a green tax reform would improve the functioning of the economy by reducing distortionary taxes and direct subsidies of polluting activities and introducing appropriate adjustments in tax systems, in particular in the energy, transport and agricultural sectors, the long-term competitiveness of the country actually could be enhanced.

Nevertheless, work at the OECD suggests that more ambitious environmental policies, for instance to reduce greenhouse gas emissions significantly, could affect the competitiveness of some sectors more severely.

In a recent paper, Cuervo and Ghandi (1998) review the literature for empirical evidence on the seriousness of a carbon's tax macroeconomic impacts. Not very surprisingly, they conclude that the effect of a carbon tax on economic growth depends on the choice of the model, the assumptions underlying the model, and the use to which carbon tax revenues are put. When models contain 'optimistic' assumptions, such as a strong response of economic agents to the tax, ready availability of cheaper alternative fuels and technologies, and efficient recycling of available revenues, the tax is generally shown to have no negative effect on growth. The effect of carbon taxes on exports could be substantial, but studies cited by Cuervo and Ghandi in their review paper show that increased costs of production can often, but not in all cases, be offset by reductions in payroll and income taxes that carbon tax revenues make possible. Fully in line with the outcome of many previous studies, the authors conclude that an international agreement to adopt carbon taxes in a co-ordinated fashion would greatly reduce the fears of a loss of competitiveness.

OECD studies also suggest that an increase in the number and level of eco-taxes could have anti-competitive effects. Moreover, structural adjustments in economies would generally take place in the longer term and transition costs might be borne disproportionately by specific sectors of the economy. Where appropriate, international co-ordination would minimise the risk of undesirable effects on the competitiveness of some sectors of the economy, as well as emission 'leakage'.

5.0   Considerations for Tax Policymakers in China

Tax policies are subject to a number of constraints -- such as efficiently raising sufficient revenue in ways that are as neutral, equitable and simple as possible. The role of environmentally-related taxes must also be seen in this context. In this section we will in turn address efficiency and design issues, where possible with a focus on the specific context of the Chinese tax system and tax collecting procedures, respectively.

5.1   Current System

Figure 1 shows China's total revenue and its share of GDP. A good starting point when reviewing options for greening China's fiscal policy may be for policymakers and their advisors to systematically review current tax policies and existing tax incentives which may directly or indirectly encourage activities that are environmentally damaging. For example, at the moment China has in place a large number of tax incentives for various industries, some of which are highly energy-intensive and contribute substantially to its pollution problems. Perhaps these tax incentives, including accelerated depreciation schemes, could be re-targeted to apply only to energy-efficient plant and equipment. Reducing distortionary features of the tax system could reap both environmental and economic benefits, resulting in a 'triple-dividend': a more efficient, simpler *and* greener tax system. This topic will be discussed extensively in Session 2.

5.2   Efficiency Issues

The introduction of environmentally-related taxes would imply that the total number of taxes in China's tax system would increase. As a consequence, scarce human resources would be diverted to administer new and unknown taxes with, in a number of cases, most probably relatively low revenue yields. Under such circumstances, the tax system becomes more complicated, while economic objectives and revenue goals may prove more difficult to attain. Paradoxically, introducing a substantial number of environmental taxes could result in a loss of revenue, if administrative resources are diverted from taxes which could -- at existing tax rates -- potentially yield substantially more revenue. This is of particular concern in the case of China where important sources of revenue, such as income taxes, are as yet not fully developed.

At this moment, direct taxes, particularly personal income taxes, bring in very little revenue as a percentage of total revenue. Even though the share from personal income taxes grew by almost 60 per cent from 1994-95, these taxes still constitute a paltry 2.2 percent of total revenue, far below OECD averages. Of course, the low share of income taxes in part reflects the present stage of economic development.

Figure 1: China's Total Tax Revenue For Selected Years
Unit: Billion Yuan

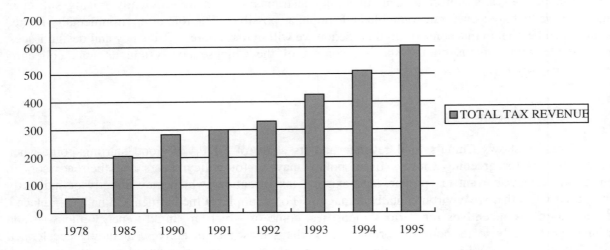

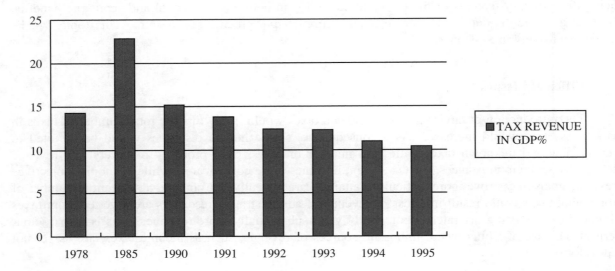

Source: Liu (1998, p.24)

OECD experience suggests that as China's economy continues to mature, direct taxes could contribute much more revenue, at least if the necessary resources are devoted to administering these taxes. Actually, this would involve two steps. First, the range and tax base of corporate and personal income taxes could be gradually expanded. Second, because generally direct taxes are more easily evaded than indirect taxes, sufficient administrative resources should indeed be allocated to guarantee that the revenue potential of income and profit taxes is realised. The revenue yield from a more effective administration of direct taxes could be quite significant, allowing China to fulfil its dual objective of reducing the number of taxes to simplify the system and improve taxpayer compliance.

Resources permitting, we feel that there could be a place for a limited number of environmentally-related taxes in the Chinese tax system. However, various policy considerations should receive due attention. First, policymakers should be keenly aware that environmentally-related taxes are largely inefficient if for political or social reasons important parts of the potential tax base go untaxed.

The natural resource tax in China seems to be a case in point. Although from a purely environmental point of view coal should be taxed more heavily than natural gas, coal is taxed much more lightly.

Second, in relative terms, the administrative costs of the government and associated compliance costs for enterprises may be excessive, in comparison to the revenue collected from environmentally-related taxes. This is especially the case if the number of taxpayers is relatively large, and tax rates and/or aggregate revenue are low/small.

Finally, in a socialist market economy such as China's, prices are not exclusively the outcome of decisions by producers and consumers. In such cases, enterprises may interpret an environmentally-related tax as additional cost to be passed on to customers, instead of stimulating technical innovation to reduce levels of pollution.

5.3   Equity issues

Any policy measure that is intended to improve the environmental situation will have distributional effects. For example, if China were to increase the tax on coal for environmental and efficiency reasons, the tax would fall hardest on lower income groups. This is because they spend a proportionately higher percentage of their disposable income on coal, their primary source of energy. In this case, suitable compensation could be adopted to reduce unacceptable effects on income distribution.

5.4   Design Issues

The experience in OECD countries is that environmentally-related taxes are sometimes difficult to design, that correct compliance is hard to monitor and that such levies may be susceptible to massive fraud due to lack of environmental expertise in national tax administrations. A very practical issue to consider is whether the State Administration of Tax (SAT) could administer any specific environmental tax under consideration. Tanzi (1991), in a paper recommending simple, transparent tax systems for emerging market economies, has pointed to the adverse effect of the transition to a market economy on the efficiency of tax administrations -- from centralised tax collection or, in some cases, appropriation under the planned regime to the new, decentralised market environment -- which requires the introduction and development of an entirely new tax administration machinery, a process which inevitably takes time. Because China is in the throes of this process, the design of environmental taxes should be guided primarily by practical considerations such as simplicity, uniformity and transparency, with a view to administrative constraints related to the newly introduced tax administration system, as opposed to design implied by optimal tax theory.

Turning now to specific design issues, the most obvious one is defining the object of taxation -- pollution in its many forms. The environmental economics literature is quite specific about the nature of the tax and tax base: it must be per-unit levies applied directly to the waste emissions or other sources of environmental damage. In other words, environmental taxes must be directly linked to the source of the pollution. Tax administrations, however, by definition do not include natural scientists and cannot undertake the necessary scientific analysis to define various types of pollution. Most then rely on their Science ministry for assistance, but often the definitions which result cannot be understood by tax administrators or even by taxpayers. Policymakers should also keep in mind that the definition of various emissions must be constantly updated to take into account technological advances. However, if the definition is not precise, the tax may fall on the unintended taxpayer or be evaded by the intended polluter.

This implies that administration of environmental taxes must be closely co-ordinated between the tax administration and environment authorities, as both have significant responsibility for the tax.

Minimising the burdens of administration and compliance will affect the choice of what to tax , often destroying at least part of the direct link between emissions and taxation. If there are many polluters, it may be both difficult and costly to measure and monitor waste emissions. In such cases, governments must adopt a second best approach and tax an input or other activity that is associated with the polluting activity. Take the pollution stream emitted by a car. Given the millions of cars on the road today, it is impossible to measure and monitor the pollution caused by each car. Instead, for practical reasons, governments adopt indirect taxes on gasoline -- the input related to the environmental damage.

Even in cases of a small number of polluters, the cost of monitoring can be prohibitive. To take a simple example: to tax a plant pipe which pollutes water it is necessary to measure the concentration of the pollutant in the water. As the rate of tax will be based on this concentration it must be monitored continuously. If the pollution concentration in water is attributable to several polluters, the monitoring task becomes even more complicated and expensive. Taking into account that the tax system in China is still very young, it may be too soon to enact ecotaxes that require elaborate monitoring schemes.

Another key design issue is the correct tax rate. When pollution taxes are used, the government sets the per-unit price for pollution. Polluters abate as long as the incremental cost of the abatement is less than the tax rate. Thus, the incentive effects are directly related to getting the rate set correctly. In order to use pollution taxes, the technology must exist for monitoring pollution streams. Environmental taxes work best where the taxpayer is easily identified, the number of taxpayers is relatively limited, and the pollution is relatively easy to quantify. As more information on pollution costs becomes available, it will become progressively easier to set the rate at the appropriate level.

Tax treaties and multi-lateral agreements, such as the General Agreement on Trade and Tariffs (GATT), can impose constraints on the optimal design of ecotaxes. These agreements require countries not to enact environmental taxes which erect barriers to trade, discriminate against imports or materially favour domestic industry. For example, China should not enact a special excise tax on large cars, if all or most large cars are imported.

Even at this early planning stage, it is not too soon to consider how to resist pressure to add a new green tax for every type of pollution. Working together, the environmental and tax ministries must ensure that each new tax has a significant and clear purpose which can be administrated efficiently, taking into consideration the existing tax mix, potential revenue from various taxes, and administrative development.

6.0   Conclusion

Tax experts may have a tendency to accentuate technical problems to be expected when the government considers introducing new taxes. Sometimes, that tendency is particularly prominent if the primary or an important goal of such new taxes is not to raise additional revenue, but to achieve 'other' goals of government policies. This paper is not written in the spirit of discouraging any tax policy initiatives not primarily motivated by revenue considerations. Our goal here is to contribute some thoughts that must not be overlooked when contemplating the introduction of environmentally-related taxes in a low- or medium-income country like China. If we have succeeded in bringing those considerations to the reader's attention, we feel this paper has served its purpose.

REFERENCES

Barde, J.-P. (1998): "Environmental Taxes in OECD Countries: An Overview". Background Paper prepared for Workshop on the Application of Environmental Taxes in China and OECD Countries. Paris, 5-6 October.

Baumol, W. and Oates, W. (1988): *The Theory of Environmental Policy*. Cambridge.

CPB (1997): *Vergroening en energie* (Working document 96). The Hague.

Cuervo, J., V.P. Gandhi (1998): *Carbon taxes: Their Macroeconomic Effects and Prospects for Global Adoption -- A Survey of the Literature*. Washington, IMF Working Paper WP/98/73.

Liu, T. (1998 forthcoming): *China's Taxation -- #A Developing System*. Directorate for Financial, Fiscal and Enterprise Affairs, OECD. Paris.

Ligthart, J.E. (1998): *The Macroeconomic Effects of Environmental Taxes: A Closer Look at the Feasibility of "Win-Win" Outcomes*. Washington, IMF Working Paper WP/98/75.

Ministry of Finance (1997): *Belastingen in de 21e eeuw. Een verkenning*. The Hague.

OECD (1997a): *Environmental Taxes and Green Tax Reform*. Paris.

OECD (1997b): *Evaluating Economic Instruments for Environmental Policy*. Paris.

Tanzi, V. (1991): *Tax Reforms in Economies in Transition: A Brief Introduction to the Main Issues*. IMF Working Paper 23, 1-23.

SEPA (1997): *Environmental taxes in Sweden - economic instruments of environmental policy*. Stockholm, Swedish Environmental Protection Agency.

TAXATION AND THE ENVIRONMENT IN CHINA: PRACTICE AND PERSPECTIVES

Jinnan Wang, Chazhong Ge and Jintian Yang
Chinese Research Academy of Environmental Sciences, China

Aiwa Song and Dongsheng Wang
Taxation Administration Department, Ministry of Finance, China

Qifeng Liu
Planning and Finance Department, State Environmental Protection Administration, China

1.0   Introduction

This paper describes current and prospective developments concerning environmental taxes in China. Although China's tax system includes several categories of taxes related to environmental resources, no environmental taxes in a strict legal sense currently exist. Proposals for incorporating environmental taxes as part of government policies are receiving greater attention, however, particularly within departments of finance, taxation and environmental protection. Within this context, the paper first provides an overview of the evolution of China's tax system from 1949 to the present. This is followed by an analysis of several environmental resource-related taxes and experience in their practical application. Finally, prospects for "greening" the tax system and establishing environmental taxes in China are examined. The authors argue that to support sustainable development the government should build upon the reform already undertaken of the tax system as a platform to introduce environmental taxes.

Before discussing China's tax system, some explanation of concepts introduced in the paper will facilitate understanding. First, the term "environmental tax" is used here as a generic term for taxes related to natural resources and the environment. Under China's existing tax system, the categories of the natural resource tax, consumption tax, vehicle use tax, urban construction and maintenance tax, fixed asset investment direction adjustment tax, urban land tax and cultivated land occupation tax are considered "environmental taxes". Second, charges and taxes are considered as two different concepts in China. A charge is made by government authorities in accordance with relevant laws and regulations. The revenue collected is used for defined purposes. A tax is levied by the national tax authority and the revenue goes into the general budget. Thus, there are differences in application and revenue destination. Since the terms charges and taxes are generally used interchangeably in OECD studies, both are discussed in this paper.

2.0   An Overview of China's Tax System

This section provides a brief introduction to China's tax system, focusing on its evolution through time, its current structure, tax revenue sources and institutional arrangements for tax collection.

2.1 Evolution of the Tax System

China's tax system has basically undergone four phases of development since the founding of the People's Republic of China (PRC) in 1949, paralleling changes in the economy.

The first phase was from 1949 to 1958 during which the socialist transformation of the ownership system was nearing completion. In 1950, a new unified tax system was established containing 15 categories of taxes which were levied nation-wide. In addition, industrial and business activities were brought within those sectors of the economy subject to taxation.

The second phase was from 1958 to 1978. Beginning in 1978, China began to implement economic reforms and adopted an "open door" policy to deepen its international trade and investment linkages. This phase was characterised by difficulties in applying the tax regime to industrial and business activities. The tax system was simplified and categories merged so that their number was reduced from 15 to 8 in 1973. However, this major contraction in the number of taxable categories seriously restricted the overall functioning and effects of the tax system.

In the third phase from 1980 to 1993, the tax system was strengthened and reformed in a comprehensive manner. To meet the challenges posed by economic reform and to attract foreign capital, individual income tax, joint venture income tax and income tax on foreign-invested and foreign-owned enterprises were introduced between 1980 and 1982. In 1982, a special tax on fuel oil was levied and a value-added tax was applied to the machinery and agricultural machine industry on a trial basis. Subsequently, a two-step "profit to tax" system (by collecting taxes instead of profits as state revenue) was introduced in 1983-1984, and a reform of taxes of industry and business activities was carried out. The reform culminated in the adoption of a product tax, a value-added tax and a business tax. Tax rates on some products were also revised to make them more rational. A natural resource tax and construction tax were also introduced during this period. In 1985 an urban maintenance and construction tax was established and in 1988 an urban land tax was first levied. These two taxes were not introduced directly out of consideration for environmental protection needs. The overall focus of tax reform in this phase was to establish a tax system based principally on the circulation tax and income tax and supplemented by other tax categories. By 1993, the taxation system comprised 37 categories.

The fourth period was from 1994 to the present. In 1994, the government undertook a comprehensive reform of the country's tax system resulting in the enactment of a new system that continues to be applied today.

2.2 Structure of the Current Tax System

By the end of 1997, there were 23 tax categories established (see Figure 1). With the exception of the inheritance tax and security transaction tax which have not been levied for the time being, the others are collected nation-wide. Among the tax categories, the consumption tax, the natural resource tax, the vehicle use tax, the fixed asset investment direction adjustment tax and the urban maintenance and construction tax are all directly or indirectly related to environmental protection. Each of these taxes is discussed in Section 3 of the paper.

Figure 1: Structure of the New Tax System

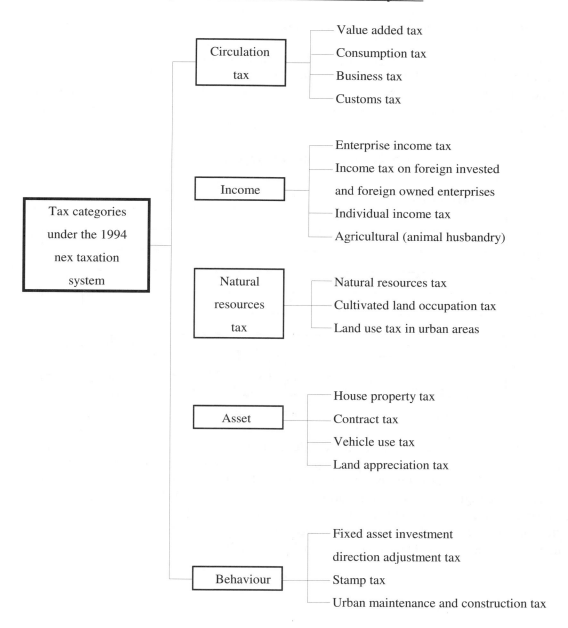

The present tax system has four characteristics. First, a new circulation tax centred around the standardised value-added tax and supplemented by a consumption tax and a business tax. Second, a common base of income tax payable by domestic enterprises, which standardises the profit distribution relations between the state and the enterprise. Third, reform of individual income tax. Fourth, the revision, merger and establishment of some new tax categories levied on industry and business. The new system basically reflects criteria of establishing a coherent and simple tax system, a fair tax burden and a rational division of authority. It creates a favourable environment for promoting fair competition among enterprises and supporting a market-based economy. It also plays a very important role in defining the relationship between the state and enterprises and between central and local government. In addition, it ensures a steady growth in national tax revenue.

2.3   Tax Revenue and Its Structure

Scale of Revenue and Structure of Tax Categories

Tax revenue has increased steadily over time in parallel with the country's social and economic development. In 1997, the total national tax revenue was approximately 8.2 billion yuan[1], which was 310 times higher than that in 1950. In particular, tax revenue has accelerated since economic reform policies and opening to external trade and investment began in 1978. For example, tax revenue in 1997 was 16 times higher than that in 1979. The trend is illustrated in Figure 2.

Figure 2: Changes in Tax Revenue, 1979-1997

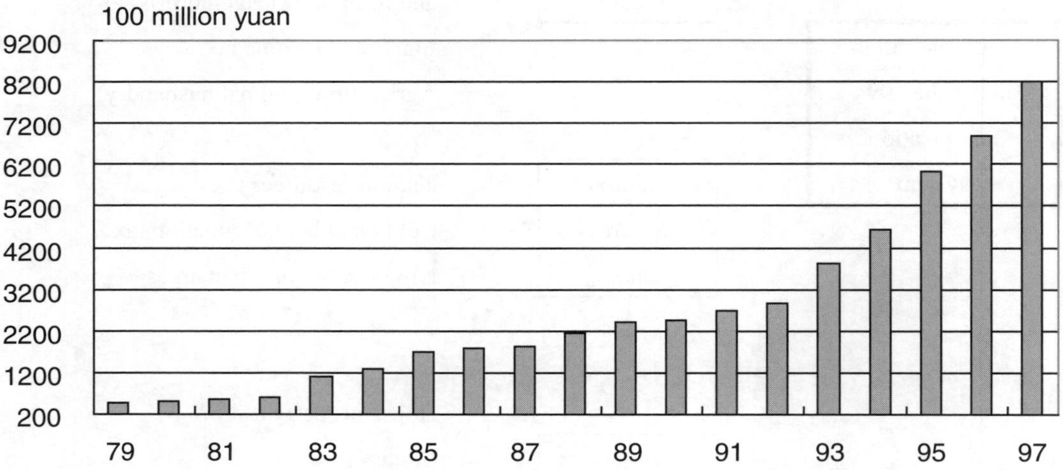

Industry and business[2] tax is the largest share of the overall tax revenue. In 1996, it accounted for 541.1 billion yuan, or 84.2% of the overall tax revenue. Considering variations of tax categories in different time periods, the structure of tax revenue in 1994 and 1996 is compared, when the tax categories were the same (see Figure 3). For simplification, the tax system is divided into circulation tax, income tax, natural resource tax, asset tax and behaviour tax (as indicated in Figure 1). Figure 3 shows that the proportion of revenue from the circulation tax decreased slightly between 1994 and 1996 but that from environmental resource-related taxes remained unchanged at 2%.

---

[1]   US$1 = 8.28 yuan (March 1999).

[2]   According to the 1994 tax system, industry and business tax includes the categories of value-added tax, consumption tax, business tax and customs duty.

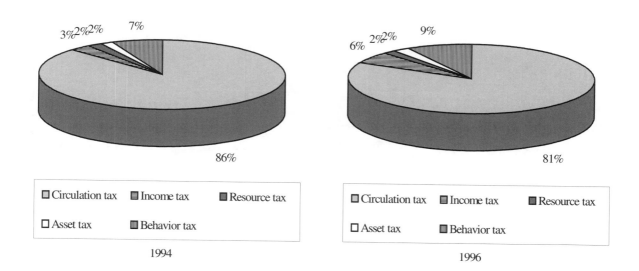

Contributions to Revenue

The main sources of revenue are income tax and non-taxation income (such as the energy and traffic priority construction fund, budgetary adjustment fund, education surcharge) collected by the tax authorities, and regulatory charges collected by other government departments. Revenue is currently the most important source of government revenue. Figure 4 shows that in 1978, tax from industry and business accounted for about 40% of total revenue. By 1997 the figure had risen to just over 70%. In 1997 this tax revenue accounted for 95% of the total sum of revenue.

Figure 4: Share of Industry and Business Tax Revenue in Total Tax Revenue and GDP

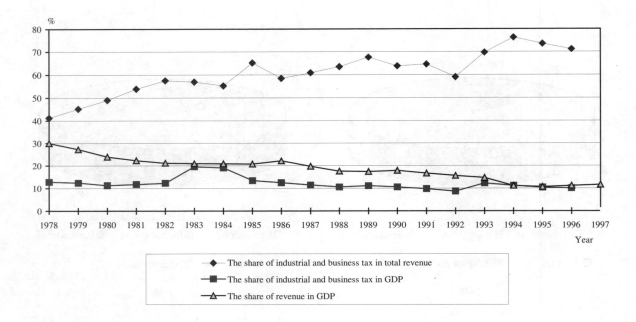

Sources: Calculated based on data from the State Bureau of Statistics (1996) and Chinese Tax Statistics (1997)

Figure 4 shows that the share of GDP of industry and business tax and that of tax revenue as a proportion of GDP have declined in the past 20 years. In particular, the latter has fallen from 30.9% in 1978 to 11.6% in 1997. In other words, national tax revenue did not rise as quickly as growth of the national economy. The major reason is increased amounts of money flowing to enterprises and individuals since the economic reform and open door policies were adopted. An increase in the number of charges linked to the tax system has added to the burden of enterprises and eroded the tax base, reducing fiscal income. It has been estimated that the share of state income in total national income dropped from 32.8% in 1978 to only 16.2% in 1990. This situation has weakened the power of the state to manage and control the macro- economy (Task Group of the Ministry of Finance, 1994).

Tax Sources

The state-owned economy remains the major source of tax revenue, although its share of total tax income decreased from 76% in 1980 to 54.6% in 1996. It is expected that this downward trend will continue with the further development of a market-based economy.

Industry is the main source of national industry and business tax revenue. In 1993, this sector's share in the overall tax receipts was 56.9%. The contribution of the service sector is steadily growing, however. From 1980 to 1996, the share of tax receipts from this sector rose from 15% to 41.5%.

2.4   Institutional Arrangements

The <u>State Administration of Taxation</u> (SAT) is the highest taxation authority in China. Its main duties are: (1) developing tax policies, laws, regulations and the detailed rules of implementation; (2) collecting and managing central government taxes, taxes shared by central and local governments and special taxes set by the state; (3) supervising and auditing the state tax office system; (4) providing tax education and training, and participating in international exchange and co-operation efforts on tax matters.

In accordance with the established division of responsibilities in the tax field, authority at the level below provinces is divided into two systems of <u>state tax offices and local tax offices</u>. The former includes branches of SAT in provinces, municipalities and counties. SAT branches have overall responsibility for office location, staffing and executive appointments and operational budget arrangements. They also assist local governments to manage local tax offices. Local tax offices operate at provincial, municipal and county levels and come under the administrative jurisdiction of the relevant local government. In order to reinforce the efficiency of tax collection and to reduce costs, the state tax office and the local tax office may entrust each other to levy some tax categories on their behalf

The taxation-related duties of the <u>General Customs Office</u> concern participation in the formulation of tariff policies and import and export tariff regulations and the overall administration of import and export tax collection.

Receipts from tax are divided into central taxes, local taxes and taxes shared by the central and local governments (see Table 1).

Table 1: Tax Revenue According to Tax Categories

Type of tax	Elements of Tax Category
Central Tax	(1) Consumption tax; (2) Value-added tax and consumption tax collected by Customs Office; (3) Income tax on state-owned enterprises; (4) Income tax on banks and non-banking financial enterprises; (5) Business tax, income tax and urban maintenance and construction tax levied on bank and insurance companies; (6) Tariffs.
Local tax	(1) Business tax and urban construction and maintenance tax; (2) Income tax on local enterprises; (3) Individual income tax; (4) Urban land tax (5) Cultivated land occupation tax; (6) Fixed asset investment direction adjustment tax; (7) Vehicle use and licence tax; (8) Real estate tax, contract tax; (9) Stamp duty tax; (10) Animal slaughter tax, agricultural tax and animal husbandry tax.
Shared tax	(1) Value-added tax, of which central government's share is 75%; (2) Natural resource tax. The resource tax on offshore oil belongs to the central government while the resource tax associated with land belongs to local government.

3.0   Environmentally-Related Taxes

3.1   Natural Resource Tax

A natural resource tax was introduced on 1 October, 1984. This followed the promulgation of a new natural resource tax regulation as part of the 1984 tax reform in which the scope of taxation was enlarged. The major objective in levying the natural resource tax is to level the playing field among resource developers and to provide incentives to manage natural resources sustainably from an economic and environmental perspective. From the point of view of state-owned resources, the natural resource tax is akin to developers "purchasing" the right to use public resources.

In practice, the natural resource tax can be considered a differential resource tax. It applies only to mineral resources, broadly defined, and salt. Taxable mineral products include crude oil, natural gas, coal, metal mineral products and other non-metal mineral products[3]. Items subject to the natural resource tax and the tax rate is stipulated in "The Provisional Regulations for Natural Resource Tax" (see Table 2). It should be noted that the amount of tax levied on a specific tax payer (such as a coal mine operator) depends mainly on the resource characteristics and is independent of the environmental effects of resource use (such as atmospheric pollution caused by combustion of the high-sulphur coal).

Table 2: Tax Items and Rates of the Natural Resource Tax

Tax Item	Rate of tax payment	Notes
1. Crude oil	8-30 yuan/ton	Crude oil refers to the natural oil, not including refined oil from oil shale .
2. Natural gas	2-15 yuan/thousand cubic meter	Natural gas refers to those extracted separately or with crude oil, not including those produced by coal mines for the time being
3. Coal	0.3-5 yuan/ton	Coal refers to raw coal, not including washed coal and dressed coal from raw coal.
4. Other non-metal minerals	0.5-20 yuan/ton or cubic meter	
5. Ferrous metal minerals	2-30 yuan/ton	
6. Non-ferrous metal mineral	0.4-30 yuan/ton	
7. Salt	2-60 yuan/ton	

Source: State Council, 1993a.

Figure 5 shows the amount of natural resource tax collected since 1984. The amount collected did not contribute greatly to the expected increase in financial revenue. Indeed, from 1985 to 1993 the share of this tax in the overall tax revenue remained constant. The situation has not improved since 1994. The reason for the substantial rise in the natural resource tax revenue after 1994 is improved tax collection. This is clearly inconsistent with the observed rapid growth in natural resource development since less than 1.5% of total tax revenue in 1997 was sourced from this tax. State-owned enterprises are the principal source of the natural resource tax reflecting their major role in the economy as resource developers and users: statistics for 1996 indicate that the proportion of the natural resource tax revenue paid by the state-owned, collective and private enterprise sectors was 83.4%, 12.4% and 4.2% respectively.

---

[3]   Although water resources are not taxed, local governments generally charge a fee for water extraction and also a water resource fee. Based on our study, some cities charge up to 12 different fees related to water supply and sewerage.

Figure 5: Natural Resource Tax Revenue, 1984-1997

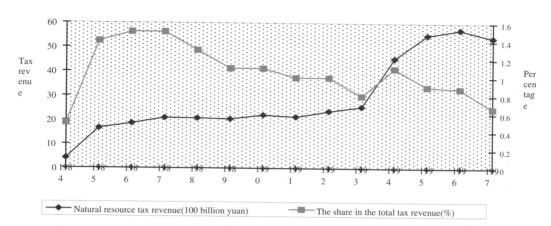

Legend:
— Natural resource tax revenue(100 billion yuan)   — The share in the total tax revenue(%)

3.2   Consumption Tax

The consumption tax was introduced as part of the 1994 tax reform to influence consumption patterns, restrain luxury goods consumption and increase financial revenue. It is composed of 5 categories, broken down into 11 types of consumption goods. The tax rates (and the amount of tax payment) of the 7 products related to the environment are shown in Table 3. However, the determination of the tax rates (or amount) does not reflect the external environmental costs of the related consumption[4].

Table 3: Tax Items and Tax Rates of the Consumption Tax

Tax item	Unit of measure	Tax rate (amount of tax due)
1. Tobacco		30% - 45%
2. Wine and Liquor		
(a) Liquor		15% - 25%
(b) Wine and beer	Ton	220 - 240yuan
3. Petrol	Liter	0.2 yuan
4. Diesel oil	Liter	0.1 yuan
5. Automobile tire		10%
6. Motorcycle		10%
7. Cars		3% - 8%

Source: State Council, 1993b.

The discussion below focuses on the consumption tax applied to petrol and diesel oil and vehicles.

---

[4] Although recently some local governments have considered charging a fee to reflect health damages from cigarette smoking. For example, Chongqing city began to charge such a fee on cigarette manufacturing and distribution businesses at a rate of 0.1% of their sales.

Petrol and Diesel Oil

Due to the close relationship between air pollution and energy consumption as well as vehicle use, imposing taxes on these items may, in theory, restrain the rise of energy related consumption or decrease the energy consumption elasticity of GNP. Compared with the situation before the 1994 tax reform, the tax burden of petrol and diesel oil increased 17.72% and 12.66%, respectively, as a result of collecting the value-added tax and consumption tax (Hao, *et al.*, 1994). Nevertheless, the upward trend of petrol consumption has not slowed. Nor has the energy consumption elasticity of GDP: it rose from 0.46 in 1994 to 0.60 in 1996. Figure 6 shows the trend in consumption tax collection since 1994[5].

Figure 6: Consumption Tax Revenue, 1994-1997

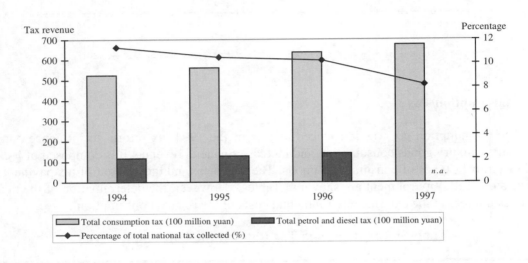

Vehicles

From an environmental point of view, limiting vehicle use can directly alleviate the problem of air pollution. However, the automobile industry has been listed as a pillar industry in the government's Ninth Five-Year Plan (1996-2000), with the economically efficient car as one of the Plan's priorities. Because the government's policy encourages vehicle production and use, the domestic production and purchase of motorcycles and cars has accelerated in recent years. This has implications for increasing urban air pollution and traffic congestion problems. Many high income families have bought cars. For example, the Beijing Youth Newspaper reported that of car sales during the fourth quarter of 1997, 75% were bought for private use. The number of automobiles (including goods vehicles) that were privately owned totalled 2.9 million in 1996, an increase of 4.09% since the consumption tax was levied on cars in 1994. This shows that the tax has had little effect in restraining car ownership. Its main function is to add to the financial revenue of the state. As private incomes grow, and given the importance placed on developing a robust domestic automobile industry, the demand for cars will increase and the consumption tax will likely be an increasingly blunt instrument to limit car ownership.

---

[5]   The amount of consumption tax to be paid on petrol and diesel is based on the previous year's consumption figure and the tax rate applicable. The specific gravity of petrol is calculated as 0.73 kg/l. The specific gravity of diesel is calculated as the average specific gravity of light and heavy diesel, giving a figure of 0.89 kg/l.

3.3   Vehicle Use Tax

Since 1951 the government has levied a vehicle use license tax. This tax was merged with the industry and business tax in 1973. In 1986, the vehicle use tax[6] was reconstituted. In accordance with "The Provisional Regulations for Collection of the Vehicle Use Tax", the tax is levied on vehicle use and strictly speaking is not an asset tax. The main objective of the tax is to provide funds for local governments, upgrading of local public roads and the maintenance of infrastructure. The tax rate applicable to motor-boats and automobiles is shown in Tables 4 and 5 respectively. From the tables, it is clear that there is no direct relationship between the vehicle use tax and the actual intensity of vehicle use (such as the number of km driven or the amount of petrol consumed) or with environmental impacts.

Table 4: Tax Rates for Motor Boats

Taxation Basis	Annual tax payment
Net tonnage ≤ 150 tons	1.20 yuan/ton
151 tons ≤ 500 tons	1.60 yuan/ton
501 tons ≤ 1500 tons	2.20 yuan/ton
1,501 tons ≤ 3, 000 tons	3.20 yuan/ton
3,001 tons ≤ 10,000 tons	4.20 yuan/ton
10,001 tons plus	5.00 yuan/ton

Source: State Council, 1986.

Table 5: Tax Rates for Motor Vehicles

Item	Taxation basis	Annual tax payment	Notes
Passenger vehicle	Per item	60 - 320 yuan	Includes trolley buses
Cargo vehicle	Per net tonnage	16 - 60 yuan	
Two-wheel motorcycle	Per item	20 - 60 yuan	
Three-wheel motorcycle	Per item	32 - 80 yuan	

Source: State Council, 1986.

Revenue collected under the vehicle use tax is shown in Figure 7. This shows that the share of the tax's share in total tax revenue has trended down even though the absolute amount of the income from the vehicle use tax has risen over time. On the other hand, the vehicle use tax is only a small part of the cost of using vehicles, making it difficult to adjust the behaviour of vehicle owners. In reality, it is traffic control instruments, such as limiting the issuance of new vehicle licences, charging a new vehicle fee and applying an "even and odd licence number" system[7] rather than this tax, which is often used to alleviate traffic congestion and reduce air pollution.

---

[6]   China currently levies a licence tax on vehicles used by foreign investment enterprises, enterprises set up by overseas Chinese and those established by Hong Kong, Macao and Chinese Taipei business persons.

[7]   In some downtown areas in large cities, vehicles with an even numbered licence plate are allowed to be used on even days of the month while those with an odd numbered licence plate can only circulate on the odd days of the month.

Figure 7: Vehicle Use Tax Revenue, 1987-1996

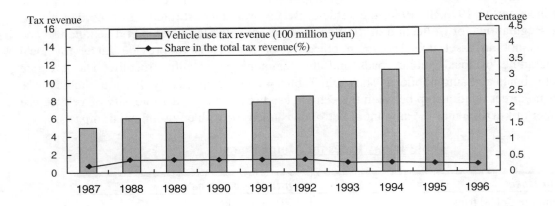

3.4   Urban Construction and Maintenance Tax

The urban construction and maintenance tax is a local tax introduced in February 1985 to enlarge and stabilise the sources of funds to finance urban infrastructure. Tax revenue is used specifically for public works such as housing, road and bridge maintenance, flood prevention structures, water supply, water drainage, district heating, ferry service, afforestation and environmental sanitation. It is also used to fund the construction and maintenance of fire stations, traffic signalisation and road lighting. The tax payers are the enterprises and individuals who pay the domestic value-added tax, business tax and consumption tax . The taxation basis is the actual amount of the above taxes paid by tax payers.

The normal process of introducing a local tax is for central government to prepare a framework law for the proposed tax and local governments to formulate detailed implementing regulations consistent with the provisions of the framework law. As a type of local tax, the urban maintenance and construction tax follows this process. According to the principle of tax burden sharing, i.e. "those who benefit pay, those who benefit more pay more tax", the tax rate is set depending on the geographical location of the tax payer and the degree of amenity received from the facilities. For tax payers located in urban areas, the tax rate is 7%. For tax payers located in counties and towns, the tax rate is 5% and for tax payers in other areas the tax rate is 1%.

Figure 8 shows the revenue collected from the urban construction and maintenance tax between 1985 and 1997. The tax receipts are quite small, less than 4% of the total tax revenue in any year. However, due to the specific local focus of the urban construction tax, it has become an important source of finance to support urban environmental facilities, including waste water collection and treatment plants, waste management, district heating system and clean fuel supply.

Figure 8: Revenue from the Urban Maintenance and Construction Tax, 1985-1997

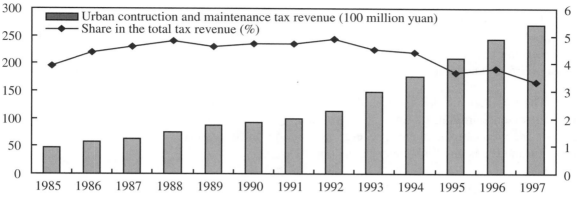

Because these types of facilities are of particular importance for improving urban air and water quality, this tax is a kind of "green" tax or a specific tax for environmental protection financing. Figure 9 shows that about 35% of total investment in environmental protection is sourced from this tax, accounting for approximately 45% of the revenue collected[8]. With further economic development and a revision of the taxation base and rates, the funds from this source are likely to rise. Hopefully, it will evolve to become a stable, sustainable financial mechanism for the construction and maintenance of urban environmental protection facilities.

Figure 9: Revenue from the Urban Construction and Maintenance Tax, 1986-1996, and Percentage Used for Investments in Environmental Protection

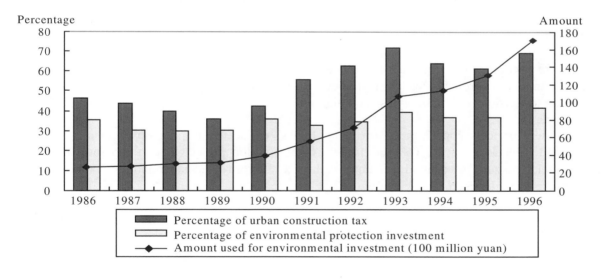

---

[8]   In Figure 9, the sources of urban environmental investment after 1991 include subsidies and other contributions in addition to the urban maintenance and construction tax.

3.5   Fixed Asset Investment Direction Adjustment Tax

This tax (abbreviated hereafter as "adjustment tax") is aimed at implementing the state's industrial policy, guiding the direction of investment, adjusting the structure of investment and promoting the construction of priority projects. It was introduced in 1991. In line with the requirements of the state's industrial policy and economies of scale, differential tax rates are applied to different investment projects.

The tax rates are designed on the basis of three principles. First, to ensure consistency with the requirement of encouraging or limiting investment types as set out in the state's industrial policy. For instance, it encourages investment in energy production but limits investment in projects associated with major pollution effects and high energy consumption.

Second, to promote economies of scale. For example, while encouraging investment in electric power projects, the projects should be evaluated and treated on a case by case basis according to their installed capacity. Projects with over 100,000 kW of installed thermal power capacity are charged an adjustment tax rate of zero percent while those with 25,000 -100,000 kW of installed capacity are taxed at 5%.

Third, to encourage modernisation of technology used by enterprises. Compared with investments in construction projects, those that focus on technological upgrading enjoy a preferential tax rate.

The adjustment tax is applied to two categories of investment projects, each with differential rates. The schedules of tax items and tax rates are revised by the State Council regularly. The first category is investment in construction projects, housing and other fixed assets. In this case, four levels of tax rates have been established: 0%, 5%, 15% and 30%. Specifically, the zero tax rate is levied on investment projects in agriculture and forestry, water conservancy, energy, traffic, communication, urban construction and environmental protection that are priorities supported by the state; the 5% tax rate applies to investment projects in the main raw material sectors of steel, chemicals, petrochemicals and cement which are encouraged by the state but hindered by energy and communications limitations; the 30% tax rate is applied to projects that are restricted by the state's industrial policy and those of small production scale, low efficiency of energy use and high pollution.

Investment projects concentrating on technological replacement and renovation comprise the second category. The tax rates are 0% and 10%. A construction project that incorporates upgraded technology is subject to zero per cent adjustment tax; the tax rate for replacement and renovation projects that do not include upgraded technology is 10%.

As a tax aimed at modifying behaviour, theoretically the revenue collected is not symmetrical with the role of the tax. Simply put, the less the actual amount of tax collected, the greater the effects of adjusting the fixed asset investment and the smaller the scale of investment in the sector or product associated with high energy consumption and pollution. The revenue collected by the adjustment tax is shown in Figure 10. This shows that the amount of tax collected increased steadily between 1991 and 1996, attributable to the continued increase in project investments and the range of activities to which the tax applies.

Figure 10: Revenue from the Investment Direction Adjustment Tax, 1991-1996

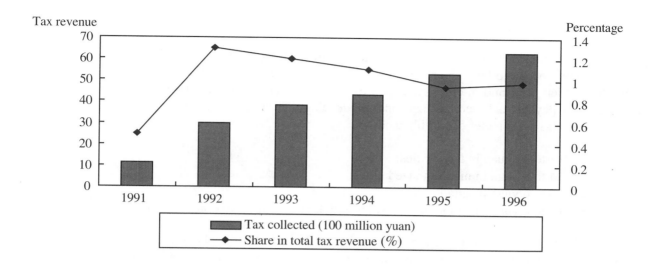

The adjustment tax provides a way to influence environmental protection efforts through the adjustment of the investment variable. This is in the nature of pollution prevention. That is, from an environmental protection point of view the adjustment tax promotes cleaner energy production, improved efficiency in energy use, and reduced pollution generation.

Limiting growth in pollution-generating sectors through application of the adjustment tax does not directly contradict China's economic development goals. When the project satisfies neither the economic benefit criterion nor the environmental benefit criterion, the adjustment tax is consistent with the industrial policy goal of limiting ineffective investments. Conversely, when the project satisfies both criteria the tax is consistent with the industrial policy objective of encouraging sound investments. For example, a thermal power project of over 100,000 kW installed capacity may be positive both in terms of economies of scale and pollution control. Accordingly, the adjustment tax rate would be zero.

When the economic and environmental criteria are not conjointly satisfied, the policy goal of economic growth takes priority in evaluating the tax rate to be applied. For example, a 5% tax rate is levied on the raw material production sectors of steel, chemicals, petrochemicals and cement which are energy intensive and generate significant pollution. This is considered a necessary choice in the primary stage of developing a market economy in China. Usually other supplementary policies and rules are needed to solve this type of contradiction. For instance, for development projects that are prohibited by government decrees measures other than the adjustment tax are used to stop further work. As soon as such a project comes to the attention of the authorities, work must stop immediately, Either the physical and financial investments are confiscated by the authorities or some mandatory measure such as "closure, stopping, merging and transfer" is undertaken to settle the matter.

3.6   Urban Land Tax and Cultivated Land Occupation Tax

Urban Land Tax

To promote effective use of urban land resources and to adjust the differential rent of urban land, the government began to levy an urban land tax from November, 1988. The tax payer is the enterprise or individual which uses land in cities, counties, townships, and dedicated industrial and mining areas. The amount of tax payable is based on the economic development in the area concerned. The annual amount payable on each square meter of taxable land is:

- 0.5 to 10 yuan in large cities;
- 0.4 to 8 yuan in medium-sized cities;
- 0.3 to 6 yuan in small cities;
- 0.2 to 4 yuan in counties, townships and dedicated industrial and mining areas.

The provincial government may vary the taxable rate for the above categories according to the economic development and urban infrastructure situation within its administrative boundary. At present, the nation-wide revenue collected from this tax is about 4 billion yuan (see Figure 11), which is less than 1% of the overall tax revenue. Therefore, this tax has no effect on protecting the urban land resource and promoting efficient land use. It is essentially a small tax category that supplements the funds of local governments.

Figure 11: Revenue from the Urban Land Tax, 1989-1997

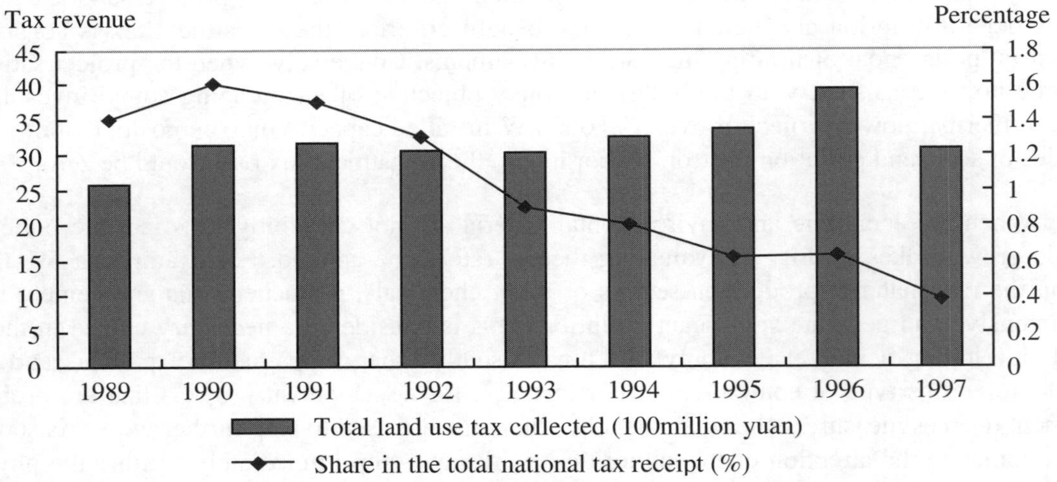

76

This tax was introduced in 1987 with the objectives of improving land use and arresting the decline in area of arable land. The tax payer is the enterprise or individual who occupies the cultivated land to build housing or engage in non-agriculture related development. The amount of tax levied varies based on the local average occupation of cultivated land and the level of economic development. The annual tax due for each square metre of taxable land is:

- 2 to 10 yuan for an area with less than 1 *mu*[9] cultivated land per head;
- 1.6 to 8 yuan for an area between 1 to 2 *mu* cultivated land per head;
- 1.3 to 6.5 yuan for an area between 2 to 3 *mu* cultivated land per head;
- 1 to 5 yuan for an area with over 3 *mu* cultivated land per head.

Revenue collected is specifically used for establishing local agricultural development funds.

The tax has proved effective in limiting the arbitrary occupation and misuse of cultivated land even though the amount of tax collected is relatively low. During the three years before the tax was introduced, land use by non-agriculture related developments averaged 3.24 million *mu* per annum. After 1987, following the implementation of the tax, the situation changed; land use by the same type of development was 2.44, 1.32, and 0.9 million *mu* in 1987, 1988 and 1989 respectively (Pan, 1994). According to statistics from the State Administration of Taxation revenue in 1997 from this tax was 3.1 billion yuan, or 0.4% of the country's overall tax revenue .

3.7   Value-Added Tax

Value-added tax is levied on the incremental value associated with goods production, merchandising, sales and service supply. It is a tax implemented in many countries. Since 1994, China has been levying this tax. Due to the wide range of goods and services potentially subject to value-added tax there is an indirect relationship between the tax and some environmental resources, such as production inputs which generate environmental pollution.

The value-added tax rates applied in China are divided into three groups based on the principle of neutrality and simplicity in operation:

- the basic rate (17%): applied to the tax payer who sells (or imports) taxable goods and services;

- the low rate (13%): applied to sales or imports of products or commodities, such as cereals, drinking water, heating, hot water, air conditioning equipment, coal gas, liquefied petroleum gas, natural gas, biogas, coal products for residential use, chemical fertilizers, agri-chemicals, plastic sheeting used in agriculture[10]; and

---

[9]   One mu is about 667m^2.

[10]   According to the provisions of the government's 1996/18 finance and tax paper, plastic sheeting used in agriculture and some chemical fertilisers and agri-chemicals were exempted from value-added tax between 1 January 1996 to 31 December 1997.

- a zero rate: applied to goods for export. In practice, tax paid on such goods is refunded.

This tax is the largest source of tax revenue in China. In 1996, the figure was 267 billion yuan, accounting for 42.9% of overall tax income that year.

From an environmental point of view, items subject to the low tax rate can be divided into two types. The first includes gas heating, coal gas and model coal products for residential use[11]. The second includes agricultural pesticides, chemical fertilisers and plastic sheeting used in agriculture. Arguably, the tax rate should be lower on those items that have an environmental protection role. However, due to the principle of "neutrality" established in the value-added tax, and the importance of agricultural chemicals and chemical fertilisers as inputs to agriculture, in the short- and medium-term it is unlikely that these two items will be subject to a higher tax rate.

4.0   Implementation and Reform of the Pollution Levy System

From an economic point of view, a pollution charge is a quasi-pollution tax based on the "polluter pays principle (PPP)". China's environmental management and finance ministries do not regard pollution charges as a pollution tax, however. The pollution levy (charge) system is the economic instrument most widely used in environmental management in China. Practical experience has shown positive results in reducing pollution and in financing environmental protection investments. However, the system urgently needs a comprehensive reform to adapt it to the conditions of a deepening market economy and new environmental objectives. In response, the State Environmental Protection Administration (SEPA) is undertaking a major reform of the system based on trial implementation of the framework proposed in a research project on the design and implementation of the Chinese pollution levy system[12].

4.1   Implementation of the Pollution Levy System

Over the past 17 years the pollution levy system has undergone three stages of trial, implementation and revision. A system of supporting regulations has been established, including state laws, administrative laws and regulations and rules and regulations applicable to departments and local governments. The pollution levy has been widely implemented in all provinces and municipalities (counties) nation-wide.

Levy Collection

As of 1996, the pollution levy had been collected from 496,000 enterprises and the total revenue obtained was just over 29 billion yuan. In 1996, the amount collected was 4.1 billion yuan. Figure 12 shows the trend in pollution charge collection between 1986-1996.

---

[11]   Comparatively speaking, central heating is more environmentally-friendly and efficient than individual household heating; coal gas and model coal products are more environmentally benign than untreated coal.

[12]   This project is supported by funds from the World Bank (Technical Assistance Project B-8-1) and is being carried out by the Chinese Research Academy of Environmental Sciences. It is the most comprehensive research project yet undertaken on the pollution levy system and sets out a wide-ranging programme of suggested reforms.

Figure 12: Pollution Charge Collection, 1986-1996

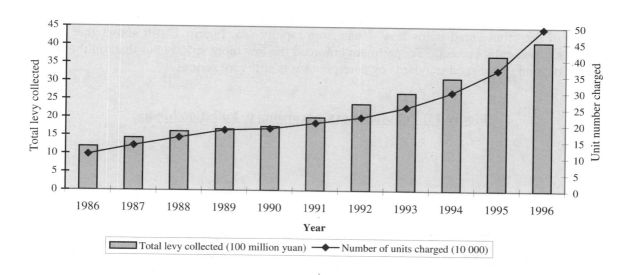

Number of Enterprises Levied

Pollution levies were applied to just over 368,000 enterprises in 1995, or about 24.77% of total industrial enterprises nation-wide (not including private enterprises). By sector, the main industries charged were metallurgy, chemicals, light industry, textiles, power and coal. Broken down by ownership, central and provincial government-owned enterprises accounted for 125,000, or 3.39%, of the total number charged and municipal and county-owned enterprises comprised 55,800 (15.2%) of the total. A rapid increase in the number of enterprises that fall under the jurisdiction of sub-county level governments is becoming evident, rising from 51,100 in 1985 to 299,900 in 1995. Accordingly, their share in the total number of enterprises rose from 57.3% to 81.5%. This was the result of the extraordinary growth of township and village enterprises (TVEs) in the past decade.

Total Amount of Pollution Levy Collected

Figure 12 shows that the amount of pollution levy collected increased by 2.13 times during the ten year period between 1986 and 1995, at an annual growth rate of 12.7% (higher than that of gross industrial production value which was 11.46%). The share of pollution levy collection in gross industrial production value decreased from 0.11% in 1986 to 0.04% in 1995. In addition, although the absolute number of township and village enterprises increased substantially between 1985 and 1995 (as noted above) the share of the pollution levy collected from this sector declined from about 0.03% in 1986 to approximately 0.01% in 1995. In 1995 alone, the share contributed by township and village enterprises to gross national industrial production value was over 50%, but they only accounted for about 13.4% of the total pollution levy collected that year. There is, therefore, great potential for improving the collection of pollution levies from this particular sector.

Structure of the Pollution Levy

The water pollution levy is the largest component of the system. In the past decade the proportion of the "four small items levy"[13] has risen rapidly (see Figure 13). It shows that, on the one hand, the environmental protection department enforced the law more strictly but that, on the other hand, discharges beyond established standards by enterprises was still very serious.

Figure 13: Pollution Levy According to Pollution Media

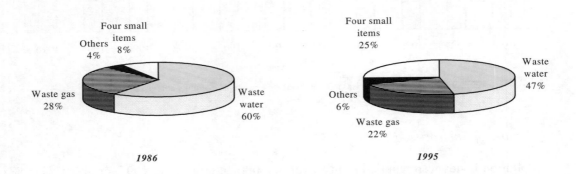

State-owned enterprises are the major payers of the pollution levy. Their contributions accounted for 60.28% of the overall pollution levy collected in 1995. The share of their contribution has trended down over time, however, while that of the township and village-owned enterprises has risen. By sector, the key ones are metallurgy, coal, chemicals and light industry.

Allocation of the Revenue

In accordance with the pollution levy policy, 80% of the revenue collected from the pollution levy is used to fund pollution abatement initiatives by enterprises while the remaining 20% and the revenue from the "four small items levy" are at the disposal of the environmental protection department and used mainly for covering operational costs of levy collection and local capacity building. Nevertheless, there are some provinces and municipalities that have adjusted this 80-20 split. Table 6 illustrates the general situation in the use of revenue raised by the pollution levy in recent years.

---

[13]   This refers to double levying, a levy following the raising of standards, overdue fines and compensatory fines.

Table 6: National Situation Concerning the Use of Revenue Collected from the Pollution Levy

Year	1991	1992	1993	1994	1995
Charges used (100 million yuan)	17.84	21.65	24.83	27.00	32.20
Percentage of the total charge collected (%)	88.71	90.78	92.44	86.68	86.42
Amount used as subsidies for pollution control (grants and loans) (100 million yuan)	12.00	13.98	15.09	16.19	17.71
Percentage of the charges used (%)	67.26	64.57	60.77	59.96	55.00
Amount used for local capacity building in environmental management (100 million yuan)	5.64	7.44	9.42	10.47	14.14
Percentage of charges used(%)	31.61	38.38	37.54	36.56	35.31

Source: SEPA statistics; China Environmental Yearbook, 1996

Balancing Revenue Expenditure on Pollution Abatement and Capacity Building

A frequently discussed topic about the use of revenue from the pollution levy system is the balance between pollution abatement and capacity building in the environmental management. The basic reason is that local budgets are incapable of financing the work of sub-national environmental protection bureaus and offices.

Figure 14 illustrates the expected and actual situations in 1995. Because of tight local budgetary constraints and various other reasons, diversion and interception of revenue occurred resulting in amounts lower than that stipulated in the government's policy available both for investment in pollution abatement and capacity building.

Figure 14: Use of Revenue from the Pollution Levy: Expected versus Actual Situation, 1995

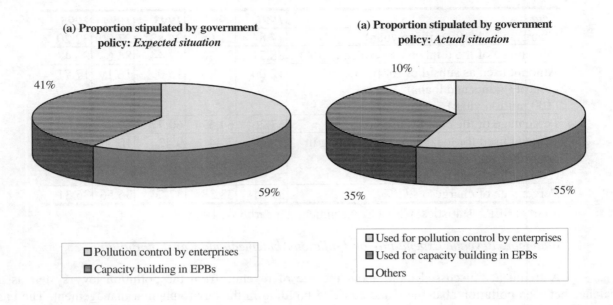

(a) Proportion stipulated by government policy: *Expected situation*

41%

59%

☐ Pollution control by enterprises
▣ Capacity building in EPBs

(a) Proportion stipulated by government policy: *Actual situation*

10%

35%

55%

☐ Used for pollution control by enterprises
▣ Used for capacity building in EPBs
☐ Others

(i) Pollution Abatement

Prior to 1988, the government's policy stipulated that "refund" of the pollution levy to enterprises was unconditional. In 1988 this was changed so that the "free" allocation back to enterprises became a loan. The share of loans within the overall revenue collected under the pollution levy system has increased each year and is now close to 40% of the total. For pollution abatement in enterprises, loans from the pollution levy system account for about 20% of their total abatement investment.

(ii) Capacity Building

To take account of the cost to the sub-national environmental protection bureaus and offices in implementing the pollution levy system[14] and the difficulties of local financing, a portion of the pollution levy collected must be used to pay for operational expenses. This situation is expected to continue for some time. In general, the share of the pollution levy revenue used for local capacity building is less than the level permitted by the government's policy.

Results

The pollution levy system has now been operational nation-wide for 17 years. It has been a remarkable success: pollution abatement has increased and local capacity building in sub-national environmental protection offices has been strengthened.

---

[14] Sub-national environmental protection bureaus and offices, including their staff, are funded by local government not central government.

(i) Pollution Abatement

By 1995, almost 9.7 billion yuan had been committed to pollution abatement. An environmental loan fund of just over 2.9 billion yuan had also been established. There were 220,000 pollution control projects financed by revenue raised through the pollution levy, of which 210,000 had been completed. These projects can process 17 billion tons of wastewater annually, 4000 billion cubic meters of waste gas per annum, process for reuse 70 million tons of solid waste, and attenuate 19,000 sources of noise pollution.

(ii) Capacity Building

Up to 1995, about 6.1 billion yuan had been used in capacity building projects. The actual expenditure for the establishment of environmental protection bureaus and offices was 5.4 billion yuan. This included the employment of 38,000 staff, of which 17,000 were employed in environmental monitoring, and the setting up of 2000 environmental supervision institutions.

4.2   Existing Problems in Pollution Levy Implementation

There are three major problems associated with the current pollution levy system.

First, levy application. The present system only charges for emissions exceeding the relevant national or local pollution standard. In addition, the charge is mainly based on the amount of pollution that exceeds the standard without taking into account the total amount of pollution discharged. Also, the present system stipulates that when there are several pollutants exceeding the standard, it is only the one that attracts the highest fee rate that is charged. Therefore, the polluter only has an incentive to focus on the pollutant with the highest charge rather than trying to reduce all of them. The collection of the pollution levy is not strictly related to the physical location of polluters, which is inconsistent with the environmental management system under which polluters are managed by local environmental protection bureaus.

Second, the rate schedules on which the pollution levy is based are too low. It is estimated that the yield of current rates is far below the operating cost of pollution control equipment, in some cases being only 25% of the pollution control cost. In recent years, the escalating rate of inflation has worsened the problem. In addition, there is incomplete coverage of pollutants within the levy system despite there being 113 chargeable items divided among five categories (wastewater, waste gas, solid waste, noise and radioactivity). For example, there is no standard for hazardous waste, household wastewater and garbage, and mobile pollution sources. Finally, the charge is levied on the pollution media rather the pollutant itself.

Third, the management and use of revenue raised by the pollution levy. In China, there is a strong view that pollution levy funds belong to polluters. This seriously impedes reform of fund collection, management and use. "Illegal" fund use is another problem. This refers to the phenomena of massive removal and hoarding of funds by some government agencies. An investigation by the former National Environmental Protection Agency (since March 1998, renamed the State Environmental Protection Administration), backed up by statistical analysis, showed that from 1981 until the end of 1996, "illegal" use of funds from the pollution levy amounted to 2.93 billion yuan, accounting for 13.76% of the total pollution levy collected in the same period.

Management responsibility for revenue raised is not coherent. The provinces and municipalities establish management arrangements to suit their particular interests, which leads to confusion in revenue management. For example, distribution of money from the "four small items levy" is problematic. Because of higher standards in collecting the pollution levy, revenue from the "four small items levy" has risen quickly and its share in total pollution levy receipts has increased each year. According to the current policy, money from the "four small items levy" is at the direct disposal of local environmental protection bureaus which therefore have a vested interest in ensuring that collection is undertaken expeditiously.

4.3   Reforming the Pollution Levy System

The overall objectives of reforming the pollution levy system are to set up a mechanism that is suitable for a market-economy, that supports the achievement of China's environmental management priorities, that promotes pollution abatement and that supports the accumulation of funds for environmental protection investments. The proposed reform focuses on three aspects: pollution levy standards, use of pollution levy revenue and revenue management.

Reform of Standards for Assessing the Pollution Levy

The principal proposed changes from the existing situation are:

- shifting from a focus on charging for discharges that exceed national and local standards to charging for any discharge irrespective of amount;

- changing from charging based on concentration only to charging both concentration and total amount of pollutant;

- moving from a single pollutant charge to multiple pollutants charge;

- shifting from a static charge to dynamic charges; and

- refocusing from low charge rates to high rates that are higher than pollution abatement costs.

In setting the goals of the pollution levy, those of stimulating pollution abatement and raising revenue are not mutually exclusive although their relative emphasis may differ in practice. For instance, if the aim is to promote pollution abatement the focus should be on the incentive function through, for example, a realistic high water-pollution charge. On the other hand, a broad-based user charge would support a revenue raising function.

In order to simplify collection of the pollution levy, the concept of "pollution equivalent" is introduced into the new standards used for charging waste water discharge and air pollution emissions. The "pollution equivalent" is defined in relation to the relative amount of specific pollutants and pollution activities, based on their environmental damage potential, toxicity to organisms and technical possibilities for control and treatment. In other words, the pollution equivalent expresses the relative relationship between the environmental damage associated with various pollutants or pollution and the abatement cost.

The suggested new pollution levy rates are shown in Table 7[15]. Based on 1995 data from 77 cities nation-wide, it is estimated that the theoretical revenue collected that year would have been between 44.8 - 55 billion yuan under the proposed new charge rates. This is 10 times more than the actual amount collected that year. Under the proposed new rates, the main pollutants charged are CO_2 and SO_2, representing 32.1% and 32.7% respectively of the share of the overall pollution levy. Broken down into the components of the levy applied only to air and water pollution, CO_2 and SO_2 pollutants represent 55.4% and 75% of the respective totals. Among the 12 pollutants subject to government controls on total releases, revenue collected from the 8 water pollutants accounts for 68% of the overall amount collected in the water sector. The revenue collected from the 3 atmospheric pollutants subject to the same controls accounts for 95.3% of the overall amount collected in the air sector. These figures illustrate the effectiveness of the pollution levy as a potential instrument for controlling total pollutant releases. Among economic sectors, the highest levies are paid by, successively, power, metal smelting, pulp and paper, chemicals, food and construction. Under the suggested new levy rates, the average ratio of pollution charge to industrial production value is 9.45‰, while the ratio of pollution charge to production cost is 12.89‰. Eighty-five percent of the pollution charge is borne by the consumer and the enterprise. The influence of the new rates on prices is considered to be small, with an average increase of 2.09%. The most significant effect is on power prices where a 0.004 yuan increase for each kWh is estimated.

If the new rate schedules for the pollution levy are adopted and the collection rate reaches 70%, then the annual leviable amount is about 36 billion yuan. This is estimated to provide 40% of the revenue needed for environmental protection investments. However, if account is taken of the annual economic and environmental losses caused by pollution, the receipts under the new rates can only cover 25% of the cost of environmental investments.

---

[15] The Chinese Research Academy of Environmental Sciences has developed four plans for proposed discharge standards covering wastewater, air, solid waste, noise and low level radioactive waste. For simplicity, only the fourth of these plans is shown in Table 7, i.e. a multiple pollutant charge standard based on total amounts of discharge/emission.

Table 7: Proposed Pollution Levy Rate Schedules: An Example

Charge item	Unit rate	Remarks
Water pollutants	Discharge not in excess of the standard: 1.4 yuan/pollution equivalent (PE) Discharge in excess of the standard: 2.8 yuan/PE Special industries(including animal husbandry, small enterprises and services): 2.0 yuan/PE	1PE = 1000g COD = 500g BOD (5 days) = 0.5g Hg (PE = Pollution Equivalent)
Air pollutants	Discharge not in excess of the standard: 1.2 yuan/PE Discharge in excess of the standard: 1.2 yuan/PE	1PE = 670g SO_2 = 480g NOx = 500g TSP
Solid wastes	Industrial solid wastes: 5 -30 yuan/ton Hazardous wastes: 1000yuan/ton	Charges levied on polluters without "Three Prevention" facilities
Noise	For every db in excess of the noise standard: 350 - 11,200 yuan/month	Calculated according to the db level in excess of the noise standard
Automobiles	100 - 1100 yuan/vehicle/year	Based on noise and emissions
Domestic sewage	0.38 yuan/ton of sewage 30 yuan/person/year	Each city can make some modification to the national average rate
Domestic refuse	60 yuan/ton of refuse or 90 yuan/person/year	Each city can make some modification to the national average rate

Under the new pollution levy system, an area coefficient, environmental capacity coefficient and time coefficient are included. The area coefficient has three values to reflect differences among developed, general and developing areas in terms of their economic development and pressures on environmental quality. The environmental capacity coefficient incorporates five values to take account of the differences among areas in environmental capacity and differences in environmental functions (e.g. land and water use). The time coefficient refers to the adjustment of the rate schedules to take account of inflation.

Reform of Pollution Levy Revenue Management and Use

The basic objectives of reforming the management of revenue raised by the pollution levy are to rationalise the allocation of money and to maximise its use. Taking account of the existing problems and the expected functions of a new pollution levy system, the following reforms are required:

- revenue from the pollution levy should be subject to standard budget management procedures. The principle of collecting money first and then using it later should be abolished gradually;

- the principle of local environmental protection bureaus collecting the pollution levy from polluters located in their administrative area should be firmly upheld to ensure a rational approach to revenue collection and management;

- greater clarity and stability is needed in the share of revenue destined for the central government in order to strengthen its ability to invest in environmental protection at a macro level.

From the perspective of the reform of China's tax system, revision of the pollution levy will inevitably affect the current charge basis. Under a market economy, strong taxes and weak charges appears to be the basic trend. Charging may be considered a temporary financial policy in the long run. Changes in the management of revenue collected under the pollution levy will intensify calls to include money from this type of charge within the coverage of the general budget system. At the same time, a special fund for environmental protection should be set up in all levels of government.

For the effective reinforcement of its role and responsibilities in carrying out environmental management, the central government should also share the revenue generated by the pollution levy. Although reform of the system may result in objections from local environmental protection bureaus, it could get their support provided the rights and obligations for environmental affairs at all levels of government are clear and upheld.

Several points can be made concerning the management and distribution of revenue from the pollution levy. First, all money collected (including from the "four small items levy") should be turned over to the finance ministry and included in the budget. Second, the finance ministry should set aside 60% of the revenue provided to establish a special fund for investments in environmental protection. The remaining 40% would be used to cover the administrative expenditure of sub-national environmental protection bureaus but in time this money would progressively revert to the finance ministry and be considered part of the general budget. Third, "environmental protection subsidies" should be abolished and the "comprehensive abatement subsidy" merged into the special fund for investments in environmental protection. Fourth, an "administration fee for environmental protection" should be established at each level of government with money from the pollution levy channelled thereto and expenditure deducted therefrom.

The special fund for investments in environmental protection would mainly finance projects concerned with pollution control facilities, the development of cleaner technology, protection of natural resources, compensation for victims of pollution and the expenditure of local environmental protection bureaus. The special fund could operate at national, provincial, municipal and county levels, with different foci but consistent with national goals for environmental management. To finance environmental investments of enterprises and local governments, low interest loans (soft loans) and credit guarantees could be used.

Consolidating the Principle of Loans

The development of improved policies for revenue use, based on the principle of repayable loans, is urgently needed. In particular, three successive initiatives should be undertaken. First, shifting from providing loans that are partially repayable to requiring full repayment. Second, changing from charging low interest rates to charging quasi-commercial rates. In the interim, projects that show strong environmental benefits should be evaluated against favourable discount rates. Third, abolishing exemptions so that the perception that revenue from the pollution levy is "refunded unconditionally" to contributing enterprises is broken.

4.4   Sequencing Implementation

Redefinition of the charge rates under the pollution levy system is at the heart of the reform process. The implementation of the new rates should be a process beginning with trials and progressively building to nation-wide implementation.

The proposed new pollution charge rate is higher than the current rate by 4 to 10 times and essentially embodies the principle of "higher than the abatement cost". Because it is difficult to implement the reform in one phase, a step-wise approach is proposed. Before the year 2000, charging 50% of the design rates is suggested. After that the rates are to be increased progressively by 20% each year until 2002 when the design rates are fully implemented[16].

In general, reform of the pollution levy should be consistent with the goals of revisions to the tax system. Synergies between reform of the use of revenue obtained under the pollution levy and changes to the financial system should taken advantage of.

5.0   Greening the Tax System and Environmental Taxes

Practical experience in OECD countries demonstrates that establishing environmental taxes or greening the tax system can be complementary to general tax reform. At present, China is deepening its reform of the general tax system, of which changes to taxes and fees are especially important elements. In this section of the paper, and based on the above analysis of tax policy and the pollution levy, several preliminary proposals for introducing environmental taxes and to green the tax system in China are outlined.

Deepening Reform of the Tax System

(i) The Need for Reform

The 1994 reform of China's tax system has yielded four achievements (Ministry of Finance, 1996; Li, 1997). First, the rule of law applies fully to the tax system, providing a necessary support for the development of a market economy. Second, the reform standardised the relationships governing the distribution of revenue, stimulated new initiatives by central and local government, promoted the rapid growth of tax income and strengthened the fund raising function of taxes. Third, the reform rationalised tax policies so that the definition of taxable sources was improved, the distribution of the tax burden was made fairer and anomalies between the taxes levied on state-owned and non-state-owned enterprises were

---

[16]   The State Environmental Protection Administration planned to undertake a trial of the proposed system in the cities of Hongzhou, Zhengzhou and Jilin in 1998. The trial was to be based on applying a charge rate of 50% of the final recommended rate.

reduced. Fourth, the reform improved the structure of taxation. In general, the new system is not only consistent with world standards but also better reflects China's domestic tax conditions. The most distinct characteristic of the new system is that taxes have become more "neutral", i.e. the role of the market in resource allocation has strengthened.

Despite these achievements, the task of tax reform is unfinished. Urgent problems that need to be addressed include enhancing revenue stability and improving efficiency and fairness. First, the low share of taxation revenue in GDP has remained unchanged. As Figure 4 showed, the share dropped from 12.3% in 1993 to 10.1% in 1996[17]. This trend at the macro level indicates that the current tax base is not very rational, that the tax burden of enterprises is decreasing and suggests little progress on deep-seated problems such as low efficiency in tax collection.

Second, the new system could be more scientific, standardised and fair. Examples include the very high share of the circulation tax; incoherent tax categories, tax base and tax rates; and an unnecessarily narrow tax base for the value-added tax.

Third, the local tax system needs improvement. This applies particularly to the tax categories established by local governments which are not always consistent with the national level groupings. The current tax system yields such a low amount of local tax receipts in some under-developed areas that it falls well below the local government's needs.

From an environmental protection point of view, the "green" element of the current tax system is small. The items subject to tax and rates applying to most of the tax categories reflect neither environmental protection nor sustainable development considerations. There is no use made of differential taxes to create incentives for modifying behaviour, such as setting a high tax rate to restrain use of "environmentally-unfriendly" goods (such as high-sulphur coal) and stimulating greater demand for those that are "environmentally-friendly" (such as clean coal and central heating) through preferential tax treatment.

(ii) Objectives

The government set out the objectives for deepening its tax reform in "The National Taxation Development Strategy for the Ninth Five-Year Plan and the Long-term Objectives for 2010" (simplified hereafter to "Strategy"). The Strategy states that the annual growth rate of tax revenue should reach 10% during the Ninth Five-Year Plan period (1996-2000). The new tax system should be coherent, ensure a fair tax burden and clearly specify the functions and division of authority between various levels of government. The functions of the tax system should be fully implemented and tax revenue should be doubled by 2000. A tax system, including appropriate revenue collection mechanisms, that meet the needs of a market economy should be established by 2010. A legally constituted collection authority system should also be set up.

---

[17]   However, if the various fees and appropriations of local government are included the overall percentage of charges and taxes in GDP has fluctuated up and down. Table 8 shows that the figures for 1985, 1993 and 1996 were 25.4%, 16.4% and 18.9% respectively.

(iii)   Scope

Based on the above objectives, the scope of deepening tax reform can be divided into five aspects (State General Taxation Office, 1996; Liu, 1997; Li, 1997). First, existing tax law should be reinforced. This includes the progressive establishment of tax legislation consistent with the needs of a market-based economy and which covers both central and local governments.

Second, a rational overall tax burden should be defined so as to ensure steady growth in revenue and a growing share of tax receipts in GDP. The main instruments available include strengthening financial budget management, refining the current tax categories and items, and levying new taxes where appropriate.

Third, a clear tax structure should be established. In particular, by simplifying tax categories, collecting social security tax, increasing the proportion of direct tax and raising the share of local taxes within the overall tax system.

Fourth, the tax categories should be revised. This could be carried out by gradually enlarging the tax base, adjusting tax rates and progressively abolishing tax exceptions. According to the principle of tax neutrality, value-added tax should be standardised and the role of the consumption tax should be consolidated and extended. Consistent with the principles of efficiency and fairness, the tax base for personal income tax and natural resource taxes should be enhanced and the asset tax improved.

Finally, improvement in tax reporting systems. The aim is to establish a reporting and monitoring system based on both computerised networks and in-field tax inspection teams.

(iv)   Shifting From a Charge to a Tax

As noted in Section 1.0, charges and taxes are considered as two different concepts in China. However, because of the financial difficulties and the lack of legislative powers in some provinces, their governments prefer to use charges as a means to make up for financial shortfalls. Three major issues have arisen from this practice.

First, in some areas, the burden imposed by charges is higher than that of taxes. The number of local level charges and their restricted distribution erode contributions to the national tax revenue. Table 8 shows that the charge burden of GDP is rising steadily. In 1996, the share was already 8.8%.

Second, the basis of some of the charges at local government level is questionable. They not only add to the financial pressures faced by farmers and enterprises but also do little to discourage corruption.

Third, a large amount of charges are managed outside the general budget. This weakens the financial function of the central and local governments. From its perspective, reform of charges is important.

Table 8: Revenue from Charges and Taxes as Share of GDP

Year	Revenue from charges (100 million yuan)	Revenue from taxation (100 million yuan)	GDP (100 million yuan)	% of charge revenue in GDP	% of tax revenue in GDP	Total % of charges and taxes in GDP
1985	233.21	2040.79	8964.4	2.6	22.8	25.4
1990	760.00	2821.83	18547.9	4.1	15.2	19.3
1993	1432.5	4255.30	34634.4	4.1	12.3	16.4
1995	3843.00	6038.04	58260.5	6.6	10.3	16.9
1996	6000.00	6901.35	67795.0	8.8	10.1	18.9

Source: Liu, 1997.

However, deepening tax reform is not about replacing the various charges by taxes. The co-existence of taxes and charges is common in financial systems in many countries, particularly in the area of environmental protection. In the case of China, taxes cannot replace all the existing charges in the near future. In practical terms, in China the two complement each other (see Table 9).

Table 9: Comparison of the Characteristics of a Charge and Tax in China

	Tax	Charge
Process	Strict legislative process, not easily changed	Administrative process, easier to adjust
Approval authority	National People's Congress, Ministry of Finance	State Development Planning Commission and provincial governments
Collection Agent	Taxation department or delegated representatives	Various, but usually not the tax department
Targets	General	Specific targets or groups
Revenue use	Goes to the general budget	Largely used for special purposes
Relationship with national economic development	Increases with national economic development and income levels	Static nature, has less relation with national economic development

The government has identified the reform of charges and taxes as one of its major areas of work. Six issues in particular require special attention.

First, the charges themselves. Although they have important deficiencies in implementation which need to be addressed, their use should not be suppressed (Liu, 1997). Indeed, abolishing charges in China is neither rational nor realistic. Some charges related to key traded technologies have a formal legal basis. They are important instruments to achieve national policy goals and cannot be easily changed into taxes.

Second, the balance between charges and taxes. Not all charges lend themselves to such a shift, for both political and pragmatic reasons. A case by case analysis is needed as well as research into how existing charges could be strengthened.

Third, sequencing of initiatives. The general direction of the reform process is to enhance the role of taxes and at the same time to retain charges (Ma, 1997). A first task might therefore be to eliminate unjustifiable charges followed by changing some local authority-levied charges into taxes, where practicable.

Fourth, clear definition of items subject to charges. This is likely to lead to some consolidation in the number of charges, including the transformation of some into taxes.

Fifth, the ability of farmers and enterprises to absorb a shift of some charges to taxes. Charges and taxes paid by farmers and enterprises should not rise unacceptably. However, this issue should be considered in the context of the overall demand on all tax payers.

Finally, responsibilities of local government. Most charges are levied by local government. Where they are transformed into taxes, the central government should provide local government with the requisite legislative authority for their collection.

5.2   Greening the Tax System

A key goal in greening the tax system is to raise the share of environmentally- favourable taxes in the overall tax revenue. Put another way, to decrease the share of environmentally-unfavourable taxes . There are two major instruments for greening tax systems: revise the current tax structure to increase the share of "green" taxes or introduce new environmental taxes.

Is China's Current Tax System "Green"?

From an efficiency and fairness point of view, the circulation tax may result in price distortions and thus affect the rational allocation of resources. While income tax can address the problem of fair income distribution, it can also have an effect on economic efficiency. Therefore, the circulation tax and income tax each have their advantages and disadvantages. Since China is still in the primary stage of developing a market economy, the government's first objective is enhancing economic efficiency. In the long term the circulation tax will play a key role in China's tax system. However, it is necessary to use income tax to reduce disparities between the rich and the poor and to distribute income more fairly as the transition to a market economy progresses and improvements in economic efficiency occur (Yuan, 1995). In this way, the role of income tax in China will be consolidated step by step.

In most developed countries, income tax[18] is an important element of overall tax revenue: its share of total tax revenue ranges between 17% and 57%. A different situation exists in China at present. In China the circulation tax has been the most important source of tax revenue and was the focus of the 1994 reform of the tax system. It can be seen from Figure 3 that in 1996, the circulation tax (principally value-added tax) receipts accounted for 81% of the overall tax revenue whereas the share of income tax was only 6%.

Judging the degree of "greenness" of a tax system by the share of income tax is not appropriate in the case of China. The fact that income tax accounts for a low share of overall tax revenue does not

---

[18]   Meaning personal and corporate income tax. For the figures, see OECD 1997: *Revenue Statistics 1965-1996*. OECD. Paris.

mean that the tax system is "green". Rather, the current tax system might be characterised as not quite "environmentally-friendly" but does have the potential for becoming greener.

For simplification, suppose that all the environmental resource-related taxes are "green". Section 2.0 of the paper identified six such taxes. Table 10 and Figure 15 show the revenue collected from them. Obviously, these taxes themselves provide a certain stimulus and fund for environmental protection and pollution abatement activities although the environment was not a major consideration in their design. The share of these "green" taxes in the total tax revenue is today around 8% and increasing annually[19].

Table 10: Income from Environmental Resource-Related Taxes, 1987-1996
(Unit: 100 Million Yuan)

Tax item	1987	1988	1989	1990	1991	1992	1993	1994	1995	1996
Natural resource tax	20.96	20.79	20.51	22.12	21.41	23.72	25.61	45.50	55.06	57.36
Consumption Tax	0	0	0	0	0	0	0	117	128	141
Vehicle use tax	5.02	5.99	5.6	7.01	7.74	8.41	9.96	11.29	13.4	15.15
Urban maintenance and construction tax	62.93	75.47	86.42	92.40	100.3	114	147.9	176.3	209.8	245
Fixed assets investment direction adjustment tax	0	0	0	0	11.49	29.8	38.48	43.22	53.40	63.31
Land use tax	0	0	25.64	31.37	31.68	30.52	30.22	32.54	33.65	39.41
Total	88.91	102.25	138.17	152.9	172.62	206.45	252.17	425.85	493.31	561.23

---

[19] Figure based on consumption tax collected on petrol and diesel oil. Because of the unavailability of data, vehicle use tax revenue does not include the vehicle licensee tax; the land tax revenue does not include the cultivated land occupation tax. In Figure 15, the number shown for 1997 is the authors' estimate.

Figure 15: Revenue from Environmental Resource-Related Taxes, 1984-1997

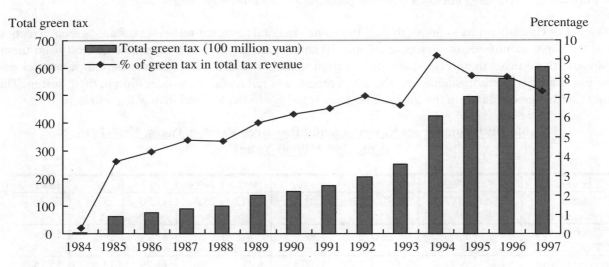

Making China's Tax System "Greener"

China's current tax system is gradually being harmonised with the needs of a market-based economy. From the perspective of tax reform, greening the tax system in China should begin by improvements to the existing arrangements. Greatest emphasis should be placed on the natural resource tax and the consumption tax. In the next section we outline proposals to "green" the range of environmental resource-related taxes.

(i) Natural Resources Tax

This tax presently emphasises revenue-raising over behaviour modification through resource savings and pollution abatement. One of the most important weaknesses is the non-imposition of the tax on water resources. Six suggestions are made for reform of this tax:

- determine the full cost of water as a basis for restructuring its pricing. The government plans to present a policy for water price reform in 1998.

- add a specific tax item covering water resources. The specific amount of tax payable could be determined based on local scarcity of water and economic development. A low tax or tax exemption should be applied to water used for irrigation given the national policy priority for agricultural development.

- enlarge the scope of the tax by adding in new items covering land, forests and pasture.

- establish a steep tax rate on high-sulphur coal (i.e. where sulphur content is over 2%).

- reinforce the view that the environment is a scarce resource by renaming the natural resources tax the environmental resource tax.

94

(ii) Consumption Tax

From an environmental perspective, the principal weakness of the current consumption tax is that it does not cover coal, the dominant source of energy and air pollution in China. It is a key input to industry, power generation and heating schemes. In this context and given that the coal sector is facing strong financial pressure, there is a reluctance to levy the consumption tax. The consumption taxes on petroleum products (petrol and diesel oil) and on motorcycles and cars are of most interest here (see Table 3 for full list of items covered by this tax). It is noted that these categories cover only a small part of overall energy consumption in China.

The following aspects should be considered in "greening" this tax:

- in the long run, and overall tax reform permitting, include coal as one of the items subject to the consumption tax. The amount of tax payable could be determined by the quality of the coal product. The tax could be set at a low rate but the base for levying it should be broad. Consumption tax should be exempted on clean coal and modelling coal.

- a tax differential should be placed on low grade and leaded petrol so as to encourage the use of high grade and unleaded petrol. The amount of tax payable could be between 0.08 to 0.3 yuan/litre.

- likewise, a tax differential should apply to health-damaging and environmentally polluting consumer goods (such as cigarettes). Alternatively, the existing tax rate on these items could be raised.

- a high tax rate should apply to luxury consumer goods.

- the consumption tax on cars and motorcycles should be revised.

(iii)   Vehicle Use Tax

This tax is levied on the basis of ship tonnage or per motor vehicle and is independent of the actual intensity of use. Reform of the tax should focus on:

- merging the vehicle use tax and vehicle licensee tax into a single vehicle tax.

- adjusting the tax rate upwards to reinforce the incentive effect and to reflect the effects of inflation.

- simplifying the existing 6 tax items applied to ships and consolidating the tax rates for ships and vehicles into a comprehensive tax.

- levying a pollution surcharge as a means of addressing environmental problems associated with vehicle congestion, emissions and noise.

(iv)   Urban Maintenance and Construction Tax

This tax provides most of the funds for the construction of urban environmental infrastructure. It is levied by local governments. Suggested initiatives for its "greening" are:

- the scope of the tax should be extended to cover rural as well as urban areas. Accordingly, the tax should be renamed the urban and rural maintenance and construction tax.

- it should have an independent tax base and differential tax rates could be applied to reflect variations in regional economic development.

- the tax rate on enterprises outside urban areas could be increased.

(v)   Cultivated Land Occupation Tax and Land Tax

The objective of this tax is to control strictly the occupation and use of the limited cultivated land resource. Changes should focus on:

- increasing substantially the tax rate to reaffirm the government's commitment to protect cultivated land.

- setting a high tax on the development of wetlands to signal the importance placed on their protection.

- including non-agricultural land uses within the scope of the tax.

(vi)   Fixed Asset Investment Direction Adjustment Tax

This tax is a powerful instrument to support national industrial policies. Suggested changes are:

- timely and regular adjustment of the tax rates to reflect the macro-economic situation.

- raising the tax rates on investments in projects for which there is an over supply and pollution- and energy-intensive projects.

(vii)   Value-Added Tax

Since this tax was established on the principle of tax neutrality, it is neither environmentally-friendly nor unfriendly. There is little scope to "green" it because explicit inclusion of an environmental aspect, for example by setting differential tax rates on the basis of environmental criteria, would bias it. However, there is a possibility to vary the three rates of this tax, as discussed earlier.

5.3   New Environmental Taxes: Challenges and Opportunities

In the previous section a number of new environmental taxes were suggested, such as a water resources tax and a tax differential on low grade and leaded petrol. All these taxes depend, however, on the present tax categories. Based on the experiences of OECD countries and the possibility of further reform of China's tax system, consideration should be given to introducing taxes on energy and water resources and ozone depleting substances, a leaded petrol tax [20] and, as appropriate, shifting from pollution charges to pollution taxes. These are discussed in further detail below.

Energy Taxes

A number of OECD countries are very interested in reforming energy taxes because the production and consumption of energy has an influence on economic growth and at the same time may seriously affect atmospheric environmental quality. An energy tax can encompass taxes levied on value-added, consumption, pollution (such as a tax on sulphur content) and carbon. Tax rates vary depending on the energy category. Research in OECD countries shows that the introduction of an energy tax (and simultaneously decreasing individual income tax and capital tax) can not only promote GDP growth but also reduce the rate of unemployment (OECD, 1996). At the same time, an energy tax may result in environmental improvements through stimulating greater energy efficiency and the substitution of "dirty" fuels with cleaner ones. A "win-win" outcome is therefore possible.

China's energy structure is dominated by coal (75% of overall energy consumption) followed by petroleum (17.5%), hydropower (5.9%) and natural gas (1.6%) (State Bureau of Statistics, 1997). At present, taxes on energy comprise:

- a value-added tax (rate of 13%) and natural resource tax are levied on coal production (including raw coal, coal washing, and coal processing). An SO_2 pollution charge[21] based on the sulphur content of coal is also collected. There is no tax preference between modelling coal and clean coal.

- a value-added tax (rate of 17%) and natural resource tax are applied to crude oil and liquefied petroleum gas. A consumption tax is levied on petrol and diesel oil, the rates being 0.2 yuan/litre and 0.1 yuan/litre respectively.

- a value-added tax (rate of 13%) and natural resource tax are levied on natural gas.

- a value-added tax is imposed on power generation (4 yuan/kWh) and power supply (1% to 3%).

It is evident that the tax categories and tax burden differ according to the energy source. The tax burden on low polluting, clean energy sources is higher than that on "dirty" ones. Current energy taxes are therefore not environmentally-friendly.

Due to the wide coverage of the energy tax base, energy producers and large consumers are likely to bear much of the burden of new or reformed taxes. In line with the concept of tax neutrality, taxes on clean, low polluting energy sources should be reduced while those on "dirty" and carbon content-rich sources increased. In addition, this change should be co-ordinated with the planned leaded petrol

---

[20]   These are not the categories as set out in China's tax law. Rather, they refer to the environmentally-related taxes on energy, natural resources and polluting products. For example, the so-called "energy tax" encompasses taxes on all forms of energy rather than being a stand-alone tax category.

[21]   The current charge rate for SO_2 is 0.2 yuan/kg, which is only 17% of the abatement cost. Based on this charge rate and the average sulphur content of coal (1.2%), the average SO_2 pollution charge per tonne of coal is 2.4 yuan.

surcharge so that the environmental cost of energy consumption can be included either within the surcharge or energy tax. The relevant government departments should set up a special project to carry out comprehensive and systematic research into the costs, benefits and trade-offs of implementing energy taxes[22].

Water Resources Tax

In the present tax structure, only drinking water is subject to value-added tax (rate of 13%). Numerous charges relating to the development and use of water resources are collected, however. Our investigations show that in Changzhou city, Jiang Su province, there are as many as 11 water resource-related charges. These include charges for wastewater discharge, overflow discharge, water use, sewerage, wastewater treatment plant construction and centralised wastewater treatment (CRAES, 1994). Not all enterprises pay the full range of charges. Nation-wide, the most important water charges are those for wastewater discharge, water resource use and sewerage.

A rational pricing system for water needs to be established. The government is beginning to reform prices for water supply and charges for wastewater treatment through a small price rise for water used in agriculture, a relatively large price rise for water used by industry and hydropower stations, and doubling the price of water used for luxury consumption goods. As noted in China Environment Newspaper (1998), the main elements of water pricing reform are:

- irrigation schemes presently supplying water without charge must set a supply price in 1998. To alleviate the serious financial losses faced by schemes directly under central government control or of a transprovincial nature, the water price should rise by 0.01 yuan/ton on average. The price of water from local irrigation schemes may rise by 0.008 yuan/ton.

- application of multiple water prices. For large industrial water users, a two-tier price system is applied based on both approved volume and measured use[23]. For urban residents, a graduated water price system is applied in which the price rises progressively on water use above a basic volume. For agricultural water use, the price should increase gradually until the accumulated revenue exceeds the cost of operating irrigation schemes.

- cities in the area of the "three rivers and three lakes"[24] should pay a wastewater treatment charge of 0.2 yuan/ton in addition to the relevant water price. Other cities may choose to levy this charge as well. In implementing the charge, the existing wastewater discharge charge levied by local environmental protection departments and the sewage treatment plant charge set by the urban construction department should be abolished.

---

[22] Use should be made of econometric approaches such as input-output modelling, macro-economic models and computable general equilibrium (CGE) models (Zou, 1996).

[23] The approved volume of water use is the basis for calculating the volume water price. This price covers the fixed costs of the wastewater treatment plant. Water use within the limits of the approved volume is priced according to the measured amount used. This price covers the operations cost of the wastewater treatment plant. Water use in excess of the approved volume attracts a higher rate penalty price.

[24] This refers to the Huaihe, Haihe and Liaohe rivers and the Taihu, Dianchi and Chaohu lakes which have been identified as priorities for water pollution control under the first phase (1995-2000) of the China Trans-Century Green Project Plan.

In addition, the following initiatives are suggested:

- transform the current water resource charge covering groundwater and surface water into a water resource tax.

- determine differential tax rates according to the local scarcity of water resources and degree of pollution. These rates should then be reflected in the water resource tax.

- raise the rates levied on water pollution so that their yield is higher than the cost of undertaking pollution abatement measures (CRAES, 1998).

Tax on Leaded Petrol

Urban air pollution from vehicle emissions is recognised by the relevant government departments as an emerging problem. The government has decided to ban leaded petrol nation-wide from 2000 and promote use of unleaded petrol. Experience in OECD countries has shown that a price differential between leaded and unleaded petrol has been a common and effective policy instrument. On the basis of this experience, the Chinese Research Academy of Environmental Sciences prepared a leaded petrol tax plan (Wang, *et al.*, 1998b). The State Council is currently examining the plan, and plans to levy a leaded petrol tax in 1999.

A leaded petrol tax focuses on modifying behaviour. As soon as leaded petrol is completely phased out, the policy usefulness of the leaded petrol tax will have ended. The purpose of this tax is to encourage consumers to use unleaded petrol, promote the production of unleaded petrol, increase its market share and reduce the discharge of lead pollutants in vehicle exhaust gases.

The proposed tax is defined as a type of surcharge and would be an item in the petrol consumption tax. It would apply to all grades of petrol (70 MON, equivalent to 82 RON; 90 RON; and higher grades). The tax payers would be the refineries that produce the different grades of petrol.

Among the higher grades of petrol available in China, the share of 90 RON is about 41% while 93 RON petrol accounts only for 6.57%. Therefore, the tax rate should be determined mainly on the basis of the 90 RON grade petrol.

The tax would account for 5.7% of the average market price for petrol. If the tax rate for all grades of leaded petrol is set as 0.14 yuan/litre while the rate for 70 MON petrol[25] is 0.17 yuan/litre, the tax is equivalent to adding 3.82% to annual vehicle costs. The most significant effect is on owners of medium-sized vehicles.

---

[25] Currently in China low grade 70 MON petrol accounts for over 50% of overall petrol consumption. 70% of the 70 MON petrol is unleaded and the remaining 30% is leaded. A tax on the 70 MON petrol may stimulate refiners to produce higher grade petrol. Given that the end result desired is the substitution of 70 MON petrol by 90 RON unleaded petrol, we have calculated the tax rates based on the difference between the production costs of 70 MON and 90 RON petrol.

Pollution Tax

This refers to the tax based on the volume of pollutants discharged or polluting products produced. It is the tax category that most directly reflects an environmental tax. The discussion in Section 4.0 showed that the existing pollution charge is a quasi-pollution tax even though China does not have a legally defined pollution tax. The pollution charge system is the key economic instrument applied to China's environmental policies.

The pollution charge has a well established legal basis. The Environmental Protection Law, Atmospheric Pollution Prevention Law and Water Pollution Prevention Law include provisions for pollution charges. In general, pollution charges are calculated according to the volume of pollutants or discharge in excess of relevant standards and based on enterprises' detailed pollution discharge declaration and data verification by environmental protection bureaus. This poses problems in revenue collection by local tax offices. Whether the levy is in the form of a tax or a charge, the main problem is how to accelerate the reform of the pollution charge system so as to stimulate effective pollution abatement measures.

In general, because of the flexibility and distinct purpose of the pollution charge system, it is a useful approach to deal with pollution problems and is more easily accepted by the public. In the long run, though, with the consolidation of state finances the pollution charge should be transformed into a pollution tax. The preconditions for such a transformation include a simplification of the current charge standards, i.e. a shift from being based on pollutant discharge to the quantity of production or consumption, or a discharge tax imposed only on a few key pollutants. For instance, the air pollution charge could be transformed into a natural resource tax and a consumption tax surcharge on coal and petrol. In order to deal with water pollution by phosphates a consumption tax or a pollution tax on detergents containing phosphates could be levied. Likewise, to address solid waste problems a disposal tax could be levied on products that create disposal problems (batteries, vehicles and non-biodegradable packaging material).

Preferential Tax Treatment of Environmental Investments

In general, investments in environmental protection improve public welfare but their return is not high. For this reason, preferential tax treatment is given in China to the following types of investment. First, for projects concerned with pollution abatement, environmental protection, energy saving and the sustainable use of natural resources, a zero tax rate applies to the fixed asset investment direction adjustment tax. Second, value-added tax is exempted for some products that make comprehensive use of natural resources. Third, for enterprises that engage in waste recycling activities 70% of the value-added tax is refunded.

To support growth of the environmental protection "industry" six aspects of the present preferential tax arrangements need to be improved as soon as possible. First, an enlargement of the type of projects subject to the zero tax rate in the fixed asset investment direction adjustment tax. Second, defining boundaries of the environmental protection "industry" and providing preferential tax treatment to enterprises engaged in this sector within a fixed time period. Third, import duties should be reduced on goods for environmental protection that cannot be manufactured domestically at present, such as pollution control equipment, instruments for environmental monitoring and research, and cleaner technologies. Fourth, lowering the consumption tax on fuel-efficient vehicles, clean energy sources and those consumer electrical appliances and vehicles that have obtained a "green" label or an energy efficiency label. Fifth, for enterprises engaged in building and operating environmental infrastructure preferential treatment should be available in the collection of the business tax, value-added tax and urban maintenance and construction tax. Finally, provision should be made for accelerating depreciation allowances for investments in projects covering clean energy, pollution control, environmental infrastructure and demonstration environmental protection schemes.

5.4   Implementing Environmental Taxes in China: Supporting and Limiting Factors

Whether one undertakes "green" tax reform or establishes new environmental taxes, issues of implementation and institutional arrangements need to be addressed. In China, the establishment of legally binding environmental taxes is supported by the favourable situation provided by the macro-economic and tax reforms but it is also constrained by many legal and institutional obstacles.

Supporting Factors

Several factors support the creation of environmental taxes in China at this time. First, the worsening trend in pollution has increased public environmental awareness.   Concern about environmental quality and the degree of public participation in environmental protection efforts have both risen. This enhances the acceptance in society of the need for an environmental tax. Second, government departments have realised that environmental pollution cannot be solved by relying only on laws and administrative interventions. Market-based approaches are increasingly seen as complements to regulation. The relevant government departments, particularly the environment and tax departments, are becoming increasingly concerned about environmental protection. Third, with the deepening of a market economy and the transformation of state-owned enterprises, there is a stronger incentive to respond to market signals. Enterprises are becoming more interested in reducing costs, including environmental costs, as well as to establish a "green" image. Fourth, the reform of the tax system in 1994 has been successful in establishing the policy framework appropriate for a market economy. Efforts are now turning to reforming local tax arrangements and the pollution charge system. This provides a good opportunity to carry out green tax reform and to introduce environmental taxes. The relevant government departments should set up as soon as possible a research project to examine feasible policy options. Fifth, the relevant regulations concerning environmental protection and tax have been enacted. They provide the basic legal foundation for the establishment of environmental taxes. In particular, the present tax system provides ample opportunity for "greening". Finally, the existing tax collection arrangements provide the institutional means to   collect environmental taxes. The environmental protection bureaus at sub-national level can supply technical support as required.

Limiting Factors

The history of environmental protection in China spans just over 20 years. Environmental taxes in the legal sense is a new subject for China. At present, the main limiting factors in establishing environmental taxes are five-fold. First, the macro-economic environment is not favourable. During the transition to a market economy, many state-owned enterprises are enduring heavy losses and laying off workers. In addition, the national economy is suffering from the Asian financial crisis and a consequent reduction in domestic demand. Thus, it is unlikely that the government will introduce new environmental taxes that will further stretch the capacity of tax payers.

Second, the objective of an environmental tax. In its design, this type of tax should have a goal of modifying the behaviour of polluters. However, considering the lack of finance for environmental purposes during the transition period and the overall economic situation, the short-run function of an environmental tax should emphasise revenue raising primarily but also take account of behaviour modification possibilities. This obviously limits the scope of the environmental tax.

Third, progress in enterprise reform. If the enterprise sector is not an integral part of the economic reform process and property rights are not clear then the market signal from environmental taxes could be weaker, which may exacerbate existing market distortions and seriously reduce the efficiency of such taxes.

Fourth, institutional arrangements for revenue collection. For technical reasons, the tax authorities find it very difficult to collect those environmental "taxes" based on pollutants (such as the SO_2 charge and the tax on ozone depleting substances (ODS)). In such circumstances, it is necessary to examine how the current system might be changed, including the feasibility of the environmental protection department carrying out the collection role.

Finally, earmarking of the revenue. Among the existing taxes, only the urban maintenance and construction tax and the agricultural (animal husbandry) tax have been designated a "special fund for specified purposes". According to conventional welfare economics, earmarking revenue may reduce the efficiency of fund use. Too many special taxes will undoubtedly destroy the integrity of government finance and erode the public budget contribution provided by taxes. Nevertheless, given the lack of funds to support environmental protection, studies should be undertaken to assess how revenue could be used to establish an environmental fund.

6.0 Conclusions

China has largely established a tax system appropriate to a market economy. In general, the new system reflects the requirements of a comprehensive tax law, a fair tax burden, simplified rules and a rational division of responsibilities. It creates a favourable tax climate to enhance fair competition among enterprises and the further establishment of a market economy. It also plays an important role in defining the relationships between the state and enterprises and between central and local government. In addition, it ensures a steady growth in national tax revenue.

In China's tax system, the environmental resource-related tax categories are the natural resource tax, the consumption tax, the urban maintenance and construction tax, the vehicle use tax, the fixed asset investment direction adjustment tax and the cultivated land occupation tax. These "green" taxes account for about 8% of the overall national tax revenue. The existing framework provides a foundation for the "greening" of the tax system.

The pollution levy system is a quasi-pollution tax system. It has played a positive role in promoting pollution control and in environmental capacity building. At the same time, its reform is an urgent task. The main elements of the proposed reform include redefining the rate schedules upon which pollution charges are set, changing the revenue distribution system and adopting a loan system to replace grants or refunds. The State Environmental Protection Administration, together with other relevant departments, is engaging in trial implementation of the proposed new pollution levy system.

The present tax system is not very environmentally "friendly". Greening of the present tax system should focus on the natural resource tax, the consumption tax, the urban maintenance and construction tax and the vehicle use tax. The scope of the reform should be to include as many environmental costs as possible within the relevant taxable categories and tax rates. At the same time, in each of the tax categories preferential tax rates for investments in environmental protection should be introduced. Greening of the tax system should be combined with the forthcoming "From Charge to Tax" reform to be carried out by the state as well as reform of local tax arrangements.

Further research is needed on proposed new environmental taxes such as an energy tax, water resource tax, leaded petrol tax, ODS tax, pollution tax and coal tax, etc. If possible, and based on the current natural resource tax, a natural resource and environmental tax category could be established. In the course of introducing environmental taxes, the relationship between taxes and charges should be clarified. Revenue from the new pollution charges should be part of local government finances. Receipts from the environmental tax should be considered either part of national tax revenue or shared between central and local government.

Green tax reform in China is a complicated process that must be undertaken systematically. The relevant government departments should actively take advantage of the deepening tax reform, enhance co-ordination and exchange among themselves and draw on the experience of green tax reform in OECD countries to develop a "green" tax system appropriate to China's circumstances.

BIBLIOGRAPHY

China Environmental Newspaper (1998): "Water Price Is to Be Raised" China Environmental Newspaper, April 16, 1998. Pg 1.

Chinese Research Academy of Environmental Sciences (CRAES) (1994): Program for the Minimum Cost of Changzhou City Urban Environment: Comprehensive Renovation and Research About Its Economic and Financial Policies. Beijing.

CRAES (1997): *Research on the Design and Implementation of Chinese Wastewater Discharge Fee*. China Environmental Science Publishing House. Beijing.

Editorial Committee of Tax Almanac of China (1994): *Tax Almanac of China 1994*. State General Tax Office. Beijing.

Editorial Committee of Tax Almanac of China (1995): *Tax Almanac of China 1995*. China Tax Publishing House. Beijing.

Editorial Committee of Tax Almanac of China (1996): *Tax Almanac of China 1996*. China Tax Publishing House. Beijing.

Editorial Committee of Tax Almanac of China (1997): *Tax Almanac of China 1997*. China Tax Publishing House. Beijing.

European Environment Agency (1996): *Environmental Taxes: Implementation and Environmental Effectiveness*. European Environment Agency. Copenhagen.

Guo, Daimo, *et al.* (1997): "Basic Thinking About Improving Local Taxation System" in *Finance Research 3*.

Hao, Ruyu *et al.* (1994): *China's New Taxation System*. Economic Science Publishing House. Beijing.

Joint Task Group of Hunan, Sichuan, Henan and Anhui (1997): "Research on the Reform of the Overall Funding System in Villages and Towns" in *Finance Research 10*.

Li, Fanwang (1997): "Positive Analysis and Countermeasure Research About the Practice of the Tax System Since 1994" in *Finance Research 10*.

Liu, Shangxi, *et al.* (1997): "A Brief Discussion on the Relationships Between Taxes and Charges" in *Finance Research 10*.

Liu, Zuo (1997): "Probe Into the Thinking of the Next Step in China's Tax System" in *Finance Research 8*.

Ma, Shanji (1997): "Supporting Tax and Restraining Charge: The Only Way for Local Tax and Charge System Reform" in *Finance Research 4*.

Ministry of Finance (1996): *China's Tax System*. Enterprise Management Publishing House. Beijing.

OECD (1993): *Taxation and the Environment: Complementary Policies*. OECD. Paris.

OECD (1994): *Internalising the Social Cost of Transport*. OECD. Paris.

OECD (1996): *Implementation Strategie for Environmental Taxes*. OECD. Paris.

State Bureau of Statistics (1997): *China Statistics Yearbook 1977*. China Statistics Publishing House. Beijing.

State Council (1986): "Temporary Regulations for the Vehicle Use Tax" in Sun Shangqing *et al.* (ed.), 1994: *New Tax Rules Handbook*. Xinhua Publishing House. Beijing.

State Council (1993a): "Temporary Regulations for the Consumption Tax in the People's Republic of China" in *Tax Almanac of China 1994*. China Tax Publishing House. Beijing.

State Council (1993b): "Temporary Regulations for the Resource Tax in People's Republic of China" in *Tax Almanac of China 1994*. China Tax Publishing House. Beijing.

State General Tax Office (1996): "The National Ninth Five-Year Plan for Taxation Development and the Long-term Objectives to 2010" in Editorial Committee of Tax Almanac of China, 1997: *Tax Almanac of China 1997*. China Tax Publishing House. Beijing.

Task Group of Ministry of Finance (1994): *Research into Financial Reform and Financial Policy*. China Economy Publishing House. Beijing.

Wang, Jinnan, *et al.* (1994): "A Probe Into China's Environmental Tax Policies During the Transition Period" in Progress in Environmental Sciences 2 (2).

Wang, Jinnan, *et al.* (1998a): "A Macroeconomic Analysis of Chinese Industrial Pollution" in General Report for Research on Economics of Chinese Industrial Pollution Control. Beijing.

Wang, Jinnan, *et al.* (1998b): "Policy Design for a Leaded Petrol Tax in China" in Chinese Population, Resources and the Environment 8 (1).

Zou, Ji (1996): "China's Finance and Tax Policy for Energy and Atmospheric Pollution Prevention and Control" in Paper Collection of the Seminar About China's Environmental Economic Policies. Beijing.

PART 2:

REFORMING ENVIRONMENTALLY-DAMAGING SUBSIDIES

SUBSIDY POLICY AND THE ENVIRONMENT IN CHINA

Chazhong Ge, Shuting Gao, Jinnan Wang, Jintian Yang and Dong Cao
Chinese Research Academy of Environmental Sciences, China

1.0   INTRODUCTION

Policy instruments are an important tool of government intervention and macroeconomic adjustment. In a market economy, the state may use such instruments to address problems arising from market failure, such as income disparity, adverse external influences on the economy, environmental pollution, the pattern and flow of investment etc. However, due to a lack of systematic knowledge about certain activities, or underestimation of their impact, government policies often also cause unwanted side-effects. Subsidies on the prices of agricultural products encourage farmers to invest more, and to adopt intensive farming methods, including the use of chemical fertilisers and pesticides, irrigation technology, and hybrid varieties. This may, however, lead to surplus production, and a consequent drop in agricultural prices, as well as land degradation or water pollution.

Since the beginning of the reform and opening-up policy, China has been moving gradually from a centrally planned system to a socialist market economy. The state's role in the economy, and hence its policy instruments, have changed accordingly. In terms of pricing policy, the sales prices of products and resources are now determined by the market, except for a few items and commodities important to the national economy and the people's livelihood; the proportion of state-controlled commodities is falling steadily. The government now intervenes in the market only for purposes of macro-economic regulation.

Subsidies are among the macroeconomic control instruments of economic policy in China. During the transitional period from the old to the new system, changes in prices and the supply and demand relationship may affect the interests of both producers and consumers as well as social stability. In order to stabilise production and consumption, therefore, the government has adopted a series of subsidy policies, which have been implemented as planned in specific conditions and have had the desired stabilising effect on the markets and society. But what is their real impact on the environment and resource utilisation? No systematic study has yet been conducted or published on the links between subsidy policy and the environment in China.

This paper examines subsidy policy during a period of rapid economic transition in China. After looking at subsidy policies in some key sectors, the paper argues that although China has worked hard to correct the irrational price structures of the planned economy, quite a few of the transitional subsidy policies, which have been designed mainly to stabilise production and people's livelihoods, have a negative effect on resources and the environment and should therefore be gradually removed.

The paper is divided into eight sections beginning with this Introduction. Section 2 describes Chinese subsidy policies during the transitional period. Sections 3 to 7 provide an analysis of subsidy policy in the following selected sectors: water, electricity, fertilisers and pesticides, transport and energy.

Section 8 offers some conclusions and policy suggestions. The paper is based for the most part on data from secondary sources which is supplemented by material from our own investigations.

2.0   MAIN FEATURES OF SUBSIDY POLICY IN CHINA

2.1   Reform of the Economic System

China has adopted an evolutionary model for economic reform, in contrast with the 'shock treatment' approach of countries in central and eastern Europe and the former Soviet Union (Li, 1997; Fewsmith, J., 1994; Naughton, 1995). The reform began with the adoption of the agricultural production responsibility system in 1978, followed by the definition of the socialist market economy at the Third Plenary Session of the 14th Central Committee Conference of the Communist Party of China, and the adoption of the principle of distribution according to production factors at the 15th Central Committee. This slow evolutionary process has now been underway for 20 years and is continuing.

The Chinese economic system has already undergone radical reforms in production, sales and distribution. In production, state administrative control and intervention have been reduced and considerable autonomy has been given to enterprises. With the adoption of the responsibility system for agricultural production, and the household contract system which guarantees farmers 30 or 50 years tenure on the land, their productive potential has been given free rein. In combination with other agricultural policies, these measures have ensured the steady growth of Chinese agriculture. The vigour of state-owned enterprises has been enhanced since they have been granted operational autonomy and a linkage has been established between their responsibilities, powers and profits. The sales system has been reformed from a centrally planned allocation system to a market-based system. The government has gradually relaxed price controls, and the prices of around 70% of all commodities are now determined by the market. The former unified policy by which natural resources were deemed to be 'free', or were irrationally priced, has gradually been abolished, and the idea that a natural resource has a value is now established. Some resources are now taxed or charged to a certain extent.

With regard to distribution, the 'iron rice-bowl' has been broken. Not only is the principle of distribution according to labour now applied, but the principle of distribution according to production factors has been clearly endorsed by the 15th Central Committee. In investment, the planned economy system of allocated funding has been replaced by repayable loans. Fund raising in civil society and individual investment are encouraged in order to increase the range of financing channels. In taxation, the profit retrocession system of the planned economy has been converted into a tax system. At the same time, a complete reform of the existing tax system was undertaken in 1994, resulting in a gradual improvement of the whole taxation system in China. Together, these measures have contributed to the gradual shaping of a market economy with Chinese characteristics. But to avoid the short term disruption which can follow the introduction of new policies, particularly as regards prices, and in order to maintain stability in production and national life, the government has introduced a series of appropriate measures, including subsidies. These counter-measures have played a positive role in reducing instability in production and economic life in the short term. Nevertheless, some have also brought new distortions.

2.2   Definition and Classification of Subsidies

According to a World Bank study, a subsidy can be broadly defined as the difference between the reduced cost of a good as a result of government support, and its cost without such support (World

Bank, 1997a). Subsidies are used by a government to alter the risks, costs and returns on markets to favour their orientation towards certain economic activities and groups (Roodman, 1996). This definition is adopted in this paper to cover various types of subsidy. The definition in fact assimilates subsidies to cost differences, which are chiefly due to prices or pricing policies (Gao, 1994). Thus a study of subsidy takes the form of a study of prices.

Subsidies can be classified according to their object into various types, including price controls, tax preferences, interest rate subsidies and enterprise loss compensation (Ma, 1996). In a pure market system, Chinese grain prices would reflect the exact balance between supply and demand. But the government sets the price higher than this market price in order to encourage farmers to produce more grain. The government also subsidises the price of some commodities in order to stabilise prices and stimulate consumption. Such subsidies are called price controls, and the difference between the two prices is called the price subsidy. Secondly, in order to stimulate development in, for example, agriculture and forestry, the government may reduce the rate of value added tax from 17% to 13% on products from those sectors. The government also offers tax deduction or exemption to foreign-operated businesses in the special economic zones (SEZ) to encourage foreign investors to invest in these areas. This is known as preferential taxation, and the resulting subsidy is called a tax preference subsidy. Lastly, to support projects in agriculture, forestry and water management, the government provides favourable bank interest rates, including grants, free loans, soft loans, etc. The government also provides low interest rate loans in support of national priority construction projects. These forms of preference measures are called interest rate preference subsidies.

Subsidies may also be divided into those in kind and those in cash. When chemical fertilisers and pesticides are in short supply, the government links chemical fertiliser supply to grain or cotton production to ensure that high-quality, low-price chemical fertiliser is available to high-grain-producing families, by offering a quota of lower priced fertiliser in proportion to the unit's grain production. This is classified as a subsidy in kind. On the other hand, to keep prices low, the government caps the prices of some production materials, farming and side-line products and other consumer goods by paying producers a subsidy to make up the price differential. This is classed as a cash subsidy. Some subsidies are explicit, being direct financial subsidies from the State to consumers, i.e. to the consumption phase of re-production, in the form of allowances to employees for grain, oil, vegetables, non-staple foods, transportation, winter heating, summer cooling, etc. Others are implicit, being aimed at the production, sales and distribution phases, such as price support for farm and side-line products, agricultural materials, coal, etc. Some are direct price subsidies, such as subsidies on chemical fertiliser, pesticides, grain and oil; others are indirect subsidies, such as the State subsidy on grain, which may indirectly influence farmers' use of chemical fertiliser.

2.3   Calculating Subsidies

The accurate determination of the level of subsidy is the key to a proper assessment of the relationship between subsidies and the environment. Several methods are currently used, each with its pros and cons: the direct method, the domestic market method, the international market method and the marginal opportunity cost method.

(i) Direct Method

This method assesses subsidy levels directly from government statistics. The method is simple, but reflects only the financial subsidy provided by the government; it does not capture the subsidy due to price distortions. Secondly, it reflects only explicit expenditure by the State, i.e. direct subsidy, or financial expenditure on products as used by government.

(ii) Indirect Methods

In these methods the amount of subsidy is measured with respect to a reference price. Indirect methods can be divided into three types according to the reference price used.

Domestic Market Method

This method reports the subsidy as the difference between the domestic market price and the government fixed price or guide price. It can measure the effective price subsidy due to government intervention, but does not take into account international market influences on the domestic market. Some products do not benefit from preferential allocation of resources since they enjoy domestic trade protection (tariff barriers). For example, in 1996 the average price of coal was US$25/ton in China as compared to US$40/ton in the United States (CIF price) (The Energy and Raw Materials Division of the Price Management Department, State Planning Commission, 1996).

International Market Difference Method

This method determines the amount of subsidy as the difference between the domestic market price and the FOB price (the latter being the reference price) plus transportation cost. It is appropriate to tradable goods, and measures the subsidy as an economic subsidy corrected for domestic market distortions and tariff barriers. However the use of the FOB price as the reference fails to take into account quality differences among goods from different nations; a more accurate value would be obtained by multiplying the FOB price by a quality coefficient. Furthermore, the effects of frequent sudden changes in international market prices make the amount and rate of subsidy difficult to determine: for instance, at one point in March 1998, the international market price of crude oil dropped to US$12 per barrel, then rose to US$16 per barrel two weeks later. Large errors may therefore result if the amount of subsidy is calculated from the international market price on a given day; this can be avoided by taking an average value over a period.

Opportunity Cost Method

This method determines the amount of subsidy from the difference between the marginal opportunity cost of the resource and its market price. The marginal opportunity cost of a resource is given by its marginal production cost plus the marginal use cost and marginal external cost (Li and Warford, 1997). The subsidy amount as computed in this way is the economic subsidy from the sustainable development point of view, and thus differs from the financial subsidy.

This paper will adopt the last method in principle, but in some cases, where marginal external cost is hard to determine, only indicative results will be given. Also, since the study concerns relations between subsidies and the environment, we consider that some proxies which indirectly describe the marginal external cost, rather than measures of the level of subsidy as such, should suffice. The correct determination of subsidy might be an appropriate topic for future studies.

A subsidy can also be expressed as a rate or coefficient. The *subsidy rate* is given by the difference between a price with and without subsidy (the latter expressed as a reference price) divided by the price without subsidy and multiplied by one hundred. According to World Bank (1997a) this captures the effect of policy changes better than the subsidy amount since the former is independent of measurements of quantity. The subsidy rate is given by the following formula:

$$\text{Subsidy rate } (\%) = \frac{\text{Amount sold x (Market Price - Non-subsidised price)}}{\text{Amount sold x Non-subsidised price}} \text{ x } 100\%$$

2.4   Main Features of Subsidy Policies in China

(i) Towards Subsidisation as a Corrective to Market Pricing

In a market economy, price is an important indicator of the relationship between supply and demand. In a fully competitive market, the supply-demand relationship is an invisible force regulating price and allocating resources to their most efficient use. But the State must consider social and environmental benefits as well as economic benefits and efficiency. The government may use appropriate policy instruments of macro-economic control, in particular controls on prices, taxation, interest rates etc. These measures may sometimes distort the market; do not necessarily achieve the desired objectives; and may result in negative effects on the environment. For example, agricultural subsidy policies in nations with sound market mechanisms (such as OECD Member countries) do not consider explicitly the effects on the environment (Potier, 1996).

Under the planned economy, prices were fixed by the planners, i.e. government departments. Due to limitations of information and knowledge among individual officials, these prices did not reflect market relations between supply and demand, or the scarcity or availability of the resources. Prices were fixed for each enterprise, financing was strictly according to budget, and resources were allocated by the plan (Jin, 1996). As a result, under the pure planned economy, resources were distributed to departments according to the plan. Efficiency in the use of resources depended entirely on the information available to the planner.

As China has moved from a planned economy towards a market economy and the reforms have intensified, the price system has changed substantially: market pricing mechanisms are gradually taking shape, moving from a system in which directive prices were dominant towards one in which directive prices, guide prices and market prices exist side by side, with market prices increasingly dominant from year to year (Table 1).

Table 1 shows that over the eighth five-year plan period, the proportion of market-determined prices rose year on year to exceed 75%. In total retail sales of products for consumer use, this ratio rose from 53% in 1990 to 88.8% in 1995, and for overall purchases of farm and side-line products, from 51.6% in 1990 to 78.6% in 1995. The proportion of market-determined prices in total revenue from sales of production materials rose from 36.4% in 1990 to 77.9% in 1995. Price distortions have been progressively eliminated and the power of the price mechanism to regulate supply and demand has been strengthened. With the implementation of market pricing and other economic policies, the subsidies of the planned economy and early reform periods have been gradually abolished. The ratio of subsidies to GNP is declining (see Figure 1 below).

Figure 1: Financial Subsidies as Percentage of GNP, 1978-96

Total Price subsidies, share in GNP

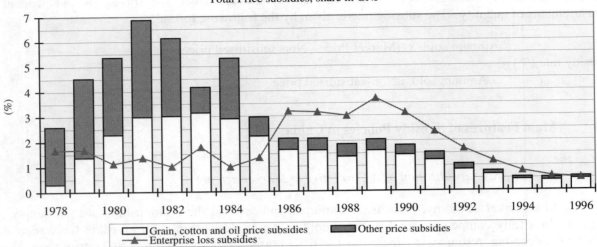

Grain, cotton and oil price subsidies — Other price subsidies — Enterprise loss subsidies

Table 1: State-Controlled Product Prices During the Eighth 5-Year Plan
(Unit: %)

Item	Price form	1990	1991	1992	1993	1994	1995
Retail sales of consumer items	Government fixed price	29.8	20.9	5.9	4.8	7.2	8.8
	Government guiding price	17.2	10.3	1.1	1.4	2.4	2.4
	Market price	53.0	68.6	93.0	93.8	90.4	88.8
Purchases of farming and sideline products	Government fixed price	25.0	22.2	12.5	10.4	16.6	17.0
	Government guiding price	23.4	20.0	5.7	2.1	4.1	4.4
	Market price	51.6	57.8	81.8	87.5	79.3	78.6
Sales of production materials	Government fixed price	44.6	36.0	18.7	13.6	14.7	15.6
	Government guiding price	19.0	18.3	7.5	5.1	5.3	6.5
	Market price	36.4	45.7	73.8	81.1	80.0	77.9

Note: Data are not available for Inner Mongolia, Guizhou and Tibet for 1994, or for Hainan and Tibet for 1995.

Source: The Price Management Department of the State Planning Commission, 1996.

(ii) The Core of Subsidy Policy: Price Support and Enterprise Loss Compensation

Price subsidy and enterprise loss compensation are the two main forms of financial subsidy in China (Table 2). During the transition, the government has had to use price subsidies to soften short-term disruptions in the economic system and stabilise production and economic life. As Table 2 shows, the absolute value of price support and subsidies to compensate enterprise losses has increased, though with some fluctuations. The bulk of price subsidies have been aimed at grain, cotton and oil prices, and their total value has increased year-on-year. Since the reforms began, Chinese enterprises have gained a relative degree of operational autonomy. Theoretically, and particularly in a market economy where property rights are clearly defined, enterprises should bear the consequences of their operational profits and losses, but some companies incur losses due to government policies (such as state control of raw materials prices) and apply for a government subsidy. This subsidy is called the enterprise loss subsidy. Also, although China is in transition towards a market economy and there are now multiple forms of ownership, state-owned enterprises are still a key pillar and the government is willing to support them (especially large and medium-sized state-owned enterprises). Because of the key status of some state-owned enterprises in the national economy, and for employment, the government is prepared to subsidise them even where their losses are due to bad management. This is known as the operation loss subsidy.

Table 2: Financial Support: Price Subsidies and Enterprise Loss Subsidies
(Unit: 100s of millions of yuan)

Year	Total price subsidies (1)	Breakdown				Enterprise loss subsidy (6)	Tax relief subsidies (7)
		Grain, cotton, oil (2)	Direct price reduction subsidies (3)	Meat (4)	Other price subsidies (5)		
1978	93.86	11.14			82.72	60.17	6.00
1979	180.71	54.85			125.86	67.33	28.34
1980	242.07	102.80			139.27	50.98	45.39
1981	327.71	142.22			185.49	64.21	49.31
1982	318.36	156.19			162.17	52.65	45.53
1983	241.66	182.13			59.53	103.00	55.28
1984	370.00	201.67			168.33	68.00	46.78
1985	299.49	198.66		33.52	67.31	121.00	74.34
1986	257.48	169.37		42.24	45.87	324.78	64.44
1987	294.60	195.43		42.74	56.43	375.49	63.72
1988	316.55	204.03		40.40	72.39	446.46	-
1989	373.55	262.52		41.29	69.74	599.76	-
1990	380.80	267.61		41.78	71.41	578.88	-
1991	373.77	267.03		42.46	64.28	510.24	-
1992	321.64	224.35		38.54	58.75	444.96	-
1993	299.47	224.75		29.86	44.69	411.29	-
1994	314.47	202.03	41.25	25.41	45.78	366.22	-
1995	364.89	228.91	50.17	24.17	61.64	327.77	-
1996	453.91	311.39	53.38	27.46	61.68	337.40	-

NB: the symbol "-" means no available data.

Source: The data in columns (1), (2), (4), (5) of the table were supplied by the Editorial Committee for the *China Finance Yearbook 1997*, except for data in column (1) and (5) for 1978 -1985, which are taken from Mei Yang (1996). Data in column (6) and (7) also come from Mei Yang (1996) except for column (6) from 1990 to 1996, which originates from the Editorial Committee of the *China Finance Yearbook 1997*.

Although the value of financial price subsidies has increased annually in absolute terms, their relative value as a percentage of GNP shows a downward trend (see Figure 1). Figure 1 shows the four main financial price subsidies as a percentage of GNP. Price subsidies increased sharply from 1978 to 1981, but have decreased annually since 1982. GNP-relative total price subsidies for grain, cotton and oil, other price subsidies and enterprise loss subsidies show a similar trend. 'Other' financial subsidies have been relatively small as a share of GNP and have tended to shrink further in recent years, indicating a steady decline in state subsides to water, electricity, other basic resources and transport. This picture was confirmed by our own survey. Enterprise loss subsidies as a percentage of GNP have also fallen in the last few years, demonstrating the positive effects of policies such as further reducing government control and intervention, and the policy of allowing more freedom to smaller firms while retaining control over the larger enterprises.

(iii) Purpose of Subsidies: To Stimulate Production and Stabilise Livelihoods

Economic reform is a difficult process. In the move from a planned to a market economy, many policies need to be altered or adjusted, and smooth implementation of these reforms without affecting social stability is a challenge for the government. Subsidy policy is one available means of allaying the short-term impact of the new policies and maintaining social stability and orderly production. The government may, for example, offer cereal price subsidies to residents to counter the negative effects of price adjustments for farm and side-line products, such as cereals and cotton, on people's livelihoods and productivity.

The state therefore uses subsidies to offset short-term confusion due to the new measures, particularly the price adjustments. In agriculture, to encourage grain farmers to invest more and alleviate their financial burdens, the government applies a system of centrally unified prices for chemical fertilisers with management functions devolved to different levels (Fee Management Department, State Planning Commission 1997). This technique reduces the grain farmers' financial burden and encourages them to invest in cereal production.

In terms of results, financial subsidies clearly have a positive effect on economic life and productivity, but the measures now in force also have major side-effects:

- an increasing burden on government finances;

- further distortion of the price and salary regimes;

- limited social and economic benefits;

- the present financial subsidy system has encouraged a simplistic idea of economic management in some people's minds (Ma, 1996).

It is therefore considered that the present subsidy policy should be reformed gradually as the Chinese market economy improves and the sustainable development strategy is implemented, in order to comply with principles of equity and efficiency.

2.5   The Analytical Framework

This section presents a framework for the analysis of subsidy policies for selected resources. Since the purpose of the study is to identify the environmental effects of subsidy policies, with a view to achieving sustainable development and utilisation of resources and the environment, analysis should be based on a sustainable development model. In such a model, environmental protection is given equal consideration with economic growth and social stability.

Figure 2: Analytical Framework for Subsidy Policy

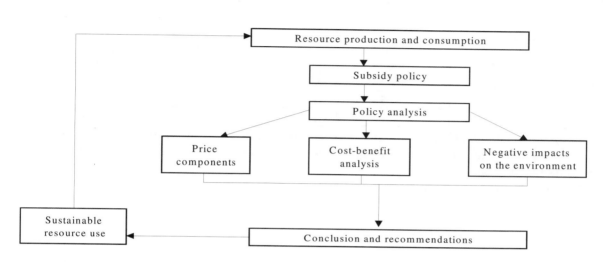

3.0   Water

3.1   Water Resources in China and Their Use

(i)   Current Situation

The total volume of surface water in China is about 2812.4 billion cubic meters (State Statistics Bureau (SSB), 1996), but the average water resource per head is only 2232 cubic meters, or barely one-fourth of the world average, and these water resources are unevenly distributed. Similarly, rainfall is uneven across China: annual precipitation is 1600-2000 mm in the southern coastal area, 1000-1500 mm in the Yangzi River basin, and only 100-200 mm in the north-western inland area. According to SSB statistics, China has 828.7 billion m^3 of groundwater, which is also unevenly distributed. These conditions underlie the regional differences in water resources: some regions suffer floods while others are afflicted by drought. In some regions water is so scarce as to jeopardise production and even survival. In addition, economic development and resulting water pollution further reduce the availability of water. The water shortage is even more acute in the big cities, where rapid economic growth and urbanisation further increases the pressure on water resources for residential and industrial use. This situation is made worse by the current low capacity of waste water processing in China. Pollution reduces the usability of the water resource and exacerbates the shortage. Table 3 shows water shortages prevailing in several major Chinese cities; shortages are anticipated in cities such as Beijing and Tianjin. Finding an effective solution to the problem of urban water shortages is now a major priority.

Table 3: Water Shortfall in Ten Major Cities in 1993

City	Population (million)	Water use in 1990 (100 million m³)	Water demand in year 2000 (100 million m³)	Estimated water supply in year 2000 (100 million m³)*	Projected water shortfall (100 million m³)
Beijing	7.00	9.7	33.5	17.7	15.8
Tianjin	5.77	6.3	27.4	17.1	10.3
Shanghai	7.83	28.7	55.5	8.8	46.7
Shenyang	4.59	5.6	10.4	1.3	9.1
Lanzhou	1.51	3.6	7.3	1.4	5.9
Guangzhou	3.58	8.6	22.4	8.4	14.0
Xian	2.76	3.5	7.5	1.8	5.7
Nanjing	2.49	10.2	18.7	2.1	16.6
Wuhan	3.75	8.5	16.6	2.8	13.8
Chengdu	2.81	4.1	9.2	2.5	6.7

*Assuming the water supply in 1990 equal to water use because of water shortage and the water supply will increase at an average rate of 5% per annum with the development of new water supply schemes and innovation of the old ones.
Source: Zhang, Q. and Zhang, X., 1995.

(ii) Water Resources Use

China, like other nations, makes extensive use of its water resources: for residential, industrial and agricultural activities, hydropower generation, water transportation and recreation. In 1996 the total volume of urban tap water supplied was 4.46 billion tons, of which 1.67 billion tons was supplied to residential users (daily average 208 litres per head), and 2.62 billion tons to industry (State Statistics Bureau 1997). China's gross potential hydropower resource is estimated at 676 million KWh, of which 379 million KWh are exploitable. Since the founding of the People's Republic of China in 1949, both large and medium-sized hydropower stations and small rural installations have been built across the nation; as of the end of 1996, the total installed hydropower capacity was 55.58 million KWh (Editorial Committee, China Power Yearbook, 1997). Water resources from natural features such as rivers and lakes are supplemented by water management projects to supply water both for power generation and for residential, industrial, and agricultural uses. Water management provides a total of 500 billion m³ of water each year (Zhang and Zhang, 1995).

3.2 Water Subsidy Policies

Under the planned economy, the construction of hydropower plant and other waterworks was controlled by the government. Water was regarded as a gift from heaven, to be freely used and exploited. The fiscal authorities allocated funds at no charge for the construction of waterworks and hydroelectric plant, and the revenue from such facilities accordingly reverted to the state. Prices for water supplied from waterworks were simply calculated at cost plus a few percentage points of profit as stipulated by the government, and were thus extremely low, reflecting low employee salaries, interest-free investment capital for construction and a low rate of depreciation. The situation was very similar for hydropower. In line with the favourable treatment granted to industry under the planned economy, the price of hydroelectric power, an industrial production factor, was set very low, indeed significantly lower than thermal power.

With reform and decontrol, the government has revised its policies for water management, hydropower and water resource utilisation. The view that the water resource does have a value has been developed and enshrined in the Water Law of the People's Republic of China. Although no policy on water charges has yet been announced at national level, some provinces, autonomous regions and centrally-administered municipalities have started to levy water resource charges (Price Management Department, State Planning Commission, 1996). Government investment in waterworks has also changed, moving from a funding allocation system to the provision of repayable loans, raising the cost of financing hydropower and waterworks projects, and this has been reflected in some readjustment of the price of waterworks water and the urban water supply. Nevertheless, the current water subsidy policy still includes price controls, funding allocation for waterworks, and preferential loans and tax conditions to water projects, of which price controls are the main component: waterworks water and urban water prices remain under state control. Although the Water Law prescribes a policy of covering cost plus a small profit, this principle cannot be applied at present since water pricing is not rational. With the perfection of the market economy, government allocations and loans to water projects and tax preferences on waterworks will be gradually reduced.

Preferential prices are also offered for energy from hydro projects, for instance for irrigation. In Shanxi Province, power for irrigation is priced at 0.068 yuan/KWh, 68% lower than for agricultural production, making the power department reluctant to guarantee supply (Electricity Price Coordinating Office, Shanxi Province, 1996). Value-added tax charged on tap water is also below the general rate[1].

3.3 Policy Analysis

(i) The Theoretical Basis of Water Pricing in China

The Water Law of the People's Republic of China clearly stipulates that water prices must reflect cost of supply plus a small profit, and allows for a competition mechanism. Thus the key to determining a rational water price is to correctly assess the total *cost* of water. In theory, prices for waterworks water should include investment depreciation, staff costs, the operational and maintenance costs of the facilities, a profit margin and a compensation levy for social and environmental damage caused by the facility. In practice, waterworks water pricing in China reflects these principles, but in fact it chiefly reflects the visible cost component. Current water pricing is based on a State Council decision promulgated in 1985 (Regulation on the Calculation, Collection, and Management of Charges for Waterworks Water, State Council Decisions No.94) issued by the State Council in 1985, which embodies the principle of covering cost with a small profit (Table 4). However, there is no comprehensive and systematic evaluation of social and environmental losses due to waterworks or any integration of this factor in cost. Although some experts consider this measure, which was drafted some time ago, to be outdated and irrational (He, 1996), it has been routinely applied.

---

[1] According to the Circular on VAT on Drinking Water issued by the Ministry of Finance and the State Administration of Taxation, as contained in the *China Tax Yearbook 1995*, the VAT rate is 6%.

Table 4: Basis of Various Rates and Prices for Water

Use	Basis of price determination	Remarks
Agricultural	For grain crops: supply cost. Can be higher for cash crops	Cost does not include depreciation of fixed asset formed by farmers' investment of labour
Industrial	Depleting use: cost + 4.6% profit. Non-depleting use: according to resulting economic benefit	Cost includes depreciation of fixed asset formed by farmers' investment of labour
Urban residential	Cost of supply or cost plus small profit	Can be lower than industrial use price
Small hydropower plant	Composite of other water use charges: can be 12% of hydropower or 8% of grid power price	
Environmental enhancement, public health	According to agricultural use price	

Source: The Editorial Committee for the Handbook on Expenditure Standards, Fee Rates, Interest Rates, and Tax Rates for the Administrative Units of Enterprises and Institutions, 1996.

(ii) Water Prices: Rationale

In 1996, the total charges due for the supply of waterworks water nation-wide were just over 5 billion yuan but the actual amount collected was just over 4.75 billion yuan. Water revenues and prices in provinces and cities for 1996 can be found in Table 5. As can be seen from the Table, water prices differed widely between provinces, from a high of 0.77 yuan/m^3 in Hainan Province to a low of 0.005 yuan/m^3 in Hunan. The question of whether these prices are rational, and whether they cover costs, must be answered in the negative. Table 6 compares water prices and costs for agricultural irrigation, industrial use and everyday domestic use in 1996.

Table 5: Water Revenue and Water Prices in Provinces and Cities

Number	City/Province/ Autonomous Region	Water supply revenue (10 thousand yuan)	Average water price (yuan/m^3)
1	Beijing City	11,833	0.026
2	Tianjin City	2,740	0.007
3	Hebai Province	17,448	0.016
4	Shanxi Province	15,051	0.100
5	Inner Mongolia Autonomous Region	13,549	0.006
6	Liaoning Province	33,526	0.025
7	Jilin Province	7,968	0.020
8	Hei Longjiang Province	10,623	0.009
9	Shanghai City	2,668	0.009
10	Jiangsu Province	26,331	0.016
11	Anhui Province	28,563	0.014
12	Zhejiang Province	20,814	0.011
13	Fujian Province	31,580	0.011
14	Jiangxi Province	19,167	0.006
15	Shandong Province	68,661	0.038
16	Henan Province	36,840	0.031
17	Hubei Province	17,610	0.006
18	Hunan Province	30,426	0.006
19	Guangdong Province	248,225	0.110
20	Guangxi Autonomous Region	12,617	0.005
21	Hainan Province	7,699	0.770
22	Yunnan Province	9,555	0.008
23	Guizhou Province	3,558	0.014
24	Sichuan Province	45,633	0.017
25	Shanxi Province	13,669	0.016
26	Gansu Province	22,229	0.011
27	Ningxia Autonomous Region	8,587	0.011
28	Qinhai Province	1,500	0.006

Source: Zhang, J., 1997.

Table 6: Comparison of Water Prices and Costs Nation-wide (Units: yuan/m^3, %)

	1988-1990			1991-1996			1997		
	Water price	Cost	Rate of subsidy %	Water price	Cost	Rate of subsidy %	Water price	Cost	Rate of subsidy %
Agricultural irrigation use	0.008	0.013	37.0	0.016	0.029	44.8	0.03	0.055	45.5
Industrial use	0.04	0.063	36.5	0.06	0.086	30.5	0.16	na	na
Source water for domestic use	0.023	0.031	25.8	0.04	0.056	28.4	0.1	na	na

na = not available
Source: Tian, 1997.

It can be seen from Table 6 that water prices are below the production cost in every case. Since such low prices cannot cover the cost of supply, financial subsidies are required to avoid water supply plants showing a deficit. For irrigation, both prices and costs have increased annually, but costs have risen faster: prices rose by 100% from 0.008 yuan/m^3 in 1988-90 to 0.016 yuan/m^3 in 1991-96, but costs rose by 123.1% over the same period, from 0.013 yuan/m^3 to 0.029 yuan/m^3, resulting in a commensurate increase in subsidies. For industrial and residential water use, the rate of subsidy declined, since prices rose faster than costs. However, in some areas, the local water price still did not even cover the depreciation of equipment. In the Beijing Municipality in 1993, for instance, water for commercial and industrial use was priced at 0.21 yuan/ton, while residential water was at 0.12 yuan/ton; but depreciation of waterworks equipment in the near suburbs was estimated at 14.8 yuan/thousand tons per km. Depreciation of the No. 8 Water Plant, 44 km away from Beijing was as high as 39.18 yuan/thousand tons per km (Gao, 1994).

(iii) Rational Water Prices

Since water price controls are the main form of water subsidy, the key to eliminating subsidisation is to price water rationally. What is a rational price for water? From a sustainable development point of view, a rational water price should include the full cost of supplying the resource, i.e. the sum of marginal supply cost, marginal use cost and marginal external cost (CCICED, 1995) (marginal use cost plus marginal external cost equals marginal opportunity cost). In some literature, the full cost is also called the marginal opportunity cost of water consumption. Marginal supply cost can be computed from the average production cost in a given sector. The opportunity cost is the revenue lost from the next best alternative use: for example, when agriculture and industry are in competition for the use of the water, the opportunity cost of agricultural water is equal to the profits lost to the industrial sector due to any shortage of water. The marginal external cost refers to the cost of water management projects to the rest of society not involved in the project, which includes economic, social, and environmental loss in the upper and lower reaches of a watercourse. According to Smil, the economic loss incurred by China in 1990 due to water shortage was 5 to 8.7 billion yuan, including reductions in crop yields (3 to 6 billion yuan) and industrial production (1.5 to 2.1 billion yuan), and the subsidy was 0.5 to 0.6 billion yuan (Smil, 1996). Assuming that the annual volume of water supplied by water plant is 500 billion m^3, as cited above, the economic loss per cubic meter is 0.01 to 0.017 yuan.

(iv) Water Resource Subsidies

The above analysis shows that water subsidies are currently very high in China, as is the subsidy rate. The current irrational water prices cannot offset the cost of supplying water, not to mention operating profits for water supply plants, resulting in a rate of financial subsidy as high as 30%. From the sustainable development point of view, the amount of subsidy should be calculated to include the economic, environmental and social opportunity costs and benefits of water use. However, due to the difficulties in calculating these opportunity costs and benefits, and limited access to data, no further analysis is made here.

(v) The Main Problems

Water pricing management problems: the existing policies are not consistent, and the government has not developed a coherent policy management system. In regard to procedures for setting, collecting and managing water charges, the central government continues to apply the 1985 regulation, which does not meet the criteria for a market mechanism. The calculation of the cost of supplying water is incomplete. For instance, under the former planned economy, capital investment was interest-free, so interest did not enter into the calculation of cost. Another problem is the value of the farmers' labour invested, which is not included in production cost. In agricultural water use, various factors complicate the calculation of water charges based on the irrigated area, such as: the efficiency of water use, the problem of water saving, and the ageing of water supply equipment.

Environmental and resource use problems: water management projects which dam, re-route, interrupt or divide the flow of watercourses all affect the ecological environment within the watershed. A large dam which divides the river into two parts will influence the redistribution of the water resource and the overall water ecology. Low water prices lead to over-utilisation of water resources. The Yellow River, for example, passes through the dry north and north-west regions of China, where water is in very short supply and the situation is worsened by the inefficiency of water use. The efficiency of irrigation in this region is only 30-50%, and the industrial recycling rate only 30%. Low water prices are the chief cause of these phenomena (Chen 1996). The 'Yellow River Water for Qingdao' Project, in contrast, has set a rational price which encourages water saving in Qingdao. In this supply project, the basic water price is 0.89 yuan/m^3, urban tap water is supplied at 1.2 yuan/m^3, and industrial water at 1.5 yuan/m^3. In some cities, groundwater is over-utilised to make up for the shortage of surface water, causing land subsidence. Table 7 lists the relevant data on groundwater locations and subsidence in major northern cities.

Table 7: Surface Subsidence in Some Major Chinese Cities

City	Use of groundwater (000m^3/day)	Groundwater level (m)	Subsidence area (000m^2)	Maximum subsidence (m)
Beijing	1390	40	600	0.59
Tianjin	274-329	94.58	400	2.46
Taiyuan	349-377	71	226	1.38

Source: Zhang, Q. and Zhang, X., 1995.

Social issues: shortages of water affect daily life and production capability. Water management projects also influence livelihoods and daily life in their host regions. Water is an indispensable input to life and production. Without water, a factory can not produce, crops cannot grow, and people cannot survive. When water is scarce, various users compete for the resource, and problems in matching supply and demand may become acute. Water management projects may affect neighbouring communities through their effects on lifestyles and production patterns. Residents of up-river regions may have to relocate. In the beneficiary region, productivity and livelihoods are improved. Price reforms for water supplied by such projects have an impact on residents' acceptance: excessive prices beyond their ability to pay will lead to rejection, while prices which are too low can have little influence on their behaviour.

4.0 Electric Power

4.1 Electricity Use in China - Present Situation

As the second most important resource in China's current energy structure, electric power plays a major role in national development and economic life. Table 8 shows power generation and consumption in China. Since the start of the reform period, electric power generation has increased year on year. The total output for 1995, at 1002.34 billion KWh, showed an increase of 233.4% over the 1980 figure. Thermal power generation is the main source of electric power in China, accounting for 80% of total output in 1995, as compared to 19% for hydropower and only 1% for nuclear.

Table 8: Electrical Power: Balance Sheet (Unit: 100s of Gwh)

Item	1980	1985	1990	1994	1995
Power supply	3006.3	4117.6	6230.4	9260.4	10023.4
Generation	3006.3	4106.9	6212	9280.8	10077.3
Hydropower	582.1	923.7	1267.2	1821.6	1905.8
Thermal power	2424.2	3183.2	4944.8	7459.2	8043.2
Nuclear power					128.3
Imports		11.1	19.3	18.5	6.4
Exports		0.4	0.9	38.9	60.3
Consumption by sector:					
Farming, forestry, animal husbandry, fishing, water works	270	317.4	426.8	530.6	582.4
Industry	2471.9	3283.4	4873.3	6983	7659.8
Building industry	47.1	71.2	65	149.7	159.6
Transport, post and telecommunications	26.5	63.4	105.9	164	182.3
Commercial, catering, materials supply and marketing, storage	16.8	38	76.2	179.2	199.5
Other	68.8	121.7	202.4	386.9	234.2
Private consumption	105.2	222.5	480.8	867	1005.6
Among which:					
End-user consumption	2763.4	3813.3	5795.8	8664.3	9278.9
Industry	2229	2979.1	4438.7	6386.9	6915.3
Losses from power transmission and distribution	242.9	304.3	434.6	596.1	744.5

Source: The State Statistics Bureau, 1997

Figure 3: Power Use in China, 1980-1995 (Unit: 100s of Gwh)

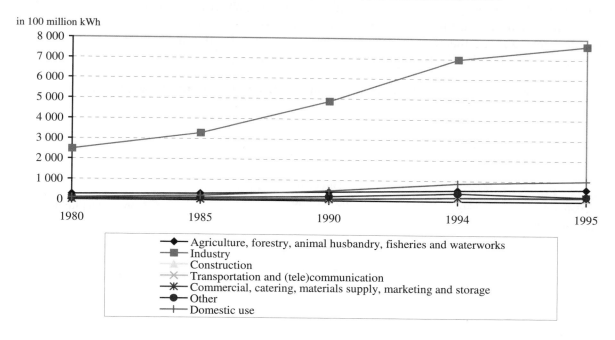

Figure 3 shows that industry is both the largest and the most rapidly-growing consumer of electric power. In 1995, industrial use of power accounted for 76% of the total, while residential use accounted for 10.9%, and farming, animal husbandry, forestry and fisheries combined, for 5.8%. The rate of end-user utilisation was 93%, with power losses amounting to 7%.

4.2   Subsidy Policies in Power Generation and Consumption

Since the reforms began, the government has made great efforts to eliminate subsidies, but in view of the unique status of power subsidies in national economic and social life, a number of them have survived.

(i) Controls on Power Prices

Electric power is one of the commodities still under state control, and is priced according to a dual-track system comprising a grid and a retail price. Power prices can also be divided into directive prices and guide prices, which are expected to coexist for some time to come. The directive price and guide price are centrally fixed by the Price Bureau of the State Planning Commission according to its principle of collective leadership and administration at different hierarchical levels (Fee Management Department, State Planning Commission, 1997) (Figure 4). Any price re-adjustments by provinces, autonomous regions or municipalities directly under the central government are subject to prior reporting, registration and approval by the Price Bureau. Power prices comprise operational costs, fuel transportation surcharges, contributions to a fund for electric power construction projects, and loan interest and principal repayments. Of these components, the standard fuel transportation surcharge accounts for about 0.12 yuan/KWh, repayment of interest and principal to the central government for about 0.0203 yuan/KWh, and the construction fund contribution for about 0.02 yuan/KWh. From January to April 1996, the listed power price for grids under the direct authority of the Ministry of Electric Power was 0.29 yuan/KWh, while the guide price was 0.50 yuan/KWh (Energy and Raw Materials Division, Price Management Department, State Planning Commission, 1996). Prices are based directly on production cost, and are therefore lower for hydroelectric than for thermal power, regardless of quality, thus creating a disincentive for the development of hydroelectric power.

Figure 4: Schematic Breakdown of Electricity Price Structure in China

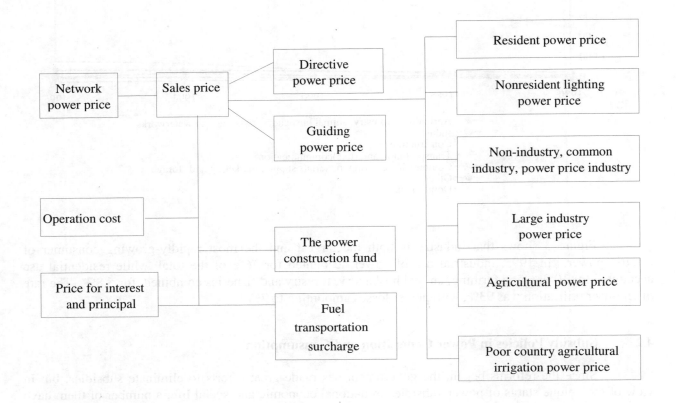

(ii) Controls on Raw Materials

Prices for power plant coal and generated electricity are interdependent: fluctuations in the price of the former will influence the cost of the latter, and thus the price of power. The price of electricity also affects the cost of producing coal. As a general socio-economic stabilising measure, the state applies a guide price for power plant coal. When the demand for coal exceeds supply, this amounts to subsidisation of the power plant, but when coal supply exceeds demand, the power utility has to pay a price above market cost to purchase this same coal. However, the coal supplied under the unified state-run system is of better quality, with lower gangue, ash and sulphur content, than the small county or township coal-mine product sold on the open market; so that, even when coal supply exceeds demand, the guide price works in favour of the environment, although not in favour of optimum economic efficiency.

126

(iii) Investment Policy and the Loan Rate

To promote power plant construction, and ameliorate power supply bottlenecks, the government has established a Power Generation Infrastructure Fund to support the development of power generation facilities. Contributions are collected as a supplement independent of the power price. Specifically, the State Council has approved a local power plant construction fund, to be financed by contributions of 0.02 yuan/KWh over the period of the 9th Five-year Plan, and the contributor base has been enlarged to include residential users (Fee Management Department, State Planning Commission, 1997). With the establishment of this fund, and in view of the key role of electric power in the national economy, power plant construction has been assigned a high priority in state investment in infrastructure projects, and will accordingly receive preference for the allocation of government funding and other preferential treatment. Of course, power plant construction is also funded by civil society, and by individual and foreign capital, which will need to be repaid with interest. In addition, to attract capital these projects will have to offer a rate of return higher than the 'average social rate'.

(iv) Tax Policy

Since tax reform began, the policy of granting tax preferences has been progressively reduced. A 1993 Ministry of Finance directive on value added tax on power products established a fixed-rate VAT of 4 yuan/1000KWh on power generation plants, and 1-3% on power transmission plant (State Taxation Administration 1995), as compared to the general VAT rate of 13-17%. Tax refunds are also offered: for example, before 1997, 90% of the VAT revenue collected from Qinshan Nuclear Power Station was subsequently refunded.

(v) Preferential Policies to Other Sectors

Power is an important factor in production. The state has established preferential electricity prices for irrigation, and for chemical fertiliser production, and the differences can be significant in some areas. The price of power supplied to the large chemical fertiliser enterprises in Shanxi Province is only 25% of that applied for general industrial use. Such a large difference has led to the unchecked proliferation of small chemical fertiliser plants in that area. Statistics show that there are now over 110 small phosphate fertiliser plants in Shanxi alone. In most of these plants, power consumption per unit of product exceeds the standard, amounting to a serious waste of power. Power is supplied for irrigation at 0.068 yuan/KWh, which is 68% lower than the general agriculture rate, working as a disincentive to power administrations against supplying power for irrigation (Electricity Price Coordinating Office, Shanxi Province, 1996).

4.3   Policy Analysis

(i) Power Prices: Present Structure

According to the Power Law which came into force in April 1996 and the associated state regulations, power pricing should be based on the principle of covering cost with a small profit. The Price Bureau of the State Planning Commission publishes a government guide price calculated on this basis, and provinces and municipalities then set their policies accordingly. Table 9 lists the published state prices for electricity from various grids, for uses ranging from 1,000-10,000 volt, on the basis of consumption figures for 1996. Differences are noted among power prices in different provinces and for different uses. The overall average price was about 0.30 yuan/KWh. In a study of thermal power costs, Zhang Shiqiu (1998) has estimated the production cost of coal-fired power at 0.3 yuan/KWh. On this basis, it might appear that the official power price is already equal or close to the actual power plant production cost, but in fact, since these prices include not only these production costs, but also government levies such as the power-plant construction fund and the Three Gorges Reservoir construction fund, they may be lower than the cost of generation. In other words, the present power pricing mechanism is indeed irrational (Zhao, 1998).

Table 9: Unit Prices by Power Grids and User Capacity (1-10 KVA) (Units: yuan KWh)

Power grid	Residential power use	Non-residential power use	Non-industrial and ordinary industrial power use	Large industrial power use	Agricultural production power use	Poor counties (power for irrigation schemes)
Beijing - Tianjin - Tangshan	0.250	0.350	0.324	0.237	0.265	0.112
Hebei Province	0.230	0.352	0.331	0.251	0.266	0.087
Shanxi Province	0.260	0.338	0.303	0.227	0.246	0.108
Inner Mongolia	0.230	0.296	0.237	0.177	0.189	0.121
Henan Province	0.265	0.327	0.241	0.175	0.188	0.093
Jiangsu Province	0.300	0.403	0.333	0.246	0.275	0.092
Zhejiang Province	0.295	0.360	0.337	0.246	0.274	0.087
Shanghai City	0.295	0.360	0.337	0.246	0.274	0.087
Fujian Province	0.235	0.267	0.168	0.114	0.129	0.064
Shandong Province	0.260	0.306	0.238	0.174	0.172	
Xinjiang	0.283	0.393	0.240	0.193	0.121	
Guizhou Province	0.265	0.365	0.285	0.215	0.228	0.109
Ningxia	0.250	0.363	0.285	0.221	0.229	0.105
Guangxi	0.265	0.297	0.205	0.154	0.159	0.090
Yunnan Province	0.265	0.361	0.296	0.226	0.243	0.117
Northeast power network	0.240	0.361	0.340	0.254	0.276	
Shanxi Province	0.220	0.381	0.294	0.126	0.242	0.068
Qinhai Province	0.205	0.269	0.170	0.122	0.132	0.083
Average	0.256	0.342	0.276	0.200	0.217	0.095

Source: The Price Management Department of the State Planning Commission, 1996.

(ii) Rational Power Pricing

A rational power price should be based on a sustainable development scenario, and hence should include the full cost of power, comprising not only the cost of generation, but also the cost of utilisation and the external environmental cost, i.e.:

Rational Price P = MPC (Marginal Production Cost) + MUC (Marginal Use Cost) + MEC (Marginal Environmental Cost) (Zhang, 1997).

The cost of power should be measured as an average social cost, rather than as any individual enterprise's generation costs. This 'average social cost' should cover both the consumption of tangible production factors and a reasonable return on capital. Capital is invested in the power sector at the expense of other sectors, so the rate of return must be higher than in other sectors in order to attract such capital. The marginal use and external costs correspond to environmental damage by SO_2 and coal combustion emissions, which may have both positive or negative social and environmental effects at local, regional or even national and global level. The environmental costs of thermal power can be calculated simply from the abatement cost of SO_2 and smoke emissions. The external environmental cost of power generation can be thus be computed from the amount of SO_2 and fumes resulting from coal burning for thermal power generation, and for hydropower, from the effects of water management projects on society and the environment. In 1996, total Chinese thermal power generation was 877.80 billion KWh (Editorial Committee, China Power Yearbook, 1997). According to data from the Chinese Research Academy of Environmental Science (CRAES, 1997), the costs of abatement are 1.26 yuan/kg for SO_2 and 0.55 yuan/kg for fumes, or 0.00969 yuan per KWh of power for SO_2 and 0.0346 yuan for fumes[2]. Assuming that all environmental damage from power generation is due to coal-fired plants, the environmental cost, on this marginal abatement cost approach, is 0.04459 yuan/KWh. A separate study, from Beijing University, estimates the external costs due to damage caused by coal-fired power generation at 0.02316 yuan/KWh (Zhang 1998). The different findings of these two studies reflect the difficulty of determining environmental cost per unit of power generated. More comprehensive and systematic studies are needed in this area.

A rational power price should also reflect the principle of equity, i.e. thermal power and hydropower of the same quantity and quality, and from the same grid, should enjoy the same price with no discrimination. The present regime, in which thermal and hydropower are differently priced (Zhang et al. 1996; Zhang, 1997), should be gradually abolished. Only thus will hydropower, which has few environmental effects in the narrow sense, become more attractive to investors. On the other hand, if no incentive in favour of hydropower is desired, then the charges for the use of the water resource, and environmental compensation levies, can be applied to hydropower on the basis of equal quantity and quality from the same grid.

(iii) Power Subsidies and the Environment

Power subsidies mainly take the form of price controls and subsidies on raw materials, supplemented by a range of investment and taxation policies and other preferential terms for different sectors. The power utilities enjoy a strong monopoly position, since power prices are controlled by the state. Currently, these prices include the costs of generation and transmission, and some government charges and levies. Although power pricing is based on the principle of cost coverage plus a small profit, it is not rational (Energy and Raw Materials Division, Price Management Department, State Planning Commission, 1996). In practice, power subsidies, in both the financial and general economic sense, are still a fact of life in China.

---

[2] SO_2 abatement cost per KWh (C) is calculated as follows: C = coal consumption per KWh x 2 x coal sulphur content (S) x discharge factor (K) x standard SO_2 levy = 0.377 x 2 x 0.012 x 0.85 x 1.26 = 0.00969 yuan. Fumes abatement cost per KWh   (C) is calculated as follows: C = [(coal consumption per KWh) x 2 x (coal ash content (A)) x (percentage of ash content in   fumes (D)) ÷ (1 - percentage of flammable matter in fumes (C))] x (standard fumes levy) = [0.377 x 0.30 x 0.5 ÷ (1 - 0.1)]   x 0.55 = 0.0346.

Two aspects of the energy-environment relationship have been described: the environmental impact of emission pollutants from thermal power generation, such as SO_2 and fumes; and the impact of water storage facilities like dams and reservoirs associated with hydroelectric generating plant. Since coal-fired generation is the major source of power in China, we have focused on the environmental effects of thermal power subsidies. From the economic point of view, subsidies reduce the price of power to consumers, encouraging greater consumption; the increased demand in turn encourages utilities to produce more, releasing more SO_2 into the atmosphere. From the generators' point of view, subsidies are a disincentive to business due to their price-controlling effect, and affect the flow of capital into the power sector (Zhao, 1998).

5.0   Chemical Fertiliser and Phyto-sanitary Subsidies

5.1   Annual Production, Import and Use of Chemical Fertilisers And Phytosanitary Products

Chemical fertilisers and pesticides are important materials in agricultural production. The intensive production of crops such as cereals needs chemical fertiliser and pesticides as inputs. Agriculture is fragile, in the sense that it is heavily affected by natural conditions. Like advanced nations, the Chinese government attaches a high priority to agricultural development; the difference is that there are far more people engaged in agriculture in China. In China, 80% of the population live in the countryside, and in 1996, about 70% of the working population was engaged in agricultural production (including county and township enterprises) (State Statistics Bureau, 1997).

(i) Chemical Fertilisers

Production: Since 1949, China has developed a substantial chemical fertiliser industry with Chinese characteristics, basically by relying on its own resources and technology but also by actively absorbing the experience of advanced foreign nations, and importing production equipment. Between 1949 and 1986 the state invested 26 billion yuan in chemical fertiliser plant, and production capacity reached 15 million tons (Editorial Committee, China National Petroleum and Chemicals Corporation Yearbook, 1991). Since the recent reforms began, chemical fertiliser production has seen major changes both in quality and quantity. In 1990, licenses to produce chemical fertiliser were held by 1897 companies nation-wide, including 1100 small-to-medium-sized, 58 medium-sized and 19 large nitrogenous fertiliser plants; 716 phosphate fertiliser plants; and 3 potash fertiliser plants (Editorial Committee, China National Petroleum and Chemicals Corporation Yearbook, 1991). National chemical fertiliser production rose from only 8.693 million tons in 1978 to 28.09 million tons in 1996 (Figure 5), showing an average annual growth rate of 17.9% over the nineteen year period. China is now a leading producer of chemical fertiliser.

Figure 5: Chemical Fertiliser Production, Import, Sales and Use, 1952-1995
(Unit: million of tons)

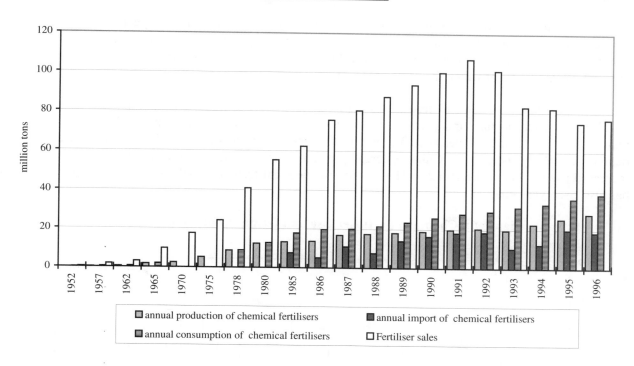

Chemical fertiliser imports: China is a major importer of chemical fertiliser, purchasing large volumes on the international market each year to make up shortages in domestic supply. In the 40 years from the birth of the People's Republic of China to 1989, the country produced a cumulative total of about 1.06 billion tons of chemical fertiliser, and imported 0.27 billion tons, i.e. 25.6% of the domestic requirement, to a total foreign exchange value of $US 18.21 billion (Jin, 1995). Since the reforms began, the level of these imports has tended to rise, with some fluctuations (Figure 5).

Sales: Since the reforms began, state policy for the distribution of chemical fertilisers has undergone major changes, in line with fluctuations in supply and demand and changes in agricultural policy. Under the planned economy, the production, importation, sale and pricing of chemical fertilisers were set within the plan. Currently, the government exercises only macro-control over production and sales of chemical fertilisers, in order to maintain equilibrium in overall volumes. Factory gate prices are set by the government and managed at different levels of the administration. Chemical fertilisers under central government control are subject to a two-tier price system for wholesale distribution, and a single price for retail sales. For sales under provincial government control, the system prescribes one price level for retail and another for wholesale. District-level farm input suppliers and grassroots agricultural co-operatives also engage in combined wholesale and retail sales, through an agent system. Farm input supplier enterprises are the main marketing channel for chemical fertilisers, supplemented at district and lower levels by local phytosanitary, production and agricultural extension stations (Fee Management Department, State Planning Commission, 1997: 131-132).

Retail prices for chemical fertiliser are set by provincial commodity pricing authorities. To ease the financial burden on farmers, and combat price inflation due to the uncontrolled levying of fees by multiple intermediaries, a policy has been adopted whereby purchases of chemical fertilisers are linked to contracted sales of grain and cotton to the state. For fertilisers not under the above policy, a comprehensive price and uniform rate of return have been set (ibid. 133-134).

Figure 5 shows the sale of chemical fertilisers in China in recent years. The figures are considerably higher than those quoted in statistics for volumes produced and traded, reflecting the effects of the Chinese distribution circuits and statistical practices. Double-accounting may arise, since there are three wholesale levels at which the sales volume may be calculated.

Utilisation: Chemical fertiliser use in China in 1996 was 38.279 million tons, an average of 251.2 kg for each hectare under crop (16.8 kg/*mu*; China Statistics Yearbook, 1997), amounting to an increase of 47.8%, or 56% per hectare, over 1990. The use of chemical fertilisers is one of the factors behind the steady increase in Chinese cereal production (Figure 6): grain yields have risen with the increased use of chemical fertiliser. The amount of chemical fertiliser applied per thousand tons of grain has also risen year-on-year.

Figure 6: Chemical Fertiliser Use and Grain Production (1978-96)

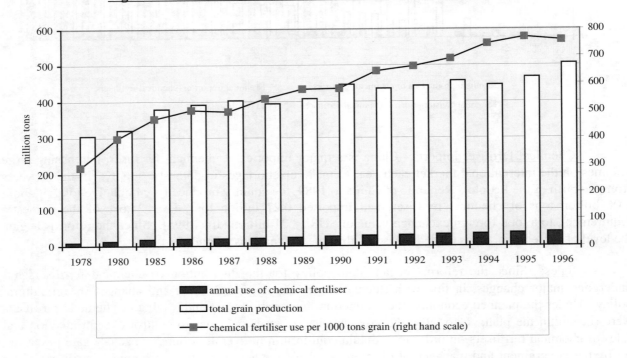

(ii)   Phytosanitary Products: Production, Trade, Sales and Use

Production: Statistics for 1994 put China's production of phytosanitary products for that year at 555,000 tons, including 404,000 tons (72.8%) of pesticides, 69,000 tons (12.4%) of bactericides, 75,000 tons (13.5%) of herbicides, and 7000 tons (1.3%) of plant growth promoters (Jin 1995). From 1952 to 1996, actual phytosanitary production fluctuated, rising steadily year on year from 1952 to peaks in 1978 and 1980, then declining for several years before picking up again from 1987.

Imports and Exports: Although domestic phytosanitary production is quantitatively adequate to meet demand, a certain volume is imported and exported, due to differences in the supply and demand structures for various products. China imported 30,000 tons of phytosanitary products per year, on average, from 1984 to 1996, with some fluctuations. In 1996, China imported 32,100 tons of phytosanitary products, to a declared customs value of US$137.55 million, or US$4285/ton (State Statistics Bureau, 1997). In 1993 China exported 148,000 tons of phytosanitary products for a total value of US$95,823,000; and in 1994 exported 70,000 tons for US$170 million (Jin, 1995).

Sales: Phytosanitary products are distributed mainly through supply and marketing co-operatives (before 1994) or the China Agricultural Materials Corporation, and to some extent by phytosanitary producers and grassroots agricultural extension stations and companies. Besides these sanctioned operators, no other unit or individual is authorised to market these products.

Sales of phytosanitary products were at their highest in China between 1980-1985, and remained stable, though showing a gradual decline, thereafter. The similar patterns in sales of phytosanitary and chemical fertiliser products further demonstrate the weaknesses in commercial statistics methodology in China.

Use: In recent years, average annual use of phytosanitary products in China has been 210,000 thousand tons (68% pesticides, 21% bactericides and 11% herbicides), or an average of 1.417 kg applied per hectare sown to crops (Jin, 1995). Phytosanitary products play an very important role in agricultural production. According to statistics from the departments concerned, in 1994 not less than 309.5 million hectares of agricultural land in China were afflicted by disease or damage due to insect and rodent pests. Pest prevention and control measures totalled 297 million 'application/hectares' (205 million received chemical protection, and 242 million biological protection). Comprehensive prevention and control, achieved primarily through the use of phytosanitary products, is estimated to have saved 42.763 million tons of grain and 1.6534 million tons of cotton (Jin, 1995).

5.2   Subsidy Policy

For many years in China the system under which chemical fertilisers and phytosanitary products were produced and sold involved industry responsibility for production while sales were the responsibility of the department of agricultural materials, and exports and imports the responsibility of the foreign trade department. As economic reforms have become increasingly far-reaching there have been definite changes, and companies which produce fertilisers and pesticides have begun to handle the sale of their products. It is Chinese agricultural policy, given the importance of chemical fertilisers and phytosanitary products, to accord some preferential policies in the area of production and controlled use. Under special circumstances loss subsidies are provided.

(i) Preferential Policies for Production Plants

Essential raw materials, electricity, fuel and foreign exchange are supplied to plants at reduced prices. Those raw materials or energy sources which fall under the aegis of central planning such as electricity and oil are supplied under specific state arrangements. Coal is supplied by the relevant local government. Working stocks required for production are allocated depending on the product, in compliance with regulations governing economic management.

A few large and medium-sized chemical fertiliser production plants (including some in the chemicals mining industry) receive loss subsidies involving one-off payments. For example, in 1991 and 1992, following several applications made by the plant, the Chinese Ministry of Finance made one-payments of 20 million yuan and 15 million yuan to the Jilin Chemical Industry Corporation's chemical fertiliser plant. In 1990 the Ministry of Finance made one-off payments of 30 million yuan in the form of loss subsidies to the Nanjing Chemical Industry Corporation and the Dalian Chemical Industry Corporation to compensate for lost production as a result of test production of ammonium phosphate equipment. In 1992 the Beijing City Financial Authority paid out a 2000 yuan loss subsidy to the Beijing Chemicals Industry Experimental Plant in order to balance the plant's end of year financial results. (Chemicals Industry Ministry, Phytosanitary Policy Research Unit, 1994).

(ii) Preferential Policies in Management

Chemical fertiliser production plants, all types of supply and marketing co-operatives, the agricultural management system and the agricultural technology promotion department are all exempt from business tax and product tax for all transactions involving chemical fertilisers, pesticides and agricultural plastic sheeting. Between January 1 1994 and 31 December 1997 plants producing chemical fertilisers were exempt from VAT. Allocation of working stocks necessary for production and management to these companies was given priority (Jin, 1995).

(iii) Preferential Policies for Imports

Financing required for central and regional imports of chemical fertilisers, phytosanitary products and agricultural plastic sheeting is guaranteed by banks. Centrally planned imports of these products continue to be exempt from or enjoy reduced customs tariffs, product tax (VAT) and cash deposits also enjoy tax exemption. The average rate of customs tariffs is around 3% for chemical fertilisers.

(iv) Preferential Policies for Farmers

Before the 1990s, in an effort to encourage farmers to grow grain and cotton, the Chinese government introduced policies which linked grain production to fertiliser use and others offering bonus schemes for cotton production. Prior to 1994 the so-called linking policy was implemented because demand for fertilisers outstripped supply. Between 1994 and 1995 supply and demand balanced out as markets for grain and cotton developed and price control was gradually reduced and consequently the state's grain-fertiliser linking policy and cotton-chemical fertiliser bonus policy were eradicated. Fertiliser price differences were considered as cost-external subsidies and directly benefited farmers.

The aim of the government's preferential policy was to protect the interests of farmers, ensure regular production and supply of chemical products for agricultural use and stimulate agricultural production. However imbalances between supply and demand and imperfections in management systems led to confusion in the fertiliser market. It was impossible to strictly limit the sale of chemical fertilisers to the major players in the industry such as the Ministry for Agricultural Materials and the supply and marketing co-operatives and hence prices were marked up excessively. According to a 1995 survey conducted by the Ministry for Agriculture's Agricultural Economy Research Centre, in some regions the volume of fertilisers circulating on the black market represented more than 80% of that on the official market while 48% of the retail price of urea was a result of mark-ups through circulation. Hence although the prices that Chinese farmers pay for fertilisers are basically market prices, most of the benefits of the government's preferential policies for fertilisers were eaten up through mark-ups, and only a small proportion of the benefits went to production companies while in actual fact the farmers themselves saw nothing of the subsidies. As a result of government intervention in 1996 the situation as described above has been rectified.

Because of the excessive number of "links" in the chemical fertiliser circulation chain, the excessive burden on farmers and indiscriminate taxation, the government issued two documents[3], document NO. 19 in 1996 and document NO. 156 in 1996, the latter dealing with price management, in order to radically overhaul the price management of chemical fertilisers. The result was the removal of several "links" in the chain, a clarification of the relationship between production, marketing and imports, producing a macro-economic system of control over fertiliser volumes.

5.3 Policy Analysis

(i) The Present Price Structure

Price structure of chemical fertilisers: The price of chemical fertilisers gradually increases as it moves through the chain from production to end use. The price structure includes cost price, allocated price and retail price. The cost price or factory price is the base price and is determined by the factory within the scope permitted by the state. The state stipulates the median permitted price of the fertilisers on leaving the factory as well as the upper and lower limits of price fluctuation. The allocation and retail prices of chemical fertilisers are calculated on the basis of business differentiation rates or profit rates. In 1994 the state determined the following median permitted price for chemical fertilisers: urea - 1000 yuan/ton, ammonium nitrate 700 yuan/ton with a 15% fluctuation permitted. The profit rate through the entire chain was less than 4% more than the purchasing price for those products which required transport or storage (including transport costs and other incidentals) and less than 1.5% more than the purchasing price for products which did not transit through warehouses (this figure includes interest).

Price structure of phytosanitary products: The price structure of pesticides is very similar to that of chemical fertilisers. However, the large diversity of types of pesticides and low levels of demand (although its use is considerable) mean that state control over the factory price is not as tight as it is over fertiliser prices. The increasing production capacity of Chinese pesticide production plants together with imports of pesticides have provoked market fluctuations. Prices of chemical fertilisers are mainly fixed by regional authorities The state, in this instance the State Agricultural Materials Corporation, still dictates the overall volume of pesticide production. A profit margin of 4.8% (factory price to retail price) is stipulated for pesticides produced in China. As for imported pesticides, no more than 4.8% of the overall domestic price differential including fixed state port fees are added to the import price (which includes CIF price in yuan, customs tariffs, commissions for import agents, insurance and inspection fees). The fixed price is then determined on a regional basis (The Fee Management Department, State Planning Commission, 1997).

(ii) Rational Prices

Rational prices are prices calculated on the basis of the principle of sustainable development. They should not only include the production costs of chemical fertilisers and phytosanitary products but

---

[3] The State Council issued Document No. 19 on June 19, 1996: "Improving the Marketing Chain for Chemical Fertilizers". The Price Management Department of the State Planning Commission issued Document No. 156 on January 1, 1996: "Improving the Price Management of Chemical Fertilizers".

also the external environmental costs of their use. Prices calculated on this basis are referred to as shadow prices.

The rational price of chemical fertilisers: The rational price of chemical fertilisers should take into account their full cost. This includes production costs, cost of fertiliser use and environmental costs. Production costs can be replaced by the overall average social cost while the environmental costs can be calculated on the basis of the economic loss resulting from the use of the fertilisers. The environmentally damaging effects of using chemical fertilisers mainly manifest themselves in decreased soil fertility and increased water pollution. However since it is difficult to accurately calculate the extent to which the use of chemical fertilisers does harm the soil and water, it is extremely difficult to establish the overall loss to the national economy that excessive use of chemical fertilisers generates.

It is difficult to obtain statistics for the entire country and hence only specific case studies can be cited to illustrate this point. According to analysis of the situation in the Dianchi Lake in Yunan Province and Dazu County near Chongqing (Jin, 1995) the cost of damage recovery in the Dianchi Lake region of Yunan Province in 1990 stood at 0.46 yuan/kg while the cost of urea in the same year was 1.44 yuan/kg. Hence the rational or shadow price of chemical fertilisers for that region was 1.9 yuan/kg. By the same calculation the rational or shadow price of chemical fertilisers in Dazu County near Chongqing in 1993 was 1.26 yuan/kg (Jin, 1995).

The shadow price of phytosanitary products: The rational price of pesticides, as with chemical fertilisers, should reflect the total cost (production, retail and environmental costs). As above, the production costs can be replaced by what is referred to as the average social cost while the environmental cost must reflect the economic losses brought about by damage to human health and the environment as a result of use of pesticides. In 1994 the average production and retail costs of pesticides stood at 56 yuan/kg while the marginal environmental cost based on agricultural value loss, labour production value loss and health cost, was calculated to be 47.55 yuan/kg. Hence the rational or shadow price was 103.55 yuan/kg (Jin, 1995).

(iii)   Chemical Fertiliser and Pesticide Subsidies

Chemical fertiliser subsidies: Over recent years the retail price of chemical fertilisers in China has been close to or on a par with the international market prices. In 1994 and 1995 the average retail price of urea on the Chinese market was 1,386 yuan/ton and 1,964 yuan/ton respectively. During the same two years the average CIF price of urea after conversion into Chinese yuan was 1,140 yuan/ton and 1,705 yuan/ton respectively (China Statistics Bureau, 1995; 1997). Thus with the addition of transport costs the CIF price of imported urea was virtually identical to the price of domestically produced urea. A special survey conducted by the Ministry of Agriculture in 1995 revealed that the average market retail price for urea varied from 2,200 yuan/ton in Anhui Province to 2,400 yuan/ton in Botou City, Hebei Province. Prices peaked at 2,800 yuan/ton during periods of intense agricultural activity. During the same year the international price of urea was US$250/ton (CIF price for spring 1995) or 2,175 Chinese yuan after conversion. Because China imports large quantities of chemical fertilisers, it is considered to be a tradable commodity whose reference price is the CIF price plus transport costs. Since its final retail price is almost identical to the reference price (price difference zero), Jin (1995) argued that calculations should be made on the basis of the international market prices and as a consequence, the Chinese chemical fertiliser subsidy rate was in fact zero. Given the frequent fluctuations in the price of chemical fertilisers on the international market, domestic prices may be higher or lower than international prices and hence the level of subsidies also fluctuates.

Pesticide subsidies: Phytosanitary products, like chemical fertilisers, are also tradables. In 1994 the price of domestically produced pesticides stood at 56 yuan/kg (Jin 1995). In the same year the CIF price of imported pesticides was US$4.3/kg, or 36.3 yuan/kg (State Statistics Bureau, 1994). In addition, transport costs of 0.32 yuan/kg have to be added (assuming transport over 500 km by road at a cost of 0.45 yuan/ton/km and transport over 1,500 km by rail at a cost of 0.0605 yuan/ton/km). Adopting the same international market calculation, the pesticide subsidy per kilo is the final price of pesticides minus the reference price (CIF price), or 56 - (36.3 + 0.32) = 19.38 yuan/kg. Hence the subsidy rate equals the subsidy per kilo divided by the reference rate and multiplied by 100%. 19.38 ÷ 36.62 X 100% = 52.9%.

(iv) The Effects of Chemical Fertiliser and Phytosanitary Subsidies on the Environment

The effects of chemical fertiliser subsidies: From an economic point of view and all other things being equal, the direct effect of subsidised chemical fertiliser is that they encourage farmers to use them more than non-subsidised ones. Because of the subsidies the fertilisers are cheaper than those which receive no subsidies and farmers do give little thought to their effectiveness. It is estimated that the utilisation rate of nitrate-based fertilisers in China is only 30% because most of the fertiliser is lost in run-off and ends up polluting rivers, lakes and ground water. This leaching of chemical fertilisers is one of the main reasons for the excessive levels of nitrates in water in China. 65-70% of the excess nitrate-based nutrients in China's Tianhu Lake can be attributed to water run-off as a result of ground pollution, mainly through agricultural use (Jin, 1995).

The effects of pesticide subsidies: All other things being equal, the direct effect of pesticide subsidies is that they encourage farmers to use subsidised pesticides rather than those not subsidised. Naturally when a farmer considers whether or not to use a pesticide, price is only one factor, others include plant diseases and pests, the agricultural economy, the characteristics of the pesticide under consideration and the farmer's knowledge of agri-technology.

(v)   The Feasibility of Applying Full Cost Pricing to Chemical Fertilisers and Phytosanitary Products

The removal of subsidies and the use of full cost pricing can help control the use of chemical fertilisers and pesticides and can be seen as an example of environmental friendliness. But because of conditions on the Chinese agricultural market and the fact that supply of fertilisers and pesticides outstrips demand, such a policy poses very real problems. If, in order to increase the prices of fertilisers and pesticides, the full cost pricing system which includes environmental cost, is implemented, the market would find it difficult to withstand. Stocks of fertilisers and pesticides are already high but such a policy would lead to even higher stock levels and consequently farmers would have to bear the additional economic cost. This would have a knock-on effect on fertiliser and pesticide production, industry management and the interests of the farming community. These issues require further examination.

6.0   Transport Subsidy Policy

Transport is the cornerstone of the Chinese economy. In the early days of reform and greater openness, the rapid increase in the movement of goods and domestic trade led many to consider the transport infrastructure as representing a major bottle-neck throttling economic development[4]. The Chinese government has adopted a variety of policies to support the development of the country's transport infrastructure (including the creation of a national energy and transport construction fund and measures to attract foreign capital using Build Operate Transer, BOT). Although transport is essential to the national economy it can have a negative effect on the environment. The transport infrastructure has an impact on the environment and the landscape (exhaust fumes, oil residues and vehicle scrap). The transport network must be developed with the minimum possible effect on the environment. A sustainable transport system must be able to combine these two aspects of the situation. In order to create such a model system, it is essential to evaluate current transport policy and develop new, effective economic policies. One novel and effective policy is to internalise transport costs making it possible to enhance the social and economic benefits of transport while simultaneously minimising the destructive effects of transport on the environment. Subsidies are one of the ways in which it is possible to influence the internalisation of transport costs. This section will therefore concentrate on an analysis and evaluation of subsidy policies within the transport sector, focusing particularly on subsidies in the areas of haulage, passenger transport and urban public transport. Haulage and passenger transport includes rail, road, water and air transport of goods. As China moves towards perfecting its market economy, the transport sector has become an independent economic entity. Government subsidies to the transport sector have basically been abandoned although some forms of financial subsidy still remain in the urban public transport system.

6.1   Goods and Passenger Transport and the Urban Public Transport System

(i) Goods Transport

Since the founding of the People's Republic of China and especially since the implementation of reforms and the moves to open up the country, China's goods and passenger transport sector has expanded rapidly with major increases in the total number and distances of goods transport routes and increases in passenger and cargo volume. The overall length of road and air transport routes has grown faster than that of railway and inland waterway routes. In 1995, the total length of paved roads and highways in China stood at 1.157 million kilometres compared to 127,000 kilometres in 1952. The total length of all Chinese domestic air routes in 1995 was 1.129 million kilometres compared to 13,000 kilometres in 1952. The total length of railway tracks was 55,000 km, an increase of 140% over 1952 while the length of all inland waterways used for transport was 110,000 km, an increase of 16% over 1952. In 1992 total passenger volume for that year stood at 1.73 billion compared to a mere 250 million in 1952. The volume of goods transport in 1995 stood at 123.5 billion tons compared to 320 million tons in 1952.

(ii) Urban Public Transport System

The rapid growth of the Chinese economy and increasing urbanisation have stimulated the expansion of urban public infrastructure. The urban public transport system, an integral part of this infrastructure, has expanded rapidly since reform began in China. In 1995 the total number of urban buses

---

[4]   Transport is considered a strategic priority in China's economic development. See Zhu 1997: "Sustainable Transport and Environmental Economic Policies" in Hu, Tao and Wang Huadong (eds.) 1997: *The Practical Application of Environmental Economics in China*. China Environmental Sciences Publishing House. Beijing.

(and trams) in Chinese cities was 136,821, an increase of 326% over 1980, an average of 7.3 buses or trams per ten thousand inhabitants - an increase of 110% over the ratio in 1980 (see Table 10).

Table 10: The Urban Public Transport System

Item	Unit	1980	1985	1990	1995
Total number of buses and trams		32098	45155	62215	136821
Proportion of buses and trams per 10,000 inhabitants		3.5	3.9	4.8	7.3
Total length of urban paved roads	km	294850	382820	978200	1,300,000
Surface area of paved roads	10,000 square meters	25255	35872	89160	135810

Source: The State Statistics Bureau, 1996.

6.2   Transport and Goods and Passenger Transport Subsidy Policy

(i) Goods and Passenger Transport

Subsidies in this sector include price controls, subsidies to compensate for company losses and a variety of other preferential policies. As Chinese economic reform expands, a market-based pricing system has gradually emerged. Annual, occasionally major adjustments to goods and passenger transport prices have been made (Zhou, 1996; Jin, 1996) and as a result today's goods and passenger transport prices generally reflect real costs. Nevertheless, the relative price of rail transport is some 20% lower than the actual cost (Zhou, 1996) and this has led to repeated losses in the rail transport sector over the years. In the early days of economic reform in China losses to goods and passenger transport caused by the pricing policy was compensated by the government. With the completion of the new pricing policy and the creation of a modern enterprise-based transport system, transport companies have become legal entities responsible for their own profits or losses, operating their businesses independently of the state. Hence loss subsidies have been abolished. Today transport subsidies and preferential policies tend to be concentrated in the rail and civil aviation sectors (Authors' own inquiries to the Ministry of Finance).

Since 1961 subsidy policies have included a preferential policy which offers tax exemption to cargo vessels of the China Ocean Transport Corporation. Since the reform of the tax system and during the last two years of the 8th five year plan, a new tax policy for ocean-going cargo vessels has been implemented - the so-called "levy first, refund later" system. (Tax Policy Department of the Ministry of Finance, 1996).

Since 1993 when the contract system was applied to the Chinese railways system, investments for railway construction were made in the form of loans from the Ministry of Railways. In other words the cost of rail transport increased while the price of rail transport did not actually go up. Consequently losses of 2.77 billion yuan, 6.41 billion yuan and 1.38 billion yuan were posted in 1994, 1995, and 1996 respectively (State Statistics Bureau, 1997). As a result of this the Chinese government issued the "Circular on Finance and Tax Issues concerning the Ministry of Railways' Penultimate Two Years of its 8th 5 Year Plan" (7 April 1994, (94) Finance and Tax File NO. 5). This circular stipulated that given budgetary restrictions for railway construction and the need to continue construction in this sector, all business tax on the railway construction fund during the last two years of the 8th Five Year Plan would be earmarked for railway construction projects in order to increase state capital construction investments. Hence during the last two years of the 8th Five year plan, railway construction investment funds were exempt from income tax. According to other relevant documents published by the Ministry of Railways, goods and passenger rail transport companies, industrial companies, supply and marketing companies and construction companies are all temporarily exempt from urban land use tax, real estate tax, vehicle tax and stamp duty. The "levy first, refund later" system, applied to the railway construction fund, has meant that the Ministry of Railways has been able to construct new lines using non-repayable loans.

Since the reform of the tax system in China, state-owned transport companies and shipping companies have benefited from income tax rebates. In order to offset the losses and alleviate the financial difficulties of civil aviation companies, a "levy first, refund later" income tax levy of 33% and refund of 15% was imposed on companies[5]. Between 1994 and 1995, the civil aviation construction funds were exempt from income tax.

(ii) Urban Public Transport

In 1993 the government paid out more than 1.9 billion yuan in subsidies to the country's public transport sector. In 1994 and 1995 subsidies totalled some 2.6 billion yuan and 3.45 billion yuan respectively (Xu, 1996). In 81 of China's major cities the average price of a standard bus or tram ticket is a mere 0.059 yuan per kilometre per person and in 72 cities the average cost of a monthly season ticket is 42.96 yuan while the average price of a ticket is 18.28 yuan, only 42.5% of the actual cost (Xu, 1996). It is the regional or local government which provides most subsidies for urban transport networks while the central government takes a back seat. The central government did provide half of the loss subsidies granted to the Beijing Underground. Between 1990 and 1995 these subsidies increased but the following year, after a rise in ticket prices, they were virtually zero while in 1997 losses were posted again (see Table 11)

Table 11: State and Beijing Municipal Government Subsidies to the Beijing Underground
(Unit: tens of thousands of yuan)

Year	90	92	93	94	95	96*	97
Central government	5300	5400	6000	11000	16000	0	2000
Beijing city	5300	5400	6000	11000	16000	0	2000

*In 1996 the price of a ticket on the Beijing underground rose from 0.5 yuan to 2.00 yuan. No subsidies were provided that year.

Source: Authors' inquiries to the Ministry of Finance

There are two major types of subsidy provided to the urban public transport system: price control subsidies and state employees' public transport subsidies. The former is a subsidy granted to transport companies to compensate for the effects of government policies. As public transport prices have increasingly reflected companies' operating costs this form of subsidy has been gradually removed. The latter type of subsidy is what is referred to as a welfare subsidy provided to state employees since increases in their earnings are slower than increases in the cost of living. Created in the early days of

---

[5] File No. 55, 17 May 1994 "Ministry of Finance, State General Tax Office and People's Bank of China Circular on Temporary Provisions on Budgetary Handling of the "Collect First, Refund Later" system applied to some companies since tax reform" (China Tax Yearbook, 1995).

reform, they still exist today. The state employees' public transport subsidy is calculated on a standard basis throughout the country although there are some regional variations in the actual amount. On average it is between 5 to 12 yuan per month per employee. Hence in 1995 with 110 million state employees and an average of 10 yuan per month per person provided in the form of subsidies, the total annual wage-earner public transport subsidy stood at 13.2 billion yuan (State Statistics Bureau, 1996).

6.3   Analysis of the Subsidy Policy for the Transport Sector

(i) Goods and Passenger Transport

The price of goods and passenger transport: With the exception of air transport[6], prices in other transport sectors are determined by the Price Bureau. Goods and passenger road transport prices are fixed on a regional basis by the relevant provincial Price Bureaus on the basis of a base price dictated by the State Price Bureau. The price of rail transport is calculated on the basis of a pricing system laid down by the State Council which takes into account operating costs and railway construction fund costs. Prices of transport on waterways is calculated by one of two bodies, either the companies directly under the control of the Ministry of Transport or the companies directly under the control of the provincial government. In the case of the former, the Ministry of Communications sets the price which is then approved by the State Planning Commission. In the case of the latter, the price is ratified by the local Price Bureau. It can be seen from Table 12 that road haulage is the most expensive form of transport while road and waterway transport prices are higher than rail prices.

Table 12: Prices of Road, Water and Rail Transport

Year	Cargo freight (0.01 yuan/ton/ km)			Passenger transportation (0.01 yuan/km/passenger)		
	Railway	Road	Water transportation	Railway	Road	Water transportation
1986	1.81	21.1	1.0	1.94	2.5	3.1
1990	2.65	26.9	1.3	4.24	4.0	6.0
1992	3.85	35.0	1.6	4.33	5.2	7.0

Source: Zhou, W., 1996.

Goods and passenger transport costs: Generally speaking maritime transport is the cheapest form of transport, followed by pipelines, rail and inland waterway transport while road transport costs are higher and air transport the most expensive of all. Figure 7 provides a comparison of transport costs by rail, road and water over the last 45 years. The figures take into account present operating costs but not the cost of investments. As a result the figures are somewhat distorted and the transport prices appear far lower than actual costs.

---

[6]   According to the circular published by the Price Bureau dealing with the management jurisdiction of air prices, the China Civil Aviation Bureau is responsible for setting standard prices. See State Planning Committee's Price Bureau's publication "Prices and Charges Management 1992 - 1994".

Figure 7: Comparative prices of Goods and Passenger Transport (Unit: yuan/millions of ton/km)

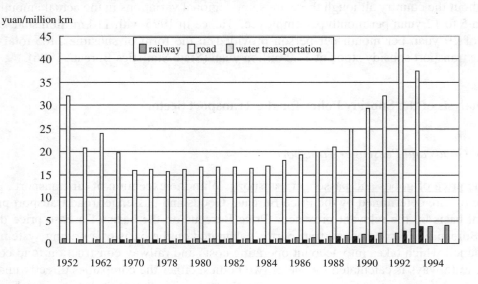

By referring to Table 12 and Figure 7 it is possible to calculate the subsidies provided on the basis of domestic market prices (see Table 13). Table 13 shows that the difference between railway transport prices and costs, is positive, implying that this form of transport is profitable and requires no subsidisation. However if one includes the transport construction fund in the calculation of the price of rail transport, the operating price, once this amount has been deducted, is actually lower than the cost. 1994 is a good example and explains the continuous deficit posted by railway companies between 1993 and 1995. In 1986, road and waterway transport prices were higher than their operational costs while in 1990 and 1992 they were lower and hence required subsidisation.

Table 13: Prices, Costs and Subsidies for Rail, Road and Water Transport for Selected Years
(Unit: yuan per millions of tons per km)

Year	Railway			road			Water transportation		
	price	cost	difference	price	cost	Difference	price	cost	difference
1986	181	123.23	57.77	2110	1926.3	183.7	100	80.1	19.9
1990	265	191.88	73.12	2690	2944.5	-254.5	130	176.1	-46.1
1992	385	232	153	2500	4221.3	-1721.3	160	261	-101
1994	535 (265)*	354.23	180.77 (-84.23)	4500			3500		

* The figures in brackets are the operating price. The difference between the price and the operating price equals the amount of the railway construction fund.

The environmental impact of transport subsidies: Transport subsidies distort transport prices which consequently do not reflect transport costs (which include operating costs and social and environmental costs). As a result the prices cannot accurately reflect supply and demand. Since the environmental externalities provoked by transport cannot be internalised, it is not possible to gain a clear picture of sustainable transport as a concept.

(ii) Urban Public Transport

Urban transport prices and cost: Urban transport mainly encompasses underground and urban public transport systems. Buses are managed by urban transport companies and prices fixed by local municipal governments. Generally fares on urban transport systems are below cost and thus require local government subsidies to prevent losses. A survey of 36 large and medium-sized cities conducted in October 1996 revealed that 25 cities had adjusted fares, increasing monthly season tickets from 14.6 yuan to 21.9 yuan. (State Planning Commission, 1996).

Li and Warford (1997) examined the marginal opportunity costs of urban transport in Shenzhen using the theory of marginal opportunity cost. The study involved calculation of the intrinsic cost and the social and environmental cost of public transport in each city and from this the so-called marginal opportunity cost was deduced (see Table 14). As a consequence of their work the authors suggested the introduction of road usage fees and congestion alleviation fees on roads which previously had been used free of charge or at very low cost, such fees being levied on the basis of cost to the road network. For polluting forms of public transport the authors suggested the introduction of strict emissions levels and pollution charges to cover pollution reduction costs levied on all forms of transport which did not meet these levels. Their work illustrates that the current price system is too low and that subsidies are provided given the fact that the present price system does not include calculation of all costs such as the environmental costs of an urban transport system.

Table 14: Breakdown of Opportunity Costs for Different Forms of Public Transport in Shenzhen Special Economic Zone, 1994 (Unit: yuan/passenger kilometre)

Form of transport	Opportunity cost	Intrinsic cost	Social cost
Taxi	2.168	1.133	1.035
Public mini-bus	0.228	0.2044	0.0236
Public bus	0.044	0.0326	0.0094
Subway train*	0.18	0.18	
Overhead light railway*	0.4	0.4	

Notes: With the exception of acquisition, operation and maintenance costs incurred by all forms of transport, borne by the owner and considered as part of the intrinsic costs, all other costs are considered part of the social costs.

* The subway system and overhead light railway are the two forms of public transport planned for the Shenzhen region which will not provoke serious environmental problems. Consequently all costs incurred are intrinsic costs.

Source: Li, Y. and Warford, J., 1997.

The environmental impact of different forms of public transport: Urban transport includes vehicles such as trams, buses, taxis, bicycles and subways (the latter are not found in all cities). Many people prefer to walk short distances but often choices are dictated by budget, time, personal preferences and government policy. With the rapid growth of the Chinese economy, improvements in standards of living and the expansion of the automotive industry, many city dwellers will soon be car owners. In cities, particularly large ones, traffic congestion, atmospheric pollution and noise are already familiar problems which are worsening with the rapid increase in the number of private cars on the roads. Public transport offers an excellent way of reducing atmospheric pollution and alleviating congestion because of the high ratio of users to vehicles and its efficiency in moving passengers from A to B. Thus developing public transport is a wise policy choice for a country such as China (Zhu, 1997). However, the low fares on public transport do not reflect the actual costs incurred by transport companies. This means financial losses and the need for state subsidies. To improve the financial health of transport companies suggestions have been made that they be run like any other business. The key to this is rational pricing. Current fares do not include a calculation of external costs and hence environmental losses which are a direct consequence of public transport, cannot be covered and the cost of repairing environmental damage cannot be recuperated.

Public transport subsidies: Given the above analysis, public transport subsidies are mainly a consequence of irrational pricing although organic management problems within a given transport company may also aggravate the problem. The internal management problems of a company are beyond the scope of this paper and will not be discussed here. Urban public transport plays a major role in the lives of the urban population and hence any fare increase will have a direct effect on passengers' personal budgets. Given that wages cannot be adjusted arbitrarily, the state has to provide urban transport subsidies to off-set any increased financial burden on users caused by fare increases. Thus although state subsidies to companies are being reduced, given the increases in subsidies provided to commuters, financial pressure is not being reduced. Recently state financial subsidies to public transport have been decreased but economic subsidies are still in place since the pricing system only includes running costs.

7.0   Energy Subsidy Policy

Energy production and use plays a major role in the expansion of the Chinese economy but also seriously affects the environment. The burning of coal and oil affects the quality of the air and gives rise to environmental pollution. Problems such as sulphur dioxide, acid rain and global warming can be traced back to the burning of fossil fuels. Consequently a detailed examination of energy production and use is an important part of China's sustainable development strategy. Naturally current economic policy affects energy generation and use. This chapter examines the affects of subsidies on energy generation and use. Power subsidies have been discussed in a previous section thus this chapter will examine policies concerning coal and crude oil subsidies.

(i) Coal Production and Sales

Coal is the major energy source in China, accounting for more than 70% of all energy consumption (State Statistics Bureau, 1996). Since reforms began in China, the production and use of coal has increased annually (see Figure 8). In 1995 coal production in China stood at 1.36 billion tons compared to 0.62 billion tons in 1980 - an annual increase of 8%. In 1995 coal consumption stood at 1.37 billion tons after an annual increase of 8.3% since 1980. In 1995 the national coal shortfall stood at 42.1 million tons. The rate of increase in coal consumption was slightly higher than the rate of increase in coal production.

Figure 8: Changes in Coal Supply, Production and Consumption in China, 1980 - 1995

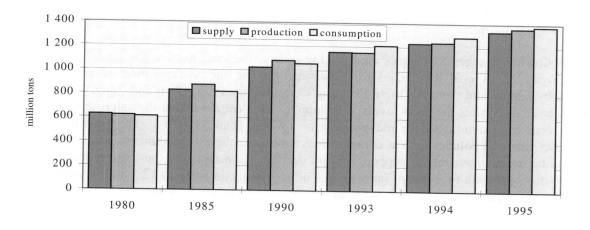

(ii) Oil Production and Sales

Oil is the second most important energy source in China, representing 17% of all energy sources (State Statistics Bureau, 1996). Since reform began in China oil production and sales have remained generally stable albeit with gradual increases over the years (see Figure 9). In 1995 Chinese oil production stood at 150 million tons compared to 110 million tons in 1980, an average annual growth of 2.4%. In 1995 oil consumption stood at 160 million tons. The annual average increase in oil consumption between 1980 and 1995 was 6.7%. The shortfall in oil for 1995 was 200,000 tons. These figures show that oil consumption in China has grown faster than production. The reasons for the slow-down in oil production are that today's oil fields have now reached maximum production capacity while newly-identified fields are in remote areas of the country which require massive investments in order to make them viable. (Chen and Zheng, 1997; Smil, 1993).

Figure 9: Changes in Oil Supply, Production and Consumption in China, 1980 - 1995

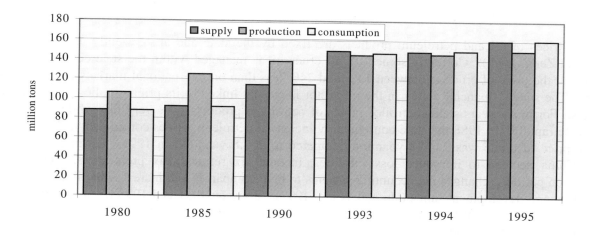

7.2   Subsidy Policy

(i) Coal Subsidies

Following changes to China's coal pricing policy, the coal market has gradually opened up. With the exception of coal earmarked for power generation, the market price of coal products is determined by supply and demand (State Planning Commission, 1996; Chen and Zeng, 1997). Present coal prices basically reflect the costs involved in supply. To a certain extent the calorific value and dust content of coal is also reflected in today's prices. (World Bank, 1997b). The central government variously uses financial policies such as company loss subsidies, interest discounts on loans for production transfer and tax reimbursements to support coal production. Consequently the total budget allocated to the industry during the 8th Five-Year Plan was 24.4 billion yuan compared to 12.5 billion yuan during the previous five-year plan. The tax reimbursement policy was implemented during the last two years of the 8th Five-Year Plan and applied to profitable plants, which received a full reimbursement given the fact that following the reform of China's fiscal system the coal sector's tax burden was considerably increased. In 1994 VAT on coal was reduced from 17% to 13% [7]. Income tax levied on state-owned coal mines was refunded.

Subsidies in the coal industry include loss subsidies because of the increased tax burden since the introduction of fiscal reform and loss subsidies granted to specific plants because of specific difficulties.

While state subsidies to those coal mines which fall within China's unified planning system have risen from 300 million yuan in 1985 to 6 billion yuan in 1990, the mines have nevertheless posted losses which have drastically checked increases in coal production and employees' pay rises. The central government, seeking to relieve financial pressure on the national budget and concerned about the situation in the coal industry, gradually phased out subsidies to coal mines between 1992 and 1996. The annual decreases in subsidies were 2 billion, 2 billion, 1 billion and 1 billion respectively (The China Coal Industry Yearbook Editorial Committee, 1993).

(ii)   Oil Subsidies

Prices of oil and petroleum products are fixed by the state and are presently on the increase (Chen and Zeng, 1997). Currently some 70% of crude oil is managed within the state central planning system and the price of crude is between 13% and 24% less than on international markets (World Bank, 1997b). The state's financial policy in the oil sector is closely linked to its pricing policy on petroleum products. For many years state-controlled prices of petroleum products were very low while production prices rose rapidly. In 1988 the state consequently increased petroleum prices considerably. In 1995 the average price of crude was 744.98 yuan/ton compared to 203.8 yuan/ton in 1991. Given this state of affairs China decided to introduce loss subsidies, income tax refunds, tax preferences, increases in depreciation periods, changes in accounting systems to help companies and increases in oil and gas field exploration and development funds (Hu and Wang, 1997). Between 1991 and 1993 fixed subsidies were implemented and the total budget earmarked for loss subsidies paid out to oil companies over the three year period stood at 12.5 billion yuan. The tax refund policy has been used for many years and during

---

[7]   File No. 22, Finance and Taxation Document, issued by the Ministry of Finance, State General Tax Office, May 17 1994, Circular on the Adjustments to VAT rates on refined products of metal and non-metal mines, China Taxation Yearbook, 1995.

1994 and 1995 a total of 6.2 billion yuan in taxes was refunded. Tax preference policies included exemption of production tax on all revenue from price differences which was reinvested in the oil and gas field exploration and development funds (before 1993). Other policies have included the possibility of reimbursing foreign loans using tax money, and in the case of some older oil fields, continued use of part cash part kind tax payment system, partial reduction or exemption from land use tax and a halving of VAT on imported goods. The state also increased the legal rate of depreciation on oil companies directly under state control from 6.34% in 1992 to 8.34% in 1993 and 10.4% in 1995 with the effect that more capital remained within oil companies during primary budget allocation. During the 8th Five-year plan government policies to support the oil industry amounted to some 166.3 billion yuan, which accounted for 70% of all investments in the industry over the same period. In order to protect oil resources and improve exploration and development of oil fields, the state has proposed the implementation of a natural resources tax and has fixed the tax rate for crude oil at 8 - 30 yuan/ton (China Taxation Yearbook Editorial Committee, 1993).

7.3   Energy Subsidy Policy Analysis

(i) Coal

Cost and price: Over the past 40 years or more, the most important state-owned coal mines (those which fall within the unified planning system) have used a highly centralised pricing system. Pricing and price management have been the responsibility of the relevant departments of the central government and the fundamental price structure was the state fixed price. The state fixed not only the base price but also a variety of price increases for excess production and coefficients for price differentials on the basis of region and on the basis of quality. Since coal is such an intrinsic part of Chinese life and is intimately linked to the success of businesses and industry, the Chinese government has for many years opted for low coal prices with the result that the gap between price and cost has increased. During the 34 years between the first price adjustments to coal in 1958 and the gradual relaxing of coal prices in the latter half of 1992 prices were adjusted eight times. After the 3rd Plenary Session of the 11th Central Committee, China began to examine more closely the coal price mechanism and implemented a multi-tiered pricing policy. The State Council decided that from July 1, 1992 the price of so-called planned and supply-stipulated coal from major state-owned mines could be relaxed. Coal mines in Xuzhou and Zaozhuang were the first to implement this new policy. The state decided that during the three year period from 1993 to 1995 coal prices in all major state-owned coal mines could be gradually relaxed while at the same time 6 billion yuan of financial subsidies would be phased out (China Coal Industry Yearbook Editorial Committee, 1993). Now coal prices are basically determined by the market.

According to the theory of marginal opportunity cost, the price for natural resources paid by the user of those natural resources should equal the social cost of the use and the cost of depletion of natural resources -- the marginal opportunity cost. If the price of the natural resources is lower than the marginal opportunity cost, this will encourage unnecessary exploitation of natural resources and harm the environment. If the price of the natural resources is higher than the marginal opportunity cost, consumption will be limited. Marginal opportunity costs consist of three parts, the marginal production cost, the marginal use cost and the marginal external cost. If we take Datong Coal Mine as an example, the actual financial cost of coal in 1991 was 54.47 yuan/ton (including 1.04 yuan environmental costs) while the actual sale price was 48.57 yuan/ton. Hence the mine lost 5.9 yuan/ton. According to the marginal opportunity cost theory, the calculated cost is 103.13 yuan/ton of which production costs account for 57.7%, use costs 37.8% and external costs 4.5% (Li and Warford, 1997).

File No. 150 of the State Council Ordinance on February 27, 1994 the "Stipulations for Collecting and Handling Mineral Resources Compensation Fees" states that a charge should be levied on minerals exploitation and that this fee be a proportion of the mining company's sales revenue. The proportion for coal was fixed at 1%. Later, the Chinese government issued a natural resources tax policy paper in which the rate for coal was fixed at between 0.3-5.0 yuan/ton (China Taxation Yearbook Editorial Committee, 1994). These two measures were designed to encourage intelligent use of coal as a natural resource.

Coal Subsidies: It can be seen from Table 15 that the average price of raw coal prior to 1994 was lower than the cost and hence coal mines were running at a loss, requiring state subsidies for their survival. All coal mines within the unified planning system are state-owned and while industrial reform has continued and companies have become increasingly independent legal entities, the coal industry nevertheless has remained under close state supervision with the result that in the long run it is still the state which bears responsibility for the mines' losses. The state therefore has had no other option but to implement tax reduction policies to subsidise the coal mines so that they may maintain normal production levels. In 1995 coal prices were slightly higher than production costs and consequently profits were posted. But because coal costs do not include the external cost to the environment, economic subsidies still exist.

Table 15: Comparison of Raw Coal Costs and Prices in Major State-Owned Mines, 1991-1995

Year	Cost of raw coal (yuan/t)	Price of raw coal (yuan/t)	difference(yuan/t)
1991	65.00	36.91	-28.09
1992	74.70	58.70	-16.00
1993	95.50	83.70	-11.80
1994	101.35	96.68	-4.67
1995	103.00	105.80	2.80

Source: Hu, T. and Wang H., 1997.

Coal subsidies and the environment: The effects of coal subsidies on the environment can be explained in the following way: subsidies distort prices and thus lead to an inaccurate reflection of the relationship between supply and demand. As far as coal consumers are concerned, since subsidised coal is always cheaper than non-subsidised coal, the consumer is encouraged to use more and more. On the other hand, as far as the supplier, or the coal mines are concerned, with a subsidy policy in place coal prices are lower than prices without subsidies and thus the mines lack any incentive to produce coal since they know they can always obtain subsidies when government policies lead to losses for the mine. A lack of sufficient data has meant that it has not been possible to conduct a qualitative analysis of the relationship between coal subsidies and the environment.

(ii) Oil

Price and cost: Oil prices have been low in China for many years. Since 1981 there has been a dual pricing system for crude oil. The first 100 million tons of crude produced were sold at a specified low price while all crude above and beyond this was sold at a higher price pegged to world market prices. As of January 1993 all crude oil which fell within the state's planning remit has been sold on the basis of international prices. In May 1994 the two-tier pricing system for crude oil and petroleum products was completely abolished and a unified fixed pricing system was implemented. Oil and petroleum products are considered to be state-controlled products in China. Following the changes introduced in 1994 the average price of crude oil was 860 yuan/ton (Chen and Zeng, 1997). Table 16 lists the producer price of several different grades of oil. In this table grade 1 oil is oil produced in old oil fields while grade 2 oil is oil from new oil fields. Because investments in old oil fields have been 100% state investments and hence non-reimbursable, the price of oil drilled in these fields has been very low. This has led to a situation in which oil of the same quality but from different fields may be sold at different prices. This is by no means an easy situation to manage. The authors believe that the same prices should be applied to the same quality oil and that relatively high drilling fees (and a natural resources depletion tax) should be imposed on oil from old oil fields.

Table 16: Producer Prices for Various Grades of Crude Oil (Unit: yuan/ton)

Item	Classification	May 1, 1994	January 1, 1996
Producer price of grade 1 oil	Type 1	754	855
	Type 2	684	830
	Type 3		785
	Type 4		755
Producer price of grade 2 oil	Type 1	1310	1280
	Type 2	1220	1220
	Type 3	1160	1150
	Type 4		1085

Source: The Price Management Department of the State Planning Commission, 1994 and 1996.

No detailed and reliable data presently exists regarding the production costs of oil but what is clear is that in the wake of a series of adjustments present prices are on a par with costs. One fact which can be confirmed is that the present price structure is not rational because the cost of exploration, resources depletion and environmental damage are not included in the price. Since prospecting and drilling are the responsibility of two separate ministries, the cost of any oil produced cannot include the exploration or prospecting costs. Furthermore the calculation of the cost of natural resources depletion and environmental damage are still at the research stage and so far no policies have been drawn up. This area therefore requires further research.

Oil subsidies: Given the lack of reliable data on the price and cost of oil, it is difficult to calculate the level of financial subsidies solely on the basis of domestic market prices. Since oil is a tradable commodity, the level of subsidies can be calculated on the basis of international market prices. The international market price for Chinese oil in 1994 and 1995 was US$15.90 (130 yuan) and US$17.94 (147 yuan) per barrel respectively. During the same two years average domestic oil prices were 134 yuan and 102 yuan per barrel. The difference between the domestic and international prices is quite clear.

Oil subsidies and the environment: The main effect that oil subsidies have on the environment is that since the subsidies produce distortions in the price of oil these prices do not accurately reflect supply and demand or the overall cost of oil production and this therefore has a negative effect on economic benefits and environmental protection - two concerns which are at the very heart of sustainable development.

8.0 Conclusions

Subsidy policy in China is the result of price distortions in a planned economy. During the transition period, these price distortions have gradually been removed as have the subsidies. The current price system is basically able to reflect supply and demand. The above analysis of subsidy policies in selected sectors has proved this argument. China is a vast country with a population of over 1.2 billion. The country's price system is equally large and the change from one pricing system to another has thrown up numerous questions and created many difficulties, impinging both on economic activity and people's lives. Consequently the Chinese government has continued to control the price of goods and commodities which are directly related to the national economy and the people's livelihoods. Although in theory these prices are designed to cover cost and include a slight profit margin, in actual fact the irrational nature of the different components of the prices mean that they do not include all costs and are even occasionally lower than production costs and certainly do not take into account environmental costs. Hence during this period of transition China is striving to streamline and rationalise its pricing system by eliminating those subsidies which harm the environment. The goal is to establish a price system which will incorporate all costs and internalise environmental costs.

While various forms of economic ownership have recently emerged in China, state-ownership is still an important component. Since economic reform, state-owned enterprises have become legally independent entities but nevertheless selected sectors of the economy still have no legal right to fix prices - this remains the sole right and responsibility of the state. This has given rise to economic losses and illustrates that legally independent companies have not gained full property rights and that the state still remains the overriding owner of companies. In order to ensure normal economic activity and protect employees affected by these policies, the state offers subsidies. From an ownership point of view this approach cannot be criticised.

It is both desirable and necessary for the state to apply macro-control over the economy. The Chinese government's subsidy policy, which is one instrument of such control, has played an important role in economic development and in stabilising standards of living in China. However, when the various policies were drafted there was no comprehensive and systematic examination of the situation, the problem was simply viewed in isolation without any regard to the impact that such policies might have on the environment or their effect on sustainable development strategies. (It could of course be argued that at that time environmental problems were not felt to be so serious and the sustainable development strategy was not as yet so widely accepted.) Some subsidy policies have had a serious effect on natural resources and the environment and in order to encourage sustainable development some of these policies need to be abandoned. Meanwhile any future subsidy policies must take into account the country's sustainable development strategy and must include a systematic evaluation of the effects that the policies would have on the economy, society and the environment.

In this paper we have shown that only two aspects of sustainable development, the economic and social, have been borne in mind in the drafting of subsidy policies. What is necessary now is to try and focus on the third aspect (environment) when drafting future policies. Trade-offs will be necessary in order to achieve sustainable development.

Some signs of a move away from subsidy policy in China include a decrease in overall state spending on subsidies. Prices for water, energy and fertilisers are been progressively relaxed. At the same time, a price adjustment fund has been set up by the state to control price fluctuations and guarantee social stability. Social welfare subsidies are gradually concentrating increasingly on the poor rather than being distributed without regard to means or need as was the case before reforms. When these subsidies were introduced in an effort to compensate for price adjustments, there was little wage disparity and it was felt that a flat rate was fairest. With economic development, wage disparity has increased and continues. The rich do not need subsidies while the underprivileged, however can greatly benefit from them. Hence the flat rate subsidy must be changed to alleviate the financial straits of the poorer sections of Chinese society.

The natural resources selected for examination in this paper all fall into the category of industries classed as natural monopolies. The state retains control over prices for all these natural resources; relevant administrative departments and offices do not have the right to fix prices for these commodities. As economic reform expands, considerable work will have to be done although some attempts at management reform in these sectors are already afoot.

8.1 Subsidies to the Water Sector

Price controls on water are the main reason for excessive use of water resources. Presently the price of water is far lower than the production cost of waterworks water and it does not therefore reflect the total cost. Hence the subsidy rate for water is very high. It is however very difficult to quantify the marginal external opportunity cost of water and hence also difficult to quantify the full cost of water.

Because the price of water only includes partial production costs it does not reveal the scarcity of water supplies. An example of this is the fixed price of water in water conservancy works which is calculated on the basis of the principle of covering cost plus a small profit margin. This form of calculation does not take into account the scarcity of water resources. Market mechanisms for managing water resources have not been formulated. Given the scarcity of water resources, it is necessary to ensure that the economic benefits of using water resources are maximised when marketing water.

The price of water should be determined on the basis of the different uses to which it is put. Then prices could gradually be increased on the basis of supply and demand until they fully reflect the full cost of the supply of water. This is the only way of ensuring that water resources are used in accordance with the strategy of sustainable development.

Given the present situation in China, we suggest that the state establish suitable methods of managing, using and pricing water resources and introduce unified national price guidelines. Each region should determine its water prices on the basis of local water resources and the situation in urban areas so as to encourage a rational use of water and ensure protection of the environment. It is up to society to handle water conservancy, solve the problem of water management monopolies and increase the economic efficiency of waterworks through competition.

8.2 Subsidies to the Electric Power Sector

Although the government has gradually adjusted prices throughout the period of transition and promoted the idea that electric power prices should cover cost and include a margin of profit, the irrational nature of the internal structure of cost and the fact that electricity and coal are closely related have meant that the two closely condition each other. Production costs of electric power cannot accurately reflect true cost. Similarly, because environmental and social costs are not included in the calculation, the co-called financial cost does not reflect the comprehensive costs of sustainable development. The difference between the comprehensive cost and the financial cost can be considered to be the electric power subsidy.

The most widely used form of electric power subsidy is price control which can be seen in electric power prices and in the natural resources used to generate electric power. As prices are rationalised and the market economy develops, financial price subsidies will be phased out although it will still be some time before the most important indicator of electric power prices, the marginal environmental cost, is taken into account.

8.3   Subsidies on Chemical Fertilisers and Phytosanitary Products

Since China's economic reform began, the production, sales, import, export and use of chemical fertilisers and phytosanitary products have increased dramatically. Chemical fertilisers have played an important part in expanding and stabilising China's grain production in recent years while pesticides have had a far-reaching effect on reducing the occurrence and spread of plant disease and pests. Nevertheless excessive use of fertilisers and pesticides has had a negative effect on agriculture, the natural environment and human health.

While the Chinese government does not have a direct subsidy policy as regards the production and management of chemical fertilisers and pesticides, some preferential policies are used in some of the links of the industry's chain. These take the form of price controls, preferential procurement of and price controls on raw materials to production plants and some investment and taxation incentives.

Since the current domestic market prices of chemical fertiliser and phytosanitary products are the same as the CIF plus freight international market price converted into Renminbi, the level and rate of subsidies, calculated on the basis of the international market price, is very low and indeed varies as international prices fluctuate. Price control has hence become a tool for stabilising domestic prices. Since China has such a huge agricultural sector and a vast population, these subsidies will remain in place for some years to come to protect farmers' interests and stimulate grain production. This is not simply an economic issue, it is also a political one.

8.4   Subsidies to the Transport Sector

Subsidies in this sector are being phased out. As China's pricing system continues to mature and industrial reform deepens financial subsidies will be eliminated. Looking at the railways as an example, since 1949 all investments in rail construction have been state-funded and the cost of rail transport has only ever covered transport costs. Since 1993 and the introduction of the contract system, rolling stock and track investment funds have taken the form of loans which has raised the cost of railway operations. After implementing several adjustments to unit transport costs, they now basically reflect cost plus a small profit, in accordance with government principles. Because of the key role that the railways play in national development the government has maintained control over pricing in the sector which has considerably stabilised the situation but the railway companies themselves have no power whatsoever in deciding prices. This has led to a lack of flexibility and response capacity in an intensely competitive market and hence to losses for the railway companies. The state has eliminated loss subsidies formerly granted to railway companies and only maintained some preferential subsidies. There are today virtually no subsidies available for road transport and waterway transport. The level of urban transport subsidies remains relatively high and mainly take the form of subsidies granted to operating companies and commuters. The situation is now being resolved.

The most common subsidy is the company loss subsidy. In the case of both the railways and public transport, subsidies are designed to offset losses provoked by prices being lower than cost. This illustrates the fact that price control subsidies and company loss subsidies are closely linked and also proves that eliminating price controls and ensuring that prices truly reflect (full) cost will increase company revenue and lead to reductions in government subsidies to companies.

Transport prices are gradually on the increase as internalisation of the social cost of transport becomes more widespread. Since reform began in China there have been continuous revisions to the prices of goods and passenger transport which have paralleled the opening up and reform to China's pricing system in general. Currently prices do reflect operational costs of transport but it will still be some time before they also include the cost of maintaining public facilities such as roads and even longer before they internalise social and environmental costs. With the development of transport networks, problems such as traffic congestion and pollution will be exacerbated. Throughout the world these problems are being examined closely in order to develop a systematic way of internalising the social cost of transport. China has made considerable in-roads in this area such as looking at the idea of levying a tax on leaded petrol or using instruments such as opportunity costs and conducting pilot schemes for a vehicle pollution tax.

The form that subsidies take should gradually change. Initially the pricing system needs to be rationalised so that prices may gradually reach the level of operational costs and eventually reach the level of opportunity costs. Furthermore, from a cost accounting point of view, given the fact that the intrinsic and social costs of public transport vehicles are the lowest, the public transport system should be massively expanded. Specific subsidies could be granted to public buses and environmentally-friendly cars to encourage the development of an environmentally-friendly transport system.

8.5   Energy Subsidies and the Environment

Energy subsidies take the form of loss subsidies. The analysis has illustrated that today's loss subsidies in the energy industry are the result of years of low price policies in the sector. Subsidies in the coal and oil sector have led to serious price distortions. Consequently prices have not been able to accurately reflect supply and demand and have provided both users and suppliers with inaccurate market information, leading to production methods and consumption habits which run counter to the principle of sustainable development. As China continues to develop a market economy the prices of coal and oil will gradually be rationalised and will slowly come into line with prices on the international market.

Financial and fiscal energy policies today are designed to encourage attempts to control pollution. As it reduces subsidies the Chinese government is at the same time levying a natural resources tax on coal and oil, directional adjustment taxes on fixed assets investments, a tax on leaded petrol and a tax on urban maintenance and technology. These fiscal policies will have a positive effect on the exploitation and utilisation of natural resources such as coal and oil and will also go some way to help protect the environment. However, present financial and fiscal policies in the energy sector fall far short in their ability to effectively influence production and consumption of energy and reduce atmospheric pollution mainly because tax revenue from these policies is too low to be able to have any effect.

Clean energy sources must be developed. The structure of China's energy sources and the country's geographical distribution of these sources of energy is such that coal remains the most important source of energy. Coal is a serious polluter and hence China needs to develop clean coal technology (such as coal washing, desulphurisation technology, etc.) while also investing massively in nuclear energy and hydroelectric power. The investments for the nuclear energy and hydroelectric industries are huge and will require state preferential policies.

It is also necessary to develop energy saving technology. At present China's energy consumption rate is far lower than that of developed countries and the government must encourage the development and application of energy saving projects and provide necessary preferential policies to encourage this.

BIBLIOGRAPHY

Bai, Yingzheng (1998): "Thoughts on the Current Situation and Reform of Chemical Fertiliser Production and Sales System" in <u>China Petrochemical Industry (1):</u> 15-16.

Chemical Fertiliser Policy Research Group of the Ministry of Chemical Industry (1994): Chemical Fertiliser Industry Development Policy Research.

Chen, Huaizhi (1996): "Using Water Pricing to Alleviate the Huanghe River Water Crisis" in <u>Water Conservancy Economics (4):</u> 59-60.

Chen, Yueming and Zeng Xiaoan (1997): "Review and Prospects of Chinese Energy Price Reform" in <u>Coal Economy Research (6):</u> 5-9.

China Council for International Cooperation on Environmental and Development(CCICED) (1995): *Proceedings, the Third Meeting of China Council for International Cooperation on Environment and Development.* Beijing.

Fewsmith, J. (1994): *Dilemmas of Reform in China: Political Conflict and Economic Debate.* M.E. Sharpe. New York

Gao, Debu (1994): *Explicit Subsidy, Implicit Subsidy.* Publishing House of the People's University, Beijing.

He, Yongjian (1996): "The Price of Water Supply to Water Works Demands Prompt Solution" in <u>Price Theory and Practice (11):</u> 32-34.

Hu, Tao and Wang Huadong (1997): *The Practical Application of Environmental Economics in China.* China Environmental Science Publishing House. Beijing.

Jin, Leshan (1995): Study on the Environmental Effects of Using Pesticides and Development of Policies. Report for the World Bank Technical Assistance Project B-8-3.

Jin, Yuzheng (1996): "Reform of Railway Transportation Price Brooks No Delay" in <u>Price Theory and Practice (7):</u> 4-5.

Li, Chanming (1997): *Study on Economic Development in China.* Economic Management Press. Beijing.

Li, Yining and Warford, J. (1997): Working Report of the Resource Accounting and Price Policy Working Group. Secretariat of International Cooperation Commission, the State Agency for Environmental Protection. *Document Collection of China International Cooperation Committee for the Environment and Development (No. 4).* China Environmental Science Publishing House. Beijing.

Ma, Haitao (1996): *An Introduction to Finance.* Beijing Institute of Economics Publishing House. Beijing.

Naughton, B. (1995): *Growing Out of the Plan: Chinese Economic Reform, 1978-1993.* Cambridge University Press.

Potier, M. (1996): The contribution of economic instruments in the environmental policies of OECD Countries. Third Expert Group Meeting on Financial Issues of Agenda 21, 6-8 February 1996. Manila, the Philippines.

Qian, Jiajun (1997): "The Control of Public Utilities in U.K and U.S.A" in International Technological Economics Research (10) : 27-31.

Roodman, D. M. (1996): *Paying the Piper: Subsidies, Politics and the Environment*. Worldwatch Paper 133. Worldwatch Institute. Washington D.C.

Shen, Zhiyu (1997): "Market Behaviour Analysis of Chinese Monopoly Industries" in China Industrial Economy (12): 55-61.

Smil, V. (1993): *China's Environmental Crisis. An inquiry on the limits of national development*. M.E. Sharpe. Armonk, New York.

Smil, V. (1996): *Environmental Problems in China: Estimates of Economic Costs*. East-West Center Special Report No. 5. East-West Centre. Hawaii.

Tax Administration Department of the Ministry of Finance of the People's Republic of China (1996): *China Taxation System*. Enterprise Management Publishing House. Beijing.

The Chinese Research Academy of Environmental Sciences (CRAES) (1997): Study on the Design and Implementation of the Pollution Levy System in China. Beijing.

The Editorial Committee for China Coal Industry Yearbook (1993): *China Coal Industry Yearbook 1993*. Coal Industry Press. Beijing.

The Editorial Committee for China Finance Yearbook (1997): *China Finance Yearbook 1997*. China Finance Magazine Office. Beijing.

The Editorial Committee for China National Petrochemical Industry Corporation Yearbook (1991): *China National Petrochemical Industry Corporation Yearbook*. China Petrochemical Publishing House. Beijing.

The Editorial Committee for China Power Yearbook (1997): *China Power Yearbook 1996-1997*. China Power Publishing House. Beijing.

The Editorial Committee for China Taxation Yearbook (1994): *China Taxation Yearbook 1994*. China Tax Publishing House. Beijing.

The Editorial Committee for China Taxation Yearbook (1995): *China Taxation Yearbook 1995*. China Tax Publishing House. Beijing.

The Editorial Committee for Handbook of Expenditure Standards, Fee Rates, Interest Rates and Tax Rates for the Administrative Units of Enterprises and Institutions (1996): *Handbook on Expenditure Standards, Fee Rates, Interest Rates and Tax Rates for the Administrative Units of Enterprises and Institution.* Economic Management Publishing House. Beijing.

The Energy and Raw Materials Division of the Price Management Department, the State Planning Commission (1996): "Thoughts about Chinese Power Price Reform" in Price Theory and Practice (9): 5-12.

The Fee Management Department of the State Planning Commission (1997): *Document Collection of Price and Fee Charge Management (1996).* China Price Publishing House. Beijing.

The Industrial Transportation Department of the State Statistic Bureau (1989): *The Development of Transportation, Post and Telecommunications in China.* China Statistics Publishing House. Beijing.

The Power Price Coordination Office of Shanxi Province (1996): "Power Price Reform in Shanxi: Achievements, Problems and Countermeasures" in Price Theory and Practice (9) 16-18.

The Price Management Department of the State Planning Commission (1994): *Document Collection of Price and Charge Management (1992-1994).* China Price Publishing House. Beijing.

The Price Management Department of the State Planning Commission (1996): *Document Collection of Price and Charge Management (December, 1994-February, 1996).* China Price Publishing House. Beijing.

The Reading and Editorial Committee for China Coal Industry Yearbook (1993): *China Coal Industry Yearbook 1993.* Coal Industry Publishing House. Beijing.

The State Planning Commission (1996). File Number 249 of The Price Management Department of the State Planning Commission. The State Planning Commission's Circular about Applying the State Guideline Price on Coal for Power Generation, February 9, 1996.

The Secretariat of International Cooperation Commission, the State Agency for Environmental Protection (1997): *Document Collection of China International Cooperation Committee for the Environment and the Development (No. 4).* China Environmental Science Publishing House. Beijing.

The State Administration of Taxation (1994): Circular for Printing and Distributing the Detailed Stipulations for Imposing Value Added Tax on Power Products.

The Editorial Committee for China Tax Yearbook (1995): *China Taxation Yearbook,* 1995. China Tax Publishing House. Beijing.

The State Bureau of Prices (1996): "Comments on the Price Reform Measures Introduce by the State in 1996" in Price Theory and Practice (12)

The State Planning Commission (1995): File Number 126 of The State Planning Commission Circular About Adjusting the Price of Railway Passenger Transportation from the State Planning Commission and the Ministry of Railway, September 25, 1995.

The State Planning Commission (1996): File Number 50 of The State Planning Commission Telegram About Adjustments of Railway Cargo Transportation Price.

The Sate Statistics Bureau (1996): *China Statistics Yearbook 1996*. China Price Publishing House. Beijing.

The State Statistics Bureau (1997): *China Statistics Yearbook 1997*. China Price Publishing House. Beijing.

Tian, Pude (1997): "Some Thoughts About Water Pricing Reform" in Water Conservancy Economy, 1997 (4): 11-14.

Wang, Jinnan (1994): *Environmental Economics: Theories, Methods and Policies*. Qinghua University Press. Beijing.

World Bank (1997a): Expanding the Measure of Wealth Indicators of Environmentally Sustainable Development. Environmentally Sustainable Development Studies and Monographs Series No. 17. World Bank. Washington D.C.

World Bank (1997b): *Clear Water, Blue Skies, China 2020: China's Environmental in The New Century*. World Bank. Washington D.C.

Xu, Qingjian (1997): "A Discussion about Public Traffic Countermeasures" in Comprehensive Transportation (9)

Zhang, Guoliang, Pang Jinwu, Zhu Ruixiang, Xu Zikai (1996): "The Principle and Methods of Fund Raising for Water Conservancy Projects" in Water Conservancy Economics (3): 1-4

Zhang, Jinong (1997): "Some Comments on Current Water Prices" in Water Conservancy Economics ((4): 7-10

Zhang, Q. and Zhang, X. (1995): "Water Issues and Sustainable Social Development in China" in Official Journal of the International Water Resources Association (20): 122-128

Zhang, Shiqiu (1997): "A Research Framework for Using Marginal Opportunity Cost Theory to Fix the Price of Thermal Power in China" in Hu Tao and Wang Huadong (eds.) *The Practical Application of Environmental Economics in China*. China Environmental Science Publishing House. Beijing.

Zhang, Shiqiu (1998): Marginal Cost Pricing for Coal Fired Electricity in Coastal Cities of China. Progress Report for Economy and Environmental Program of Southeast Asia, April, 1998.

Zhao, Xinyan (1998): "The Heel-and-toe Walking Race in the Maze of Power Prices" in The Chinese Reader of the Capital Market (1): 16-23

Zhou, Wangjun (1996): "Studies of the Relative Prices of Communication and Transportation" in Comprehensive Transportation (12): 1-4

Zhu, Zhongbin (1997): "Sustainable Transport and Environmental Economic Policies" in Hu, Tao and Wang Huadong (eds.) *The Practical Application of Environmental Economics in China*. China Environmental Science Publishing House. Beijing.

GAINS FROM REDUCING COAL SUPPORT,
WITH PARTICULAR REFERENCE TO THE UK EXPERIENCE

Jan Pieters[1]
Environment Directorate, OECD

1.0   Summary

In OECD countries there is a trend towards reducing support and changing the nature of support towards less environmentally harmful forms. Coal is no exception in this respect. There are many good reasons for reducing support.

This paper first takes a "political economy" perspective, which points to the negative effects of support on technological change and flexibility. It is extremely difficult to estimate the effects of support on technical change – and, consequently, on the economy. After all, the responses of economic agents to support removal often cannot be foreseen. In fact one of the benefits of a free market economy is that prices induce constant technological and institutional innovations and unexpected solutions.

This "political economy" perspective also draws attention to the fact that support often does not end up with the intended recipient sector, but instead leaks away to suppliers and customers. As such, many of the support measures that are used are inefficient policies for transferring funds to the sectors they are meant to support.

Finally, this perspective stresses the need for a comprehensive approach to support removal, including many sectors and as many of the relevant support measures as possible, including those embedded in institutional arrangements and the taxation regimes.

Although analytically impeccable, this approach does not help with prioritising support measures to be removed. For this purpose a micro-economic framework is developed. It describes in more detail "how subsidies to coal work" and how they might affect the environment. It suggests the possible existence of a paradoxical situation, namely: *support may not be effective in achieving its economic objectives, even though it still damages the environment significantly.* The approach can then be used to analyse under which conditions this paradoxical situation may occur. It is especially the following types of support that are likely to lead to such a paradox (largely because they lock-in present day technologies):

1. *Support that is directly contingent on the volumes of energy (coal) production and use, such as market price support;*

---

[1]   Although this paper is essentially based on previous OECD publications, it does not necessarily reflect the views of the OECD or its Member countries.

2. *Support that lowers the cost of capital, including measures such as low rate of return requirements in state-owned industry,, low interest rates on loans and tax reliefs on corporate income.*

One of the most interesting examples of the reduction of coal support in an OECD country is provided by the UK experience. The UK approach was comprehensive: liberalising the gas, electricity and coal markets within a period of roughly 8 years. Because these measures were undertaken simultaneously, it is impossible to disentangle the particular effects of the different changes made. Moreover, it is impossible to know the situation which would have prevailed if all these actions had not been taken. The effects of autonomous technical and economic changes are particularly difficult to separate from the effects of policy actions. Although it is not possible to quantify the effects of support removal with any precision, the UK experience suggests important beneficial environmental effects of support removal and the importance of a comprehensive approach, including changing institutional arrangements to increase transparency and create new markets.

2.0   Political Economy of Energy Support

2.1   Motives for Support

We define energy support[2] in this paper as:

all kinds of financial support and regulations that are put in place to enhance the competitiveness of certain forms of energy production or use, and that, together with the prevailing taxation system, (unintentionally) discriminate against other types of energy production or use, or energy saving, or both.

There are many motives for such support. Widely cited (and somewhat overlapping) motives include:

1. *enhancing economic development of certain industrial sectors, certain regions, or even the economy as a whole;*

2. *securing employment levels in the energy sector, which is often concentrated in certain regions;*

3. *equity – making (cheap) energy available for the poor;*

4. *securing the supply of energy (including a prudent management of reserves);*

5. *stimulating the development or application of certain energy technologies for energy production and energy use; and*

6. *reducing the need for imports;*

Often there are better means for achieving these objectives than supporting energy production or use, especially in the view of technical change and external (environmental) effects, and in view of the

---

[2]   In this paper we avoid the use of the word "subsidies", because it has a very distinct (more limited) meaning in trade negotiations.

fact that using some energy support measures may be in violation of WTO rules. Nevertheless, these motives tend to carry political weight because the benefits accrue to specific interest groups, which defend their interests with vigour, while the costs are often borne by large groups of anonymous tax payers or consumers. The experiences with support removal in the UK provides an interesting example of the struggle to strike an appropriate balance between particular group interests and the general public interest.

Although support has many disadvantages, the absence of *any* government intervention in energy markets, however, is unlikely. First of all, energy production and use often require complementary government investments and regulation. These will favour some energy form over others. They don't fall within the definition of support given above if their *objective* is not to distort competition. This is a rather elusive distinction, since the effects will be the same. If the objective is not to favour one energy form over another, the measures taken should be scrutinised carefully to see what their effects will be and if the objectives cannot be achieved by means that discriminate less among the energy forms.

A second (related) reason why there will be a need for government intervention in energy markets is that markets left to themselves do not automatically guarantee an optimal allocation of resources. This is often referred to as "market failures". Market failures typically occur in the presence of external costs (such as costs of pollution that are not incorporated in market prices), or when the social benefits of certain investments exceed their private benefits. This can be the case if expanding a particular type of energy production and use would result in economies of scale. For example, it is often argued that renewable energy at present is in an unfavourable position to compete with fossil fuels, because their production and application do not benefit from the economies of scale that have already been achieved by the latter forms of energy production and use.[3]

2.2 The Need for a Comprehensive Approach

Energy carriers are often rather close substitutes, especially in the long run. Consequently, the largest improvements in allocative efficiency will be obtained if the markets for all energy carriers are liberated at the same time (taking the external effects into account). To reduce support for one of them – especially support that increases user prices – while leaving other market distortions in place will often not make much sense. In fact, it may leave the share of each energy carrier in total energy use more or less unaltered and may have only a small effect on total energy use. It might, however, lead to increased imports.

Much support is (willingly, or unwillingly) given through institutional arrangements, such as defining and granting monopoly powers. This type of "support" is not financial, but may be very effective. If this type of support is not removed as well, the removal of financial support measures may be of little effect.

It is not only the alternative energy forms that must be taken into account. Since support measures often include tax elements, and interact with statutory rates of taxation, the effects of taxation regimes must be taken into account as well.

---

[3]   A word of caution is in order. Sometimes support for technical development is just support to operating costs in disguise. Moreover support to a particular type of renewable energy may lock in this type of energy, giving rise to the same inefficiencies that characterise present day energy support.

2.3   On the Effects of Support: A Dynamic Perspective

2.3.1   *Technological change lead times and sunk costs*

Typically, energy support is conditional on certain *"transactions"*, such as buying or selling particular energy carriers, or equipment. Since the use of a particular fuel or equipment is closely related to certain technologies, support to a given fuel tends to lock-in the related technologies, blocking the production and use of more efficient and less polluting alternatives. From a dynamic perspective, such support is counterproductive in many respects. For example, if a particular energy source is supported, this support does not stop technical improvements in the production and use of alternative, competing, energy sources[4]. The support does however effectively block technological improvements to the production and use of the supported energy source. Consequently, the support has to make up the ever increasing difference between the actual costs of the supported fuel and its opportunity costs, being the costs of alternative energy sources. This leads to the need to give ever increasing amounts of support money in order to ensure the same levels of production and use of the supported energy source. The same holds true with respect to the environmental effects of the production and use of energy sources: as time passes, the gap between the emissions associated with alternative energy sources compared with the emissions of the supported energy source increase, rendering the supported energy source relatively more and more polluting compared with available alternatives

Investments in coal production and use (notably electricity generation and steel production) is characterised by long lead times (construction), very long life spans and a relatively high capital intensity. Therefore the technology-fixing effect of most types of support to coal production and use carries a very heavy weight. A corollary is that support in the form of low interest rates, or low required returns on investment are particularly effective – and favoured – forms of support. Consequently, privatising coal production, electricity generation and the steel sector will have significant effects on the effective levels of support.

The high capital intensity, long lead times and life spans of coal-associated investments and related investments in infrastructure (notably in transport facilities), lead to large "sunk costs." Once these investments are made, it is often cheaper to continue their operation than to replace them with new, more efficient equipment. This means that the marginal costs of coal-fired plants tend to be low. In addition, coal is a relatively cheap fuel compared with gas or oil. On the other hand, if coal investments are made on the basis of overestimated demand, coal producers and users will be stuck with expensive over-capacity for a long time. Simulations with micro-economic models (such as Markal) suggest that the inflexibility of investments in coal-based electricity generation is often an incentive for private companies to opt for technologies such as combined heat and power (CHP) generation, in spite of their higher operating (marginal) costs. This reflects higher discounted rates of return applied by private investors, compared with the discount rates typically applied for government investments. Privatisation of the coal and electricity sector therefore tends to favour such alternatives. It should be noted that the application of higher discount rates may, in the end, result in lower costs of energy production and use if technology improves at a rapid pace. High discount rates, and short depreciation times, allow investors to reap the benefits of technical change earlier and to adjust capacity more rapidly in accordance to changes in demand.

---

[4]   Although, of course, competitively the unsupported one will suffer compared with the supported one

Pervasiveness of Support

Support to a sector has effects on (upstream) suppliers and (downstream) customers. Particularly in the case of energy, this may lead to "support clusters", where a number of industries group together to reap the benefits of the support. In the case of support to coal these sectors may include transport, mining equipment, steel and electricity generation. Consequently, support to energy tends to have pervasive effects on relative prices throughout the economy. Moreover, support removal will generally face resistance not only from the (intended) recipient sector but also from its suppliers and customers.

2.3.2   *Environmental Effects*

The non-internalisation of the full environmental and social costs of economic activities takes place in all sectors of the economy, which is sometimes referred to as an 'implicit subsidy'. The non-internalisation of external costs means that some of the damage caused by these activities is not paid for by those undertaking the activities. These implicit transfers, from those who suffer from the social and environmental damage to those who produce it (but do not pay for it) are often significant. Considerable research has already been undertaken, particularly through the OECD 'green' tax reform programme, into the implementation of economic policies for internalising these costs and 'getting the prices right'.

In general, there is no straightforward link between the size or type of support, or the nature of the recipient sector, and the environmental damage. Instead, the negative effects of a support measure on the environment will depend on a number of characteristics, both of the support itself and the nature of the:

1. *relevant input and final product markets,*

2. *availability of substitute technologies, products or services with more favourable environmental profiles,*

3. *prevailing taxation regime,*

4. *regulatory and institutional framework (including environmental policy), and the*

5. *local bio-physical characteristics of the recipient environment.*

It is only once all of these factors are considered that both the potential negative effects of the support on the environment and the effects of the support on the intended recipient sector can be understood.

The first three factors determine the effect of support on the relative competitiveness of energy forms relative to each other. The fourth factor may enhance or diminish the actual effects on emissions and pollution due to changes in the composition of energy production and use that result from the support measure.[5] The fifth factor may enhance or diminish the effects of changes in actual emissions on the

---

[5]   A support measure that increases the use of sulphur-rich coal in electricity generation, for example, will have little effect on So_x emissions if all the electricity plants have already been equipped with scrubbers that remove SO_x.

environment. Coal production and use, however, leads to significant emissions of greenhouse gases (GHGs) which are global pollutants.[6]

2.4   Efficiency of Support

Support, while possibly having positive regional and sectoral effects in the short run, will generally not achieve the stated objectives in terms of growth and employment in the long run and for the economy as a whole in an efficient (cost effective) way. The most important reasons for this are:

- *Support must be paid for, either out of taxes or directly out of consumers' pockets. This money cannot be spent on other (more profitable) uses, reducing in general the overall efficiency of the economy. In the view of increased openness of economies and technological change, this will lead to less income and often less employment in the first place. In addition, the amount of money spent on support must increase in order to maintain the same effects.*

- *Often support does not end up with the intended recipient sector. Due to price elasticities of demand and supply, large proportions of support may "leak away" from the initial recipient sector to other sectors in the economy. Support to coal for instance will also benefit the suppliers of equipment for coal mines and coal users (mainly the steel industry and electricity producers). If the support leads to lower coal prices (which is not the case with market price support for coal production, as seen in the UK and in Germany), the customers of the recipient sector will benefit. The magnitude of these leakage effects depends on many factors, including the precise conditions under which the recipient sector is eligible for the support.*

- *Support that is conditional on the volumes bought or sold of a product is often ill-targeted. This type of support is often motivated by an intention to ensure that the poor have access to the supported commodity (coal or electricity) and typically takes the form of a reduction in consumer prices (e.g. through low VAT rates). Generally, these measures will not only benefit the poor, but also the high income groups (often even more* so because the better off tend to consume more). It is preferable to support the poor by other means, such as a general tax reduction, or support for energy-saving options.

On the other hand, although it is a second best policy in terms of efficiency, support may be the only option that is available to policy makers in some circumstances. It may be the only practical way to immediately reduce the hardships in depressed areas, or to help the poor. It should be stressed, however, that the costs of such support measures are to a large extent hidden and in the long run may be counter-productive. The support to the German coal miners, for example, became untenable. Its effect has been a postponement of inevitable adjustments. In the meantime, the money spent on support could possibly have been used in more productive ways which would have led to higher levels of employment even in the regions that are heavily dependent on coal mining.

---

[6]   A number of these gases, notably CO_2 and methane (from deep coal mining) are difficult to control and have global effects. This is why this fifth factor is not particularly relevant in analysing the effects of support to energy on some GHGs.

A paradox: Support that is ineffective in economic terms, yet detrimental for the environment

Unfortunately, support that is ineffective in achieving economic objectives may still have serious detrimental effects on the environment. This is because the conditionality of the support may very well induce economic agents to engage in environmentally harmful activities, while not improving their economic conditions. This paradox is analysed in some detail in Section 3.

2.5   Motives for "Support" Removal

In general, support to all kinds of economic activities (such as agriculture, industry, energy, transport) in OECD countries seems to be decreasing, and its composition is becoming potentially less harmful for the environment, but it remains high and predominantly directed to less sound environmental practices and it continues to stimulate higher levels of pollution and resource use. Support for coal is to some degree an exception in this respect. It has been significant in a number of OECD countries, but it has been rapidly reduced during the last decade in a number of countries (such as the UK), although there are sharp differences between countries. In Germany, for example, coal support levels will mainly be reduced only in the early years of the next decade. Stated motives for reducing support for coal are indicated below.

1. ***Government budgets****: presumably amongst the most compelling motivations for governments to reduce coal support are budgetary reasons. The most striking example might be Germany, where the estimated total level of support to maintain desired levels of employment in the coal mining industry soared to US$ 90 200 in 1990 per coal miner employed, several times the yearly earnings of a coal miner. In light of increasing budgetary pressures, this is an untenable position. Not surprisingly, the German government has decided to cut back the support drastically.*

2. ***Inefficiency in achieving economic objectives****: related to the previous point is the recognition that support may not be effective, let alone efficient, in achieving its economic objectives.*

3. ***Support counteracts environmental objectives****: the relatively strong negative external environmental effects of coal production and use, as compared to other energy sources and energy saving measures, has made support for coal less popular. For example, when the UK committed itself to adhere to stricter European standards for emissions for electricity plants, it became clear that achieving the same employment objectives in the coal industry would require considerably higher sums of support.*

2.6 Remarks on Obstacles to Support Removal and Implementation Strategies

Interest groups; support clusters

Support removal creates winners and losers, at least in the short run. The initial losers from coal support removal are, of course, the coal, steel and electricity sectors as well as their suppliers (capital equipment and transport). On the other hand there are winners, notably the providers of electricity generated by means of CHP (and/ or renewable energy in the longer run), presumably because of both the greater flexibility of this form of electricity generation and its relatively favourable environmental impacts. This in turn will lead to other "winners", notably gas supply, gas-associated capital equipment and the electricity generators that prefer gas (electricity companies as well as industry). The more comprehensive the support removal programme, the more likely spontaneous shifts in the economy will occur. Temporary compensating measures can be used to ease the transition towards the "non-supported-situation."

These changes may have severe economic impacts, especially on a local and regional scale.[7] Implementation strategies often include programmes to increase employment opportunities where they will be lost (due to the support removal). Such programmes generally include training and schooling of those on the work force that become redundant, as well as certain government investments (such as in infrastructure) and support to industries conditional on investments.[8] Such schemes have been applied in the UK. In some cases (such as in Wales) they have not succeeded in eliminating relatively high levels of unemployment. On the other hand, it is believed that the comprehensive policy reforms since the 1980s, of which reducing coal support has been a part, have benefited the UK economy as a whole to a significant extent. The level that unemployment (including that in depressed areas) would have reached without the policy reforms is not known, but presumably it would have been higher.

In order to avoid dramatic shocks, in most countries support is reduced gradually and compensation packages are designed to ease the transition for the affected sectors and their workers.

International competitiveness

The continuation of support is often seen as indispensable for maintaining the competitiveness of favoured sectors, especially if foreign competition is believed to receive support. Removing support will certainly have negative effects on the recipient sector in the short run. However, most support to ailing industries has not been effective in preventing their decline. In addition, the financing of the support will generally place a burden on other sectors. Comprehensive support removal in New Zealand, for example, is believed to have benefited the entire economy and to have even led to an increase in the competitiveness of sectors that lost their support. Ensuring the transparency of the support mechanisms and evaluating their likely effects on the economy as a whole are therefore important elements of implementation strategies.

---

[7]   On the other hand, the long depreciation periods allow for some advance planning.

[8]   One could argue that such support would merely be replacing one ineffective and environmentally damaging support for another. This, however, does not need to be true. If the new support is conditional only on once-off investment decisions, it will have less detrimental effects on the environment.

2.7   Conclusion

Support often locks-in prevailing technologies. Especially in an era of "globalisation" and rapid technological change, such support may very well be counter-productive. Unfortunately, while such support is ineffective (or even counter-productive), it may still stimulate environmentally harmful practices. In those cases, its elimination would yield a "double dividend": being beneficial for both the economy and the environment. To single out these forms of support requires a micro-economic analysis. The next section provides the outline of the required type of analysis. It is based on *Improving the Environment Through Reducing Subsidies* (OECD 1998)

3.0   A Micro-Economic Based Analysis of Support

3.1   A General Overview of Support to Coal and Electricity

Support measures come in a wide variety of forms, such as direct and indirect payments, tax expenditures through tax concessions to specific industries or regions, market price support and other regulations that enhance the competitiveness of certain sectors or products. Given the focus of our analysis, support can be classified according to its immediate effects on government budgets and the elements of the firm's balance sheet that are affected by the support (points of impact, or conditionality) (see Table 1). The points of impact are key factors that influence the economic as well as the environmental effects of the support.

3.1.1   *Two Basic Formulae*

To better understand which points of impact really matter, it may be helpful to keep the following formulae in mind.

Let D_t be the total demand for energy; Y, national income; P_e, the average price for energy and T, the applied technologies. Then D_t can be written as:

$$D_t = f(Y, P_e, T),\qquad\qquad\text{(a)}$$

indicating the fact that support to a particular energy form will increase energy use in the economy, with all its associated environmental consequences, including the emissions associated with increased use of materials.

Support to a certain energy form will change the composition of energy production and use. The composition of energy production and use is a very crucial variable from the environmental perspective since energy forms differ considerably in their environmental impacts. Let D_i denote the demand for a particular energy carrier;   R, the revenues that an energy carrier can command because of its characteristics; C, the capital costs; NP, the non-price factors, like time preference, or objectives concerning optimal depletion of reserves; the suffixes i, a particular energy form and t, the average for all energy carriers. Then the share of energy form i in total demand (and supply) resulting form investment decisions can be written as:

$$\frac{D_i}{D_t} = f(\frac{R_i}{C_i}, \frac{R_t}{C_t}, NP, T)\qquad\qquad\text{(b)}$$

The first conclusion is that when analysing the effects of support, one must take all the factors that influence R and C, for all energy forms, into account. For example, the repeal by the European Council of the directive that had limited the use of gas for base load power generation changed the R of gas, and implicitly changed the R_{gas} relative to R_{coal} in the UK and other European countries. R_i is also influenced by the existing infrastructure, and by all kinds of government regulations, such as market price support, the allowance of insufficient provision for future environmental liabilities (a very significant factor favouring nuclear power) and environmental standards.

The other important variable entering the equation is the cost of the necessary capital. This is dependent on the relative capital intensity of the various energy forms and regulations as well as market circumstances determining interest rates.

These basic formulae may contribute to an understanding of the weight that various government interventions carry in influencing the relative shares of energy forms in total energy demand (and supply)

Table 1: Classification of Principal Support Measures by Budgetary Effects and Points of Impact

Points of impact / support conditionality	Effects on government budgets	
	On-budget	Off-budget

Outputs	• Deficiency payments
	• Sales premiums
	• **Preferential sales tax and VAT rates**
		• **Market price support**
		  - Border Protection (tariffs, quantitative import controls)
		  - Market access restrictions
		  - Government brokered sales contracts

Raw material and intermediate product inputs	• Support to material and energy input (e.g., energy, fertilisers, irrigation water) • Provision of infrastructure below long run marginal cost	• Material and services in kind
Capital and labour inputs *or* **Income or profit**	• **Support to non-material and non-energy inputs (e.g., labour, capital equipment)** • Accelerated depreciation allowances (if selective) • **Income tax concessions** (if selective) • Concessional credit • **Debt write off** • **Support to research and development on production techniques, safety or environmental protection**	• **Concessional credit** • **Royalty concessions** • **Low rate of return requirements** • **Exemptions from environmental standards** • Allowing insufficient provision for future environmental liabilities

a. There are many regulations which are not obvious support measures, and their financial effects may be indirect and difficult to assess, such as restrictions on third party access to electricity distribution infrastructure. Such a measure may have profound effects on competition (essentially ensuring a monopolistic market), but its precise pecuniary effects on corporate balance sheets is difficult to calculate. Only the more conspicuous support measures have been listed in Table 1 above. The "implicit" subsidies, that result from the non-internalisation of externalities are also not listed.

b. The off-budget forms of support may have second order effects on the budget. Increased efficiency of the economy as a whole, which will generally result from lower support levels, may increase revenues without increasing the tax burden as a percentage of GDP. Off-budget support measures are also often part of larger integrated support policies, and so are often accompanied by other support policies which do have direct budgetary effects.

c. The entries in bold print in the Table indicate those forms of support that are common in many countries and often imply large transfers to the coal and electricity suppliers, with considerable effects on the relative competitiveness of these forms of energy.

Sources: OECD (1998b), adapted from Steenblik (1995) and Centre for International Economics (1988).

The mix of support measures varies over countries and interacts with country-specific elements of the prevailing taxation regimes. Nevertheless it is a safe conclusion that two types of support stand out as particularly important in affecting the relative competitive position of domestic coal (and lignite) vis - à - vis its direct competitors - imported coal, gas, oil and nuclear. They are:

– *Market price support*

– *Support that lowers the cost of capital, including measures such as low rate of return requirements, low interest rates on loans and tax reliefs on corporate income.*

Market Price Support

Market price support typically takes the form of *government brokered* sales contracts, stipulating the purchase of certain quantities of domestically produced coal at a price well above world market levels. The higher costs of the domestic coal are then translated into higher electricity prices, to be paid by the consumers. These higher costs will generally be borne only by households and small businesses that do not (yet) compete on world markets – giving rise to substantial cross subsidisation. These brokered contracts ensure production levels of domestic coal production that are significantly above the levels that otherwise would occur, and they reduce the incentives for electricity generators to increase the thermal efficiency of their plants – or to shift to other technologies altogether.

The *environmental effects* of this kind of subsidy is very strong as it directly fixes a certain quantity of coal production and use, with its associated environmental consequences. The effects, however, may be local. If the alternative to the use of domestic coal would be the use of imported coal, then the global effects would be limited. In the case of the UK and Germany, domestic coal would be replaced, at least partly, by imported coal from Australia and South Africa.[9] The environmental effects of this shift would be the effects of the use of coal with a lower sulphur content, less methane emissions from deep coal mining, but more emissions from transport. If support removal would only lead to the use of imported coal instead of domestically produced coal the net effects would be mainly local, or, as in the case of CO_2 emissions, very small.

Support to Capital

Support that lowers the cost of capital, including tax reliefs on corporate income, may take several forms. Governmentally owned electricity generators do not pay corporate income taxes, which increase the relative after tax rate of return compared with electricity generation by private enterprises (decentralised CHP). This is, therefore, a strong incentive for centralised, capital intensive energy supply.

Very often publicly owned companies can borrow at interest rates well below market rates. Especially because electricity generation using coal is capital intensive, these support measures have a considerable impact. If anything, it favours capital intensive energy forms and will lead to over-investment.

Low rate of return requirements are often introduced to curtail monopoly powers. However, if they are set sufficiently low, which is often the case, they allow electricity generators to set their selling

---

[9]   In the case of the UK where these support measures have indeed been reduced, domestically produced coal has been substituted to a large extent by natural gas, not by imported coal.

price below what would have been "normal" for privately owned companies. This is believed to lead to over-investment.

Once energy markets are deregulated, these kinds of support disappear.

The *environmental effects* of this kind of support depend on how much it blocks the transition towards the use of less polluting fuels and energy savings. These questions are very difficult to answer in a quantitative way, because the answers are strongly dependent on all kinds of assumptions regarding technological changes. Moreover market price support and "low discount rate" forms of support tend to have opposite effects on consumer electricity prices (at least in the short run), leading to a difficult analytical disentangling problem. In spite of the difficulties in precisely calculating the effects, however, one can safely assume that low discount rates effectively deter the introduction of CHP-technology.[10] CHP-technology may have higher operating costs, but because of its lower capital intensity and higher flexibility (which allows supply to follow demand more closely), it may be the preferred option for privately owned electricity generators. It is believed that this is one of the reasons why the UK, after the reduction of support and deregulation of energy markets, experienced a "dash for gas". Because of lower emissions per Kwh., of course, this dash for gas has resulted in a considerable environmental improvement.

Support to R&D

Rather substantial amounts of money are spent on *R&D support* for nuclear and fossil fuels, notably coal, while relatively little is spent on renewable energy (Ruijgrok and Oosterhuis, 1997), in spite of the fact that there is a relatively strong case for R&D to renewables, because of its limited environmental impacts and the fact that renewables have not yet developed their full potential for economies of scale.[11] To the extent that this support is biased against renewables, it has a negative effect on the environment. Moreover, some of this R&D support may very well be support to operating costs in disguise, with effects similar to the effects of market price support and support that lowers the cost of capital.

Towards a more comprehensive analysis

Different forms of support, such as market price support and support that lowers the cost of inputs, have different effects on companies' behaviour and therefore will have different environmental effects. In the following paragraphs these differences will be explored in a more general way, drawing attention to the conditions under which support will not be effective in economic terms, while still having negative effects on the environment. Unfortunately, there is a gap in our knowledge, both conceptually as well as data wise. The previous remarks on the effects of coal support to firms' balance sheets and their likely responses have been derived from detailed micro-economic (linear programming) models such as Markal. This, however, can only be a starting point for a more comprehensive analysis. There will be all kinds of feedback mechanisms through market adjustments that require extensive general equilibrium modelling. So far it has proven to be extremely difficult to combine both approaches. The next section

---

[10]   One of the reasons is the relatively lower capital intensity of CHP. This argument would not hold in general, however for energy from wind.

[11]   As a consequence, support for renewables will probably lead to lower marginal (societal) costs in the future, which is one justification for the support.

tries to translate micro-economic reasoning as applied above into concepts that are more familiar to micro and macro-economists alike. There is very little empirical evidence on coal support at this level of analysis.

3.2   Support that increases the marginal revenue of a sector by market price intervention

<u>Example: minimum purchase requirements of coal by the electricity generating industry and accompanying measures (import restrictions)</u>

Effects on the output market

Market price support is provided through mechanisms that increase selling prices – normally by erecting border protections, guaranteeing minimum prices, or both. Typically, such market interventions are complemented by other measures, such as import and export restrictions and/ or purchase obligations. These measures support producers by ensuring a market price for the product that is above the market price that would have prevailed in the absence of the support. Figure 1 gives a simplified representation of how such support works in a closed economy.

The primary stated objectives of market price support are to support the incomes of producers, or to ensure a certain level of production and employment in the intended recipient sector. Market price support of these types usually consists of two parts: the transfer from users/ consumers to producers through the higher prices they pay for the products, and the money spent by governments to buy any excess production that results from fixing prices above market-clearance levels. In return, the government often acquires a quantity of product that must be stored, sold on the world market or otherwise prevented from re-entering the domestic market. Selling the product on the world market, often at prices below world market price levels, is often the least-cost option for governments. It is because of these accompanying measures that minimum price support, although increasing consumer prices generally, often leads to the over-production of the supported product (Steenblik and Coroyannakis, 1995).

For a given demand curve, a shallower supply curve (reflecting a larger price elasticity of supply) will yield larger volume effects to a certain change in price compared with a steep supply curve[12]. This can be seen by comparing Panel B with Panel A in Figure 1. With the larger quantity of production, and assuming the same technologies, there will be more associated waste and pollution with the shallower supply curve. This will, of course, aggravate the government burden of addressing environmental problems. In addition, there will be a larger quantity of "excess" product for the government to purchase or to dispose of, by some other means. In general, supply levels will respond more to changes in price in the longer run (i.e., there will be shallower long-term supply curves than short-term ones). Figure 1 therefore, shows how there may be a tendency with market price support measures to require increased environmental protection expenditures over time in order to achieve the same environmental objectives.

Regardless of the motivating factor — whether to support producers' incomes or to fix a certain quantity of production — both types of market price support have strong effects on international trade. The higher levels of domestic production that are guaranteed tend to block cheaper imports or lead to an excess level of production — with the excess often sold abroad by the government at prices below the prevailing world market price.

---

[12]   Similarly, a shallow demand curve --a large price elasticity of demand – reflects a large volume response to a given change in prices.

Figure 1: Revenue Raising Support in a Closed Economy

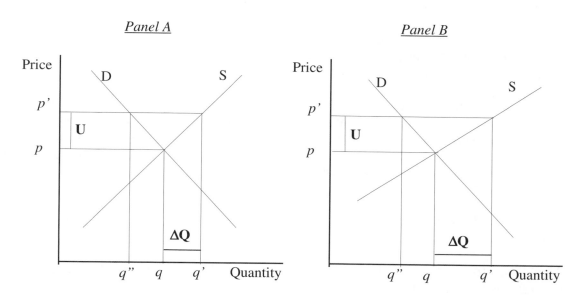

Panel A   *Panel B*

Key

D is the demand curve, S the supply curve, p is the price before and p' the price after a minimum price regulation is introduced. U is the difference between the two prices (i.e., the support). The quantity produced before and after the minimum price regulation are q and q' respectively, and the difference between the two is ΔQ.

q' can also be interpreted as the quantity the government wants the sector to produce. In order to ensure that the recipient sector does not lose money by producing this quantity, a minimum price equal to p' is necessary. In order to ensure q' can be sold at this price, however, additional measures will be used to guarantee the purchase of the extra quantity (q' - q'') which will not otherwise be in demand at this price. Such measures may include government-brokered minimum domestic purchase agreements, support to sell the extra quantity on the world market, or government purchase and disposal.

Source: OECD 1998

Not effective in economic terms, while still damaging the environment

In order to produce the quantities that correspond with the minimum price regulations and accompanying measures, the producer has to acquire additional inputs. Some of the money spent on these inputs 'leaks away' from the intended recipient sector, depending on the marginal productivity of the required inputs and the price elasticities of supply of these inputs.[13] The support that is leaked to these input providers will not benefit the intended recipient sector in terms of increased income or employment. In the meantime, however, the production is expanded by ΔQ (Figure 1), giving rise to increased potential

---

[13]   In the longer run, technological responses that increase the marginal productivity of the inputs will boost total production relative to input requirements. Accordingly, in the case of minimum price regulations, production at a given price will generally increase over time, necessitating government intervention to ensure the purchase of the extra production in order to maintain the specified prices and quantities.

pollution by the intended recipient sector proportional to ΔQ, or perhaps even more if the marginal productivity of the inputs decreases. Moreover the leakage effect will encourage upstream activities to expand, giving rise to potential pollution in those sectors as well. It is especially when the leakage effects are large (which is often the case, see Figure 2) that the economic benefits to the intended recipient sector are small, while the potential pollution effects from the intended recipient sector and upstream activities will be large compared with the level of support.

There are further inefficiencies involved. The higher prices at which the products of the supported industries are sold will generally put downstream industries at a competitive disadvantage. To limit or offset these negative effects on the competitive positions of the downstream industries, there is often a strong tendency to support them as well, thus leading to a chain of (expensively) supported industries (sometimes referred to as 'subsidy clusters').

3.3 Support conditional on the purchase of a product or the use of a particular production process

Example: Low interest rates on borrowed capital; low rate of return requirements; preferential sales tax and VAT rates (if the consumer is to be supported).

Price and volume effects on the market for the finished product (downstream effects):

A producing sector that uses an input, the purchase price of which is supported, will realise lower marginal costs of production. As a result, this sector will be able to offer its finished product at a lower selling price than it otherwise could have. Or, if producers are price takers and too small to affect world prices, they may expand production at the expense of imports. If a lower selling price is offered, buyers will generally buy more of the finished product. But this increased demand for the finished good may push up the market price of the product, partly offsetting the price-reducing effect of the support conditional on the input. This is depicted as ΔP_f in Panel A of Figure2. Given leakage ΔP_f, with respect to support, U, the portion of the support that results in a change in the price of the finished product can be defined as β^f (where $\beta^f = \Delta P_f / U$). It can then be expressed as a function of the absolute values of the price elasticities of demand (η^{Df}) and supply (η^{Sf}) as follows (see OECD 1998 for a more complete exposition)

$$\beta^f = \frac{\eta^{Sf}}{\eta^{Sf} + \eta^{Df}}, \qquad (0<\beta^f<1) \qquad (1)$$

If the absolute values of the price elasticities of demand and supply are equal, half of the support will leak away to the consumers. If the price elasticity of supply exceeds the price elasticity of demand, the leakage with respect of the support will be between 0.5 and unity.

The volume effects on the finished good market (γ^f), associated with support U, can be expressed as a function of β^f and η^{Df},:

$$\gamma^f = \eta^{Df} * \beta^f \qquad (2)$$

The volume effects with respect to support, U, increase with larger values for both the price elasticities of demand and supply. Taking the volume effects as a proxy for the potential pollution effects, comparing β^f and γ^f indicates that one can have rather substantial leakage effects and large adverse potential environmental effects at the same time. This effect is magnified if the price elasticity of supply of the inputs is small (see below).

Price and volume effects in the market for the input (upstream effects)

The increased sales of the downstream product to consumers will increase production of the product, and so demand for the supported input. Where possible, the producer of the product may use more of the supported input instead of other inputs which are now less cost-efficient. These two factors will generate an increased demand for the supported input, which will in turn tend to force the sales price of the favoured input upwards. This again will result in a reduction in the share of the support that accrues to the producing sector, as some is transferred to the input producer. Panel B in Figure 2 illustrates this transfer effect. Of course, both panels are related. The effects of the input market elasticities on input supply will be incorporated into the elasticity of supply of the finished product on the output market. Similarly, the effects of demand and supply in the finished product market will be incorporated into the producer's demand for the input as well.

Figure 2: The Price, Leakage and Volume Effects in a Closed Economy of a Support that is Dependent on the Use of a Particular Input

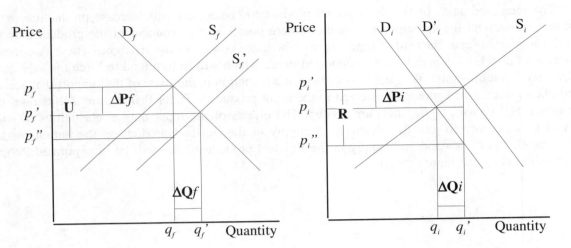

Panel A:
Market for the finished product

Panel B:
Market for the input

Key

Both markets

D represents the demand curve, S the supply curve, p is the price before and p' the price after support, ΔQ is the change in volume produced. The subscript f denotes the market for finished goods and the subscript i refers to the input market. The slope of S_f' is dependent on the slope of S_i, and thus the effects of support leakage to the input suppliers is already included in the after-support supply curve of the finished product market.

Market for the finished product (Panel A)

U represents the downward shift of the supply curve due to support of the input ($p_f - p_f''$), S_f' is the new supply curve after the support, ΔP_f is the price change ($p_f' - p_f$) that is proportional to the amount of support that is leaked to the consumers of the finished product.

Markets for the inputs (Panel B)

D_i' is the demand curve for the supported input, ΔQ_i is the change in the quantity of the input used due to the expanded sales of finished products, R is the price effect on the input market of the shift to the right of the demand curve, and ΔP_i is the resulting change in the price of the input ($p_i' - p_i$) which is proportional to the support leakage to the input suppliers.

Source: OECD, 1998

Leakage effects:

When support is conditional on the use of a particular input, the total support given will be divided between the supplier of the input, the producer of the finished product (the purchaser of the input), and the consumer of the finished product. The portion of the support that remains with the intended recipient sector reflects its transfer efficiency. A general equilibrium model would be needed to calculate precisely the relative shares each will receive for any particular support measure. However, a general rule can be developed for measuring the leakage effect since ΔP_i is proportional to the inverse of η^{si}. The total leakage β^T then becomes a function of:

$$\beta^T = f(\eta^{Df}, \eta^{Di}, \frac{1}{\eta^{Si}}) \qquad (3)$$

If the objective is to increase the profit of the finished-product producing sector, there will be a leakage of support to consumers as measured by any reduction in the selling price of the finished product, and a leakage to the input producers indicated by any increase in the price of the inputs. Conversely, if the intention is to support the input producer, any reduction in the price of the inputs sold to the downstream, input-using producer will constitute a leakage of the support to this downstream industry.

A Quick Scan for Prioritising Support Measures to be Removed

Table 2 below summarises the transfer efficiency and potential environmental effects of different combinations of supply and demand elasticities on the finished product of a support measure which reduces the cost of inputs.

Table 2: Effects of Price Elasticities in the Finished Product Market on Transfer Efficiency and Environmental Effects : Support that is Dependent on Inputs

Price elasticity of demand	large	large	small	small
Price elasticity of supply	small	large	large	small
Transfer of the support to the recipient sector	effective	moderately effective	ineffective	moderately effective
Potential environmental effects	moderate to small	large	moderate to small	small

Source: OECD 1998

The Table suggests that when some information on demand and supply elasticities is available, a quick scan of various support measures can reveal whether their removal would have significant effects on the environment or not. Given the rather inelastic demand for most energy forms and uses, at least in the short run, most support that reduces the costs of producing and selling energy will have significant effects on the environment. These effects are exacerbated by the "downstream effects" on materials consumption (including deterring recycling) that low energy prices tend to have.

4.0   Some Observations Regarding Support Removal in the UK

4.1   Comprehensive Reform, Gas, Electricity and Coal

Until the mid 1980s the major part of the UK energy sector was publicly-owned. The Government exercised much influence over the state-owned energy industries. Since the late 1980s and early 1990s the gas and electricity industries have been privatised, with British Coal privatised in 1994. There has been a considerable shift in emphasis in the sector towards greater reliance on market forces, with the Government's primary role being to set the framework within which markets operate. Detailed decisions on operational issues such as investment are left entirely to the companies concerned. The Government characterises its energy policy objectives as:

1. *encouraging competition among producers and choice for customers, and establishing a legal and regulatory framework to enable markets to work well;*

2. *ensuring that service is provided to customers in a commercial environment in which consumers pay the full cost of energy;*

3. *ensuring that the discipline of the capital markets is applied to state-owned industries by privatising them where possible*

4. *monitoring and improving the performance of the remaining state-owned industries, while minimising distortion;*

5. *having full regard to the impact of the energy sector on the environment, including measures to meet the Government's international commitments;*

6. *promoting a wider share of ownership and energy efficiency, and safeguarding health and safety.*

An important feature of the British reform is its comprehensiveness, including all energy sectors, and the simultaneity of the reforms. On the other hand, the reforms have so far taken already more than a decade. As a result of the reforms, new (energy) markets emerged and they have become more transparent. The reform has provided a regulatory framework that is presumably more neutral towards various forms of energy. Nevertheless, at present the distribution companies are required to contract 20% of their supplies from non-fossil fuel generating capacity, compensated out of a fossil fuel levy. R&D expenditures also constitute support measures. The future of government brokered contracts between the coal industry and the electricity generators seems to be uncertain.

In the following paragraphs some important elements of the British reform of energy regulations are briefly summarised.

Gas

The Gas Act of 1986 privatised the gas industry and established a regulatory regime for gas-based supply. Monopoly powers were curtailed in the Competition and Services (Utilities) Act of 1992. Important changes include:

1. *The introduction of competition in both the tariff market (residential and commercial sector) and the industrial market (above 2 500 therms per year), by offering customers a choice between suppliers. By the end of 1996, it was estimated that 65 % of the industrial market was served by independent suppliers.*

2. *Separating trading from transport and storage. On 1 March 1995, a new company was created (BG Transco), that performs transport and storage functions without discriminating against other companies.*

3. *The creation of the Office of Gas Supply (OFGAS), whose main functions are to monitor the activities of British Gas as a public gas supplier and to enforce compliance with the requirements of the Gas Act 1986 and subsequent amendments.*

Coal

Following the adoption of privatisation legislation (1994), British Coal's mining operations were sold to the private sector. Also in 1994 the Coal Authority was established, whose main responsibilities follow from owning the coal reserves and the obligation to make them available for coal mining and coal-bed methane operation. It also has responsibility for the physical legacy of past mining activities to the extent that this arises out of its ownership of coal.

Electricity

The main changes have been those related to the vertical unbundling of the electricity sector. They are listed below. The relevant Secretary of State and the Director of the Office of Electricity Generation (OFFER) are the principal regulators of the industry.

Generation

The bulk of the electricity supply industry was privatised in 1990 and 1991. In the UK, generation is now mostly carried out by 7 large companies, almost all of whom are privately-owned. However, in addition to the established generating companies, new independent entrants to the market are emerging, notably in gas-fired generation (CHP).

The building of a new power station with a capacity of more than 50 MW requires consent of the relevant Secretary of State. Environmental assessment is mandatory in most cases. In considering an application for consent, the need for the station, its capacity, choice of fuel and type of plant will generally be treated as commercial matters. However, there has been debate on a recent Government's decision (December 1997) to block further gas fired power plants.

Although the generating companies are free to make their own decisions on the fuel to be used in generation, three generators were bound until 1997 to purchase substantial amounts of domestic coal (at prices well above world market levels). Continuation of this kind of support at some level is presently being discussed.

Independent generation (including CHP) is encouraged.

Transmission and Distribution

Distribution is carried out by 12 privately owned regional distribution companies (REC's), some of which have been taken over by the generators, water companies and foreign electricity interests since 1995. The REC's jointly owned the National Grid Company (NGC), until it was floated on the stock exchange in late 1995. The distribution companies are required to contract approximately 20% of their supplies from non-fossil fuel generating capacity (i.e. nuclear and renewables). A fossil fuel levy is paid to the public electricity supply companies to compensate them for extra costs incurred in complying with the non-fossil fuel obligation.

The NGC operates a Pool pricing system. NGC estimates the demand for electricity on a half hourly basis and generators then submit bids to supply that demand. NGC calls on the cheapest plant available to satisfy the demand. The operation of the pool is subject to scrutiny by OFFER.

An REC not only distributes its "own" electricity, but also that of another REC, destined for a customer within its authorised area, or a customer who requires delivery through the REC's area.

4.2   Results

Support to British Coal

Support to British coal fluctuated considerably between 1982 and 1994 – largely due to grants (1988-1989) for restructuring British Coal– but decreased overall. Moreover, these grants can be considered transitional (Michaelis 1997).

Table 3: Financial Support to British Coal, 1982 to 1994

(in million Pound Sterling)

Year	Grants	Price Support	Total PSE[1]	Other[2]
82-83	385	217	640	248
83-84	888	587	1513	494
84-85	2232	205	2437	423
85-86	71	904	975	1100
86-87	306	1094	1400	1232
87-88	219	1545	1764	827
88-89	2986	1502	4488	511
89-90	1205	1200	2425	1258
90-91	12	1163	1175	433
91-92	28	1101	1129	694
92-93	21	1061	1082	857
93-94	12	212	225	597

1) Producer Subsidy Equivalent, including special grant for write-off of assets
2) Assistance, not benefiting current production

Source: IEA, 1991,1994, 1995; Michaelis, 1997

It should be noted that these figures do not reflect all the changes in support. They do not include many other effects of changes in institutional arrangements, nor do they cover support to other energy forms.

Environmental Effects

Vollebergh (1998) has summarised a number of case studies, following a standardised framework for analysis. His findings as far as the UK is concerned are reported below.

The *focus* in the UK case study is the effect of the removal of support measures (subsidies and market distortions) in the UK electricity industry on carbon dioxide (CO_2), sulphur dioxide (SO_2) and nitric oxide (NO_x) emissions. These effects were analysed through the impact of support removal on supply decisions in the electricity supply industry (ESI). The *method* used was a simulation analysis of cost efficient power generation decisions using projections of energy use and CO_2 emissions employed by the UK government. The major characteristics of this study are summarised in Table 4.

Table 4: Support Removal in the Electricity Sector in the UK

	Examples	Mechanisms explaining environmental effects of support reduction
	Characteristics of support measures:	
Producer subsidies	- Purchase obligations for coal inputs through long-run contracts (negative subsidy to ESI); - Fossil fuel levy to finance excess market price of nuclear energy; - Capital facilities to nuclear power plants (low Required Rate of Return, limited liability); - High R&D funding to nuclear power.	- Capacity planning for ESI dominated by fuel costs; - Penetration of environmentally less damaging gas technology (CCGT) due to the higher net-of-subsidy price for coal; - Low RRR essential to capital intensive plants (like coal and nuclear power plants); - Increased electricity supply (due to the artificially high selling prices including subsidies).
Consumer subsidies	- No VAT on electricity.	- Increased prices through raising VAT leads to lower consumer demand for electricity.
	Characteristics of the recipient sector:	
Electricity producers	- Transitory phase from monopolistic ESI and input delivering industries (coal, gas) towards privatised and market-based industry.	- Lack of competition creates over-investment in generating capacity and therefore high-priced electricity.
	Circumstances:	
Environmental policy	- Flue Gas Desulpherisation (FGD) required (for UK to meet acid rain agreements); - Upper limit on gas consumption by the ESI; - No CO_2 policy assumed.	- Competitiveness of gas simply due to high efficiency of CCGT technology and low (net-of-subsidy) fuel cost (at current prices).
Subsidy phase-out assumed in the status quo	- Considerable, though gradual, phase-out already agreed upon in practice; - and included in the reference scenario.	- Effects shown relative to unsubsidised reference scenario; - Reference path already includes non-renewal of coal contracts (reducing SO_2 and NO_x emissions considerably).

This study found that:

1. as found in other case studies, subsidies are crucial for power plant (investment) decisions through their impact on the relative prices of the various fuels;

2. if the pollution intensity of the status quo technology employed by the 'recipient sector' is high (e.g., based on coal), the removal of subsidies can reduce the negative environmental effects considerably;

3. subsidies to long-run marginal costs (especially capital facilities) prevent the penetration of environmentally less damaging technologies as (currently) the environmentally malign technologies tend to be more capital intensive;

4. the savings from emission reductions due to phase-out of support tend to dominate downstream indirect effects through lower electricity prices;

5. lack of competition due to monopolistic power supply causes over-investment in the recipient industry.

Michaelis (1997) estimated the effects on CO_2 emissions. He finds that the monetary equivalent of the distortions of grants, price support and VAT rates on electricity below the general rate only —not taking into account the effects of below market required rate of return to investment for the ESI — amounted to US$ 2.5 million per annum (various years 1988-95). He finds that removal of the support would reduce CO_2 emissions by a range of 0-40 million tonnes (equal to 0-8% of the emissions of the concerned sector). These figures represent differences between various support reducing scenarios, compared with the base line scenario in which support was assumed to be neither removed nor reduced.

5.0   Conclusions

1. Unleashing market forces can have significant effects on both the efficiency of the economy as well as the improvement of the environment. *Institutional arrangements*, hindering technical change, will also block the road towards environmentally less harmful energy supply.. *Financial* support may equally hinder technical change and lock-in environmentally harmful practices. An example is the institutional arrangements and support measures that hinder (or have hindered) the application of more efficient CHP technologies.

2. In general the economic and environmental effects of institutional arrangement and financial support, however significant, can be difficult to predict and to quantify, since they depend largely on technical and organisational changes that will be brought about by many economic agents. An evaluation of changes that are likely to result from financial and non-financial (institutional) support reduction or removal and that render themselves to quantitative estimations, suggest several general conclusions:

3. Support can be ineffective in achieving its economic objectives (employment, growth, equity), while being harmful to the environment, depending on the relative elasticities of demand and supply. Adequate information on these elasticities can help to select those forms of support that should be prioritised for reduction or removal.

4. In the energy sector, two forms of financial support are likely to be *especially* harmful for the environment, both because of their magnitude as well as their immediate effect on environmentally harmful practices:

   - *market price support and*

   - *low discount rates, low required rates of return on investment and corporate income tax reliefs.*

REFERENCES

IEA (1996): The Role of IEA Governments in Energy: 1996 Update. IEA. Paris.

Michaelis, L. (1996): "Case Study on Electricity in the U.K." in OECD Environmental Implications of Energy and Transport Subsidies Volume 2: Supports to the Coal Industry and the Electricity Sector. OECD/GD(97)155. OECD. Paris.

OECD (1996): *Subsidies and Environment: Exploring the Linkages*. OECD. Paris.

OECD (1997a): *Reforming Energy and Transport Subsidies: Environmental and Economic Implications*. OECD. Paris.

OECD (1997b): *OECD Report on Regulatory Reform: Synthesis Report*. OECD. Paris.

OECD (forthcoming): *Improving the Environment Through Reducing Subsidies Parts I, II and Part III*. OECD. Paris.

Pieters, J.H.M. and Mountford, H. (forthcoming): "Can We Tell a Perverse Subsidy if We See One? in *Greening the Budget*. Edward Elgar, Cheltenham Glos, UK.

Ruijgrok, E. and Oosterhuis, F. (1997): *Energy Subsidies in Western Europe*. Greenpeace International. Amsterdam.

Steenblik, R.P. (1995): "A Note on the Concept of 'Subsidy'" in *Energy Policy*, Vol. 23, No. 6, pp. 483-484.

Steenblik, R.P. and Coroyannakis, P. (1995): "Reform of Coal Policies in Western Europe and Central Europe: Implications for the Environment" in *Energy Policy*, Vol. 23, No. 6, pp. 537-553.

Verbruggen, H. and Oosterhuis, F. (forthcoming): "Competitiveness and Reduction of Support Measures to Industry: The Prisoners' Dilemma" in OECD *Improving the Environment Through Reducing Subsidies (Part III)*. OECD. Paris.

Vollebergh, H. (forthcoming): "Energy Support Measures and Their Environment Effects: Decisive Parameters for Subsidy Removal" in OECD *Improving the Environment Through Reducing Subsidies (Part III)*. OECD. Paris.

REFORM OF SUBSIDIES TO THE ENERGY SECTOR: THE EXPERIENCE OF RUSSIA

Alexander Golub and Elena Strukova
Environmental Policy Consultants, Russia

with contributions from E. Gurvich and E. Tsigelnik

1.0   Introduction and Context

1.1   The Energy Sector in the Russian Economy

Russia has significant deposits of mineral resources including fossil fuels and natural gas. In this century the main attention of the Soviet Government was aimed at ensuring a sufficient energy supply for the needs of basic industries and the military sector. The significant role of energy resources in the Russian economy is clear from the high level of energy intensity. This is illustrated by Gurvich et al. (1995, pg. 13), who compare energy intensity in Russia with other economies.

Table 1: GDP and Energy Consumption of the European Regional Aggregates (1990)

	A	B	EEU	West-CIS	Russia	Rest of ex-USSR
GDP, billion $88	4900	540	260	130	350	80
PPP*-GDP, billion $87	3870	670	610	370	1030	240
GDP per capita, thousand $	16	4.6	2	1.9	2.4	1.2
PPP-GDP per capita, thousand $	12.6	5.7	4.7	5.7	7	3.5
Primary energy consumption, MTOE	1065	182	382	269	832	205
TOE per capita	3.5	1.5	2.9	4.1	5.7	3
KgOE per 1 $ GDP	0.22	0.34	1.45	2.1	2.35	2.49
KgOE per 1 $ PPP-GDP	0.28	0.27	0.63	0.72	0.8	0.85

Notes: * = purchasing power parity
TOE = tons oil equivalent
A refers to the EEC 9 (Germany includes former GDR)
B refers to Greece, Ireland, Portugal, Spain
EEU refers to Albania, Bulgaria, Czech Republic, Estonia, Hungary, Latvia, Lithuania, Poland, Romania, Slovak Republic, ex-Yugoslavia
West-CIS refers to Belarus, Moldova, Ukraine
Rest of USSR refers to Trancaucusis, Central Asia, Mongolia

It is clear from Table 1 that direct comparison of energy intensities per unit of GDP produces misleading conclusions: the figure for Russia appears to be 10.7 times higher than that for the European Union, which is unrealistic. The picture becomes clearer when GDP is corrected by PPP (purchasing power parity) multiplier (see Table 1). Then it is about 3 times higher than in Western Europe.

Since 1990 the energy intensity of the Russian economy increased by about 20% due to the economic crisis, low energy prices, structural changes of the economy to the benefit of basic industries and low payment discipline of the energy consumers (calculation based on data in IEA, 1995, pp.50) . Based on the official forecast contained in the energy strategy of Russia developed in 1994, energy intensity should decline by 9 % in 2010 in comparison with 1990.

At the same time, continued exploitation of fossil fuels is important to ensure export earnings. The share of mineral products (including fuels) in export earnings was about 50 % (from 1992 to 1996 it reduced from 52.1 % to 48 %) (OECD, 1997, pp. 257).

The demand for primary energy in Russia in 1990 is shown in Table 2 (Gurvich et al., 1995, pp.12):

Table 2: Primary Energy Demand in Russia, 1990

	MTOE	%
Oil	245	27.5
Gas	320	36
Coal	180	20.5
Primary power	125	14
Total	890	100

Projected energy demand in 2010 was also estimated by these authors as shown in Table 3.

Table 3: Projected Primary Energy Demand, 2010 (%)

Coal	Gas	Oil products	Primary power
15.5%	55.2%	20.1%	9.2%

The data above is almost the same as that cited in IEA, (1995, pp.55).

Table 4 is based on data from the Energy Strategy of Russia, prepared in 1994. It includes energy supply projections out to 2010.

Table 4: Energy Supply

	1990 (MTOE)	1990 (%)	2010 (MTOE)	2010 (%)
Oil	516	40	340	28
Gas	526	41	705	58
Coal	184	14	105	9
Primary power	63	5	64	5
Total	1289	100	1214	100

2.0   Economic Reforms In The Energy Sector

Reforms in the energy sector lagged that in other sectors. At present reforms are on-going but constrained by the slowness in payments for energy and the existence of natural monopolies.

The main element of reform was price liberalisation. Energy price control was the focus of the government's attention throughout the reform period. The main points of government policy in this area can be summarised as follows:

- energy prices and trade liberalisation lagged compared to most other products. Some of these prices are still controlled.

- the government endeavoured to raise the real price of energy with the intention to increase tax collected from this sector and to expand exports, reducing energy use by domestic sources.

Energy consumers were unprepared to accept the increase in fuel prices and tried to resist it. They resorted in particular to arrears in payment to exert pressure on producers. The paradox is that fuel producers in many cases were not interested in increasing their prices. Higher prices encouraged late payment for energy supplied as well as informal pressure from consumers. There was an easier way to increase revenues: to claim privileges from the government. This approach far overweighed losses from the lower domestic energy prices. These circumstances made energy prices develop rather inconsistently.

The main points of price control in the energy sector during 1991-1994 are briefly presented below.

New wholesale prices were introduced in January 1991. They implied higher than average price increases for fuels. At the same time, the price system was made more flexible by putting into practice a new category of "negotiated" prices. These were agreed by suppliers and consumers and then reported to the Price Committee, instead of being set by the latter (as regular prices). The negotiated prices could not be applied to the energy sector, so oil, gas and coal were cheaper (in real terms) in 1991 than in the previous year.

At the beginning of 1992 most prices were liberalised. Fuel prices remained regulated, but were twice significantly raised. Oil prices were almost fully liberalised in September 1992 (profitability was limited to 50% of costs, but this constraint proved to be of minor importance). The same refers to oil products. In October-November 1992, oil prices reached their peak. Nevertheless, fuel prices decreased over the next two years. This can be explained by insufficient demand from a domestic industrial sector undergoing restructuring and the effect of government quotas on oil exports. In addition, users and producers had common interests here as noted above.

Coal prices were freed in July 1993. In August 1993 they increased by more than four-fold but then changed approximately in line with inflation. Delivery prices increased more significantly because of rising transportation costs.

Gas prices still remain under government control. The relevant decree, linking price changes to the reported industry wholesale price index, is still in effect.

Electricity prices are controlled although their establishment is decentralised. These prices are reviewed on a regular basis by special regional boards, which include spokespersons for producers, users, and local authorities. As a result agreed prices are set by the boards, taking into account operating and capital costs.

In order to improve energy pricing and to make the energy sector a substantial source of budget revenue, the government introduced excise-type taxes for oil, oil products, and gas. Several other taxes were also adopted, such as a royalty for oil and gas extraction, and a road tax for refinery products.

Domestic fuel prices were significantly affected by the regulations governing energy export. Oil, gas, and coal enterprises were given the right to export fuels on their own account and to retain the extra profits. Only in 1995 were constraints on export volumes eliminated. There were export quotas for oil and oil products before this date.

A large difference arose in 1992 between the prices of fuel for export and for domestic use. This did not matter before when all exports were totally controlled by the government. With trade being decentralised, export duties on exporters were introduced to cover the gap between domestic and world market prices. They amounted to $30/ton for oil in 1993, and $25/ton in mid-1995. In 1993, major exemptions from export duties were introduced.

Another important component of market reforms was institutional reform. The principal governmental agencies changed in both their number and functions. The State Planning Committee was transformed into the Ministry of Economy and given more analytical functions. It no longer had the task to set production targets for the different economic sectors. In the energy sector, the Ministry of Fuel and Energy supervises the oil, gas, and coal industries and the non-nuclear energy sector. Nuclear energy production is the responsibility of the Ministry of Nuclear Energy. Electricity production is mainly carried out by the Federal Joint Stock Company "RAO UES".

The privatisation process has been based on the 1992 "Law on privatisation of state and municipal enterprises". Almost all enterprises were transformed into joint stock companies with gradual distribution of shares to private parties. Some shares remain in the ownership of the state represented by the Real Estate Committee. Privatisation was very intensive in the oil sector. About 300 oil production and processing enterprises were transformed into joint stock companies with 38 % of their shares controlled by holdings. The biggest holding "Rosneft" is 100% state owned. There were several attempts to sell it, but the process was hindered by the drop in world oil prices and the corresponding fall in the valuation of Rosneft's assets. Other holding companies have a much lower share of state ownership (less than 50 %).

Privatisation in the coal sector was hindered by the very low profitability of coal production. About 300 coal mines became joint stock companies. They are mostly controlled by the state holding company "Rosygol", which is responsible for restructuring the coal industry.

Natural gas production and distribution is controlled by the state joint stock company "Gasprom". This company is formally under the direct supervision of the state. However, its executive bodies are autonomous and pursue monopolistic policies.

"RAO UES" controls 35% of electricity production (including the largest power and hydro stations) and 100% of electricity transmission. It is seeking a majority position in electricity production that is currently under the supervision of regional electricity companies. Monopolistic behaviour is evident here as well.

Because of the monopolistic character of the energy sector in Russia the major task was to create a policy framework that supported competition. However, the policy succeeded only in the oil sector. The coal sector has important problems related to the low profitability of coal production, and the relative ease of switching to other fuel sources. The natural gas and electricity sectors still behave as natural monopolists.

Further restucturation is hindered by payment crises afflicting the Russian economy. These crises create preconditions for cross-sector subsidies and governmental subsidies to the energy sector.

1.3   Non-payment Crisis And Its Implications For The Energy Sector

The combination of a high energy intensity and increased energy prices results in financial problems for enterprises and impacts upon their economic performance. A high level of non-payment for energy has led to the introduction of adjustment measures. For example, the government provides subsidies to the energy sector in different forms. At the economic sector level, cross-sector subsidies are apparent. We consider below the main subsidies to the energy sector in Russia.

Along with direct subsidies from the state there are a number of indirect factors which have the same impact on the economic performance of enterprises in the energy sector. In the Russian economy the following mechanisms are the most notable.

First, subsidies to enterprises in the energy sector during transfers to and from public organisations due to soft budget constraints. The subsidy appears as a result of an overestimation of energy prices by the suppliers of public organisations. By overestimating the price (for example, by sale of poor quality fuel at the price of high-quality fuel), the enterprise lowers the risk of non-payment. They incorporate in the price of actual production the premium for possible non-payment by some buyers, especially public sector organisations, whose potential for non-payment is greatest. If all public organisations pay their bills late then the benefit resulting from the price overestimation accrues to the supplier.

Subsidies could also be generated through overexpenditure of fuel and energy by public organisations. They do not care about cost effective performance, and exceed limits for energy use. Both factors have implications for energy production. For example, the potential for public organisations to save energy was calculated as 30% of their heat consumption and up to 15-17% of electricity consumption. The size of this kind of subsidy cannot be calculated precisely. An indirect comparison of public enterprise's payments with payments made by commercial organisations is possible, however, categorising them into groups according to sector, production volume and other parameters. The energy sector is the basic supplier of public enterprises and therefore subsidies due to soft budget constraints could be easily identified here.

Second, delaying payments on loans and other obligations. In this case the enterprise itself determines the size of the subsidy, the exact period in which subsidies will be given and terms of pay back (if any) depending on the financial state of the enterprise. Basic components of this type of subsidy are:

- difference between delaying payments to suppliers and delayed debts of buyers (cross-sector subsidies);

- delaying payment of wages to the staff of enterprises;

- delaying tax payments.

Third, it is possible to define a subsidy equal to delayed payments for credits and loans. In this case the enterprise does not pay the principal and interest to banks, using resources like subsidies.

Fourth, the most obvious subsidy from the state is deferred payments. The deferral is in the form of a contract between an enterprise and the Ministry of Finance where the enterprise is temporarily exempted from payment of past taxes under condition of duly meeting the current tax demand. In fact the state provides a subsidy to the enterprise for the amount of unpaid taxes. According to the Law on the Federal Budget such deferrals on debts are given annually for a period not exceeding six months. In each new year it is necessary to sign a new contract for granting the deferral. Although there are some longer contracts (under the Decree of the President of RF N65), their number is quite small. At the beginning of a year, the number of contracts is less than in subsequent months. The number of such contracts in the fuel sector is much higher than in the industry sector. In the electricity sector, the number is small. Thus, subsidisation of the fuel sector is more intensive than in industry or in electricity generation.

Fifth, direct subsidies from the state budget. They are provided based on the amounts assigned by the Law on the Federal Budget. Within the energy sector the major share is for the coal sector (96.7% in 1997; 99.7 % in 1998). Resources have to be spent for social programs, closing of unprofitable mines with social support for unemployed miners. Thus the major part of direct subsidies is targeted on the reduction of social tension, not to production. Thus we should exclude direct payments to the coal sector in our analysis of subsidies.

Sixth, enterprises receive subsidies through participation in mutual offsets for tax payments to the federal budget. This can occur in two ways. One is by signing fictitious contracts to get a discount. In this case, a profitable enterprise buys debts at a discounted price in a loss-making enterprise. The discount represents the price for transforming the debts into cash. With a mutual offset the debtor pays back the debt completely. It receives the discount for free, which can be interpreted as a type of subsidy. The second way is during repayment of a future debt. The scheme works as follows: within the framework of one agreement the debtor enterprise must provide information from the tax authorities about debts to the federal budget (in amount T), a certificate of verification of the public enterprise and other documents to confirm the debts of a public enterprise to a loss-making enterprise (in amount A). Then debts equal to the minimum between amounts T and A will be extinguished. If T = A then the loss-making enterprise will clear the whole debt within the framework of a single agreement. By signing contracts with several public enterprises under different agreements, a loss-making enterprise could receive more money than it owes. The excess is then paid into the federal budget against future non-payments and the loss-making enterprise is then exempted from taxes to the federal budget for a certain period. This approach could be considered as a form of subsidy.

Enterprises in the energy sector have the possibility to carry out offsets because they are the main suppliers to public organisations and, because of that, the main creditors of the state budget. For the energy sector special offsets were carried out as well as offsets of current tax payments. Therefore, this sector receives the majority of subsidies. However, an accurate figure of their value is impossible to obtain because of the confidentiality of the data and the illegal character of most of these subsidies.

Since 1995-1996 it is obvious that there are particular schemes of subsidy in Russia with no comparison elsewhere. With more accurate information it is possible to produce indirect estimations of parts of the subsidies received by enterprises. However, the essential part of subsidies comes from the "grey" sector. Approaches to reveal the full extent of subsidies are needed.

2.0   Reform Of Subsidies And Other Support Measures To The Energy Sector

Subsidies have a theoretical rationale if they are given to sectors with significant positive external effect. As an example one could consider state support for social programs or environmental projects. The same is true for subsidies to environmental funds in Eastern Europe, different types of support from trust-funds in the US, etc. These subsidies are Pigovian ones, named after the economist who proposed the internalisation of external effects through taxes or subsidies.

Unfortunately, in practice different subsidies operate. They result in an artificial reduction of natural resource prices in the cost structure of goods and services. A well-known example is pricing of primary energy sources. Below we describe the negative impact of such subsidies and benefits from their elimination.

Direct and indirect subsidies to basic industries were common in Russia until 1990. The critical element was low prices for raw materials in the planned economy. The major part of rental income from natural resources use was replaced by the central allocation of raw materials and reduced prices for inputs. Essentially, there was a hidden subsidy to consumers of raw materials. Direct subsidies also existed, for example, in the coal sector, but they were much less. Thus, we deal with three types of subsidies:

- direct subsidies to consumers or producers;

- Pigovian subsidies;

- hidden subsidies (reduced prices for natural resources).

The first two types of subsidies have the same result in theory. The main issue is to calculate their external effects. As we noted above the rationale for subsidies is internalisation of the positive external effects. For example, pollution abatement projects might receive subsidies if they are useful not only to the implementing enterprise, but for society as a whole. Subsidies could be either to the producer or consumer. We show both types of subsidies in Figure 1.

Figure 1: Pigovian Subsidies to Consumer or Producer

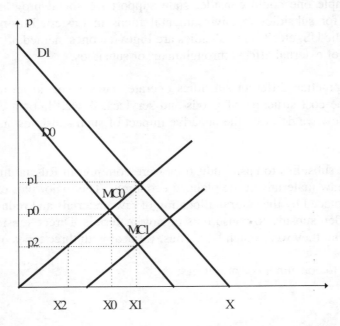

p = prices; D0 = initial demand for energy resources; D1 = subsidised demand of consumer;
MC0 = initial marginal costs for energy resources production;
MC1 = marginal costs after subsidy to producer.

If we would like to get from optimal point X0 to X1 (society prefers X1 to X0) then we could either subsidise the consumer to increase demand and move the demand curve upwards. Another option is to give a subsidy to the producer, reducing costs for commodity production. Thus we will reduce price and move the supply curve down.

In both cases the growth in demand is the same. The difference is in the market price. In the first case demand will increase with the growth of price to p1, whereas in the second case price will reduce to p2.

The third type of subsidy has a different explanation. Both in the centrally planned economy, and in transition period (1992-1994) a variety of extensive energy subsides existed in Russia. They were created by:

- direct budget subsidies for coal producers, amounting to about 1% of GDP during 1990-1994;

- price controls (though its scope is gradually being reduced and only covers gas prices and, to some extent, electricity prices at present);

- export quotas (eliminated in 1995);

- export duties on oil, oil products, and gas (for instance, export duty on oil amounted to $25/ton in mid 1995);

194

- exemptions from export duties, and some other taxes (thus subsidising domestic supplies from trade revenues); and

- setting preferential gas and electricity prices for households, covered from local budgets or by charging other users higher prices.

Gurvich et al. (1995) provide some estimates of such subsidies. Based on conservative calculations, subsidies from lower energy prices were equal to 8.4% of Russia's GDP in 1990.

Table 5: Domestic Energy Prices (for Industrial Users) Compared to World Market Prices (1990)

	Domestic delivery price, $/toe (nominal exch.rate)	Domestic/World market price (nominal exch. rate), %	Domestic/World market price (PPP-based conversion), %
Oil	52	34	27
Gasoline	310	154	119
Diesel oil	101	63	50
Heavy fuel	63	79	62
Gas	56	47	36
Coal	43	104	81
Electricity	340	95	74

Source: Estimates, based on Russian Federation Ministry of Energy reports and IEA statistics.

Gurvich et al. (1995) proposed an approach to calculate unsubsidised energy prices. The subsidy-free price levels for oil and gas were assessed based on net-back prices. They converted border prices from dollars to roubles using purchasing power parity (PPP) rather than the current nominal exchange rate. World market relative prices were then used as a baseline assuming that in the long run the exchange rate converges to the PPP level. The unsubsidised prices for refinery products were evaluated by comparing the costs of unsubsidised crude oil supplies with the price of imported oil products. Projected prices for coal were derived from their assumed proportions to the gas prices (for which coal is a close substitute). For power, subsidy-free prices were defined using production costs for thermal stations under unsubsidised fuel inputs.

Table 6: Unsubsidised Price levels for Industry (1990=100%) in per cent

	1994 (actual)	1995	2000	2005	2010
Crude Oil	187	247	279	299	327
Oil Products	156	196	185	175	168
Natural Gas	128	196	212	236	263
Coal	161	246	246	246	275
Power	188	238	250	258	272

Subsidies in the form of artificially low prices are far from Pigovian subsidies. A forced price reduction to p2 without direct subsidies to the producer and no move down of his marginal cost curve supply level should reduce the level to X2 (see Figure 1). However that is not necessarily a consequence of price regulation in a planned economy where there is no competition in the energy sector. Under such conditions producers will regulate themselves the profitability level of the whole sector. Only in this case both producers and consumers are interested in such subsidies (See Figure 2).

Figure 2: Subsidies through Price Reduction

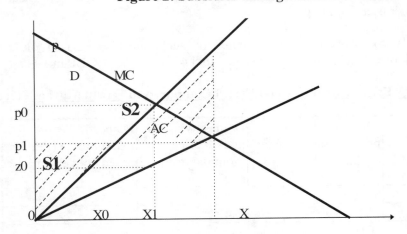

Under perfect competition the optimal sale is X0 and the optimal price is p0. Economic rent is (p0-z0)*X0. If the producer is not interested in gaining more profit and his main concern is to increase production volume then he may increase production to X1. The price will then drop to p1. Then the rent, S1, will be used to cover losses shown as S2. S2 occurred due to oversupply in the market. The hidden subsidy was thus distributed among both consumers of energy resources and loss-making enterprises in the energy sector.

Privatisation and demonopolization of the energy sector hinders the mechanism described above. The coal sector is the best example of failure of the subsidisation mechanism. Demonopolization is occurring very quickly in this sector. The natural gas sector is still a monopoly and the scheme still operates there.

Price discrimination was associated with the above mentioned mechanism. Consumers had unequal access to the hidden subsidies. At the same time, price discrimination helped to subsidise householders. Subsidies associated with earmarking also had features of Pigovian subsidies.

Thus subsidy reforms are not yet complete in Russia. We can identify a number of basic elements of reforms :

- elimination of energy subsidies under hard budget constraints;

- increase in pollution fees;

- control of greenhouse gases emissions.

3.0   Modelling Of Subsidies Elimination

Here we essentially simplify the problem and consider only hidden subsidies. Growth of real price for energy resources ensure subsidies elimination.

196

An input-output model was used to analyse the consequences of subsidy elimination. The model had already been used in a number of studies for OECD, the Harvard Institute for International Development (HID), and the World Bank. We present a short description of the model below. Further details can be found in Gurvich et al. (1995).

3.1   Model Description

The analysis is based upon an economy projection model developed by the World Bank Environment Policy Department. It is aimed at describing the performance of an economy in transition. The model incorporates 3 major components:

- simulation of economic development, including capital turnover process,

- estimation of emissions (both from industrial sources and from households),

- simulation of the impact of alternative environmental policy tools.

The general assumption of the model is that after market reforms start, gradual replacement of outdated technologies with more efficient modern technologies will take place. The latter are characterised by less resource use and improved pollutants removal. Lower emission levels can be expected as a result of carrying out market reforms. During the transition period "old" and "new" equipment operate in parallel. Their economic performance is described by input-output tables. As a starting point for the "old" equipment actual data on specific use of materials, energy, and labour in the Russian economy in 1990 were used. For "new" technologies corresponding data referring to the US, the UK, western Europe or Spain can be utilised.

The capital turnover process is simulated as follows. "Old" equipment undergoes depreciation by regular ageing, and lack of competitiveness due to trade liberalisation. Fixed investments are directed to those sectors where available capacities are insufficient to produce goods in sufficient quantity to meet expected demand. It is assumed that all investments are in "new" efficient technologies.

Emissions from production activities are divided into two groups. First, those related to fuels combustion. Rates, differentiated by sector and fuel, are given specifying emissions of major pollutants resulting from the use of 1 ton of oil equivalent (t.o.e.) of a particular fuel. Second, those related to processing. This is analysed on the basis of given emissions per $1000 output in each industry (at world market prices). Emissions produced by households are based on the volume of fuels used, other sources and to the population size. Emission rates have been estimated for Poland. It is suggested that technologies used there are similar to those used in Russia.

The following economic responses are incorporated into the model:

- production at the "old" capacity adjusts to changing relative prices. The adjustment takes place at two levels. First, the structure of energy, materials and labour is adjusted depending on their relative price levels. Next, industries modify the proportion in which various fuels are used according to their prices. In both cases reactions are evaluated based on addilog cost functions.

- energy price increases leads to accelerated turnover of equipment. This effect is assumed to be the more pronounced the greater the gain to an industry sector by replacing old technologies with new ones. The model reflects two effects: some proportion of equipment can become unprofitable with rising fuel prices, and incentives increase to use new energy-saving equipment instead of the old.

- higher energy prices for households result in a contraction in consumption, controlled by demand elasticities.

- enterprises may respond to pollution fees by investing in cleaner technologies. It is suggested that the result will be a fall in emission rates to levels typical for "new" equipment. The share of retrofitted "old" equipment is fixed as an element of the overall model. This share is differentiated by sector in proportion to the percent of pollution fees in production costs.

The model provides long-term projections for the following values:

- output volumes by sector;

- energy use;

- emissions of major pollutants;

- emissions composition by source (by sector, by enterprise type, by fuel burnt, etc.).

Some macroeconomic assumptions are presented below. The major assumptions on the GDP path were as follows:

- the trend of GDP decline stops in 1997, and growth resumes in 1998;

- annual per capita growth rate is 4.5% by 2000 and remains at this level to 2010.

Additional assumptions about the transformation of GDP structure and trade balance were also included.

Comparing unsubsidised levels of energy prices, estimated above, we come to the conclusion that the elimination of subsidies requires substantial by increasing most prices above their 1990 level. On the other hand, we established that in 1994 most energy prices for industrial users were already higher in real terms than in 1990. Taking this into account, we considered 3 levels of energy prices for industrial users:

- unsubsidised levels;

- levels actually reached in 1994; and

- initial levels in 1990.

Real energy prices for households in 1994 were lower than in 1990. But this fact hardly affected household demand (except for gasoline) because the formerly low prices did not really constrain consumption. Hence only two price levels were considered for households, namely the unsubsidised levels and the initial levels of 1990.

Eliminating subsidies from energy prices can be implemented by including into prices increased rent payments or excise taxes, abolishing tax exemptions, and liberalising trade. Higher prices imply higher budget revenues, which raises distributional issues. These revenues can be partly allocated to environment protection. The major share, however, can be used for two purposes. First, to reduce an existing budget deficit and thereby contribute to economic stabilisation. This approach can have a substantial adverse effect on industry. Currently, most enterprises have limited capacity to adjust to higher costs: their financial "health" is very poor, there is little flexibility to modify technologies, and investments are scarce. Consequently, uncompensated raising of energy prices would result in considerable output decline.

Second, to cut other taxes by the amount of extra revenue gained from the higher energy prices. This will reduce the impact on the industrial sector. Our view is that a mixed approach should be taken. Ruling out explicit subsidies in the coal industry can decrease federal expenditures and thus lower the budget deficit by 1.3% of the GDP. At the same time it may be possible to compensate for extra taxes and rents for other fuels by reducing general taxes (income, profit tax, etc.).

4.0   Scenario Development

The parameters in the scenarios prepared under the modelling exercise differ from each other in several respects:

- availability or absence of subsidies;

- the amount of pollution fees;

- presence or absence of a CO_2 tax.

Two options were considered. The first case was based on fees as of 1994. The second case (designated as "high fees") is where the 1990 level is not only retained in real terms but also is increased 3 times. This implies raising the real charge rate about 70 times compared to its actual 1994 level.

In the scenario S7, where a CO_2 tax is introduced its rate is raised in several steps during the period 1995-2000 up to approximately $10/ton. In scenario S8, the CO_2 tax is twice as high as in the previous case.

Table 7 presents the scenarios for which simulations were made.

Table 7: Simulation Scenarios

SCENARIO	SUBSIDIES	Pollution Fees			CO2 Tax
		TSP	SO2	NOx	
S1	Retained (at the 1990 level)	l	l	l	No
S2	Reduced (at the 1994 level)	l	l	l	No
S3	Eliminated	l	l	l	No
S4	Reduced	h	h	h	No
S5	Reduced	l	l	h	No
S6	Reduced	l	h	l	No
S7	Reduced	l	l	l	Up to $10/ton
S8	Reduced	l	l	l	Up to $20/ton

Key:

"l" stands for fees at the 1994 level;
"h" implies that the real fee rate is 3 times the 1990 level.
S1 is the baseline scenario.
TSP = total suspended particulate emissions

We noted above that subsidy elimination has major impacts. An increase in pollution fees would increase them. Below we analyse the effects of subsidy elimination and then consider additional implications associated with environmental regulation.

5.0   Impact of Subsidy Elimination

We compared the environmental effects from complete and partial subsidy elimination compared with the baseline scenario. In order to evaluate the impacts a comparison was carried out of scenarios S1, S2, and S3.

The forecasts of primary energy demand are presented in Figure 3. The energy use projection is affected by three major factors: real GDP trends, efficiency gains as new technologies replace old ones (see Figure 5) and adjustment to changing energy prices. The first factor accounts for energy demand growth after the year 2000. The second factor is responsible for decreasing GDP energy intensity in all scenarios (Figure 4). If economic stabilisation is achieved in the mid 1990-s and then growth resumes, a 21% decline in energy use can be expected by 2010 even if high subsidies are kept.

The elimination of energy subsidies influences energy use in two ways: accelerating the replacement of old technologies and restraining energy demand. The full impact of subsidy elimination amounts to half of the 'background effect' (so that energy demand falls to 32.5% of the initial level of 1990). Maintaining reduced subsidies, as observed in 1994, provides additional energy savings of only 3.6% of the initial level. In other words, the effect of retaining partial subsidies amounts to only one-third of the total effect of subsidy elimination.

Figure 3: Projected Primary Energy Use (1990=100%)

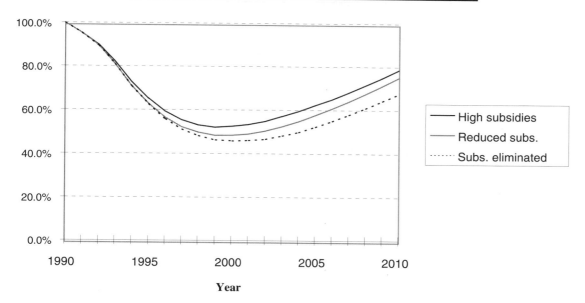

Figure 4: Projected Energy Intensity of GDP (1990=100%)

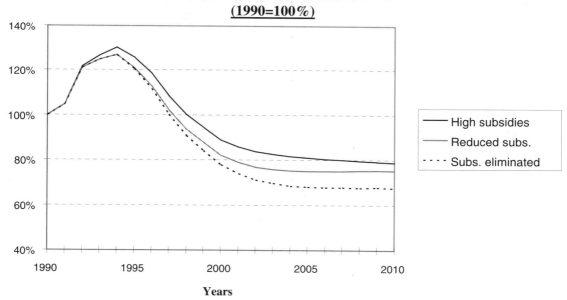

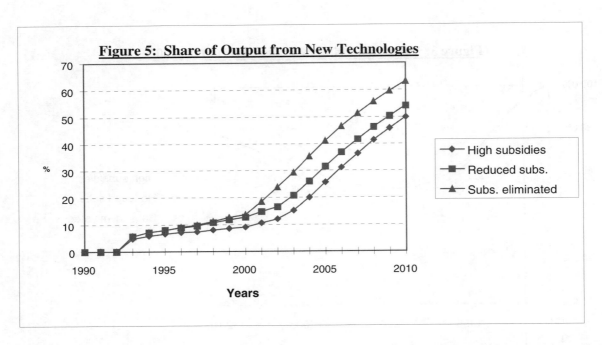

Figure 5: Share of Output from New Technologies

The elimination of subsidies results not only in a decrease in total energy demand but also in changes of fuels composition in the energy balance. As shown in Table 8, the share of coal in energy use declines whereas that of primary power and (to a minor extent) gas increase.

Table 8: Projected Fuel Composition in Primary Energy Demand for 2010

	Coal	Gas	Oil products	Primary power
High subsidies	17.0%	55.0%	20.1%	7.9%
Reduced subsidies	17.1%	54.7%	19.9%	8.2%
Subs. eliminated	15.5%	55.2%	20.1%	9.2%

The projected development of major pollutant emissions is presented in Figures 6 to 9. It is mainly affected by two factors: changing energy use, and new technologies with lower emission rates. The relative importance of these factors differs: the former is significant for NOx and CO_2, and the latter for SO_2 and TSP emissions. This accounts for the differences in the dynamics of their emissions. CO_2 and SO_2 emissions are estimated to grow after 2000, whereas NOx and total suspended particulate (TSP) emissions decrease or stabilise (if subsidies are retained). The projected emissions decline is shown in Table 9.

Figure 6: Projected TSP Emissions

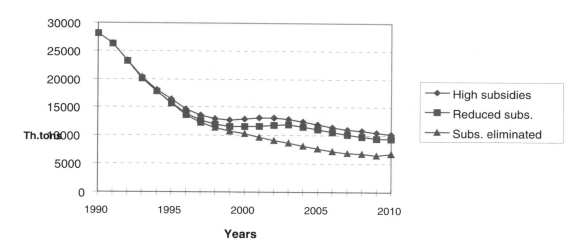

Figure 7: Projected SO$_2$ Emissions

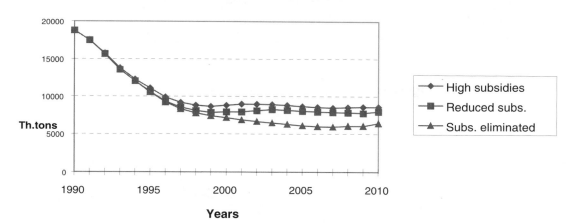

203

Figure 8: Projected NOx Emissions

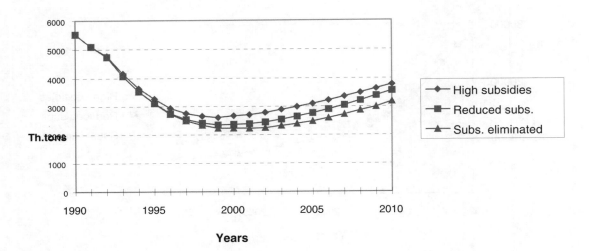

Table 9: Projected Level of Emissions in 2010 (1990=100%)

	TSP	SO,	NOx	CO,
High subsidies	36.3	45.8	68.5	73.1
Reduced subsidies	33.5	42.7	64.4	69.5
Subs. eliminated	24.1	34.3	57.4	61.7

Figure 9: Projected CO$_2$ Emissions

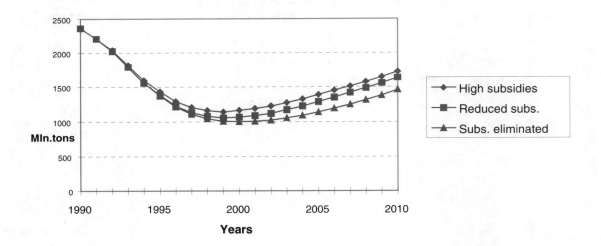

The general conclusion is that the elimination of subsidies produces an emissions decrease of 11-12% compared to their 1990 level, while maintaining reduced subsidies results in a 3-4% emissions drop.

The above simulation results demonstrate that the elimination of energy subsidies can have a beneficial impact on the environment. There is a reduction in emissions related to, *inter alia*, the generation of power and consumption of fuel. Lead emissions are also reduced. This reduction can be accounted for by the fact that higher fuel prices result in lower consumption of leaded fuels while favouring an increase in consumption of unleaded gasoline. Emissions of other pollutants, for instance, phosphorus, will be similar both in the baseline scenario and in the scenario where subsidies are removed.

6.0 Analysis of the Impact of Pollution Fees on Emissions

The model simulation gave us the possibility to analyse different scenarios of environmental management. A brief description of the existing environmental management system in Russia is presented here. The basic scenario for analysis is the same as above.

6.1 Environmental Management in Russia

Russia's system of environment management has developed over the last 25 years. There are two main periods of its development:

- administrative period (1964-1980), in which a number of legislative acts covering environmental protection and natural resource use were adopted.

- introduction of economic tools into environmental management practice after experimenting with pollution charges in 1989-1990 and under the new Environment Protection Act (1992).

Here we present only a few elements of the current system of environmental management. A more detailed description is to be found in Golub and Strukova (1995).

(i)   Environmental quality standards

The most important are Maximum Allowable Concentration (MAC) of hazardous substances in the atmosphere (water reservoirs, soils).   These standards establish maximum values for one-time concentrations and daily average concentrations. Air quality standards are divided into two sets, one for residential areas and another for industrial areas. Standards for industrial areas are stricter than those for residential areas. Introduced in 1969, MAC standards complied with medical requirements and were very severe. For example, the MAC for SO_2 according to GOST (state standard) is 0.05 mg/m^3, as compared to 0.26 mg/m^3 in the US. Such strict standards were practically unattainable. Based on the MAC values, Maximum Permissible Levels of Emissions (MPL) for enterprises (stationary sources of pollution) were established. Standards for concentrations of harmful substances in emissions from mobile sources were also set. However, in practice only automobile emissions of CO_2 have been controlled. MAC standards were applied to both new enterprises and existing ones. They were determined by the State Hydro-Meteorological Committee and the Ministry of Public Health. The strictness of the standards was offset by the lack of compliance. The most obvious example is the calculation of an MPL that does not take into account background pollution, the distribution of emissions and the total amount of emissions from other companies. Therefore real concentrations of harmful substances in the atmosphere exceed MAC's significantly. In addition, MPL's are difficult to use because, according to legislation, maximum allowed emissions are established for each source of emissions, that is, for each pipe. There are companies which have dozens of pipes, and the standards are set for each of them respectively. However, it would be more practical to consider the factory as a point source using the bubble principle. Analysis of this standardisation system is a separate issue which is beyond the scope of our research. It should be noted that many companies were not and are still not able to reach the MPL emissions standard. Therefore, after their introduction temporary standards were also set which have become *de facto* the emission control level. They have played a significant role in the process of introducing pollution charges.

(ii)   Pollution fees

From 1991, fees for air emissions, water discharges and solid wastes became the main element of environmental management in Russia. The rate of the fees was fixed by the state authorities (Resolution of the Russian Federation Council of Ministers, January 9, 1991) as per unit of emissions of the hazardous substances. There were two types of charges rates for water and air pollution: (i) for discharges within the appropriate MPL ;and (ii) for emissions above the MPL. Penalty fees for emissions above MPL were 5 times higher than the base rates.

As a result of the indexation carried out in 1993, a three-tier system of charges was established in practice: (i) charges for emissions within the MPL; (ii) charges for emissions that exceed the MPL but meet the temporary standards; and (iii) charges for emissions that exceed the temporary standards. Only the first two types of charges are relevant here. Because of the decline in production output practically all companies do not exceed the temporary emissions standards.

(iii)   Environmental funds

The system of environmental funds was established at the same time as pollution charges. These charges are the main source of income for the funds. Ten per cent of the collected revenue goes to the federal budget. The remaining 90% is distributed as follows: 60% goes to district environmental funds, 10% goes to the federal environmental fund and 30% is channelled to the regional environmental fund.

(iv)   Tax policy

Although there is a special provision in the Environmental Protection Law concerning tax discounts for firms undertaking pollution abatement, it is not implemented in practice. The same is true for the additional taxes for environmentally hazardous types of production and goods. Any proposals by the environmental authorities for tax discounts or additional taxes meets strong resistance from the Ministry of Finance or the industrial lobby in the Parliament, respectively. The only benefit which exists in practice is the reduction of charges by the amount invested by the company in nature protection.

6.2   Evaluating the Impact of Pollution Fees on Emissions

Here we take scenario S2 as a baseline, and compare scenarios of increased pollution fees with this scenario and with scenario S3 (subsidy elimination). The projected emissions levels in 2010 are presented in Table 10.

Table 10: Projected Level of Emissions in 2010 (1990=100%)

Scenario	SO2	NOx	CO2
S2	43%	64%	69%
S4	37%	59%	65%
S5	40%	62%	67%
S6	37%	60%	66%
S3	34%	57%	62%

These figures show that pollution payments result in a 6-7% drop in the initial emissions. Hence, they have about half the effect of eliminating subsidies. When combined with a partial reduction in subsidies, pollution payments exert a significant impact on emissions, comparable to the effect of subsidy elimination (though smaller than the latter).

Figures 10-12 show that the introduction of pollution fees has a much greater initial effect than subsidy elimination but by the end of the period it is inferior to the impact of subsidy elimination.

Figure 10: Projected SO$_2$ Emissions (000 tons)

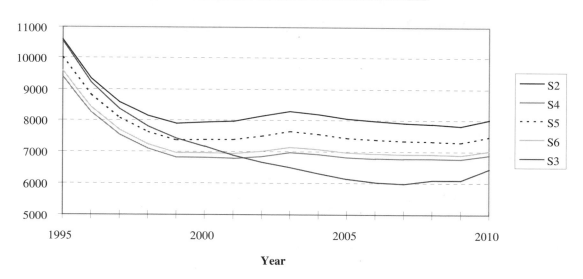

207

Figure 11: Projected NOx Emissions (000 tons)

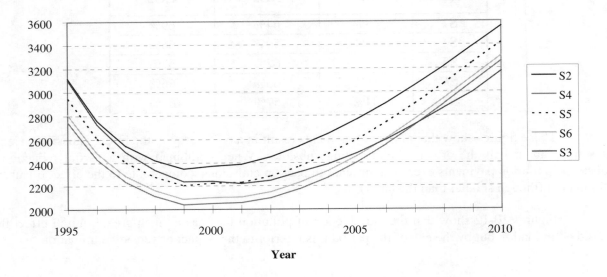

Figure 12: Projected CO₂ Emissions (mill. tons)

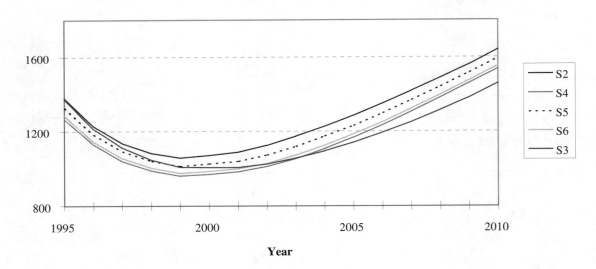

It is interesting to compare Figures 10 and 11. SO_2 emissions are decreasing not only when compared to 1990, but also when compared to 1995, i.e. emissions are decreasing throughout the entire period. The trend for NOx emissions changes after the year 2000.

Also, we can see that in scenario S3 (in which subsidies are eliminated) NOx emissions growth after the year 2000 is smoother than in the baseline scenario and in scenario S4 (in which pollution fees are introduced). It should also be noted that NOx curves in scenario S4 and in the baseline scenario (S2) are practically parallel. This means that in 1995 a certain effect appears because of the introduction of pollution fees. It affects performance throughout the entire period, but its impact is neither strengthening nor weakening. On the other hand, the elimination of subsidies results in emissions reduction with a longer-term character.

The factor could be related to the intensity of environmental activities (retirement of older plant, implementation of new environmental measures, use of cleaner technologies).

Pollution fees may encourage enterprises to move from end-of-pipe to cleaner technologies. In addition, the elimination of subsidies can support stronger interest in replacing older, more polluting and energy-intensive equipment. Such replacement is likely to be gradual. Thus, both the decrease of emissions followed by their future growth are slower than in scenario when fees are applied.

We now analyse CO_2 emissions (see Figure 12). In their orientation, they are very similar to the pattern of NOx emissions but the increase in CO2 emissions by the end of the period under consideration (2010) is steeper than that for NOx emissions. The explanation might be that NOx emissions are treated while CO2 emissions are not. NOx treatment technologies have certain limitations, however. For example, they do not apply to motor vehicles, which are likely to be the main source of increase in emissions. Emissions from motor vehicles are basically taken into account in the household sector.

The impact of the fee system on the emission characteristics of certain elements has also been considered, in particular the effect of increased charges for NOx and SO_2. Simulation results are presented in Figures 10-12. Projected SO_2 emissions, shown in Table 11 are somewhat unexpected.

Table 11: Projected SO_2 Emissions (1990=100%)

	No pollution fees	High pollution fees	High NOx tax only	High SO_2 tax only	Subsidies eliminated
1995	56.5%	50.1%	53.4%	51.1%	56.2%
2000	42.3%	36.3%	39.3%	37.1%	38.2%
2005	42.9%	36.3%	39.6%	37.2%	32.6%
2010	42.7%	36.7%	39.8%	37.4%	34.3%

An initial reduction of SO_2 emissions is more conspicuous when fees for all pollutants are introduced. This means that apart from having a direct impact, fees also have an indirect impact. In the scenario, the direct and indirect impacts are approximately equal in value.

Table 11 also shows the impact on SO_2 emissions from a tax on NOx. The results show that SO_2 emissions decline faster under the impact of a high NOx tax compared to the baseline scenario. Therefore, we can speak about a cross-impact of taxes on harmful emissions.

Comparing Figures 10 and 11 we conclude that an SO_2 tax has a more significant impact on CO_2 emission characteristics than one on NOx. In all probability, it can be accounted for by the fact that an SO_2 tax stimulates lower coal consumption.

7.0   Analysis of the Impact of a CO_2 Tax

At present Russia does not have a CO_2 tax. However, the possibility of introducing such a tax has been discussed several times by the government. In this context, we examined the implications through a scenario.

A CO_2 tax on pollutants such as NOx and SO_2 has a number of impacts. Emissions of such pollutants decrease faster than in the base scenario. However, for both SO_2 and NOx emissions, subsidy elimination would result in a stronger reduction of emissions by the end of the simulation period. The impact of the various pollution fees and the CO_2 tax do not differ significantly. The difference observed at the beginning of the simulation period (fees cause a sharper reduction) gradually disappears. It is almost equal to zero for NOx and is very small for SO_2 emissions. Fees result in a somewhat steeper drop in emissions of these pollutants compared to the CO_2 tax.   The CO_2 tax has a weaker initial impact than pollution fees but later their impact is equal. In essence, the CO_2 tax should have the same impact as subsidy elimination. Figure 13 indicates that this is not true. The reason is the need for the tax to be subject to indexation.

Figure 13: Projected CO_2 Emissions (Mill. tons)

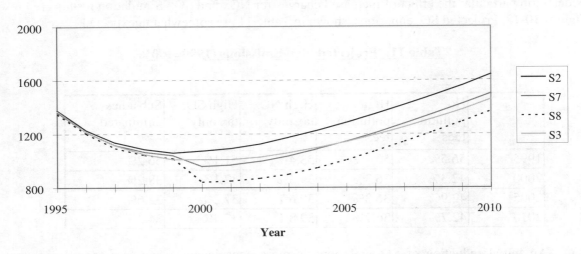

Analysis of CO_2 emissions characteristics in scenario S7 gives the impression that the tax does not provide a motivational impact. In order to test the sensitivity of the results to the tax rate, we doubled the rate in scenario S8. Figure 13 shows that CO_2 emissions are quite sensitive to the tax rate.

8.0   Other Benefits From Subsidy Elimination

8.1.   Potential Supply to Greenhouse Gas (GHG) Offsets Market

The economies in transition are potential GHG offset suppliers. It was assumed before the Kyoto Conference of Parties to the UN Framework Convention on Climate Change that these countries would become sellers of GHG offsets. The situation has now changed. Most of the economies in transition will probably have difficulties meeting their own obligations because their commitments under the Kyoto Protocol are stronger that anticipated (see Table 12).

The only large seller of GHG offsets in the early stage could be Russia (an Annex 1 country under the climate change convention). Optimistic forecasts of GHG emissions show some potential for emissions trading in other economies in transition (Czech Republic, Slovak Republic, Hungary and Poland) but in comparison with Russia and Ukraine their potential impact will be negligible. Thus, as a seller Russia might generate a considerable amount of money through emissions trading.

Table 12: Potential in the Period 2008-2012 under various factors: Russia (Unit is Gt CO_2)

Total Potential	3.92
Including:	
Due to macroeconomic factors	0.92
Due to policy measures and structural changes	1.54
Due to additional projects in energy and industry (joint implementation/activities implemented jointly)	1.12
Due to additional forest sequestration	0.34

Data presented in Table 12 are based on preliminary calculations. Policy responses include, but are not limited to, the introduction of a CO_2 tax, subsidy elimination, sector-specific bands, and emission permits allocation.

The Clean Development Mechanism (CDM) provided for in the Kyoto Protocol is likely to be of particular interest to developing countries since they could receive investments from developed countries for greenhouse gases emissions reduction. Countries such as China have great potential to implement energy saving projects and others aimed at the reduction of greenhouse gases emissions. Only the incremental costs for GHG reduction can be financed within the framework of the CDM. Elimination of subsidies will increase the internal rate of return of such projects.

8.2   Total Suspended Particulates (TSP) and their Health Effects

TSP emissions merit comment. The PM10 fraction of TSP is the main reason for increases in morbidity and mortality. Based on preliminary estimations about 8 % of mortality could be explained by the impact of this pollutant. Air pollution as a whole contributes about 20 % to mortality rates. Research by the Harvard Institute for International Development demonstrated that PM10 is the main pollutant practically in all cities where health risk analysis was carried on.

A faster reduction of TSP emissions, including PM10, is one of the results of subsidy elimination due to a reduction of coal in the energy balance. This reflects the fact that coal combustion produces a significant amount of TSP. At the same time pollution fees also have an impact on reducing TSP emissions. They create incentives to implement low-cost control measures.

9.0   Economic Effect Of Subsidy Reform Measures

9.1   Establishment Of Environmental Funds

From 1988 to 1990, fifty regions within the former Soviet Union experimented with pollution charges and used the revenues to create the first environmental funds. In 1991, pollution charges were formally introduced throughout the Russian Federation. The 1992 Environmental Protection Law gave legal recognition to the new system, financed mainly by pollution charge payments. This system has three tiers of environmental funds: local funds, which could retain 60 per cent of all pollution charge revenues collected within their territory; regional funds, which receive 30 per cent of all pollution charge revenues within their region; and a Federal Fund that receives 10 per cent of all pollution charge revenues.

To date, the revenues of environmental funds in Russia are not large (See Table 13). However, they have had a significant impact on the intensity of environmental investments. Environmental funds have an important role in promoting environmental investments, mobilising the commitment of resources by enterprises, and for providing loans.

Table 13: Revenues of the Environmental Fund System, 1991-1997

Revenues	1991	1992	1993	1994	1995	1996	1997 **
In billions of current roubles	1.1	7.7	79.8	403	930	1250	1500
In billions of 1990 roubles	0.51	0.21	0.24	0.30	0.25	0.25	0.30
In millions of US$, at the PPP exchange rate	802.9	329	345	424	351	344	417

** = estimated

We have discussed earlier reform of pollution fees in Russia. Such reform will increase the money flow to environmental funds and improve the effectiveness of their disbursement procedures.

An important factor is the share of tax revenues in GDP. The scenarios with high pollution fees indicate a significant increase in this share (see Figure 14). In this respect the "pollution fees scenarios" perform worse than the case of subsidy elimination.

Figure 14: Revenues from Pollution Payments

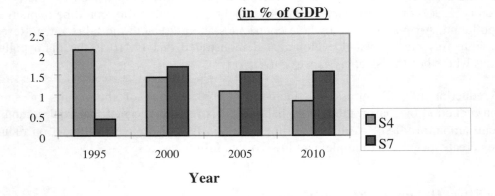

For easier comparison we present data about the actual share of environmental expenditures (see Table 14). The data presented show that environmental investments could be increased if subsidies were eliminated simultaneously with an increase in pollution fees.

Table 14: Environmental Investments in the Russian Federation, 1991-1995

YEAR	1990	1991	1992	1993	1994	1995
In current prices, (billion roubles)	1.94	3.3	52.9	592.8	2368.3	6403.6
In constant 1990 prices (billion roubles)	1.94	1.52	1.44	1.78	1.8	1.7
As % of GDP	0.3	0.24	0.28	0.35	0.39	0.37

Experience of environmental funds in eastern Europe and in Russia shows a gradual substitution of Pigovian subsidies for soft loans from environmental funds. To facilitate this process in Russia a National Pollution Abatement Fund was established (see Box I).

Box I: The Russian National Pollution Abatement Fund (NPAF)

The NPAF is an innovative new financing mechanism, created through a US$50 million loan from the World Bank. Its purpose is to provide small loans -- between US$30,000 and $7 million -- to Russian enterprises that implement environmentally friendly investment projects. These loans have an interest rate of 11.5% (in dollars), and must be repaid within 8 years. This means that projects financed by the NPAF must be profitable. The NPAF has an extensive screening procedure; applicants must follow a detailed application process to prove that their project will yield both financial returns and environmental benefits.

This trend supports the idea that any subsidies, including Pigovian ones, should be substituted by other instruments that are more effective.

9.2   Sectoral And Regional Aspects Of Subsidy Elimination

Our model also considered sectoral and regional aspects of subsidy elimination. Different sectors have different potential to reduce emissions in both absolute and per centage terms to the level in 1990. As an example we consider the potential for CO_2 reduction.

Figures 15 and 16 show the share of selected sectors in CO_2 offsets for (i) the period 2008-2012; and (ii) beyond 2012.

Figure 15: Sectoral Share in GHG Offsets for Period 2008-2012

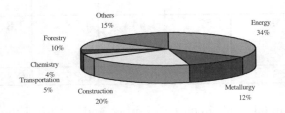

Figure 16: Sectoral Share in GHG Offsets beyond 2012

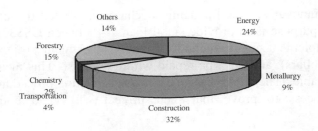

The data shows the potential for Russia to sell GHG offsets. GHG reductions resulting from subsidy elimination and other policy measures illustrate the sectoral impact of reforms. As the figures show, the energy sector has the largest potential followed by the construction and metallurgy sectors, and "others" (which includes households). Similar data exists for other pollutants.

Concerning the regional aspect, we considered four regions: European part, Urals, Siberia and the Far East. Subsidy elimination has different economic impacts for each of them. It would hinder economic development in the Far East but create additional incentives in the Urals region. The location of industries might therefore change, which will also influence the spatial distribution of emissions.

In general, the regional implications of subsidy removal are positive. However, there are some problems in those regions where subsidy elimination might encourage economic growth (in our model the Urals). In this case, subsidy elimination should be complemented by strict environmental regulation.

10.0   Conclusions

In the long run, subsidy elimination could have a positive economic and environmental impact. It could create incentives for sustainable development in the energy and other economic sectors, and also produce significant ecological benefits.

The negative impact of subsidies may be exaggerated in a transition economy because subsidies do not always reach their intended target. The only one exception seems to be natural monopolies such as Gasprom.

Subsidy elimination is necessary for further economic development, effective allocation of resources and income, and for promoting a switch to cleaner technologies. The continued availability of subsidies may result in economic growth being largely based on older, dirtier technologies.

The elimination of subsidies is complementary to the introduction of environmental taxes. Nonetheless, it must be recognised that the establishment of environmental taxes is complicated.

Subsidy elimination creates conditions for structural change in the long run. An increase in pollution fees has a short-term impact and favours the adoption of end-of-pipe technologies. Limited financial resources could be used in a more effective way. In particular, subsidy elimination is a higher priority than the introduction of pollution fees.

The elimination of subsidies has a major positive external effect on environmental quality and reduction of health risks. For countries such as China this might strengthen incentives for foreign direct investment in the energy sector within the framework of CDM. Subsidy elimination also increases the internal rate of return of energy efficiency projects.

There are significant institutional obstacles for subsidies elimination in a former centrally planned economy. Special mitigation measures may be required. They should take into account regional, sectoral, social, and psychological factors.

Different types of subsides exist, including those associated with environmental funds. To limit the potential for distortions in economic development, environmental funds should adopt a clearly defined project cycle. At present, there is a tendency to substitute grants for soft loans. That means a general phase out of Pigovian subsidies.

Subsidy elimination has different sectoral and regional impacts. In general, the impacts are positive. However, there are some problems in those regions where subsidy elimination might encourage rapid economic growth and a concomitant growth in pollution emissions. In this case subsidy elimination should be complemented by a clear environmental policy framework, including enforceable regulations.

BIBLIOGRAPHY

Averchenkov, A.; Radio I Svjas. M., (1995): Environmental Funds: Theory and Practice.

Environmental and Natural Resources Policy and Training Project, (1993): Environmental Protection and Economic Reform in Russia (Policy Brief). EPAT/MUCIA. No 2 July, 1993, p.p. 1-6.

Golub, A. and Strukova, E., (1994): "Application of a Pollution Fee System in Russia" in Ger Klaassen and Finn R.Forsund (eds) *Economic Instruments for Air Pollution Control*. Kluwer Academic Publishers. Dordrecht/ Boston/ London. p.p.165-184.

Golub, A. and Strukova, E., (1995): "Financing Environmental Investments in the Russian Federation" in Ger Klaassen and Mark Smith (eds) *Financing Environmental Quality in Central and Eastern Europe: An Assessment of International Support*. IIASA. Laxenberg. p.p. 113-132

Golub, A., (1996a): Environmental Financing in Russia. Paper to the CPPI- OECD International Conference in Nizhni Novgorod.

Golub, A., (1996b): Sources of Environmental Funds (Environmental Financing). Paper to an OECD International Conference in Almaty.

Golub, A. and Gurvich, E., (1997): Options for Revising the System of Pollution Charges in Russia: Results of an Aggregated Modeling Analysis. Environment Discussion PaperNo.21, July 1997, NIS-EEP Project. Harvard Institute for International Development.

Golub, A.; Larson, B.; Strukova, E.; and Shaposhnokov, D., (1997): Applying Cost-Effectiveness Analysis to Risk Management in Russia: A Case-Study of Air Pollution Health Risks in Volgograd. Environment Discussion Paper No.24, August 1997, NIS-EEP Project. Harvard Institute for International Development.

Gurvich, E.; Golub, A.; Mukhin, A.; Uziakov, M.; Ksenofontov, M., (1995): Effect of Russian Energy Subsidies on Green-house Gas Emissions. OECD/US EPA/World Bank.

Gurvich, E.; Golub, A.; Mukhin, A.; Uziakov, M.; Ksenofontov, M., (1996): Impact of Russian Energy Subsidies on Green-house Gas Emissions: Environmental Implications of Energy and Transport Subsidies. Rome. pp.109-123.

International Energy Agency (IEA), (1995): *Survey of Energy Policy of the Russian Federation*. IEA. Paris.

NUMS Goscomecologii of Russia, (1997): Ecological Funds of the Russian Federation.

OECD, (1995): *Environmental Funds in Economies in Transition*. OECD. Paris.

OECD, (1997): *Economic Survey of the Russian Federation*. OECD. Paris.

REFORMING AGRICULTURAL POLICIES AND THE ENVIRONMENT: THE EXPERIENCE IN OECD COUNTRIES

Wilfrid Legg[1]
Directorate for Food, Agriculture and Fisheries, OECD

1.0   Introduction

The impact of agriculture on the environment has become an important consideration in agricultural policy in OECD countries. This is partly the result of increasing awareness of the mounting pressure on the environment throughout the economy, and the commitments being made by countries within a range of international conventions and agreements (for example, on biodiversity, greenhouse gas emissions, and desertification). Given the long period of government intervention in agriculture, in most OECD countries, there is a particular interest in the environmental effects of agricultural policy reform, which aims to increase the market orientation of the sector and liberalise agricultural trade while taking account of the multiple roles played by agriculture. The reform of agricultural policies was agreed by the OECD Ministerial Council in 1987, and most recently in March 1998 by OECD Agriculture Ministers, and have been underpinned by the commitments within the Uruguay Round Agreement on Agriculture.

For the past 15 years the OECD has been in the forefront of analysing, monitoring and evaluating agricultural policies in member countries. This work is widely known, and the annual measurement of support due to agricultural policies, using the "Subsidy Equivalent" methodology, is central to the analysis. Since the early 1990's, reflecting developments in agriculture and the changing priorities for policies, the OECD has also been examining the linkages between agriculture and the environment from a policy perspective, drawing on the range of expertise available in the OECD.

Work on "agri-environment" issues in the OECD seeks to identify and analyse ways in which governments might encourage market solutions, and design and implement appropriate policies to achieve environmentally and economically sustainable agriculture, with least resource cost and trade distortions, in the context of agricultural policy reform.

This paper offers an overview of the OECD country experience on reforming agricultural policies and the environment, drawing on work in the OECD. It starts with a brief look at some of the important aspects of the relationship between agriculture and the environment, followed by a summary of developments in agricultural policy reform in OECD countries. It then makes some observations concerning the links between agricultural policy reform, and the environment. Finally, it identifies the areas of work on agriculture and the environment currently underway in the OECD.

---

[1]   The views expressed in this paper are those of the author and do not necessarily reflect those of the OECD or its Member countries.

2.0 Agriculture and the Environment in OECD Countries

The basic long-term *environmental sustainability issue* is whether agricultural activities can efficiently and profitably produce food to meet growing world demand without degrading natural resources—productive soils, clean and sufficient supplies of water, biodiversity and attractive landscape. Increasing food production has often been associated with environmentally damaging cropping and animal husbandry practices, which have led to soil degradation, salinisation, the pollution of groundwater, the farming of environmentally fragile land, greenhouse gas emissions, and loss of genetic diversity. In some of the drier areas of the OECD water for irrigation is being pumped from groundwater aquifers at rates that far exceed its natural replenishment. In other areas, surplus plant nutrients from animal wastes and fertilisers have led to eutrophication in surface waters, and excessive pesticide use has poisoned wildlife. But farmers, as "stewards of the countryside", have also shaped landscapes and contributed to the maintenance of rural communities. Agricultural land often provides important habitats for wildlife. Agriculture also plays a role in the hydrological cycle, cleansing the air of noxious gases, and in preventing flooding.

3.0 Diversity of Environmental Problems and Perceptions

Because of differences in climate, agro-ecosystems, population density and levels of economic development, the relative importance of particular environmental issues varies widely from one OECD country to another — and within countries. For example, surplus manure production and water pollution is a major problem in the densely-populated areas of northern Europe, Japan and Korea. Australia, on the other hand, along with New Zealand, suffers from extensive damage caused by rodents and other pests. Soil erosion is a concern in Australia, Canada, Mexico, the United States, and Mediterranean countries, while many of these countries are also concerned with the effects of agricultural practices on water resources.

These differences are also reflected in perceptions across and within OECD countries as to what is meant by the "environment" in agriculture. For some, the "environment" covers only biophysical and ecological aspects. For others, landscape, cultural features, and the rural development aspects of agriculture are also important. In recent years, some aspects related to the quality and safety of food, and the welfare of farm animals, have become more prominent policy issues, and have links with the environment. More generally, agriculture is increasingly considered as having multiple roles (the concept of "multifunctionality"), not only a "food producing" activity, but an activity in which food production is an integral part of the production of environmental services.

4.0 Markets and the Environment

Some of the environmental impacts from agricultural activities occur on the farm where they originate and are confined to the farm itself (for example, the quality of the soil on the farm). In such cases, the impacts will be taken into account by farmers, and will influence farmers' behaviour and decisions, to the extent that the present value of farming costs and revenues is affected, and they have sufficient information and financial resources to undertake the necessary remedial action. Some of the environmental services may be provided by farmers which raise the current value of farm receipts through, for example farm tourism, or from sales of higher valued produce that has been produced in "environmentally friendly" ways (which can be indicated through labelling, certification, place of origin, for example).

But many environmental impacts extend beyond the farm. If agricultural activities generate pollution outside the farm generating it, and there is no mechanism to charge the farm (or trade the property rights), then the farm costs of production do not include these external costs. If, however, other groups in the economy benefit from environmental services provided by farms (through the farmer's provision of landscape, or wildlife habitats for example), and there is no mechanism to value such services through charging those groups, and remunerating farmers, then this reduces farm revenues. In the former situation, the level of agricultural production and pollution is likely to be higher, and in the latter situation, the level and type of environmental services is likely to be lower, than would otherwise be the case.

The implications of farmers' actions with harmful environmental effects that are not incorporated in farming costs, for example, agricultural chemicals leaching into groundwater, can be seen in higher costs of treating water for drinking. Similarly, when farmers services are not valued, farmers refrain from taking actions that would add to public goods — such as conserving land as habitat for wildlife, or preserving other landscape features such as hedgerows — because effective ways of making the beneficiaries compensate farmers for the costs of such services are lacking.

Particularly from a policy perspective it is crucial that a distinction is made between those agricultural activities that benefit and those that harm the environment. Whichever "baseline" is chosen the direction of change of an environmental effect will indicate whether there has been an improvement or deterioration in environmental performance.

The OECD has been exploring the concept and operational use of a *reference level*, as an aid to identify "appropriate" policy responses. The reference level is defined in terms of the environmental outcomes from farming activities for which farmers or society are responsible. In other words it reflects the distribution of property rights over environmental resources, and thus the situations in which the polluter pays principle (PPP) applies (farmers responsible for any pollution they generate), and the situation in which farmers should be paid for unremunerated environmental services. There are a number of possible ways in which the reference level could be expressed in an operational way, in terms of environmental outcomes or agricultural practices, such as "codes of good agricultural practice". This requires information and indicators, on which the OECD has made significant progress.

5.0   Agricultural Policies and Policy Reform in OECD Countries

Agriculture in OECD countries has generally been a success story — in terms of increasing output, largely achieved through higher yields, rather than an increase in land devoted to agriculture. Agricultural output in the OECD region has, over a long period, tended to increase faster than demand in OECD countries and in world markets.

But that increased output has often been achieved at a high cost for both consumers and taxpayers: agricultural production has been heavily supported, mainly through commodity programmes and associated trade barriers, although the range of support varied considerably across OECD countries and commodities. Excess production has been frequently exported or stored with subsidies creating severe tensions, which characterised international trading relations from the end of the 1970s, and growing public concern over the environmental damage caused by agriculture in many countries.

The essential elements of agricultural policy reform are to reduce support levels, liberalise agricultural trade, and shift to better targeted measures to achieve those policy objectives for which markets might be inadequate. The commitment of OECD countries to reform was further reinforced by the 1994 Uruguay Round Agreement on Agriculture, which obliged countries to replace non-tariff barriers with bound tariffs, increase access for imports, and reduce subsidies to exports and -distorting domestic policy measures.

Starting with New Zealand, which had already undertaken a comprehensive reform of its agricultural policies in 1984, other OECD countries have begun to shift support away from output levels, towards more direct means of income support, such as replacing price support by area-based payments, and various forms of income safety nets. Such reforms have been evident in the United States (FAIR Act), in Mexico and Canada, in the 1992 reform of the European Union's Common Agricultural Policy, and most recently in Japan, for example.

The overall cost of support to agriculture in the mid-1980's accounted for around 2.2 per cent of GDP in the OECD area, and support was equivalent to about 45 per cent of the value of agricultural production, as measured by the OECD's Producer Subsidy Equivalent (PSE). Two-thirds of the support was channelled through measures that kept domestic market prices paid by consumers about 60 per cent on average above comparable world prices. The OECD PSE has since fallen sharply, and in 1997 it was equivalent to 35 per cent of the value of OECD agricultural production, while the share of overall cost of support in GDP was around 1.3 per cent. Over the last decade there has been a decrease in the numbers of people working in agriculture and support per "full time farmer equivalent" which was on average $14,000 in 1986-88, is currently around $17,000, which is roughly unchanged in real terms, given inflation. As in the earlier period, the same wide disparities in support remain across OECD countries and commodities. However, support that is to a degree "decoupled" from specific commodities or inputs now accounts for over 40 per cent of total agricultural support, whereas a decade ago the share was around 35 per cent. This is also reflected in the fact that domestic market prices have on average fallen to 30 per cent above world prices.

But the OECD average figures disguise the wide range of developments among countries and commodities. In 1997 the PSEs in Australia and New Zealand were below 10 per cent, while they were just below 70 per cent in Iceland and Japan and just over 70 per cent in Norway and Switzerland. PSEs were 42 per cent in the EU, 20 per cent in Canada, and 16 per cent in the United States. The milk, sugar and rice sectors have been heavily supported in many OECD countries for a considerable time, and currently register the highest PSEs of about 50 per cent for milk and sugar and 80 per cent for rice.

In many cases environmental problems have been aggravated by agricultural and trade policies that distort price signals through support increasing the prices of agricultural commodities, or reducing the costs of agricultural inputs. The economic distortions created by such policies can lead to environmentally inappropriate farming practices with environmentally harmful use of inputs, and discourage the development and adoption of farming technologies less stressful on the environment.

In New Zealand there is good evidence, given the relatively long period of fundamental policy reform, that illustrates the reduction of pressure on the environment, in particular the shift from inappropriate agricultural production on environmentally fragile land, and decreasing intensity of fertiliser use. It should be noted, however, that New Zealand's agricultural policy reforms were accompanied by economy-wide environmental measures (in the 1991 Resource Management Act).

6.0   Policy Measures Targeted to Environmental Issues in Agriculture

Over the last decade, an important component of the wider package of agricultural policy reforms in most of OECD countries has been the introduction of new programmes addressed to environmental issues.

For example, the *European Union* has a wide range of agri-environmental measures, co-financed and implemented by member states, with three general purposes: to accompany the changes introduced to market organisation rules as part of the 1992 reforms of the Common Agricultural Policy; to contribute to the achievement of the EU policy objectives regarding agriculture and the environment; and to contribute to provide an appropriate income to farmers (Council Regulations 2078/92 and 2080/92). Concerning the environment, the main aim is to introduce or maintain production methods compatible with reducing agricultural pollution, maintaining the landscape, and promoting biological diversity and rural development. Various direct **payments** are given to reduce cattle stocking density, encourage extensive farming practices, maintain abandoned farmland, afforest marginal farmland, establish wildlife habitat and ecosystems on long-term set-aside, compensate farmers for providing public access to their land, and train farmers. The proposals contained in the European Commission's *Agenda 2000* place a heavy emphasis on measures to improve the environment in agriculture, but it is obviously too early to pass judgement, both in terms of the environmental outcome and in relation to economic efficiency in agriculture.

Under *Norway's* "acreage and cultural landscape scheme" farmers receive area-based payments if they grow specified crops and refrain from making major changes to landscape features, such as streams, stone fences, paths, and forest edges. In *Switzerland*, annual payments for various types of "ecological services" support integrated production methods and organic farming.

Because of its hilly terrain, heavy rainfall, intensive agriculture, and high population density, *Japan's* approach to sustainable agriculture is oriented towards hydrological aspects: preventing flooding and water erosion, minimising nutrient leaching, and protecting forests. Its "Comprehensive Program for the Promotion of Sustainable Agriculture", begun in 1994, seeks to promote environmentally friendly, low-input agriculture in ways that minimally affect the productivity of agriculture.

In *Canada,* the Permanent Cover Program aims at reducing soil deterioration on high-risk land, through payments to shift from annual crops to grassland. The *United States* supports the adoption of more sustainable farming methods through numerous programmes. One of its main programmes, the Conservation Reserve Program (CRP) pays farmers on an annual basis for keeping environmentally sensitive land out of production in order to reduce erosion and sediment loading in streams, protect water resources and wildlife. Other programmes award cost-share or incentive payment contracts to farmers who adopt approved land management practices or install structures for controlling animal waste, or encourage farmers to adopt integrated strategies for managing their farm resources, while assisting them in meeting environmental quality standards.

Australia and *New Zealand* (and Canada, to some extent) place great stress on **community-based approaches** to agricultural resource management. The aim of these approaches is to motivate farmers to take on greater responsibility for the local management of land, water and related natural resources. *Australia's* National Lancer Program is the oldest and largest of its kind, and channels much of its financial assistance through farmer-led community groups. Much stress is placed on improving information flows, upgrading skills and using peer pressure to attain results. In this context approaches such as Linking Environment and Farming (LEAF) in the United Kingdom, and FERTIMIEUX in France are ways to manage farms and adopt practices that respect the environment, by using farm chemicals in a responsible way (part of "agriculture raisonnée" in France -- the rational use of agricultural resources).

Most of OECD countries have passed laws to deal with problems relating to pollution of air and water, and damage to ecologically sensitive areas. The European Union's Nitrate Directive is a good example. Activities that create high levels of pollution — such as dumping slurry, aerial pesticide spraying or burning straw — are frequently proscribed via **regulations,** which have also been used to limit risks of serious damage to human health and the environment. Regulations for example are used to constrain the use of new biotechnological products and on particularly toxic or persistent pesticides. Regulations also set limits on animal stocking densities, to circumscribe periods during which the manure spreading is permitted, and to forbid the collection of endangered plants and animals.

Another approach is to set *minimum standards* for farm practices and to tie them to existing agricultural support programmes. Such "cross-compliance" measures have been used for several years in the *United States* and are becoming increasingly important in European countries.

Research and development (R&D) into technologies and farming methods that are less environmentally stressful (such as crop rotation, intercropping, conservation tillage, agroforestry and silvipasture, precision application of fertilisers, and integrated pest management), and on improving scientific understanding of the physical and biological links between agriculture and the environment is an essential component of promoting agricultural sustainability. R&D is helping to reduce risks from pesticides, for example, through the development of new strains of crops that are more naturally resistant to attack by pests (and less dependent on pesticides); methods for growing crops that rely on safe yet effective biological processes or agents; and chemical agents that are environmentally safe yet effective and affordable.

Continuing technological innovation in the agricultural sector will be crucial to meeting the goals of sustainable agriculture. But if farming is to become more sustainable, it is certain to become more management-intensive, and possibly more labour intensive, focused on precision techniques.

Educated and informed farmers (who rely on the market for their incomes) are more likely to be motivated to look after the productivity of their land, to be receptive to policies that constrain their activities in the interest of environmental protection, and to be able to implement any changes required of them. *Extension services* play an important role in this process. Improved information on the proper timing of fertiliser application, for example, has already helped reduce the loss of nutrients into water systems in several countries. Technology (including the Internet) is helping to facilitate such communication, both among farmers and between farmers and government agencies.

7.0   The Environmental Impact of Agricultural Policy Reform

By decoupling support from agricultural commodities and inputs, the reform of agricultural policies should improve the domestic and international allocation of resources, reduce incentives to over-use polluting chemical inputs and to farm environmentally sensitive land. In other words, through reducing output and input use (through a reduction in output and input price distortions, and changes in relative factor prices), the reforms would tend to reverse the harmful environmental impacts associated with commodity and input-specific policy measures. But in those cases where agricultural policies are associated with maintaining farming activities that provide environmental services, reform of such policies can reduce environmental performance.

However, some caution needs to be exercised assessing the overall environmental effect. Agricultural policy reforms have been relatively recent in most countries. There are few examples of fundamental or radical policy reforms, and the degree of decoupling of policy measures is limited as, for example, compensation payments are still linked to land use in the European Union. The environmental effects of policy measures are complex, often site-specific, take some time to become evident, and the data and evidence to quantify them are extremely patchy. And many other developments have been occurring at the same time, which may or may not be linked to policy change: for example technological advances, farmer information and behaviour, consumer demands and environmental group pressure, environmental regulations, industrial pollution, climate change, and, not least, the relative prices of farm inputs (including chemicals) and outputs.

OECD work has outlined some of the trends in the environmental effects of agricultural policy reform. By lowering price support and input subsidies, shifting to policies that are less linked to production, and implementing agri-environmental measures, policy reforms have in many cases generated a double benefit: they have resulted in a more efficient allocation of market resources, and they have reduced negative environmental externalities. They have also increased transparency as to the remaining externalities that have the potential to be addressed through targeted environmental measures. The economic gains resulting from a better resource allocation could be used to support such targeted measures.

In particular, reductions in price support and input subsidies have in many cases lowered the demand for chemical and mechanical inputs, as well as for irrigation water, and have led to a de-intensification of crop production. Yet, some land may have been shifted into the production of fruits and vegetables, which are sometimes produced in input-intensive ways, or into other input-intensive crops. In some cases, the use of farm chemicals has again increased after an initial decline, largely linked to increases in world commodity prices. The effects on the environment are not only driven by policies but depend also on the developments of markets and technical progress. Positive environmental effects may, for instance, result from a switch to environmentally-friendly production methods induced by consumers' choices.

Reforms in the livestock sector are likely to have resulted in reduced grazing pressure and manure surpluses and, as a consequence, soil erosion and nutrient leaching. However, where direct payments per head of animal have been provided and the stocking density limits set by governments have exceeded the original densities in the area, increases in stocking densities may in some cases have occurred.

Policy reform has also slowed down or brought to a halt the conversion of environmentally fragile or ecologically valuable land to agricultural uses in OECD countries. Significant areas of wetland, forest and natural grassland have thus been preserved. In countries where support had previously favoured cropping over grass-based activities, shifts out of crop production into grazing and forage production have taken place. The grass or tree cover established on erodible land as a result of such shifts has reduced soil erosion rates and, in some cases, has helped restore already degraded soils.

Changes in land use have sometimes been aided by land diversion schemes, which have paid farmers for idling land or replacing arable crops by less intensive forms of production and woodland. Over time, incentives to remove the environmentally most sensitive or ecologically most valuable land from production have been introduced, and farmers have been required to make environmental improvements on the diverted land. As a result, substantial areas of land have been improved, wildlife habitat has been created or restored, and the risk of nutrient leaching has diminished. Some of these improvements appear to have been sustained, while others have disappeared when the land was brought back into production.

However, in certain countries, agricultural support has allowed farmers to maintain farming systems that support a rich variety of flora and fauna as well as scenic landscapes that are valued by the population. Such production systems, which would be unprofitable without support, can extend over large expanses of semi-natural land. Elsewhere, support has maintained agricultural activities that have been associated with land conservation, including landslide and flood prevention. There are concerns that such positive environmental externalities of agriculture could be reduced if reform causes agricultural activity to shrink.

Where reform drives farms out of business and the land is not taken over by other farms in the area for lack of profitability, the land may be abandoned. In some cases, abandoned land will revert back to nature and may actually benefit the environment, as vegetation and wildlife continue to develop along the path of natural succession until a new ecosystem has developed in the absence of agricultural activity. In other cases, environmental degradation including soil erosion, irreversible damage to wildlife habitat, biodiversity and landscapes, and loss of the flood controlling function of the land may occur.

Agri-environmental measures appear to have been effective when: the environmental objectives are clearly specified and the actions required of farmers are closely targeted to the objectives; the measures are tailored to the environmental, economic and social situation prevailing in a given area; the lands accepted into the programmes have a high conservation value; the incentives provided to farmers are linked to the size of the benefits or the income foregone by adhering to the restrictions; farmer compliance is closely monitored and the effects on farming practices and the environment are continuously assessed against the stated goals; and training and advice are provided to insure that farmers are sufficiently informed about the measures and the best ways to implement them.

In particular, it is not evident that environmental externalities have been taken into account through policy: there is a risk that more attention has been given to "environmental cost compensation" and payments for environmental services of a "public good" character, and less attention has been paid to recovering pollution costs originating in agriculture (the application of the polluter pays principle).

Where markets do not fully internalise harmful or beneficial environmental externalities, there can be a divergence between economically efficient agriculture and desired environmental outcomes, in the absence of appropriate agricultural policies.

8.0   Indicators of Environmental Performance

Part of the work on agri-environmental issues in the OECD is to develop a set of environmental indicators for the agricultural sector, which could be of use in the policy domain. A framework has been established, and it is intended that indicators will be calculated by 2000 for a set of 13 "policy issue areas", namely nutrient use, pesticide use, water use and quality, land use and conservation, soil quality, greenhouse gases, biodiversity, wildlife habitats, landscape, farm management practices, farm financial resources, and socio-cultural issues. Preliminary quantitative work is underway, and there are some interesting results in the areas of agricultural nutrient (nitrogen) and agricultural pesticide use.

In many OECD countries, as shown by Table 1, the trend in nitrogen balance surpluses[2] over the last decade is downwards, or constant, especially for countries with a high surplus (in excess of 100 kg/ha), including Belgium, Finland, Japan and the Netherlands. Of course, the absolute levels of surplus vary considerably across and within countries. Concerning pesticide use (in terms of active ingredients), as shown in Table 2, a similar downward or constant trend is observed, also with considerable variation across countries and crops. The reasons for these trends are not only related to the effect of agricultural policy reform on input demand, but also to the price of energy, technical change and farmers' knowledge.

---

[2].   The residual of nitrogen inputs — mainly chemical fertilisers, livestock waste, atmospheric deposition and nitrogen fixation minus outputs — mainly nitrogen uptake by crops and pasture -- passing into the environment.

Table 1: Agricultural Nitrogen Surplus
(% change 1986-88 to 1994-96)

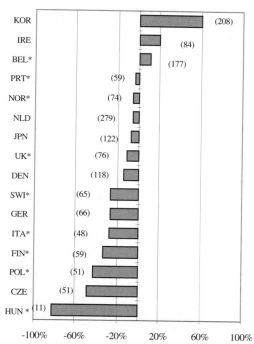

(..) kg N surplus / ha of agricultural land 1993-96
Nitrogen (N) use = N inputs (fertiliser, manure, etc.)
minus N plant uptake, which if > 0 = N surplus; if < 0 N
deficit
* 1986-88 to 1993-95

Table 2: Pesticide Use in Agriculture
(% change 1986-88 to 1993-95)

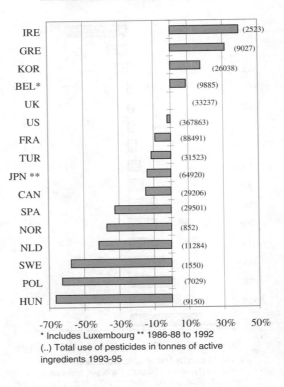

IRE (2523)
GRE (9027)
KOR (26038)
BEL* (9885)
UK (33237)
US (367863)
FRA (88491)
TUR (31523)
JPN ** (64920)
CAN (29206)
SPA (29501)
NOR (852)
NLD (11284)
SWE (1550)
POL (7029)
HUN (9150)

-70% -50% -30% -10% 10% 30% 50%
* Includes Luxembourg ** 1986-88 to 1992
(..) Total use of pesticides in tonnes of active
ingredients 1993-95

9.0   Preliminary Conclusions

A number of preliminary conclusions emerge from the OECD work on analysing and quantifying the effects of agricultural policy on the environment. Together with the on-going work in this area, this will contribute to examining the implications of the options facing policy makers in helping to achieve an efficient and sustainable agricultural sector.

- The reform of agricultural policies, through reducing the level of support from commodity and input linked policies ("decoupling"), and associated trade measures, will improve resource-use efficiency, tend to reduce inappropriate farming practices on environmentally fragile land and the excessive use of farm chemicals, and thereby benefit the environment.

- Switching to agricultural policy measures which provide payments "coupled" to targeted environmental outcomes, have the potential to reward farmers for those environmental services from agriculture that are not taken into account in their receipts from their commercial activities.

- The current combination of market price support and targeted agri-environmental measures may in many cases not be the most effective and least-cost way of achieving environmental objectives.

- The "baseline" to assess environmental performance in agriculture has often been distorted by a long period of significant levels of support in many countries, and it is not clear which environmental services the market would deliver if support were removed.

- The degree to which farmers are held responsible for agricultural pollution, or compensated for improving the environment depends on a "reference level", which varies across and within countries depending on agri-environmental situations, public perceptions, and the specification of property rights; however, if policies impose charges on farmers for non-marketed externalities that harm the environment, and pay farmers for non-marketed public goods that benefit the environment, then the "lower" the "reference level" is set, the higher the cost to taxpayers for producing the desired environment.

- To be consistent, a balanced policy approach is needed: when payments are given for the provision of environmental services over and above those that are remunerated through revenues from agricultural activities, then farmers should also be required to meet the costs of any off-farm environmental damage they cause (polluter pays principle).

- The variety of agri-environmental situations and policy priorities across and within countries suggests that appropriate policy measures and market solutions are likely to differ. This is even more relevant when also considering non-OECD countries. But, in general, there is probably a greater potential for developing innovative market solutions, more attention to localised policy measures, co-operative approaches by farmers, and the dissemination of information from scientific research. many of the latter are likely to be among the least cost, and least distorting policy approaches to achieving many environmental objectives.

10.0   Future Work

While the work on the linkages between agriculture and the environment in the OECD has made a significant contribution to the policy debate, there are a number of important areas on the agenda to further advance the work. In brief, future work below should help to find ways to deal with the fundamental question of knowing how we can obtain the amount of food needed with better environmental performance and less government support.

- Completing the methodologies for all of the thirteen indicator areas, collecting data and calculating indicators, and using them as a tool in monitoring and evaluating policy developments.

- Integrating the modelling work in the OECD, in particular the projections for agricultural markets through the AGLINK model and the work underway in developing the Policy Evaluation Matrix, to undertake scenario analysis of the possible environmental implications (such as greenhouse gas emissions) of market developments, the agricultural implications of meeting environmental standards, and to help identify the policy measures which can achieve the combination of sufficient (and efficient) agricultural output and good environmental performance.

- Establishing criteria and guidelines to determine the appropriate level of remuneration for farmers in cases where environmental services are jointly produced with agricultural products, and to analyse alternative policy options.

- Exploring the effects of agricultural policy reform and trade liberalisation on environmental performance in agriculture, and the effects of different domestic environmental standards on trade, and policy measures to minimise possible conflicts between different domestic environmental standards and trade liberalisation.

- Analysing the environmental impacts of different agricultural structures (such as large or small, extensive or intensive farms) and farm practices (such as conventional or organic farming), and technological developments (such as genetically modified organisms) from a policy perspective.

- Exploring the economic implications for the agricultural sector in implementing sustainable farming practices, and identifying the appropriate mix of market solutions and policy measures to achieve agricultural sustainability.

11.0   A Final Comment

A more market oriented agriculture through policy reform is a necessary, but not necessarily a sufficient condition to improve the environmental performance of agriculture. Markets may need to be complemented by policies to reach that goal, but many of the policy measures do not necessarily emerge as the most cost-effective way. Given the diversity and site specificity of agro-ecological conditions, local, farmer-based approaches, coupled with good research, development, training, information and advice would appear to be high on the list of "good policy practices". These types of approaches focus on the "public good" aspects of agriculture, reflect the differences across farming, and allow for the development of market based, innovative approaches.

SELECTED BIBLIOGRAPHY OF RECENT OECD PUBLISHED WORK

Agriculture and Environment

OECD (1998): *The Environmental Effects of Reforming Agricultural Policies.*

OECD (1998): *Agriculture and the Environment: Issues and Policies.*

OECD (1998): *Sustainable Management of Water in Agriculture — The Athens Workshop.*

OECD (1997): *Agriculture, Pesticides and the Environment: Policy Options.*

OECD (1997): *Agriculture, Trade and the Environment: Anticipating Policy Challenges.*

OECD (1997): *Environmental Indicators for Agriculture.*

OECD (1997): *Co-operative Approaches to Sustainable Agriculture.*

OECD (1997): *The Environmental Effects of Agricultural Land Diversion Schemes.*

OECD (1997): *The Environmental Benefits from Agriculture: Issues and Policies — The Helsinki Seminar.*

OECD (1995): *Forestry, Agriculture and the Environment.*

OECD (1995): *Sustainable Agriculture — Concepts, Issues and Policies in OECD Countries.*

OECD (1994): "Agricultural policy reform: environmental externalities and public goods", in *Agricultural Policy Reform: New Approaches — The Role of Direct Income Payments.*

OECD (1994): *Towards Sustainable Agricultural Production: Cleaner Technologies.*

Related Publications

OECD (1998): *Environment Performance Reviews — Denmark .*

OECD (1998): *Environment Performance Reviews — Switzerland*

OECD (1998): *Agricultural Policies in OECD Countries — Monitoring and Evaluation 1998.*

OECD (1996): *Environment Performance Reviews — Sweden.*

OECD (1996): *Environment Performance Reviews — New Zealand.*

OECD (1996): *Subsidies and Environment: Exploring the Linkages.*

OECD (1996): *Amenities for Rural Development — Policy Examples.*

OECD (1995): *The Uruguay Round — A Preliminary Evaluation of the Impacts of the Agreement on Agriculture in the OECD Countries.*

OECD (1995): *Environmental Performance Reviews — Netherlands.*

OECD (1997): *Environmental Data Compendium 1997.*

OECD (1994): *The Contribution of Amenities to Rural Development.*

Articles in the "OECD OBSERVER"

Bonnis, Gérard and Steenblik, Ronald (1998): "Water, Agriculture and the Environment" (No. 212, June/July).

Legg, Wilfrid and Potier, Michel (1998): "Reconciling Agriculture and the Environment (No. 210, Feb/March).

Legg, Wilfrid and Portugal, Luis (1997): "Environmental Benefits from Agriculture" (No. 206, May/June).

Parris, Kevin (1996): "Environmental indicators for agriculture" (No. 203, December).

Steenblik, Ronald (1996): "When farmers fend for the environment" (No. 203, December).

Maier, Leo (1996): "Letting the land rest", *The OECD Observer*, (No. 203, December).

Bonnis, Gérard (1995): "Farmers, forestry and the environment", (No. 196, October/November).

Maier, Leo and Ronald Steenblik (1995): "Towards sustainable agriculture" (No. 196, October/November).

Legg, Wilfrid (1993/94): Direct Payments for Farmers? (No. 185, December/January).

PART 3:

DESIGNING AND IMPLEMENTING
ENVIRONMENTAL TAXES
IN THE ENERGY AND ROAD TRANSPORT SECTORS

SO$_2$ CHARGE AND TAX POLICIES IN CHINA: EXPERIMENT AND REFORM

Dong Cao, Jintian Yang and Chazhong Ge
Chinese Research Academy of Environmental Sciences, China

1.0   Introduction

Although China does not strictly speaking have an SO$_2$ tax, a trial SO$_2$ charge has operated in two provinces and nine cities since 1993. Through this experiment, China has accumulated considerable practical experience that will support the longer term goal of introducing an SO$_2$ tax. With the deepening of the country's economic and fiscal reforms and the deterioration of acid rain and SO$_2$ pollution problems, the SO$_2$ charge will be revised and extended on the basis of the trial programme. Meanwhile, the introduction and establishment of environmental taxes, including an SO$_2$ tax, has attracted considerable attention among relevant government agencies.

This paper focuses on: (1) practical experience in implementing the SO$_2$ charge; (2) the framework for reform of the SO$_2$ charge system; (3) establishment of the charge rate schedules; (4) institutional issues; (5) the management and use of charge revenues; and (6) the potential benefits of applying more widely in China the experience from the experimental SO$_2$ charge.

2.0   Practical Experience in Implementing the SO$_2$ Charge

The SO$_2$ charge is a major component of China's pollution levy system and an important instrument to control acid rain and atmospheric pollution. An SO$_2$ charge trial program has been conducted in China since 1993. Experience has been accumulated in the design and implementation of an SO$_2$ charge, including the charge rate schedules and utilisation of collected revenue. This provides a solid foundation for extending the charge system nation-wide in the future.

2.1   The Pollution Levy System

The pollution levy system was applied nation-wide from 1982. In February 1982, based on the experience of trial programs in 22 provinces, autonomous regions and municipalities the State Council promulgated the "Temporary Management Rule on the Pollution Levy System". This set out a series of clear and specific rules on the objectives, approach, management and use of revenue of the pollution levy. The pollution levy system is based on the amount of emissions that exceed pollutant discharge standards, i.e. the charge is levied only when pollutant discharge is beyond the corresponding national standard. Emissions of SO$_2$ are included within the air pollution category of the pollution levy system; a uniform charge rate of 0.04 yuan/kg[1] SO$_2$ emitted applies. The charge applies only to SO$_2$ emissions from industrial processes. Boilers used in power plants, industry and heating are exempted from the charge. However, because of weaknesses in monitoring and measuring SO$_2$ emissions from industrial processes the SO$_2$ charge rate schedule issued in 1982 was not implemented nation-wide but rather tested in several provinces.

---

[1]   US$1=8.28 yuan (March 1999).

At the end of the 1980s and the beginning of the 1990s, China's coal consumption increased significantly as its economic development accelerated. Industrial pollution became increasingly serious. SO_2 emissions from sources under the authority of county-level government amounted to 15 million tons in 1985, climbing to 18.91 million tons in 1995. The emission of SO_2 from industrial sources is the major contributor to this form of pollution in China: in 1991, industrial-based SO_2 emissions were 11.65 million tons while in 1995 the figure had reached 14.05 million tons (see Figure 1). It has been projected that without strict pollution control, China's coal consumption could reach 1.5 billion tons in the year 2000 and SO_2 emission could attain 27.30 million tons (State Environmental Protection Administration, (SEPA), 1998). A recent study of township and village enterprises by SEPA, the Ministry of Agriculture and the China Statistics Bureau, showed that nation-wide SO_2 emissions from this sector amounted to 4.41 million tons in 1995, accounting for 23.9% of the total national emission of SO_2 by industry.

Figure 1: SO_2 Emissions in China, 1985-1995

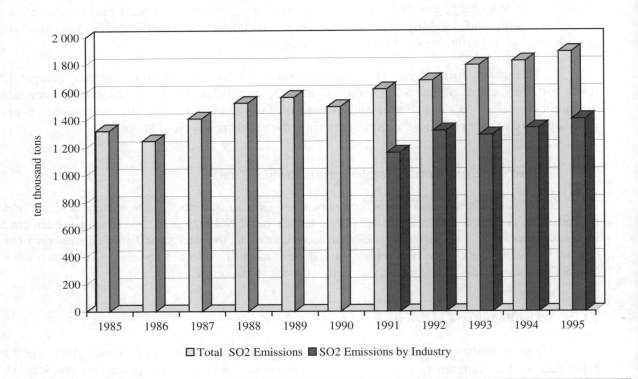

SEPA analysis of monitoring data from 2177 environmental monitoring stations over a 13 year period (1981-1993) indicates that the number of cities exceeding the national SO_2 ambient standard is increasing. Currently, 62.3% of cities have an annual average SO_2 concentration above the national Class II standard, and a daily average concentration exceeding the Class III standard. (The Class II SO_2 standard is an annual average concentration of $0.06mg/m^3$ and that for Class III is a daily average concentration of $0.25mg/m^3$).

The increase in SO_2 and other atmospheric pollutants as well as the impacts of acid rain gradually caught the public's attention. Since the initial discovery of acid rain problems in the mid-1980s, the area affected has gradually extended. In particular, spreading from small areas in southwestern China in the 1980s to the majority of the southwest, central, southern and northeastern parts of China. Currently, areas with an annual pH value lower than 5.6 cover approximately 40% of the country (SEPA, 1998).

Acid rain and SO_2 pollution threatens human health, erodes building materials, damages the ecological system and causes major economic losses. In some areas, it has become a limiting factor to social and economic development. In this context, the prevention and control of SO_2 pollution is becoming a key element of air pollution control in China. This also poses new challenges for environmental management in China.

2.2   The Trial SO_2 Charge Program

China's government attaches high priority to tackling the worsening problems of acid rain and SO_2 pollution. In December 1990, the 19th meeting of the Environmental Protection Committee (EPC) of the State Council endorsed the Suggestions on Control of the Spread of Acid Rain. In 1992, the 20th meeting of the EPC passed the "Plan for Levying Charges for SO_2 Emission from Industrial Coal-burning".   In light of these initiatives and upon approval by the State Council, the then National Environmental Protection Agency (NEPA, renamed the State Environmental Protection Administration in 1998), the Ministry of Finance, the State Planning Commission (renamed the State Development and Planning Commission in 1998) and the Economic and Trade Office of the State Council jointly promulgated the "Circular on Conducting A Trial Program of SO_2 Charges Levied on Industrial Coal-burning" (Huanjian No. [1992]361) in September 1992. The trial program was initiated in 1993-1994 in the provinces of Guangdong and Guizhou and 9 cities (Chongqing, Yibin, Nanning, Guilin, Liuzhou, Yichang, Qingdao, Hangzhou and Changsha) where SO_2 emissions are high and the local economy is sound. To provide guidance in implementing the program, NEPA issued "Suggestions on Conducting the Trial SO_2 Emission Charge Program".

The major objectives of the trial SO_2 charge program were to promote the control of SO_2 emissions through the use of economic instruments, to promote resource and energy conservation, to control acid rain pollution and improve the quality of the environment, to establish a fund for financing SO_2 pollution control measures and to use the accumulated experience to design a nation-wide SO_2 emission charge system.

The current policies applying to the SO_2 charge, its administration and the use of revenue collected follow the principle of the pollution levy system. However, there are some characteristics of the trial SO_2 charge program that differ from other pollution charges.

First, reliance on the principle of total quantity emission control (TQEC). Since the development of TQEC in China in the early 1980s, pollution control has been shifting from a concentration basis to TEQC. With regard to the pollution levy system, its emphasis on charging only for emissions above the relevant standard is not consistent with the requirements of TQEC.   Accordingly, TQEC rather than concentration control has been selected as a parameter in the trial SO_2 charge design.

Second, the share of the revenue used in financing pollution prevention investments.   The original pollution levy rules stipulated that 80% of the revenue is to be used for funding pollution prevention measures. Under the trial SO_2 charge program this rate was increased to 90% for revenue from SO_2 emissions.

Following studies led by Tsinghua University, the trial SO_2 emission charge rate was set at 0.2 yuan/kg. This figure was based principally on considerations of affordability and practicality. Judging from the results of implementation, the charge rate basically met the demands of TQEC. However, there is a large gap between the charge rate and the average cost of SO_2 emission control.   In addition, the charge rate is not sufficiently high to stimulate enterprises to reduce SO_2 emissions significantly

In October 1994, NEPA convened an Appraisal Meeting on the Trial SO_2 Charge Program in Two Provinces and Nine Cities. The meeting concluded that the trial program had been successful and that it had provided useful experience to support extension of SO_2 emission charges to cover the whole country. Despite some deficiencies, the trial program had demonstrated that SO_2 charges could play an effective role in controlling existing and new pollution sources, encouraging the adoption of pollution management measures, controlling acid rain pollution and funding environmental investments.

2.3   Current Status of the SO_2 Charge

The SO_2 charge is currently collected by local environmental protection bureaus and offices in the area where the polluting enterprise is located. Based on SEPA statistics, in 1996 the total amount of charge collected was 146 million yuan. The charge rate, scope of application and amount for the 2 provinces and 9 cities that took part in the trial program are listed in Table 1.

Table 1: Data for the Provinces and Cities Taking Part in the Trial SO₂ Charge Program

	Charge Rate (yuan/kg)	Scope of Application	Start Date	Charge Collected in 1997 (million yuan)
Guangdong province	0.2	Coal and oil for industrial and commercial purposes	1994	59.52
Guizhou province	0.2	Coal for industrial and commercial purposes	1993 (July)	15.97
Chongqing city	5 yuan/ton coal	Coal for industrial and commercial purposes	1990 (January)	7.34
Yibin city	0.18	Coal for industrial and commercial purposes	1993 (October)	7.36 in total for Sichuan province
Nanning city	0.2	Coal for industrial and commercial purposes	1994	Total for 3 cities = 8.45
Liuzhou city	0.2	Coal for industrial and commercial purposes	1994	
Guilin city	0.2	Coal for industrial and commercial purposes	1994	
Yichang city	0.2	Coal for industrial and commercial purposes	1993 (May)	11.43 in total for Hubei province
Qingdao city	0.2	Coal for industrial and commercial purpose	1993 (July)	39.41
Hangzhou city	0.18	Coal for industrial and commercial purposes	1993 (May)	9.19
Changsha city	0.2	Coal for industrial and commercial purposes	1993 (January)	3.89

Source: Statistics from the Department of Supervision and Management, SEPA.

On the basis of the trial program, the charge rate has been maintained at 0.2 yuan/kg and the scope of the charge's application concentrated on coal for industrial and commercial purposes. As Table 1 shows, the revenue collected in 1997 varied considerably.

Other provinces have now implemented SO₂ charges: Hebei in 1995 and Shaanxi in 1996. Figure 2 illustrates the trend during the period 1993-1997 in the total amount of SO₂ charge collected in the trial 2 provinces and 9 cities and as a percentage of the revenue collected nationally for air emissions.

Figure 2: Change in SO$_2$ Charge Revenue Collection, 1993-1997

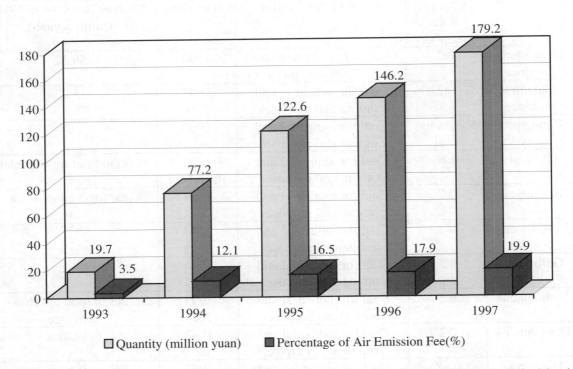

Quantity (million yuan)   Percentage of Air Emission Fee(%)

It is clear from Figure 2 that revenue from the SO$_2$ charge for the 2 provinces and 9 cities in the trial program has increased consistently since 1993. After exceeding 100 million yuan in 1995, the total was just over 179 million yuan in 1997. It is projected that the total in 1998 for these provinces and cities will exceed 200 million yuan. A parallel development has been the increase in the share of the SO$_2$ charge from these provinces and cities to the national air emissions charge category; this increased from 3.5% in 1993 to just under 20% in 1997.

Since 1993, the total revenue collected nation-wide from the SO$_2$ charge is 544 million yuan. Under the trial SO$_2$ charge program 90% of the collected revenue must be used for pollution control. This is 10% greater than the figure for other charges that fall within the framework of the pollution levy system. Even when the 80% figure is used, the SO$_2$ charge should already have provided just over 435 million yuan for controlling acid rain and SO$_2$ pollution.

2.4   Existing Problems with the SO$_2$ Charge

Since the implementation of trial SO$_2$ charge in 2 provinces and 9 cities, there has been progress in controlling air pollution; institutional support has been forthcoming from SEPA, the Ministry of Finance and the Economic and Trade Office of the State Council; and more local governments have been willing to introduce the charge. This has provided a good basis for extending the spatial coverage of the SO$_2$ charge. Nonetheless, some problems have also arisen which require attention. Most of these problems relate to the charge rate and revenue usage.

Concerning the charge rate, the current level of 0.2 yuan/kg was established to develop a fund for controlling new sources of pollution and failed to address adequately the marginal social cost for SO$_2$

reduction and the average cost of controlling SO_2 emissions. The present rate cannot effectively stimulate polluters to reduce their emissions, and an increase is urgently needed.

Currently, expenditure of the collected revenue is inefficient. In particular, recycling money to the polluters or exempting them from repayment of loans does not support improved efficiency in revenue usage. Nonetheless, the formal arrangements for revenue usage have been set: 90% of the SO_2 charge is to be used for pollution control and the remaining 10% used for capacity building in sub-national environmental protection bureaus and offices. This arrangement has strongly influenced the allocation of revenue. The linkage between the charge item (SO_2 emissions) and the majority of the collected revenue being returned to the polluter results in a loss of economic efficiency. Given that the control of SO_2 pollution is an inter-regional problem, which requires a large amount of financial resources, the demands for reform of the current method of revenue use have intensified over time.

3.0   Reform of the SO_2 Charge System

China's SO_2 charge system is not very different to the SO_2 taxes applied in OECD Member countries. Indeed, its SO_2 charge system can be considered a quasi-SO_2 tax. Given both that China has accumulated some experience in implementing SO_2 charges and that the charge scope is increasing, there is a foundation for and an urgency in carrying out a reform of the current SO_2 charge. According to our analysis, the trend might be: in the short to medium term, the reform will be focused on the SO_2 charge system which will be retained until the acid rain problem is effectively controlled; in the long term, an SO_2 tax will be established on the basis of a reformed SO_2 charge system and in combination with changes to the overall charge and tax system and energy tax reform.

3.1   Context

In November 1995, four ministries including NEPA jointly reported to the State Council on the status of the trial SO_2 charge program. It was proposed that the program not only be continued in the initial 2 provinces and 9 cities but also be extended from 1996, subject to the approval of the relevant provincial governments. The SO_2 charge was to be levied on all coal and oil used for commercial and industrial purposes and on enterprises, individuals or institutions that generated SO_2 emissions. The charge rate was determined by the provincial price management agencies in consultation with financial agencies, environmental protection bureaus and economic management agencies, based upon the experience of the trial program. The final plan was to be submitted to the appropriate department serving the State Council. The charge rate, administrative management and use of revenue were to be in conformity with the regulations governing the pollution levy system. Investment in cost-effective and proven SO_2 emission control technologies was encouraged.

In 1996, the State Council issued the "Reply on Questions Regarding the Extension of the Trial SO_2 Charge Program" (Guohuan No. [1996]24) on the basis of the report on the trial SO_2 charge program by the four ministries. The reply agreed in principle with the proposals in the report to extend the areal coverage of the SO_2 charge, in particular by first concentrating on the Acid Rain and SO_2 Pollution Control Areas (ASPCA). In 1998, SEPA, the State Development Planning Commission (SDPC), the Ministry of Finance and the State Commission for Economics and Trade jointly promulgated the "Circular on Extending SO_2 Charges to Acid Rain and SO_2 Pollution Control Areas" (Huanfa No. [1998]6) (hereinafter referred to as "the Circular"). Thus, the program will be extended to ASPCA initially and subsequently nation-wide.

3.2 Potential Impacts of Reform

At present because of insufficient income from taxes and limitations of the national tax legislation, many local governments tend to use charges as a means to increase their revenue. Three major problems in this approach have been identified (Wang et al., 1998). First, the burden of charges in some areas is obviously higher than that of taxes, eroding the contribution to national tax revenue and imposing important administrative costs. Table 2 shows that the share of charges in GDP has increased steadily over time, rising from 2.6% in 1985 to 8.8% in 1996.

Second, some charges are unreasonable or unjustified. They have not only increased the financial pressure on farmers and enterprises but also provided scope for corrupt behaviour.

Third, a large amount of money raised by charges and flowing to government agencies has been "off budget". This has seriously impacted on the financial function of the national government.

Table 2: Comparison of Charges and Taxes in GDP, 1985-1996

Year	Charge Collected (100 million yuan)	Tax Collected (100 million yuan)	GDP(100 million yuan)	Percentage of Charge in GDP (%)	Percentage of Tax in GDP (%)	Percentage of (Charge+Tax) in GDP (%)
1985	233.21	2 040.79	8 964.40	2.6	22.8	25.4
1990	760.00	2 821.83	18 547.90	4.1	15.2	19.3
1993	1 432.50	4 255.30	34 634.40	4.1	12.3	16.4
1995	3 843.00	6 038.04	58 260.50	6.6	10.3	16.9
1996	6 000.00	6 901.35	67 795.00	8.8	10.1	18.9

Source: Liu, 1997.

Recognising these problems, the government has determined to make charge and tax reform a major element of financial reform. The SDPC has proposed a basic framework for reform of the charge system in which only four major types of fees/charges will be retained: registration fee, license charge, environmental protection charge and judicial charges. In addition, following an interview with officials in the Ministry of Finance it is concluded that the pollution levy system will not be affected by reforms to the charge system nor undergo major change in the short term.

The government has started experiments with the pollution levy system based on total discharge quantities in the cities of Hangzhou, Zhengzhou and Jilin. This also indicates that the probability of transforming the pollution levy system (within which SO_2 charges are implemented) to one of an environmental tax is extremely small. However, this does not exclude reforms to the current tax system to influence the use of inputs contributing to, and emissions of, SO_2, such as the resource tax, consumption tax and adjustment tax on fixed asset investment direction adjustment.

3.3 Energy Tax Related to SO_2

Arguably, SO_2 pollution in China is a problem related to the structure of energy consumption and energy pricing. Zou (1996) developed a model based on provincial data from 1986 to 1994, and provided an explanation of the relationship between atmospheric pollutant emissions, the structure and level of economic development and energy consumption. The study concluded that the total increase in SO_2 emissions since 1986 was not the result of a change in the structure of the industry sector but rather was caused by a steady increase in overall energy consumption and inadequate controls on emission. Accordingly, characteristics of energy production and consumption are important elements in determining the status of atmospheric pollution. Therefore, policies that influence energy production and consumption will inevitably have effects on atmospheric pollution, including direct and indirect effects of SO_2 pollution control (op. cit.).

In this context, finance and tax policies can play an important role in adjusting the behaviour of economic agents and their generation of pollutants. Policies to control SO_2 emission should consider the contribution of tax policies, especially in the broader framework of reform of energy pricing.

China's current tax system does not include an explicit energy tax category. Rather, taxes on energy are spread among several categories. These include the consumption tax, the natural resources tax, the vehicle use tax and the fixed asset investment direction adjustment tax . These taxes are described in some detail in Wang et al. (1998) for this workshop.

3.4   Long-Term Possibilities for Establishing an SO_2 Tax

From the above, it can be seen that China has already established some tax categories related to energy production and consumption. However, these tax categories have limited effectiveness in controlling air pollution and SO_2 emissions given that their share of the total tax revenue is very small. In the longer term, an SO_2 tax could be established based upon modifications to the existing SO_2 charge system. The objective of the tax would be to strengthen incentives for SO_2 emission control.

Some officials and experts have noted, however, that although it is probably not feasible to establish an SO_2 tax in the short term the introduction of an element that covers SO_2 emissions into current energy-related taxes could be possible, especially if it forms part of a comprehensive strategy of longer term reform of energy-related taxes and the SO_2 charge system. Below we analyse alternative approaches for introducing an SO_2 tax within the different existing energy-related taxes. This does not imply that an SO_2 tax can be included in these existing tax categories simultaneously. Also, it should be noted that the tax on SO_2 emissions referred to here is a generic term covering the taxation of SO_2 emissions, taxes on SO_2 from energy products (such as coal) and taxes to encourage the production and use of low sulphur coal and clean energy sources.

(i)   Inclusion Within the Consumption Tax

This tax is levied on the production and import of 11 types of consumer goods divided among 5 categories of petrol, diesel, tyres, motorcycles and cars. At present, the tax does not cover coal, the major source of energy in China.

Currently, the annual production of coal with sulphur content higher than 3% is approximately 90 million tons, accounting for 7% of total national coal production. Mines producing this grade of coal are mainly located in the southwest. This is also the region where acid rain is most serious (SEPA, 1998).

To control SO_2 emissions and acid rain pollution, efforts should be made to tax the mining, transportation and use of high sulphur coal. Revenue from such a tax could be used to fund coal screening and washing facilities. The coal production management, planning and transport agencies should give priority to the designated acid rain and SO_2 pollution control areas (ASPCA) in the supply of low sulphur and washed coal to be used in power generation as well as wider availability of low sulphur coal in these areas to ensure the realisation of both SO_2 emission control and environmental protection objectives.

An SO_2 tax based on coal consumption should aim to limit the use of coal and heavy oil with high sulphur content used in power generation so that their supply and use is in compliance with the environmental protection objectives of local governments. Limits should also be set on the import of high sulphur fuels. In addition, the implementation of an SO_2 tax would support SEPA's policy goal of requiring that by the year 2000 household stoves in urban areas are to use only coal that has been screened and washed.

The logic of introducing an SO_2 tax as part of the existing consumption tax would be to ensure that coal was an explicit item of this latter tax. Air pollution in most areas of China is related to coal burning. Therefore, a tax that includes coal could strengthen incentives for producers and consumers of coal to protect the atmospheric environment. Such a tax could also provide a stable and growing source of revenue as well as help limit the use of high sulphur coal.

If the SO_2 tax were to cover all types of coal, strong resistance may be encountered because of the economic impacts that would result. Limiting the tax to coal with high sulphur content may be more acceptable. If this category of coal is included within the consumption tax, the SO_2 tax could then be collected along with the tax on gasoline and diesel tax. The SO_2 tax rate could be determined according to the sulphur content of different fuel types. The taxation of fuels based on sulphur content can have a significant impact in controlling the consumption of high sulphur coal.

(ii) Inclusion Within the Natural Resources Tax

This tax aims to reflect the different profit levels for developers arising from variations in mining conditions, natural resource quality and geographical conditions across the country and to provide incentives for the sustainable management of natural resources. It applies to mineral resources and salt. Taxable mineral products include crude oil, natural gas, coal, metal mineral products and other non-metal mineral products.

To realise the pollution control objectives for the year 2000 and the year 2010 in areas subject to acid rain and high SO_2 emissions, SEPA has stipulated that from 1 January, 1998 (i) government agencies in these areas are to prohibit the development of new coal mines where the sulphur content of the coal is higher than 3%; (ii) existing mines where the sulphur content of coal is higher than 3% shall gradually impose production limits and then phase out production; (iii) in developing new mines or upgrading existing ones where the sulphur content of coal is higher than 1.5%, coal screening and washing facilities shall be installed; (iv) existing mines shall install progressively coal screening and washing facilities according to plans developed by the designated mine management agencies of the State Council and other relevant government agencies.

There appear good opportunities for including within the Natural Resource Tax an SO_2 tax or an element that takes into account SO_2. In particular, crude oil, natural gas and coal are already included in this tax. The sulphur content of these different fuels could thus be added as a taxable item.

An SO_2 tax established on the basis of differences in the sulphur content of fuels is actually a re-pricing of the resource based on its quality. The tax rate could be set at a uniform level (e.g. a single rate on all high sulphur coals) or be scaled (e.g. a graduated rate scale related to increases in the sulphur content). An SO_2 tax as part of the Natural Resource Tax could limit effectively the production of high sulphur coal and contribute significantly in controlling SO_2 emissions. This would be of major benefit in the areas currently affected seriously by acid rain problems and SO_2 pollution.

(iii)   Inclusion Within Other Tax Categories

The Vehicle Use Tax is related to energy consumption although the energy sources it covers are fuels for vehicle use. It has no direct relation to the major source of SO_2 emission - coal consumption. Accordingly, difficulties exist in establishing a linkage between an SO_2 tax and the Vehicle Use Tax. Also, there are plans to introduce a leaded gasoline charge within the consumption tax. Therefore, if it is necessary to levy an SO_2 tax on vehicle fuels, a similar approach might be taken.

The Fixed Asset Investment Direction Adjustment Tax (FAIDAT) aims to implement the government's industrial policy by guiding investment, adjusting the structure of investment and promoting the development of priority projects. In setting the tax rate, national environmental protection goals can be taken into account, especially those concerning acid rain and the control of SO_2 pollution. The FAIDAT rate is currently 5% for the iron and steel, chemicals, petro-chemicals and cement industries, all of which consume large amounts of energy and generate significant pollution. For example, SO_2 emissions from the chemical, metallurgical, non-ferrous and building material industries accounted for about 20% of total SO_2 emissions in 1996 (ECCEY, 1997). The FAIDAT rate for these industries should be revised to take into account both SO_2 emissions and control measures.

The above analysis of energy-related tax policies shows that the introduction of an SO_2 tax within several existing taxes is basically feasible, or at least that SO_2 emissions could be a factor in setting the tax rates. In the long term, an explicit SO_2 tax might be established in China; such an idea has already been proposed by the fiscal authorities. In the interim, introducing an SO_2 tax into the current natural resource tax would support this longer term goal.

4.0   Determining the SO_2 Tax Rate

Generally speaking, the functions of economic instruments in environmental policies are to create an incentive for polluters to modify their behaviour and hence reduce pollution; and to generate funds for investments in environmental protection.

Although there are some differences in revenue use between an SO_2 charge and an SO_2 tax, determination of the rate is crucial to the operation of both. An effective rate should not only raise revenue but also encourage enterprises to reduce their emissions of SO_2.

The current SO_2 charge rate of 0.2 yuan/kg is mainly aimed at raising revenue, in which it has been relatively successful. It has had lesser effect in stimulating enterprises to reduce their SO_2 emissions.

4.1   Defining the Cost of Reducing SO_2 Emissions

To determine the cost of reducing SO_2 emissions, a cost function had to be derived. For this purpose, the Chinese Research Academy of Environmental Sciences (CRAES) carried out an investigation of air pollution control facilities in 4000 enterprises across the country in 1994. The enterprises investigated were located in over 300 cities and covered 20 types of industry. Based on technical and economic analysis of air pollution control facilities in these enterprises, a cost function for SO_2 emissions reduction was obtained as follows:

$$Cost = e^{\substack{5.143-1.335(S10)+2.307(S34)+0.855(S36)+1.509(S38)-0.993(S45)+0.61(S48)+2.464(S49)\\+1.57(S53)-7.58\bullet10^{-6}(Staff)-0.281(B)+1.151(C)}}$$
$$\bullet(A\_tre)^{0.399}\bullet(\frac{SO_2\_out}{SO_2\_in})^{-0.124}\bullet(\frac{SD\_out}{SD\_in})^{-0.076}\bullet(\frac{Oth\_out}{Oth\_in})^{-0.0002}$$

in which:

Cost = treatment cost of air pollutants in yuan

A_tre = annual treatment volume of waste gas inNm^3

Staff = employee number

SO_2_out, SD_out, Oth_out = effluent concentration of SO_2 smoke and other pollutants in mg/m^3

SO_2_in, SD_in, Oth_in = influent concentration of SO_2 smoke and other pollutants in mg/m^3

Other variants are integer variants to reflect the industry characteristics and enterprise ownership type.

Figure 3 shows the cost function diagrammatically[2]. It can be seen from this Figure that the cost increases more than proportionately with the rate of reduction in SO_2 emissions. For example, if SO_2 emissions are reduced by 60%, the corresponding cost is 420 yuan/ton; with an 80% rate of reduction the cost is 800 yuan/ton.

Figure 3: Marginal Cost of Reducing SO$_2$ Emissions

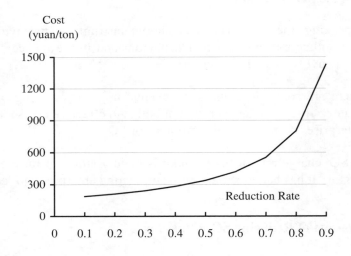

Only a limited number of coal-fired power stations in China have installed flue gas desulfurization equipment. Because of data gaps, however, it is difficult to obtain an accurate value for the marginal cost of controlling SO_2 emissions from these plants. Therefore, we used the average cost of SO_2 control to provide a basis for determining the rate of an SO_2 tax on coal-fired power stations[3].

Currently, representative flue gas desulfurization processes under demonstration trial or full application are wet flue gas desulfurization, phosphorous-ammonia composite method, spray dryer desulfurization, and furnace and boiler sorbent injection. Direct annual costs of these technologies (including depreciation and operations cost) are 839 yuan/ton,1485 yuan/ton, 770.2 yuan/ton and 665.6 yuan/ton respectively (Hao et al., 1997). By-products produced by the phosphorous-ammonia method can be sold to offset partly the cost of desulfurization. If this method is excluded from consideration, the average annual cost of the other three methods is 760 yuan/ton. We use this figure as the average cost of SO_2 control in coal-fired power stations in China.

4.2 Differentiating Sources of SO_2 Emissions for Purposes of Establishing the Tax Rate

Coal-fired power stations are major contributors of SO_2 emissions in China and thus a focus for national air pollution control efforts. However, when determining the SO_2 tax rate it is necessary to distinguish between this group and small coal-fired facilities.

SO_2 emissions from the latter are significant in terms of both volume and area affected, posing major challenges to environmental management. Investment in SO_2 emissions control in these facilities is small compared to that required for power stations. The primary objective of an SO_2 tax on small coal-fired facilities should be to stimulate reductions in emissions, with revenue-raising a secondary goal.

Figure 4 shows diagrammatically the result of our analysis of the rate of SO_2 reduction in over 4000 enterprises. It can be seen that 40% of enterprises achieved an SO_2 reduction rate of 85%; 75% of the enterprises attained a rate of about 50%; and around 10% of the enterprises did not undertake any emissions reduction. The figure also shows that 50% of the enterprises achieved an emissions reduction rate of about 80%. Referring to Figure 3, at this rate the marginal cost of SO_2 control is shown as 800 yuan/ton.

---

[3]   Research on, and trial installation of, major types of flue gas desulfurization (FGD) facilities has taken place in China. Several desulfurization processes have shown promising results. Based on economic analysis of desulfurization projects in power plants of China, investment in wet flue gas desulfurization for a 100MW plant and spray dryer desulfurization for 200MW plant costs 480 million yuan and 95 million yuan respectively. Desulfurization using the furnace and boiler sorbent injection method for a 100MW plant requires an investment exceeding 20 million yuan (Hao et al.,1997).

Figure 4: Rate of SO₂ Emissions Reduction within Enterprises

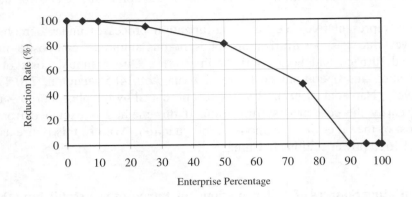

SO₂ emissions control in large coal-fired power stations requires major investment. Accordingly, the major function of an SO₂ tax applied to this sector should be to generate revenue to fund control measures, with a secondary result of stimulating a reduction in emissions. Because of data limitations we use the average cost of SO₂ control as the basis for determining the tax rate: as noted in section 4.1, this is estimated at 760 yuan/ton.

The average costs of SO₂ reduction in large coal-fired power stations and small coal-fired facilities are not widely different. For the former the figure is estimated at 800 yuan/ton and for the latter it is 760 yuan/ton. Although these figures could be used to set the initial SO₂ tax rate, they should be reviewed regularly to reflect changes in the marginal cost of SO₂ control and broader air pollution management objectives.

Obviously, different tax rates will promote different objectives. For example, the 0.2 yuan/kg rate (1990 prices) developed by Tsinghua University was aimed primarily to meet a revenue raising objective. By contrast, the Chinese Research Academy of Environmental Sciences has proposed[4] a rate of 0.52 yuan/kg (1995 prices) to generate revenue as well as a rate of 1.05 yuan/kg (1995 prices) to stimulate behaviour modification by polluters. The latter figure is based on consideration of the average cost of SO₂ control in all facilities that emit this gas.

To facilitate the introduction of an SO₂ tax we can transform the existing SO₂ charge based on emissions to one based on the sulphur content of coal and on coal consumption. Currently, there are mines in 19 provinces and cities producing coal for centralised distribution, each of widely different average sulphur content. The best quality coal is from Heilongjiang province where the average sulphur content is only 0.4%; the worst is from Guizhou province with an average sulphur content as high as 3.2% (Tsinghua University, 1993). The average sulphur content of coal for centralised distribution is 1.21-1.79%. To determine the SO₂ tax rate we can define three types of coal: low sulphur coal, medium

---

[4]   In 1997, the Chinese Research Academy of Environmental Sciences completed a study under the World Bank Technical Assistance Project on "The Study on Design and Implementation of Pollution Levy System of China". This study proposed approaches for reforming China's existing pollution levy system.

sulphur coal and high sulphur coal. Medium sulphur coal has a sulphur content of 1.2-1.8%. If a tax rate of 800 yuan/ton is used, the schedules[5] corresponding to the different coal types are as listed in Table 3.

Table 3: SO₂ Tax Rate Schedules (yuan/ton coal)

Low Sulphur Coal		Medium Sulphur Coal		High Sulphur Coal	
S content (%)	Tax Rate Schedule	S content (%)	Tax Rate Schedule	S content (%)	Tax Rate Schedule
0.4	5.6	1.2	16.7	2.0	27.8
0.6	8.4	1.4	19.5	2.4	33.4
0.8	11.1	1.6	22.3	2.8	39.0
1.0	13.9	1.8	25.1	3.2	44.5

The impact of an SO₂ tax on the production and sale of coal is closely related to the sulphur content and price of coal. For example, in Shanxi province, the coal production base of China, the local price of coal within the province is about 100 yuan/ton (Shanxi Coal Management Bureau, 1998) and the average coal sulphur content is approximately 1.3% (Editorial Committee of China Coal Industry Yearbooks, 1991-1993). From Table 3, one ton of coal with a sulphur content of 1.3% corresponds to a tax rate schedule of 18.1 yuan, or about 18% of its sale price. This is likely to have a significant impact on the production and sale of coal, especially the mining and use of high sulphur coal.

5.0   Reform of the Existing SO₂ Charge

The existing SO₂ charge will remain the major policy instrument within the national pollution levy system to control acid rain pollution and SO₂ emissions. In particular, it will be applied in the Two Control Zones[6]. A key task in the short and medium term is to revise the operation of the SO₂ charge to take account of new requirements in China's environmental management and air pollution control policies. This work will also support the long term goal of establishing an SO₂ tax.

---

[5]   We have adopted the SO₂ emission factors developed by Beijing Academy of Environmental Sciences: 0.9 for boilers in power plants and 0.85 for industrial and household boilers. Based on the weighted average of coal consumption in the three types of boilers in 1995, the national average SO₂ emission factor is 0.87.

[6]   The total area of the newly identified Acid Rain Control Zones and SO₂ Control Zones is 109 sq. km, or 11.4% of China's total land area. The area of the Acid Rain Control Zones is 80 sq. km, or 8.4% of the total territory area while the area of the SO₂ Control Zones is 29 sq. km, or 3% of the total land area (SEPA, 1998). SO₂ emissions in the two control zones were about 14 million tons, or 60% of the total of 23.7 million tons for the whole country in 1995. Thus a focus on controlling acid rain and SO₂ pollution in the two control zones can have a major impact in addressing these problems.

5.1 Specific Tasks

(i) Clarifying Administrative Responsibilities

Despite the number of different charge systems operated by local governments, most charges are organised by regional jurisdiction. In order to achieve co-ordination with the local environmental management structure and enhance the efficiency of collecting the SO_2 charge, municipal and county environmental management bureaus should be designated the responsible agency. Village and township authorities could also be entrusted to carry out this task.

(ii) Widening the Scope and Target of the Charge

After 5 years of applying the SO_2 charge in two provinces and nine cities, valuable experience has been accumulated. On this basis, the scope of the charge and the target sources of pollution should now be revised.

Concerning the scope of the charge, SEPA, the State Planning and Development Commission, the Finance Ministry and the State Economic and Trade Commission jointly published in January 1998 a "Circular on Expanding the SO_2 Charge Demonstration in the Acid Rain Control Zones and the SO_2 Pollution Control Zones" (Document [1998] No. 6). According to this circular, the charge will be promoted first in the Two Control Zones and then nation-wide.

SO_2 pollution is concentrated in urban areas at present, with coal-fired facilities being the main sources. Charging for SO_2 emissions from these facilities is imperative to address the problem. Since the start of the trial program in 1993, the charge has been targeted on industrial and commercial coal-fired plants. No charge has yet been levied on other sources of SO_2 emissions.

However, some of these sources contribute an important share of SO_2 emissions. Statistics show that in recent years such emissions from industrial and residential sources account for about 74% and 12% respectively of the total for the whole country (China Statistics Bureau, 1994-1997). Thus, the sources subject to the SO_2 charge should be expanded to all coal and oil burning facilities that emit this pollutant.

(iii) Strengthening the Monitoring of SO_2 Emissions

The SO_2 charge is based on the quantity of emissions. This differs from the other types of pollution charges established under the pollution levy system which apply only to emissions exceeding the relevant standard (i.e. the charges relate to non-compliance with the designated standard). Therefore the monitoring of SO_2 emissions is the key in implementing the SO_2 charge.

Three methods can be used to determine SO_2 emissions. The first and most direct method is to monitor emissions on site. The second approach is to establish a material balance or pollutant emission coefficient, such as an emission coefficient per unit output value, to calculate the level of emissions. The third method is to rely on the reporting data submitted by the polluters or specifying emission limits for individual polluters. All of these methods have their advantages and disadvantages.

Currently, the material balance and pollutant coefficient method is used in defining the SO_2 charge. Considerations of the amount of coal burnt, its sulphur content, combustion characteristics and the efficiency of de-sulphurization facilities in place are used to calculate the level of SO_2 emissions. This method can also be used in the future in setting an SO_2 tax. Where possible, such as for large power stations which have the necessary technical and financial resources, on site monitoring of emissions should be the preferred approach to determine SO_2 emissions. For other operations monitoring data should be used as the basis for setting the charge, where possible. For counties and townships which have small-medium sized power plants and other sources of SO_2 emissions, insufficient monitoring powers available to local authorities may require that the charge rates be obtained by using the material balance method. In particular, based on the pollutant emission coefficients and SO_2 emission coefficients per unit product.

Further efforts are needed to strengthen and promote more widely the charge method based on pollutant emission data reported by enterprises[7].

(iv)   Legislating for Charging on the Basis of Quantity of Pollutant Emitted

The SO_2 charge is an important component of China's pollution levy system. The pollution levy system itself has a legal basis, implemented through regulations. The regulations set out the scope and targets of the charges, the tasks of responsible institutions, the standards against which charges are levied, the procedure for implementing the charge and the method for collecting the charge and disbursing the revenue.

In 1995, the People's Congress revised the Air Pollution Prevention Act. The revised Act still requires charges for emissions exceeding the defined standards but it has expanded the pollution prevention focus from dust to SO_2 and other noxious gases. The Act also stipulates that the Acid Rain Zone and SO_2 Control Zone are to be identified; this task was completed in 1997.

The State Council's "Decision on Several Issues of Environmental Protection" requires that "effective measures to control the deteriorating trends of acid rain and SO_2 pollution be taken". In addition, the State Council has recently published its "Reply to the Related Issues on Expanding Trials of the SO_2 Charge System". The State Environmental Protection Administration, the State Development and Planning Commission, the Ministry of Finance and the State Commission for Economics and Trade have jointly issued a circular on this matter (see section 3.1). Revision of the existing "Regulation on Pollution Charges" is also under way.

All of the above provide a legal basis for an SO_2 charge. However, there is no explicit provision in the Air Pollution Prevention Act, the basic law for air pollution control in China, for setting a charge based on the quantity of pollutant emitted. It is suggested therefore that this concept should be included as part of a future revision to the Law in order to facilitate the implementation of charges for SO_2 and other pollutants based on quantity emitted.

(v)   Capacity Building

Capacity building involves both the environmental supervision and management personnel and inspection teams in sub-national environmental bureaus and offices. The environmental supervision teams are the main institution for implementing the SO_2 charge at the local level (collection of SO_2 charges).

---

[7]   The emission data measured and reported by polluters should be verified by the local environmental protection bureaus (EPBs) before being used as the basis for charging. Environmental monitoring stations or other monitoring stations appointed by the EPBs also carry out monitoring. Their results also need to be approved by the EPBs.

The key need for capacity building here is training of personnel to improve the teams' effectiveness. The main role of the <u>inspection teams</u> is to ensure that compliance with the legal requirements for environmental management is achieved by relevant enterprises and activities. This is carried out through routine, special and random inspections.

(vi)   Standardising Aspects of the SO_2 Charge

To enhance acceptance of the SO_2 charge, especially in the Two Control Zones, various elements of the charge system need to be standardised. This should draw upon the experience from the trial program. In particular, standardisation of procedures used to calculate and collect the charge, and the documentation required.

The former includes pollutant reporting and registration, emissions auditing, charge calculation, transmission of charge demands, mechanism for collecting the charge and penalties for late payment.

The latter refers to the adoption of a standard system of documentation. It includes forms for recording pollutant emissions, charge demands and payment, and deadlines for payment.

A computerised management information system related to pollution charges generally has been developed in China and is applied nation-wide. It comprises 3 elements: levying of charges, financial analysis, and management and decision-making. The SO_2 charge should be included within this system for administrative efficiency.

5.2   Complementarities Between the SO_2 Charge and a Possible Future Tax

The SO_2 charge and, in the long term, SO_2 tax, are somewhat different in concept. The SO_2 tax to be established in the long term should be incorporated into the state tax system and its management procedures. As discussed earlier, a future SO_2 tax could be included as part of energy-related taxes such as the consumption tax or the natural resource tax. Environmental protection bureaus could be authorised by the state tax administration to collect the SO_2 tax, whether this is incorporated into the consumption, natural resource or another tax category.

In the long term, the incorporation of an SO_2 tax into China's general tax system will most probably be within the framework of a revised consumption tax that includes coal and the natural resource tax. These two taxes could include as part of their respective goals influencing the extraction rate and use of coal, and control of SO_2 emissions from multiple sources.

The target group of the SO_2 charge are emitters of this gas. These emissions are sourced not only from coal burning but also industrial processes and other activities. The charge aims to encourage polluters to treat pollution and to compensate for damages because of the effects of SO_2 pollution. It favours end-of-pipe approaches to pollution control.

From the view point of SO_2 pollution control, the tax and charge do not overlap and could be adopted simultaneously. In particular, given that coal generates SO_2 only when it is burned emissions from industrial processes could be subject to the charge while the SO_2 tax could be levied on coal-fired boilers and furnaces.

As the SO_2 charge cannot be transformed into a tax in the short term, a new mechanism combining elements of both is suggested. For enterprises and public institutions, the charge could continue to be collected by local environmental protection bureaus, of which 90% of the revenue would go into local environmental funds. A sulphur-content based tax could be added to the consumption tax and natural resource tax categories. The revenue collected would go to national or local finance authorities as defined by the administrative procedures for these two tax categories. The money would be used as an SO_2 pollution prevention fund.

These proposed arrangements require the assent and co-operation of the environment, finance and taxation authorities. The objective is to limit the development and use of high-sulphur coal and to reduce SO_2 emissions. The SO_2 charge rate could be based on existing research work while the rate of the SO_2 tax should be decided following consultation among the finance, taxation and environment authorities and taking into consideration the tax situation of affected consumers and enterprises.

5.3   Main Barriers to Reform of the SO_2 Charge

(i)   Economic Impacts of Raising the Charge Rate

This paper has suggested that a charge rate of 800 yuan/ton SO_2 is a reasonable figure to both stimulate behaviour modification by industry and generate revenue for environmental investments, especially in coal-fired power stations. In 1998, three demonstration cities are using an SO_2 charge based on total quantity of emissions. They have applied charges between 0.32-0.63 yuan/kg, which is lower than the rate proposed in this paper. If the rate we propose is implemented, the financial burden on enterprises will increase. As shown earlier in the example of Shanxi Province, the introduction of an SO_2 tax will result in an 18% increase in the price of coal. In the short-term, this has important economic implications for coal producers and consumers.

Implementation of the SO_2 charge and, ultimately, the tax, rate could be achieved in a graduated fashion. Enterprises would be informed in advance of the future rate increase so that they can plan their responses as early as possible, whether this is in the form of process changes or new investments. For those enterprises unable to pay the new rate, the approach of "levying first and exempting later" might be adopted.

(ii)   Redefined Resource Needs

Human, physical and financial resources are needed to support implementation of the SO_2 charge and future tax. This issue is directly affected by the approach adopted for revenue collection. If in the long term the SO_2 tax is collected by environmental protection bureaus under the devolved authority of the tax department, the issue becomes one of enforcement capacity among the environmental monitoring teams. Statistics for 1995 show that there were 2603 provincial, municipal and county-level environmental supervision and management institutions in China. They employed 27,300 staff, collected 140,000 yuan per staff in pollution charges and each staff member was responsible for 15 enterprises[8] (Chinese Research Academy of Environmental Sciences, 1997). With the strengthening of environmental enforcement and a new emphasis on total quantity emission control, the capacity and quality of the current environmental

---

[8]   The collection of pollution charges is one of the responsibilities of the supervision and management institutions.

supervision and monitoring institutions is inappropriate to the new situation. This will affect the speed of implementation of the SO_2 charge and tax.

(iii) *Revenue Use*

The mechanism for using the collected revenue is one of the major problems to be resolved. It needs to be strengthened and standardised. The number of local environmental protection funds based on the pollution levy should be gradually expanded and their operation improved. Considering that SO_2 and acid rain problems affect several regions in China, a state environmental protection fund should be established as soon as possible.

(iv) *Legislative Base for Charging on the Basis of Total Quantity of Emissions*

As distinct from other pollutants, the charge on SO_2 is currently based on the total quantity of emissions. As there is no explicit provision for this approach in the existing Air Pollution Prevention Act, its legal foundation is weak. It is hoped that the national legislative agencies will prepare the necessary amendments as soon as possible to ensure the smooth introduction of an SO_2 charge nation-wide.

The prerequisite for legally introducing the SO_2 tax is to make provision for a coal consumption tax within the consumption tax. This requires an amendment to the Consumption Tax Act and the Resource Tax Act.

6.0 Use and Management of Revenue Collected from the SO_2 Charge and Tax

Revenue use and management of the SO_2 charge and tax are not identical. For the SO_2 charge, these aspects will be in accordance with the existing requirements concerning the pollution levy system, which may be revised in the future. For the future SO_2 tax, the revenue will be incorporated into the state tax system. The finance authorities will be responsible for the management and distribution of the funds.

6.1 SO_2 Charge: Revenue Use and Management

(i) *Policies Concerning Revenue Use and Management*

Policies for revenue use and management stem from the relevant environmental protection laws and regulations. Several policies concerning revenue use have been adopted, i.e. (1) using funds raised by the charge to invest in pollution source control, comprehensive pollution prevention measures and the development of an environmental industry; (2) shifting from charging a low loan rate to a quasi-commercial loan rate, applying a suitable discount rate, setting realistic loan interest rates for projects with an obvious profit potential, and gradually phasing out the policy of revenue exemption; (3) incorporating all charge revenue in the fiscal budget but with a proportion dedicated to a specific fund for pollution control and for funding capacity building in environmental departments; (4) incorporating the SO_2 charge in production costs.

Policies for the management policies of revenue collected under the SO_2 charge are: (1) the incorporation of the money raised by the charge within the fiscal budget; (2) levying the charge according to defined jurisdictions and establishing a nation-wide system for the overall management and distribution of funds; (3) the finance authorities are to share responsibility for distribution of the revenue, with a proportion of the money to be used to strengthen the state's investment in environmental protection.

(ii)   Expenditure

As for other pollution charges in China, the expenditure of revenue raised by the SO_2 charge should be determined according to central and local environmental management responsibilities. The current distribution of pollution charge revenue raised from enterprises does not meet regional pollution treatment goals. Considering the current status, the total charge revenue should be incorporated into the fiscal budget. A proportion of the revenue (e.g. 70%) could be set aside as a specific fund for pollution control and used to establish environmental protection funds at various levels of government. The remainder of the revenue could be used for capacity building in environmental protection departments.

(iii)   Establishment of Environmental Protection Funds

Various types of environmental funds, mainly under the responsibility of government administration, have been established in China. By the end of 1996, the total revenue of environmental funds in 31 provinces, municipalities and autonomous regions was 3.5 billion yuan. Eighteen provinces, municipalities and autonomous regions have set up provincial environmental funds, and 15 sub-provincial cities have set up urban environmental funds. Environmental funds at provincial and sub-provincial levels had revenue of 1.4 billion yuan, representing 40% of the total revenue of China's environmental funds.

Currently, the main difficulty in establishing national, provincial, city and county environmental funds is at the national level. As the environmental fund cannot be fully funded by government contributions, a self-funding mechanism with the introduction of market mechanisms needs to be established. The scale of economies and the lack of management capacity in county governments means that the provincial and city level governments are the focus of local environmental funds.

To ensure compatibility with the needs of a market economy, the specific fund for pollution source treatment that was established under the planned economy should be completely reformed. In recognition of the "public welfare" characteristics of environmental protection, mixed funds could be established aimed at meeting national environmental protection objectives and creating incentives for environmental investments.

(iv)   Including the SO_2 Charge Within Production Costs

The inclusion of the SO_2 charge within production costs means that the polluters should have an incentive to internalise the external costs of pollution. In doing this, the biggest beneficiaries are the enterprises themselves since they can reduce their tax bill. Otherwise the burden on enterprises will increase because they will pay not only the charge but also 33% in income tax. This double incentive should encourage enterprises to adopt pollution control measures. However, the inclusion of the SO_2 charge in production costs is not easily implemented from the viewpoint of the current status and management system in enterprises.

6.2   SO₂ Tax: Revenue Use and Management

The nature of the revenue from a future SO_2 tax, its management and use are different from those of the SO_2 charge. The SO_2 tax will be part of the state finance system and distributed by the finance authorities in accordance with the relevant policies. During the transition period, it is suggested that most of the revenue will continue to be used for SO_2 pollution prevention.

If in the long term the SO_2 tax is incorporated into the energy consumption tax and natural resource tax and the environmental protection departments are entrusted to collect the tax, part of the revenue will be used to fund the administrative costs of the environmental protection departments and the remainder will be available to the general budget. As revenue from the energy consumption tax goes to local government while that from the natural resource tax is shared between local and central government, money raised by the SO_2 tax will also follow this differentiation. However, it should be noted that revenue from the SO_2 tax should be used specifically for establishing an SO_2 pollution prevention fund or contribute to an environmental fund.

7.0   Potential Benefits of Implementing an SO₂ Tax

China is experiencing rapid economic development. This is reflected, *inter alia*, by the accelerating trend in energy consumption. From 1995 to 2010, coal consumption is expected to increase by up to 0.5 billion tons, resulting in a large increase in SO_2 emissions. With the increase in coal consumption and SO_2 emissions, the acid rain problem will become increasingly serious. Currently, acid rain impacts on one-third of China's total land area.

SO_2 is the main source of acid rain and urban air pollution. The economic loss from SO_2 pollution includes damage to human health, decrease in crop yield and quality of produce, reduction in water quality and corrosion of materials and buildings. At present, there is no comprehensive analysis of the extent of economic loss caused by air pollution. Some estimates have been made, however. Sun (1997) reported that the annual loss from air pollution in China is 50-90 billion yuan, with the majority due to SO_2 pollution. In recent years, the annual economic loss from acid rain in Guangdong Province exceeds 2 billion yuan, while the loss in Sichuan and Yuannan Provinces and Guangxi Autonomous Region is 16 billion yuan and in Chongqing it is more than 0.5 billion yuan (Zhang, 1997).

China has developed acid rain and SO_2 pollution control objectives up to the year 2010 for the two control zones. On the basis of current per capita GNP of US\$620, extensive financial and technical investments are needed to reduce significantly SO_2 emissions and to control effectively acid rain and SO_2 pollution. The promotion of an SO_2 tax will undoubtedly provide support for achieving these objectives in the two control zones.

If the SO_2 tax is first implemented in the two control zones using a tax rate of 800 yuan/ton, the revenue is estimated at 6.72 billion yuan (1995 prices). This assumes that 14 million tons of SO_2 are emitted in the control zones and that the tax coverage is 60% of leviable entities. If the SO_2 tax were applied nation-wide, the expected revenue would be 11.38 billion yuan (1995 prices). It can be seen that the smooth implementation of an SO_2 tax would produce obvious economic and environmental benefits. The revenue raised would offset about 17% of the economic loss caused by air pollution.

In 1995, investment in air pollution control in China was only 3.24 billion yuan. The revenue raised by the air pollution charge that year was 0.74 billion yuan (China Environmental Yearbook, 1996). If 90% of the SO_2 tax is applied to preventing emissions, about 6 billion yuan could be invested in SO_2

pollution control in the two control zones, providing a solid financial foundation for the realisation of environmental protection objectives.

8.0   Conclusions

On the basis of a comprehensive analysis of SO_2 charge trial projects in China, the concept of a future SO_2 tax in the two acid rain and SO_2 pollution control zones, and ultimately nation-wide, has been discussed in this paper. The conclusions are as follows.

The successful trial of an SO_2 charge system in 2 provinces and 9 cities since 1993 has yielded valuable experience to support the future promotion of an SO_2 tax. As of 1997, the total revenue raised by the SO_2 charge in the demonstration provinces and cities was 0.544 billion yuan.

At present, the two roles of the SO_2 charge are to (i) stimulate emissions reduction in industrial processes and in small and medium-sized power stations; and (ii) to raise revenue for SO_2 reduction in large power stations.

The existing SO_2 charge system, its implementation and use of revenue raised should be further strengthened and extended in the two control zones.

A realistic charge rate for SO_2 emissions would be 800 yuan/ton. This rate is 4 times the current rate. The new rate should be introduced gradually.

Building on the trial SO_2 charge system, in the short and medium-term the focus should be to introduce the system on a nation-wide basis and in the longer term to introduce an SO_2 tax within the existing natural resources tax and consumption tax categories. The SO_2 tax rate should be linked to the sulphur content of coal to limit the exploitation and utilisation of high sulphur coal.

Levying an SO_2 tax will promote social and environmental benefits. If a charge rate of 800 yuan/ton is adopted the annual revenue raised in the two control zones will be about 6.7 billion yuan, which would provide significant resources for SO_2 pollution control.

The use and management of revenue from the SO_2 charge need to be improved. On the basis of existing local environmental funds, a national SO_2 pollution prevention fund or environmental fund should be established as soon as possible to resolve the cross-regional acid rain problem and to provide money for controlling SO_2 emissions.

At the same time as the SO_2 charge is promoted, a new combined tax and charge system could be established to integrate objectives of controlling sources and emissions of SO_2.

Pollution charges and environmental taxes are two types of economic instruments increasingly used in environmental management. Pollution charges are a particularly effective economic instrument in an economy in transition. The charge can modify the behaviour of polluters, reduce part of the environmental damages and raise revenue for pollution control. Although there are no differences in the function and operation of an environmental tax and pollution charge, their approach to revenue management and use are different under China's current financial system. As economic reform deepens in China, together with improvements in the fiscal system and increased resources for environmental investment, it is envisaged that an environmental (or pollution) tax will be gradually introduced for some pollutants.

The implementation of an environmental tax in China is complicated as it is linked to reform of the overall tax system. An environmental tax cannot replace fully a pollution charge; it should be integrated with the pollution charge system. A new combined tax and charge system is suggested by the authors. Money from the charge would be destined principally for local government purposes while the revenue from the tax would be for national purposes. For pollutants with wide and deep impact on the environment, an environmental tax should be levied, e.g. carbon tax and SO_2 tax. For pollutants with regional and local impacts, a pollution charge could be levied to promote the achievement of local pollution prevention objectives.

BIBLIOGRAPHY

China Statistics Bureau (1991-1997): *China Statistics Yearbooks 1991-1997.*China Statistics Press. Beijing.

Chinese Research Academy of Environmental Sciences (1997): Study on the Design and Implementation of China's Pollution Levy System. Unpublished report. Beijing.

Chinese Research Academy of Environmental Sciences (1998): Study on Funding of, and Capacity Building in, Environmental Protection Departments. Unpublished report. Beijing.

Editorial Committee of China Environment Yearbook (1992-1997): *China Environment Yearbooks 1992-1997,* China Environmental Sciences Press. Beijing.

Editorial Committee of China Coal Industry Yearbooks (1991-1993): *China Coal Industry Yearbooks 1991-1993.* Coal Industry Press. Beijing.

Hao, Jieming, Lu Yongqi and He, Kebing (1997): "Current Status and Economic Analysis of Flue Gas Desulfurization Technologies in Coal-fired Power Stations in China" in *Proceedings of China Environmental Sciences.* China Environmental Sciences Press. Beijing.

State Environmental Protection Administration (SEPA) (1998): "Defining the Acid Rain Control Zones and SO_2 Pollution Control Zones" in *Environmental Protection. March 1998.* Beijing.

Sun, Binyan (1997): *Estimation, Projection and Thinking of Pollution Loss in China this Century.*

Tsinghua University and Shanghai Academy of Environmental Protection (1996): Study on SO_2 Charges and their Implementation in the Industrial Coal Burning Sector. Unpublished report.

Wang, Jinnan, Ge, C., Yang, J., Song, A., Wang, D. and Liu, Q. (1998): "Taxation and the Environment in China: Practice and Perspectives". Unpublished Background Paper to Workshop on Environmental Taxes in China and OECD Member Countries (Held at the OECD, Paris on 5-6 October, 1998).

Wang, Tianxiang and Zhao, Yong (1997): *Acid Rain and Energy Strategy Planning.*

Zhang, Huiming (1997): "SO_2 Pollution Control in Chian's Power Industry" in <u>Progress of Environmental Sciences 12</u>.

Zou Ji (1996): Study on Integrated Environmental and Economic Policies. Unpublished PhD Dissertation. Institute of Environmental Economics, Renmin University, Beijing.

Zou, Ji (1997): "Energy, Finance, Tax Policy and Air Pollution Prevention in China" in *Proceedings of the China Environmental Economics Policy Conference.* Beijing.

ENERGY TAXES - THE DANISH MODEL

Hans Larsen
Ministry of Taxation, Denmark

1.0 The Danish Taxation of Energy is Comprised of Three Elements:

- energy taxes on oil, coal, gas and electricity, where an attempt has been made to balance the rate for the different fuels according to the gross energy content of the fuels

- a CO_2 tax on energy, where the rate for the different fuels is balanced according to the fuels' CO_2 emissions on combustion

- an SO_2 tax on energy, where the rate depends on the S-content of the fuels or the net SO_2 emission on combustion.

There are a number of common elements in the three types of taxes, but there are also a number of differences in the rules for refunds, exemptions, etc.

2.0 A Brief History of Energy Taxes in Denmark

2.1. Evolution of Tax Rates

Until 1978 Denmark had no tax on energy, apart from a tax on petrol which was introduced in 1917.

In 1978 a tax was introduced on electricity, and later that year a tax was introduced on light and heavy fuel oil. In 1979 a tax was introduced on bottled gas and town gas. This tax on town gas was lifted again in 1983, however. In 1982 a tax was introduced on coal. In 1996 a tax was introduced on natural gas. Over the years this tendency to tax has been extended to cover more oil and coal products, etc.

The first energy taxes on oil and electricity were modest in amount, and were introduced because of the two oil crises in the 1970s, although there were also fiscal grounds for the taxes.

Denmark was hit particularly hard by the first oil crisis, because a very large proportion of the Danish energy consumption was based on oil.

The energy taxes on oil, gas and petrol, in particular, were increased substantially in the mid-1980s in connection with the fall in international oil prices and the drop in the dollar exchange rate. These tax increases were carried out in connection with a tightening of fiscal policy. The tax increases were set so that the absolute consumer price could be kept unchanged. In this way, an attempt was made to maintain the incentive to continue energy savings, which had become an important political objective during and after the oil crises in the 1970s, as well as to increase the use of energy sources which were exempt from taxation, such as sustainable energy, bio-fuels and waste heat, in addition to surplus heat from industrial plants, etc.

Lastly, this was a way of ensuring a future for the new forms of collective energy supply (natural gas and combined heat and power generation (CHP)) which it had been decided to develop after the energy crises in order to reduce the dependency on oil.

The drop in the consumer price of oil also led to a drop in the consumer price of natural gas. The import price of natural gas also fell, although not by quite as much, and the gas utilities' profit margin was therefore reduced. It also became evident that the higher energy prices had reduced the consumption per customer installed, so that the financing charges ended up weighing heavier than expected in relation to sales.

These financial difficulties with the natural gas supply, which was established in the mid-1980s, were a contributory factor to it being only the tax on oil which was increased, whilst no tax was introduced on natural gas. However, the gas utilities were able to continue selling their gas at the same prices as oil with the tax, as a result of their monopolistic position. The additional price which the gas utilities were able to demand for the gas as a result of the rival fuels being taxed, the shadow tax, was collected according to the same principles as the oil tax, the difference being that the revenue went to the public gas utilities rather than the treasury.

The change in international energy prices in the mid-1980s also meant that the competitive strength of CHP compared to other forms of energy supply was reduced. The prices for fuels which were used for CHP supplies fell less than those for other fuels, such as light oil.

As CHP has a fiscal advantage, higher taxation would increase the competitiveness of CHP.

The international oil prices exclusive of tax fell more than coal prices, and the tax increases for oil were therefore greater than those for electricity and coal. The former balance in taxation in relation to the gross energy content of the fuels was thereby altered. Before 1986 the level was about 10 Danish kroner (DKK) per Gigajoule (GJ) energy in the fuels. After the increases, the oil tax rose to DKK 50 per GJ, whilst coal and electricity were taxed at about DKK 25 per GJ. The net effect, despite the large tax increases on oil, was that the price inclusive of tax was just about unchanged for oil, whilst the price of coal and electricity rose.

When the CO_2 tax was introduced in 1992 the oil tax was reduced by a similar amount, to a level of about DKK 41/GJ, whereas there was a certain net increase in the tax on coal and electricity, where the energy tax amounted to DKK 25-30/GJ.

Balance was again restored to the energy taxes in connection with a tax reform implemented in 1993 and phased in from 1994 to 1998.

The tax on oil remained at the same level, but the tax on coal and electricity was gradually increased to the same level as for oil, i.e. to around DKK 41 per GJ.

In connection with a new tax adjustment, it was agreed that the taxes should again be increased in the period from 1st July 1998 to 2002. The rates for the energy taxes will be increased by about 25 percent, and will therefore reach a level of about DKK 51 per GJ once they have been phased in.

In 1996 a tax of DKK 0.25 per GJ or DKK 0.01 per m3 was introduced on natural gas, and natural gas also became subject to the CO_2 tax. The tax on natural gas has been increased considerably with effect from 1998, and at the end of 1998 it will amount to DKK 1.47 per m^3. (If this rate were to be fully balanced with the oil tax, the rate ought to be DKK 1.88 per m^3). The rate for natural gas will be equivalent to the tax on oil by the year 2009 at the latest.

The reduction in the difference in tax between natural gas and oil does not affect the consumer prices, but only the earnings of the gas utilities (see above). The gas utilities have set the price of gas as if it were subject to the same tax as oil, but in the future the revenue will go to the treasury.

The tax burden from all green taxes is shown in Appendix 1. Appendix 2 summarises past and projected energy tax rates.

2.2   Tax Assessment, Refunds and Exemptions

Basically all sales of oil, gas, coal and electricity from the energy suppliers are taxed, as is consumption by the latter. This tax must be shown on the invoices sent by the energy suppliers. There are, however, certain applications where tax is not levied.

This is true for:

- fuels used for the production of electricity

- energy for air and sea transport

- energy for collective traffic (trains and buses)

- energy for use outside of Denmark, including for the extraction of oil from the North Sea.

The energy consumers, apart from those applications which are exempted, therefore pay the energy supplier (the electricity plant, the coal dealer, the oil company, etc.) for the energy as well for the tax. The energy supplier pays this tax to the state once a month.

A large number of energy applications are, however, entitled to have this tax refunded by the tax authorities.

From the beginning, it was implicit that VAT-registered companies could have their energy taxes reimbursed if they were entitled to have the VAT on the energy refunded. This was possible if the energy was used commercially for the production of goods and services which were subject to VAT. However, it has never been possible to obtain a refund of the tax on petrol, regardless of whether or not the petrol is used commercially. In the past it was possible for agricultural concerns to obtain duty-free petrol to run their tractors. This possibility has now been ended.

The net tax burden of these energy taxes therefore fell only on households and non-VAT-registered companies (primarily the financial sector and private health care, as well as the public sector).

For companies which sold heat, however, the tax could not be refunded. Here, the heat supplier (the heating plant) was able to add the energy tax burden to the heating bill (the invoice) to the heating client, which made it possible for companies selling district heating to pass on the indirect tax burden.

In many ways the refund system for the energy taxes operates in the same way as VAT refunds. In order to be reimbursed, the tax must be shown on the invoice, and it is the date of the invoice which determines when the refund can be paid.

The question as to whether the energy is used for commercial purposes or private purposes must always be clarified, in order to be able to correctly declare the VAT. The same distinction is used for the energy taxes.

Both the VAT receivable and the energy tax refunds are declared on the periodic VAT declaration, and it is the same authority which checks them.

The energy taxes are refunded by offsetting them against the VAT total, or by a payment being made according to the same procedures as for the payment of negative VAT, if that is the case.

Very large companies can be registered in accordance with the Energy Tax Acts on the consumption of fuel. These companies can purchase fuel tax-free, and will only have to pay tax if they consume fuel for applications for which no refund can be given.

For other companies with a large energy consumption, the energy taxes can be refunded monthly, rather than waiting for the VAT declaration which, to date, has normally taken place once every quarter or once every six months.

The refunds to trade and industry are justified in respect of the competitiveness of this sector.

The principle of unconditional reimbursement of the energy taxes to VAT-registered companies was broken by two restrictions to the exemptions/refunds.

Firstly, the possibility for having the tax refunded on oil, etc., for the operation of motors refunded, was abolished in connection with the harmonisation of taxes in the single European market as of 1st January 1993.

Since 1993 a higher tax has been levied, and it has not been possible to obtain a refund on oil used to operate motors. This higher tax does not only apply to motor vehicles, but to almost all types of motors (development machines, mine operations, stationary motors, etc.) The tax on oil used for the operation of motors for agricultural purposes, however, is still refunded.

Secondly, the possibility of having the tax on energy for space heating and hot water refunded was restricted during 1996 and 1997, and was abolished entirely as of 1st January 1998 (see below).

2.3 The Organisation of the Various Energy Taxes

Electricity

The assessment basis for the electricity tax is electricity consumption in Denmark outside of the electricity plants and the electricity supply utilities. This electricity consumption is calculated on the basis of sales of electricity for which invoices are made. The electricity supply utility adds the tax to the price, and is responsible for paying the tax to the state.

The same electricity tax is levied, regardless of whether or not the electricity is produced in Denmark or abroad. (It is not possible to determine the origin of the electricity which is supplied from the normal electricity network anyway.) In the same way, the tax is exactly the same, regardless of how the electricity has been produced (coal, nuclear power, hydropower, natural gas, wind turbines, etc.) when the electricity is supplied via the electricity network.

Fuels used for the production of electricity are exempt from taxation. This is, however, conditional on an electricity tax being paid on the electricity. Tax is not levied on electricity produced at small electricity plants for the producers' own consumption and supplied without using the normal electricity network. Tax may, however, be levied on the fuel in this case.

Electricity which is sold abroad is not subject to tax. The electricity which is used by the electricity supply utility for the actual manufacture of electricity is also tax-free. The electricity is exchanged tax-free between electricity plants, to electricity supply utilities, and to and from other countries. The tax only becomes payable when it is sold to customers outside of the electricity supply system. The tax is collected when the consumer is invoiced. No tax is therefore levied on network losses arising before the customers' meters.

There are two rates of electricity tax:

- that on electrical heat; and

- that on "other electricity".

The rate for electrical heat can be used for consumption over and above 4,000 kWh annually in permanent residences which are registered as being heated by electricity. "Other electricity" is taxed at a higher rate.

An attempt has been made to balance the electrical heat tax with the coal tax, such that the rate corresponds to a fuel tax on the fuels used in producing electrical heat, as in the following example.

Tax rate for coal	DKK 20/GJ
Tax rate for coal (DKK 20/GJ ´ 0.0036 GJ/kWh)	DKK 0.072/kWh
Efficiency of the electricity plant	40 percent
Burden of electricity price ex. works (0.072 GJ/kWh/0.4)	DKK 0.18/kWh
Network losses from plant to consumer	5 percent
Burden of electricity price ex. consumer (DKK 0.18/kWh/0.95)	DKK 0.189/kWh
Electrical heat rate, rounded off	DKK 0.19/kWh

The tax on electrical heat corresponds to the increase in price which would have been incurred if the fuels used in producing the electricity had been subject to the normal tax rate, and if the tax had then been passed on in full in higher prices, assuming an electricity efficiency of 37.5% ex. consumer (the degree of electricity efficiency is equal to the amount of energy sold, divided by the amount of energy in the fuels used). Most of the electricity produced in Denmark comes from coal.

There are a number of reasons which made Denmark choose to levy the tax on the consumption of electricity and to exempt the fuels used in its production. The tax on fuels would exempt electricity imports, but place an extra burden on electricity exports. This would lead to a distortion of trade such that production in Denmark would be reduced and imports increased. In the same way, exporters to Denmark would probably be able to increase their prices for electricity by up to about the amount of the indirect tax burden in Denmark, whereby Denmark would experience a loss in its terms of trade. This effect was very probable in the past, before the liberalisation of the electricity market, where the international trade in electricity was carried out between monopoly/monopsony.

Normally, this type of distorting tax is neutralised by border equalisation of the tax. The tax is reimbursed on exports, whilst it is levied on imports.

However, the Danish opinion is that it would not be in line with international tax regulations regarding the border equalisation of taxes, to refund indirect goods-related taxes on exports if the individual tax burden cannot be determined unambiguously.

As it is impossible to determine how the exported electricity is produced, either in theory or in practice, it is impossible to unambiguously decide how much fuel tax should be refunded.

The electricity in the network is comprised of a non-divisible mixture of electricity produced at different plants with different degrees of efficiency, and where different fuels are used, some of which will be tax-free, whilst others are taxable. It may be possible to calculate an average, whereby the tax on fuel has, on average, burdened the export by say DKK 0.273 per kWh, but the export may have been caused by the start-up of an extra wind turbine, which is not subject to taxation.

If this was the case, the tax refund could be called an export subsidy.

Similar conditions apply to imports, where the tax levied on goods must not exceed that levied on the same goods produced domestically.

As there is no fuel tax on hydropower, bio-fuels or wind turbines it would not be possible to levy an equalisation tax on electricity imports which may be produced from hydropower, etc., abroad.

Average tax burdens would not meet the conditions for the border equalisation of tax either, and they would also lead to a serious trade distortion.

Combined Heat and Power (CHP) Production

A distinction is made between centralised and decentralised CHP plants in Denmark. The centralised CHP plants are operated by the electricity supply utilities, which supply heat as a bi-product, whilst the decentralised CHP plants are heating plants which supply electricity as a bi-product.

In CHP production, both electricity and heat are produced by using the same fuel. Moreover, the consumption of fuel is lower than if the heat and electricity are produced separately.

With the tax exemption for fuel used in the production of electricity, and tax levied on fuel used for the production of heat, a decision has to be made as to how the fuel should be distributed.

There is no unambiguous, technically correct solution to this question. However, there are certain outer limits.

The fuel benefit from CHP production, i.e. the fuel saving obtained from combined production compared to the separate production of the same quantities of heat and electricity, can be calculated.

Under certain conditions, one could argue that this entire benefit reduces the fuel consumption for the production of heat. This would be the case if electricity needed to be produced at electricity plants as well as at CHP plants, as in the following example:

	1	2	3	2+3
	Electricity plant	CHP plant	+Electricity plant	Total
Electricity production	40	30	10	40
Heat	0	50	0	50
Loss	60	20	15	35
Fuel	100	100	25	125

This means that if a plant had to supply heat, in addition to electricity, from 100 fuel, it would be possible to supply 50 heat and 30 electricity. If electricity production had to be increased to 40 again, 1/4 electricity plant would also have to be started, which would use an extra 25 fuel. The heat supply of 50 will therefore be able to be produced with an extra fuel consumption of 25, without electricity production falling.

On these grounds, the CHP plant's total fuel consumption of 100 can be distributed with 75 for electricity and 25 for heat. This approach is natural for electricity plants which have also become heat suppliers over the years.

On the other hand, it would be just as correct to argue that this entire benefit reduces the fuel consumption for the production of electricity. This would be the case if heat needed to be produced at a heating plant as well as at the CHP plant. This approach is illustrated in the following example:

	1	2	3	2+3
	Electricity plant	CHP plant	+Electricity plant	Total
Electricity production	0	18.75	0	18.75
Heat	50	31.25	18.75	50
Loss	12.5	12.5	4.69	17.19
Fuel	62.5	62.5	23.44	85.94

In this instance the starting point is a heating plant. When this plant produces electricity as well, the heat production falls by 18.75. This 18.75 can be produced by using 23.44 fuel in a heating plant (18.75/0.8).

On these grounds 62.5 percent of the fuel will go to heat production and 37.5 percent will go to electricity production. The fuel is distributed pro rata.

On the basis of such theoretical considerations, it can be determined that, from a given amount of fuel of 100, between 25 and 62.5 fuel would go to heat, and between 75 and 37.5 would go to electricity. The difference of 37.5 is the fuel benefit from combined production.

It is technically complicated to determine this interval, and technical impossible to determine where in the interval the division should be made. Conditions are different from plant to plant, and the choice of plant depends on the economics of heat and electricity sales, amongst other things. In addition to the purely technical conditions, the determination will also depend on the market conditions for electricity and heat.

Centralised Plants

In Denmark, electricity and heat may not be sold at more than cost price. The monopoly pricing commission monitors the market to ensure that this does not happen. The commission authorises/accepts a distribution of the fuels so as to be able to calculate the price of heat and electricity without taxation. The monopoly authority must base this distribution on reasonable operational principles.

The monopoly pricing commission has decided that the distribution should be calculated on the basis that the fuel saving should be attributed equally to both electricity and heat (i.e. 25 + 18.75 = 43.75 to heat and 75 - 18.75 = 56.25 to electricity), (see the example above).

The tax legislation prescribes that this distribution of fuel should also be used when calculating the taxation. However, the monopoly authority has given permission for the entire fuel saving to go to the production of heat if the price of heat is very high. The typical case is therefore that in the first years after the heat network has been established, tax is only paid on 25 fuel, but when the network has almost been paid off, tax is paid on 43.75 fuel.

The heat from the centralised CHP plants is therefore typically levied with a somewhat lower tax than heat from other sources. The tax on heat from decentralised CHP plants, for example, is paid on 62.5 fuel.

Decentralised Plants

Other tax rules apply for the so-called decentralised CHP plants. The latter sell their electricity at prices determined by the market, and are typically supplied with natural gas in Denmark.

According to these rules, the fuels are distributed pro rata. If 30 electricity and 60 heat are produced, 1/3 of the fuel will be tax-free and 2/3 of the fuel will be taxable. However, there are certain cases where concessions are given. For certain plants with an overall efficiency of typically over 83.5 percent, a certain tax concession is granted.

Considerations as to the Level of CHP Taxation

It has been found reasonable for CHP to be levied with a lower tax than other heating suppliers, naturally under the condition that the tax benefit is passed on to the consumers and not the producers.

The operation of a CHP plant is similar in nature to that of a natural monopoly, in that it is difficult to imagine several CHP plants in the same urban community.

In a system where electricity and heat prices are determined by the market, a profit maximising company with the city's CHP plant at its disposal will set the price such that it corresponds to the prices of alternative heat. The plant will therefore benefit from the alternative forms of heat being levied with higher taxes than the CHP plant.

This effect has already been seen for the natural gas-fired plants, where the gas supplier, who has a monopoly, sets the price of the gas so that the fuel saving goes to the utility selling the gas.

There is therefore a *pro rata* distribution of the fuels for decentralised CHP plants which corresponds to tax being paid on 62.5 fuel, (see the example above). If tax concessions were given here, the consumers would not receive any benefit, because the gas utility would be able to raise the price of gas accordingly.

In the longer term, when the electricity market is liberalised, it will be difficult to maintain the different principles for assessing CHP for decentralised plants and centralised plants respectively.

The way in which the final distribution will be calculated has not yet been determined.

The advantages in taxing a large quantity of the fuels used for CHP production include:

- there being no unjustified profits for the owners of monopolies

- it providing an incentive to change to technology which saves fuel

- it providing an incentive to change to fuels which pollute less.

- equity

The advantages in taxing a smaller quantity of the fuels used for CHP production include an incentive for the establishment of more CHP plants, whereby energy consumption and the environmental burden will be reduced.

It is likely that the final system will involve:

- tax being levied to a certain extent on the entire fuel consumption, including that used for the production of electricity.

- the tax on fuels never being so great that the heat is taxed more highly than alternative sources of heat

- the taxable quantity of fuel in a CHP plant being set at approximately 10 percent less than that which applies to the most efficient heating plant.

- the granting of a reduction in taxation to new heating networks/subsidies for the connection of new CHP customers.

2.4   The Incentive Effects of the Energy Taxes

The high energy taxes have clearly prompted a continued incentive for energy savings and the spread of other, tax-free energy. But the high taxes have also helped to promote the use of certain fuels which were not originally considered as fuels, just as they may have helped to push through certain investments which have not been profitable in socio-economic terms.

The taxes have affected behaviour in the following ways:

- less energy consumption at the end users, through the use of insulation, a reduction in room temperature, more energy efficient equipment, newer, more efficient boilers, etc.

- a change from taxed fuels to tax-free fuels

- a greater spread of CHP

- a greater spread of natural gas

This change in behaviour has yielded a socio-economic benefit in that the rates have mirrored society's appreciation of a lower consumption of the taxable fuels. But the energy taxes probably involve a considerable fiscal element as well. Some of the changes in behaviour have notably been considered inexpedient.

If fuel oil cost DKK 3,000 per tonne inclusive of tax, and DKK 1,000 exclusive of tax, for example, whilst tax-free fish oil cost DKK 2,000 per tonne, it would have paid to use fish oil instead of fuel oil in district heating plants on the personal financial level. But in socio-economic terms it will not be profitable to use an expensive good as fuel instead of a cheaper one.

In some cases, therefore, high energy taxes may promote the use of tax-free fuels in a way which is socially neither expedient nor desirable.

Moreover, unwanted distribution effects may arise between different heating customers, depending on whether the heat is produced from taxable or tax-free fuels, or whether it is surplus heat from power plants or industrial companies.

Over the years it has been necessary to expand the range of taxable fuels. Tax has, for example, been introduced on tall oil, wood tar, wood tar oil, vegetable pitch and other products extracted from wood sap, which are used, or intended for use for heating, as, at one time, there was a major importation of this kind of fuel to heating plants.

The increase in energy taxes which came into effect on 1st July 1998 lead to an even greater advantage for the alternative fuels which are not levied with the increased taxes. A greater fiscal incentive for the combustion of waste would mean that the balance between the political objective for waste disposal and the fiscal incentive would be upset. Higher prices for alternative fuels therefore mean that the combustion of waste is rewarded fiscally, in preference to the political objective of recycling as much as possible.

In order to offset the increased incentive for combustion in preference to recycling, a tax corresponding to the increase in energy taxes on coal and oil has been levied on heat produced from the combustion of waste. This tax amounts to DKK 4.9 per GJ inclusive of VAT, and will be increased to DKK 12.9 per GJ exclusive of VAT by the year 2002. The tax will be levied on the amount of heat supplied from the combustion plant. This rate is calculated on the basis of an efficiency of 75 percent of the energy in the waste.

The influence of the taxes on the net energy consumption should be seen in light of the fact that the large increase in taxes occurred at the same time as prices fell. The actual consumer prices after the taxes were increased considerably were therefore no higher than they had been previously. The taxes have therefore maintained the incentive to save, rather than creating new incentives.

The net consumption of space heating thereby fell by 10-15 percent from the start of the 1970s to the start of the 1990s. Without the higher prices and taxes, consumption would probably have increased as the number and size of residences has increased.

This net consumption of space heating has also been supplied with a considerably better utilisation of the gross energy. In this way productivity in the conversion of fuel, etc., to net energy has increased by about 20 percent from the start of the 1970s to the present day. In total, the gross energy consumption for space heating has therefore been reduced by about 30 percent.

If there had been no taxes / high prices, consumption would probably have increased.

This improved utilisation of the energy in the fuels is due not least to the greater spread of CHP supply. There has also been a change in the fuels used over the period towards fuels which are less environmentally damaging.

In practice, the energy taxes, which are balanced according to the gross energy content, place the heaviest burden on fuels which have the greatest CO_2 emissions. The energy in coal is utilised less than the energy in heavy oil, and a lot less than that in light oil. The energy in natural gas is utilised better than the energy in oil.

In summary, it can be very difficult to quantify the effects of the taxes. The effects often become apparent in the slightly longer term, and should be calculated as the difference between the price development with and without tax.

The impression given is that the taxes have had their most marked effect in the spread of new supply systems (gas and CHP) and in the change in fuels, whereas it has become more difficult to reduce the net energy consumption.

2.5 Use of the Revenue

In general, the revenue from the energy taxes goes to the treasury. That part of the revenue which comes from the space heating tax on VAT-registered companies, however, is included in the calculation of the special retransfer to trade and industry.

3.0 The CO_2 Tax

At the end of the 1980s the political discussion changed from being concerned only with energy savings (less dependency on imported energy), to also being concerned with the energy sector's contribution to the global environmental problems, in particular those connected with the emission of CO_2 from the combustion of fossil fuels, but also that of air pollution from sulphur and other substances.

The politicians put forward requests for a readjustment of the tax system such that it could better support the long-term political objectives for energy, transport and the environment. The request was for the tax structure to be adjusted so that part of the taxes should depend on the environmental burden of the fuels combusted, and that trade and industry's energy consumption should be taxed, but in such a way that trade and industry's competitiveness in relation to other countries would not be reduced.

The criticism of the energy taxes was based on the fact that the balance between the various fuels which had been introduced in 1986 did not reflect the environmental burden of the individual fuels, amongst other things. Oil was taxed at DKK 50 per GJ, and natural gas with an equivalent shadow tax, whilst the tax on electricity and coal, which involve greater CO_2 emissions, was DKK 25 per GJ. Criticism was also directed at the fact that the differences in taxes favoured those who were able to be connected to coal-based CHP in particular, compared to those who used individual oil-firing or natural gas. The favourable rules for the taxation of coal-based CHP could also lead to a fiscal incentive to expand the CHP areas over and above that which is socially expedient, and thus reduce the market for natural gas to decentralised heating plants and CHP plants. Lastly, the fact that trade and industry were not affected by the energy tax was criticised, as the pollution from this sector had the same environmental effects as household consumption. There were probably opportunities to reduce the environmental burden in the untaxed trade and industrial sectors at less socio-economic expense than from even higher taxes for households.

Over the next few years, then, the task was to find solutions to the requests and criticisms stated above.

In 1992 a CO_2 tax was passed which aimed at taxing the fuels according to their CO_2 content on combustion, with a view to creating a more substantial basis for realising the objective to limit CO_2 emissions by 20 percent in the year 2005 compared to the year 1988. In contrast to the energy tax, the CO_2 tax was levied on trade and industry.

In 1993 a green tax reform project was implemented with the aim of increasing taxation on the consumption of resources, including energy, and reducing the high marginal taxes on income. The tax reform, which was phased in from 1994-98, restored the balance in the energy tax to a level of about DKK 41 per GJ.

In connection with the implementation of the tax reform, whose energy effects primarily affected households, it was decided that trade and industry should also help in reaching the objective of limiting the CO_2 emission. It was concluded that a great deal of energy savings and CO_2 reductions could be implemented in the trade and industrial sectors at less socio-economic cost than letting households initiate additional reductions. With the high tax levels on households' energy consumption, it was estimated that the latter could only implement further energy savings if very expensive investments were made. Furthermore, the CO_2 tax act from 1992 included some inappropriate factors which could only be solved effectively by carrying out considerable changes to the law. A major readjustment of the CO_2 tax act was implemented in 1995, which led to an increased taxation of trade and industry.

3.1   The CO₂ Tax in 1992

The CO_2 tax was introduced with effect from 1st January 1993 for trade and industry (and from 15th May 1992 for households).

The CO_2 tax covered all fuels on which there was an energy tax, apart from petrol. The reason for this is that a CO_2 tax on petrol would have the same effect as a higher petrol tax, so that the rate only needs to be set at the level required. The exemptions are limited, and correspond to the exemptions in the energy tax, i.e. the production of electricity, fishing, air and sea transport and collective transport.

The tax rate was DKK 100 per tonne CO_2, and was balanced between the various fuels in proportion to their CO_2 content on combustion. The CO_2 tax rates are shown in appendix 2.

According to economic theory, the rate should reflect the marginal external costs of the CO_2 emission. It has not been possible to assess these external costs, and the rate of DKK 100 has therefore been set on the basis of political considerations.

At the same time as the CO_2 tax was introduced, the energy tax was readjusted. The energy tax on heavy and light fuel oil was reduced, so that the overall tax remained unchanged, whilst the overall tax on coal and electricity was increased. In this way, the former inequality in the taxation of oil, electricity and coal was more or less evened out.

A CO_2 tax of DKK 100 per tonne was found to be too high for industry, and it was decided that industry should only be charged with DKK 50 per tonne. This was more or less equivalent to the starting level at that time of a future CO_2 tax which was considered within the context of member states of the European Union. As the CO_2 tax is collected from the energy supplier, and as one good cannot be levied with two different taxes, the differentiation was implemented as a normal refund paid together with the energy taxes.

Apart from the fact that the rates are balanced differently in a CO_2 tax compared to an energy tax, the CO_2 tax differed from the energy taxes in that trade and industry also had to pay the CO_2 tax.

For the most energy-intensive production companies, a CO_2 tax of DKK 50 per tonne CO_2 would mean a serious reduction in their international competitiveness. It was therefore necessary to introduce a special refund scheme for the energy-intensive companies.

In this refund scheme it was possible to obtain a 50 percent refund of that part of the CO_2 tax which made up between 1 and 2 percent of the refund base, 75 percent of that part which made up between 2 and 3 percent of the base and 90 percent of that part of the CO_2 tax which made up more than 3 percent of the base. The refund base was the company's sales, including exports, subject to VAT, minus the purchases, including imports, subject to VAT. This base corresponds to the VAT base with regard to the principle of origin, and was considered to be a much better measurement of the size and level of activity of the company than the traditional VAT base, where export companies have a modest base and import companies have a large base. The refund base chosen was also considered to be more appropriate than the companies' turnover, which would place a particularly large burden on those companies which were not vertically integrated.

At the same time, a law was passed whereby subsidies could be given to cover the CO_2 tax which was not refunded for companies whose CO_2 tax amounted to more than 3 percent of the refund base. However, such companies would always have to pay a minimum of DKK 10,000 per year. This subsidy was conditional on the company having an energy audit carried out by an energy consultant, and on the company effecting suitable energy saving measures.

Electricity

As far as electricity is concerned, consideration was given as to whether taxation should be levied on the fuel, or on the electricity.

In Denmark the marginal consumption of electricity is supplied from coal-fired electricity plants. The theoretically correct price signal to the consumers is therefore given by calculating the rate on the basis of CO_2 emissions from coal-based electricity.

However, if the CO_2 tax is to give the theoretically correct price signals to the electricity producers, the tax should be levied on the fuel used.

CO_2-bearing fuels will thereby tend to be replaced by fuels containing less CO_2, or even by fuels which give off no CO_2. The electricity plants will also have more of an incentive for greater efficiency.

After weighing the same considerations regarding problems with the border equalisation of taxes as for the energy taxes, it was decided to levy the CO_2 tax on the electricity and exempt the fuels in Denmark. This solution was then supplemented with a subsidy scheme for electricity plants which use fuels with little or no CO_2, and which are not otherwise linked to other environmental burdens.

A subsidy equivalent to the CO_2 tax on electricity produced by wind turbines, biogas, straw, and other fuels which have no CO_2, is therefore given to electricity producers per kWh produced. A subsidy is also given to electricity produced at decentralised CHP plants which use natural gas. These decentralised CHP plants were originally heating plants which were ordered to produce electricity at the same time, and which are rewarded for using the surplus heat for the production of electricity via the subsidy scheme.

This subsidy scheme provides basically the same incentives with regard to the use of sustainable sources of energy and fuels which have little or no CO_2 as could have been achieved by a fuel tax.

Use of the Revenue

Some of the revenue was used for measures to further ensure that the objective of energy savings and CO_2 reductions is met. Subsidies could therefore be given to energy-saving investments in certain companies with a large energy consumption, and support could be given to promote decentralised CHP production and the use of bio-fuels, as well as to the completion of some district heating networks.

3.2   The CO_2 Tax in 1995

There were a number of weak points in the refund scheme for energy-intensive companies, however. The refund was organised according to a cursory and somewhat crude measurement of the company's energy intensity. There was an inaccurate limitation of the activities or companies which the concession was aimed at. The tax burden therefore depended on whether the company was vertically integrated (the company could involve tile burning, or it could involve a whole group which included a tileworks, for example). Companies which produced the same goods could therefore have a different tax burden on the same activity, which distorted competition.

Furthermore, there were incentives to separate the energy-intensive parts of a company into independent units, in order to obtain the tax concessions. As the incentive for reducing the tax would increase, so would the tax burden. Lastly, in some cases the 3 percent limit led to less of an incentive for energy savings if they meant that the company came under the 3 percent.

Energy Initiatives by Trade and Industry

The Danish government has retained its objective of reducing CO_2 emissions by 20 percent in 2005 compared to 1988. In 1994-95 it was found that the initiatives which had been implemented until then were not sufficient to meet the objective. A further 5 percent was needed. It was decided that trade and industry should contribute with the necessary CO_2 reductions. The households had already implemented comprehensive energy savings, and it was concluded that it would be less expensive in socio-economic terms to make use of the savings potential in trade and industry rather than let households carry out further, and thereby more expensive, energy savings.

The government therefore decided to carry out a reform of the CO_2 tax, and to introduce an SO_2 tax. It also became possible for companies to enter into voluntary agreements with the state with a view to further energy efficiency measures which could increase trade and industry's contribution to CO_2 reductions. In concession the companies obtain a special tax rebate which is increased in line with the phasing in of the CO_2 and SO_2 tax from 1996-2000. Lastly, it was decided that the revenue from trade and industry should be transferred back to trade and industry, in order to avoid unacceptable effects on employment and on the earnings of trade and industry, in such a way as to support the environmental objectives. The SO_2 tax and the changes in the CO_2 tax corresponded to an average levy on trade and industry of 0.5 percent of labour costs, which would be neutralised after the tax is retransferred.

If trade and industry were to contribute with a 5 percent CO_2 reduction, it was calculated that the CO_2 tax from 1992 would have to be multiplied by about 6, which is equivalent to an increase from an average DKK 35 per tonne CO_2 to about DKK 200 per tonne CO_2, or to approximately 1/3 of the total tax burden for households in 1998.

As energy consumption in trade and industry is distributed very unevenly, a uniformly high rate would lead to such a great tax burden for the most energy-intensive companies, that they would close down and move production to another country. This would reduce the Danish CO_2 emission, but would just be followed by increases abroad.

The objective must therefore be to reduce the Danish CO_2 emission, but in such a way that the Danish reductions are not just replaced by increases abroad.

In a small open economy such as Denmark's, a high uniform rate will lead to CO_2 reductions as a result of a different factor composition (the substitution effect), which is desirable and beneficial, whereas some of the other CO_2 reductions would arise as a result of the decrease in Danish production due to reduced competitiveness, which is not desirable.

Allowance was made for the considerations mentioned above in a differentiated CO_2 tax, which was formulated so that the lowest rates were used for the most energy-intensive processes, but in such a way that the tax burden per unit produced continues to increase with the energy intensity. In spite of the low marginal taxes on the most energy-intensive processes, the average tax burden per unit produced will therefore be greater than for the less energy-intensive processes. In addition, some of the tax concessions are made conditional on the companies having an energy audit carried out, and on their effecting the energy efficiency measures which would have been profitable to carry out if the tax rate had been "normal". The more theoretical considerations which underlie the differentiation in the Danish CO_2 tax system are described in more detail in appendix 5.

3.3   Current Status of the CO_2 Tax

The CO_2 tax amounts to DKK 100 per tonne CO_2, and companies can have the taxes on process energy reimbursed with differentiated rates of refund, depending on whether the energy is used for light or heavy processes, and depending on whether the company has entered into a voluntary agreement with the state in respect of energy savings. Companies' space heating consumption is taxed in the same way as for households, i.e. after a phasing-in period, there will no longer be refunds offered on either the CO_2 tax or energy tax. The CO_2 tax is refunded in connection with the VAT declaration, as are the energy taxes. It is up to each individual company to determine whether it wants the tax refunded. If the company wants a refund, it must be able to document what the energy is used for. In practice, companies base their request for refunds on a meter reading of the energy consumption.

The tax burden of the various energy applications is shown in the table below.

The Tax Burden under the New Tax System

	1995	1996	1997	1998	1999	2000
CO_2 tax, DKK per tonne CO_2						
Heavy process, with agreement	0-2	3	3	3	3	3
Heavy process, w/o agreement	0-2	5	10	15	20	25
Light process, with agreement	0-2	50	50	50	58	68
Light process, w/o agreement	50	50	60	70	80	90
Space heating[1]	50	200	400	600	600	600

1) In 1998 a further increase was adopted.

The tax on energy used for light processes (lighting, office inventory, machines, etc.) is to be increased up to the year 2000 from DKK 50 per tonne CO_2 to DKK 90 per tonne CO_2. However, it will be possible for companies which enter into voluntary agreements in respect of energy savings to be levied at a lower rate.

For energy used for heavy processes, a tax of DKK 5 per tonne CO_2 is payable in 1996. This will rise to DKK 25 in the year 2000. For companies which enter into an agreement with the state in respect of energy efficiency measures, a subsidy can be obtained thus reducing the tax to DKK 3 per tonne CO_2.

For energy used for space heating, there will be a gradual increase in the tax burden from about DKK 200 in 1996 to about DKK 600 in 1998. The total energy and CO_2 tax will vary between DKK 550 and DKK 850 per tonne CO_2, depending on the type of energy. The space heating tax will be increased to around DKK 725 per tonne CO_2 with the new energy tax increases.

3.4 Space Heating

Space heating demand by trade and industry is very similar to households' use of energy. It was therefore decided that trade and industry's former refund of the energy and CO_2 tax should be gradually terminated from 1996-98. As of 1998, energy used for space heating will be taxed at the same rate, regardless of whether the energy is used in households or in trade and industry.

The space heating tax is equivalent to about DKK 600 per tonne CO_2. The CO_2 tax is DKK 100 per tonne CO_2, and the energy tax is equivalent to a tax of about DKK 500 per tonne CO_2, but this will vary in proportion to the actual CO_2 content of the various fuels. From 2002 the energy tax will be raised to about DKK 625 per tonne CO_2.

The distinction between energy used for space heating and energy used for processing is laid down in the legislation. All fuels (coal, mineral oil and natural gas) are considered, in principle, as being used for heating, unless they are used for processing purposes. Process heating arises if the manufacturing of a raw material involves it being washed, rinsed or cleaned in special equipment, or if it is subject to increases in temperature of at least $10°C$ in relation to the room in question, such as heating, boiling, roasting, distillation, sterilisation, pasteurisation, steaming, drying, dehydration, evaporation or condensation in special equipment, as part of the manufacturing process.

If the process is carried out in the production hall itself, the processing space is limited to special rooms which are heated to more than $45°C$. The heating of some greenhouses in market gardens, and stables is considered to be process heating.

Electricity is basically considered to be used for production processes, unless it is used for heating purposes, such as in radiators or water heaters.

(i) Surplus Heat

In the event that energy used for processing also contributes to an unavoidable heating up of the production hall, it is not considered to be space heating. But if heat is also removed by special installations which supply radiators, etc., in connection with the energy applications in the special production processes, then the amount of energy which is removed for space heating will be taxable as space heating. This applies, regardless of whether the space heating is consumed in the same building as the process consumption, in other of the company's buildings, or if it is sold to other companies or to a district heating network.

This specification of the rules for the taxation of surplus heat aims at a balance between the intention of avoiding surplus heat which can reduce the overall energy consumption from being wasted, not least for energy and environmental reasons, and the intention of avoiding a fiscal "production of surplus heat". In practice, it would not be possible to distinguish the one from the other.

There is an incentive to avoid surplus heat whose use may reduce the overall energy consumption from going to waste, if the value of the total energy saving is greater than the costs of the operation, depreciation and the interest on such equipment. This incentive is not removed by taxing the heat removed from the production process. The introduction of the space heating tax increases the value of the total energy saving, because the alternative to using the surplus heat, i.e. normal space heating, will be more expensive. There is a further incentive in that the taxation of the heat removed from the production process is assessed as if the heat were produced in a boiler plant where there are no conversion losses in the form of chimney losses, etc.

These rules may contain an incentive for the deliberate production of surplus heat by removing the insulation of production equipment. But in a number of cases the company will put themselves to extra expense for heating than otherwise. Just the fact that the heat is only required in the heating season will, in most cases, make it uneconomical to deliberately produce surplus heat. It is also difficult to control the heat production by removing insulation or by leaving the light turned on or letting the electric motor run more than is absolutely necessary. The overall costs of heating from lighting or motors will normally be greater than those from using normal fuels, as electricity is a more expensive source of energy than fuel oil. It is estimated that the scale of the deliberate production of surplus heating is not very large.

A balance is sought between, on the one hand, uses of surplus heat that are justifiable on social, energy and environmental grounds and, on the other hand, the intention not to provide incentives for the deliberate production of surplus heat. By taxing the surplus heat as if it were produced by a boiler system which uses the energy 100 percent efficiently, there will be an incentive to make use of the surplus heat, as the energy efficiency in normal boiler systems is 75 to 90 percent.

The surplus heat is levied by a tax of DKK 50 per GJ, both when it is used internally in the company, and when it is sold outside of the company. If the heat is sold, however, the tax will amount to a maximum of 50 percent of the payment received.

If surplus heat from processing plants were exempted, the incentive would be greater, which in some cases would be appropriate, on the basis only of environmental and energy political considerations. But this incentive could very easily become so great that disproportionately large investments would be made in making use of the surplus heat. There would also be incentives to produce more surplus heat than is absolutely necessary. The surplus heat cannot often be used in the companies where it is produced, and is sold to a nearby district heating network. As the heat can be sold at almost the same price as the heat produced at a normal district heating plant which uses taxed fuels, processing companies which use low-taxed fuels would be given unreasonably preferential treatment. With high energy taxes unreasonable distortions would arise.

3.5   Process Energy

Most of the energy consumed by trade and industry is used for process applications. This use of energy differs from households' use of energy, and a refund of the CO_2 tax is offered, its size depending on whether the energy is used for heavy or light processing. The concession also depends on whether the company has entered into a voluntary agreement with the government in respect of energy savings.

(i)   Heavy Processes

The heavy processes are carried out in energy-intensive companies. These processes are described in more detail in a list attached to the act, covering 35 specific processes (see Appendix 6).

A heavy process is, for example, defined as energy which is used directly in the production of cement or glass or starch or paper, or for the refining of mineral oil, or for the smelting of metals, but not for further processing. By defining energy intensity in relation to a process concept, there is a more robust limitation than a limitation based on the increase in value or the turnover in a company. The process concept is unaffected by the company's organisational circumstances, and is therefore less able to be manipulated. It is much more difficult to separate a process into an independent activity than it is to divide up a company and its turnover, or its value added.

Process energy which is not a heavy process in the company, is considered to be a light process.

The present concession system provides concessions for heavy processing for specifically named energy-intensive applications of energy, regardless of where or in which company this application arises. This means that only energy which is used for a particular purpose (a process) is given a concession, and that this concession does not cover any of the company's other energy applications. In this way, competition is not distorted between energy-intensive domestic companies which produce the same goods under different organisational configurations.

Importance was attached to a number of considerations when the process list was drawn up.

The main aim of the process concession is to ensure that the companies' competitiveness is not reduced in relation to other countries. The process list is also drawn up so that the tax does not distort competition between companies. The aim is therefore for competing products to be taxed at the same rate.

The processing concession should never be so comprehensive that the companies or branches which consume the most energy have an overall net benefit (where the tax after concession is less than the general retransfer).

Moreover, it has been important for a company's tax burden to increase if its energy consumption increases. Companies with the same process description should therefore pay twice as much in tax if their energy consumption is twice as large.

Apart from the consideration given to competition, the most important criterium is whether or not the production is energy-intensive. Energy intensity is not an unambiguous concept, however, as the energy intensity can be 100 percent if only a suitably small part of the production process is considered. The energy consumption must therefore be evaluated in relation to a relevant final or intermediate product, which, if occasion should arise, could be moved abroad. As an indicator for whether or not a production is energy-intensive, one could start with whether the energy consumption per unit of value added to the relevant production unit amounts to at least 3 percent with a tax of DKK 50 per tonne CO_2, and whether the tax burden amounts to more than 1 percent of the sales value. Other factors have also played a role. For example, an evaluation has been made as to whether or not the tax can easily be passed on, or whether or not the tax will affect the company's competitiveness. Further evaluation has been made as to whether an eventual processing concession would distort competition in relation to rival Danish companies which are not energy-intensive, and lastly, consideration was given to the administrative aspects.

The list should not be seen as a final and inflexible list, however, but as a list drawn up on the basis of current experience.

The Minister for Taxation therefore regularly draws up a statement about the process exemptions for the Danish Parliament. This includes an assessment of trade and industry's applications with regard to the process list in relation to the criteria named. Consideration will then be given to whether the list needs to be revised. If this is the case, a bill will be put forward on this matter. When the act was passed, it was decided that the green taxes on trade and industry should be evaluated in 1998.

The principle behind the process list can be illustrated by the manufacture of sugar. The sugar beet are subject to a number of processes at the sugar factory. The production of the finished pack of sugar can be divided up into two processes: the first part is the actual manufacture of the sugar, which includes the beet being rinsed and heated up, for example. This part ends at that point in the process where, in principle, a sample of the sugar can be taken. The second part involves the finishing, including the production of different qualities and packaging.

No. 17 of the appendix to the act states: "Used directly for the production of cane and beet sugar falling under pos. 17.01 in the EU's combined nomenclature, made from sugar beet or cane." The energy consumption covered by no. 17 will therefore include the energy used directly in the machines used in the first part of the process, i.e. until the production has reached the point where a sample would be tariffed as sugar in respect of the EU's combined nomenclature. In practise the process covers energy consumption until the product is in such a form that it can be sold Energy which is used indirectly in production, such as for lighting and ventilation in the production hall, will not be included in the energy which is used directly in production. The energy consumption in ventilation systems which are coupled directly to the actual production plant is considered to be part of the actual manufacturing process, however.

The tax on electricity is not paid back at the increased rate for applications nos. 1-14 in the appendix. In these processes it is not the electricity which is used in the energy-intensive part, but oil, coal or gas.

A random limit has been introduced, so that the special increase only applies to greenhouses of more than 200 m^2, and only for plants with an annual production of at least 10 tonnes for other applications.

3.6 Agreements In Respect of Energy Efficiency Measures

The government's proposal opens up for the use of agreements between the authorities and companies as a means of promoting energy efficiency measures in trade and industry. The agreements are a contribution to the next few years' work in increasing trade and industry's input to reducing the CO_2 emission.

The agreements are well suited to the most energy-intensive companies. The Danish Energy Agency can enter into agreements with the following types of company:

1. Companies with particularly energy-intensive processes ("process list" companies).

2. Companies with light processes where the corrected tax burden amounts to more than 3 percent of the company's sales minus the company's purchases, but at least 10 percent of the company's sales. The corrected tax burden is the sum of the CO_2 tax, the SO_2 tax and the space heating tax calculated at the rate for light processes. The total tax payment must, however, amount to a minimum of DKK 10,000 annually, increasing to DKK 20,000 in the year 2000.

With these two criteria, the opportunity for entering into agreements in respect of energy efficiency measures is extended to a greater number of companies than just those which have heavy production processes.

The tax payment on energy which is consumed in the energy-intensive processes (see the list in Appendix 6) can be subsidised (given an agreement rebate) so as to bring down the actual cost to DKK 3 per tonne CO_2. The other companies which are able to enter into agreements could obtain an agreement rebate on their CO_2 tax for process purposes at DKK 50 per tonne CO_2 in 1996, increasing to DKK 68 per tonne in the year 2000.

The experience gained from the agreements is to be evaluated in connection with the overall evaluation of the proposal in 1998.

(i)   Conclusion of Agreements

The agreements are entered into between the Danish Energy Agency and the individual companies. There are often a number of similarities in the energy consumption of small companies within the same branch. It is therefore appropriate to let the trade association, or a group of companies together, draw up a draft action plan for the companies in that branch. The draft is negotiated with the Energy Agency, and the individual companies can then enter into the agreement if they want a tax subsidy. Large, energy-intensive companies, or companies with atypical energy consumption can negotiate individual agreements with the Energy Agency.

It takes time to draw up a draft agreement and to negotiate agreements. Companies which meet the criteria to conclude agreements (i.e. heavy processing and light processing companies) can therefore apply to the Energy Agency and sign a declaration of intent with regard to wanting to conclude an agreement in respect of energy efficiency measures. The companies will obtain a conditional undertaking for subsidisation for a certain period (approximately 6 months) on the basis of their declaration of intent. During this period the company must draw up a draft action plan for energy efficiency measures, and negotiate this with the Energy Agency.

The company's draft action plan for energy efficiency measures should be drawn up on the basis of a detailed analysis of the company (an energy audit carried out together with an authorised consultant). Action plans for whole branches should be drawn up on the basis of an analysis of selected companies within the branch.

The energy audit involves an examination and mapping of the company's energy consumption with a view to identifying technically feasible possibilities for effecting energy savings and making the company more energy efficient, which are estimated to have a simple payback period of less than 5 years when they apply to different energy consumption. Taxed energy prices, i.e. the price which is the sum of the company's actual purchase price, plus energy and CO_2 and SO_2 taxes on energy according to the refund rates in the year 2000, should be used to calculate the payback period.

The company draws up an action plan on the basis of the energy audit, and this will form the basis for the negotiations with the Energy Agency as to the final agreement.

In the final agreement, companies consuming energy for heavy processing undertake to carry out all the energy savings and efficiency measures which have a payback period of less than 4 years, whilst companies which enter into a light processing agreement must carry out energy savings which have a payback period of less than 6 years.

An agreement for a final action plan for the individual company will be concluded on the basis of the draft action plan. The agreement can be concluded for a maximum period of 3 years, and should include the following main elements:

- An audit of the individual companies which are attached to a trade agreement. This audit should be carried out by an authorised consultant who can point out the energy saving measures which are relevant for the company in question on the basis of the trade action plan.

- Plans for carrying out the energy-saving measures which are identified in the company audit.

- Completion of the special analyses of those parts of the company's energy consuming equipment which were not analysed in the first audit.

- The establishment of energy management and control systems in the company.

- Guidelines for the purchase of energy efficient equipment, as and when the existing equipment needs to be replaced.

- Training and motivation of relevant employees.

- Reports of energy use and production to be sent to the Energy Agency.

The action plan concludes with a number of points/actions which make the company more energy efficient, and which can be controlled. Actual efficiency objectives can be included in the action plan in certain, limited areas.

The Agency issues an undertaking to subsidise part of the tax on the basis of the agreed action plan.

The companies report on progress in achieving the action plan to the Energy Agency once a year. The Energy Agency may choose to let certain parts of the report be reviewed by a consultant.

If the company deviates substantially from the action plan, without the Energy Agency authorising this, the subsidy for the period in question may be required to be paid back, or the undertaking to pay subsidies may be revoked.

All expenditure incurred in drawing up the action plan, and in writing up the annual reports shall be defrayed by the company.

The company's agreement rebate on the sum which exceeds DKK 10,000 per year, and rising to DKK 20,000 in the year 2000, shall be paid by the Central Customs and Tax Administration.

3.7   Retransfer of the Revenue to Trade and Industry

At the same time as the decision was made to tax trade and industry in 1995, it was decided that trade and industry's share of the additional revenue from the CO_2 and SO_2 taxes should be transferred back to trade and industry. The tax revenue and retransfer is shown in the table overleaf.

The effect of the tax on space heating is neutralised primarily by the repayment in labour costs and employment. The tax on process consumption, including the SO_2 tax, is neutralised in particular by the retransfer via investment subsidies.

	1996	1997	1998	1999	2000
		Phase 1		Phase 2	
			---------------- DKK Mill. ----------------		
TAXES					
Trade and Industry					
1. Tax on space heating	420	750	1050	955	910
2. CO_2 tax, inc. Voluntary agreements	65	245	425	585	775
3. Sulphur tax	225	235	255	360	390
4. Total, trade and industry..................	710	1230	1730	1900	2075
Households					
5. Sulphur tax	195	190	195	280	325
6. Total tax revenue	905	1420	1925	2180	2400
RETRANSFER					
7. Investment subsidies........................	300	500	500	500	0
8. Pool for the self-employed..............	180	210	255	255	295
9. Lower social security supplementary pension contribution from employers	200	200	200	200	200
10. Lower social security contribution, etc..	0	290	745	915	1550
11. Administration costs........................	30	30	30	30	30
12. Total to trade and industry..............	710	1230	1730	1900	2075
13. Compensation to electric heating customers	30	30	30	30	30
14. Surplus to households.......................	165	160	165	250	295

NB:
The revenue effects are stated after quantity adjustments.
The revenue from the natural gas tax is included under the CO_2 tax and the space heating tax.

The retransfer is carried out by giving investment subsidies for energy savings. A pool has also been set aside to support smaller companies, including agriculture. Lastly, some of the revenue was retransferred by reducing the employers' social security supplementary pension payment and their social security contribution (which is paid as a proportion of labour costs). The reduction in the social security contribution will be increased in the period 1996-2000, whilst the investment support will be gradually phased out.

Subsidies can be granted for up to 30 percent of investments in energy efficiency measures which companies have undertaken to carry out in connection with voluntary agreements with the Energy Agency in respect of energy efficiency measures. However, support cannot be given to projects with such a short payback period that the profitability of the project ought to be sufficient incentive in itself for the companies to carry out such measures. In practice, no support is given to projects with a payback period of less than 3 years. Support can also be given for energy saving measures which are not carried out in connection with an agreement. In these cases, subsidies are not given to projects with a payback period of less than 2 years. The stricter requirement as to payback period in connection with agreements should be seen in light of the fact that a special agreement rebate on CO_2 tax is given when a voluntary agreement is concluded.

4.0   The Sulphur Tax

A tax is levied on the sulphur content of fossil fuels (mineral oil, coal and natural gas) which contain more than 0.05 percent sulphur. A tax is also levied on the sulphur content of wood, straw, waste and other sulphur-bearing fuels which are combusted in plants with an output of more than 1000 kW.

The tax rate is DKK 20 per kg sulphur, and the tax burden for the different fuels is shown in Appendix 3.

The tax is collected from the suppliers of coal, oil and natural gas, whilst it is the companies which use wood, straw or waste which have to assess and pay the tax. Companies which measure their sulphur emission can choose to pay tax on the company's actual sulphur emission, rather than paying tax on the sulphur content of the fuel used. Companies which limit their emission of sulphur by means of smoke purification, or by binding the sulphur to other materials can thereby have the tax on the amount of sulphur purified refunded. If the company limits its sulphur emission, it will not have to pay as much in tax.

The tax is being phased in the period from 1996 to 2000 by reducing a tax-free basic allowance for the sulphur content in the various fuels. In this way, tax is only payable on that part of the fuel's sulphur content which is above the basic allowance. For example, the tax-free basic allowance for coal was 0.28 percent in 1996. This was then reduced to 0.21 percent in 1997 and 0.14 percent in 1998. It will be reduced to 0.07 percent in 1999 and will be done away with completely in the year 2000.

At present, coal containing 0.54 percent sulphur would be liable for tax only on 0.4 percent sulphur.

In the period 1996-1999 electricity production is exempted from the actual sulphur tax. Instead, a special tax is levied on the electricity, calculated from the expected sulphur emission in the permissible sulphur quotas for electricity plants. The reason for this construction is the same as that described under the sections on both the energy and CO_2 taxes. The rate is DKK 0.009/kWh up to and including 1998, and DKK 0.013/kWh in 1999. From the year 2000 onwards, sulphur tax will be payable regardless of whether the sulphur emissions are caused by the production of electricity or heat.

In order to reduce the tax burden for companies which have a large energy consumption, and which are vulnerable to large increases in energy costs, and which are also expected not to want to change

282

fuel on the basis of the sulphur tax alone, special concession rules have been put forward for coal. In this concession scheme, the company can use the basic allowance for 1996 for a longer period. This is conditional on the coal being used in boilers or ovens which were erected or renovated for at least DKK 10 million in the period 1st January 1976 to 1st April 1995. This basic allowance can be used until the year 2000. If the boiler was built or renovated before 1st January 1986, the basic allowance applies until 2005. For boilers erected after 1st January 1986, or renovated for at least DKK 10 million, this condition stops at the end of the 20th year after the boiler was erected or renovated. Another condition is that the company has entered into an agreement in respect of energy efficiency measures with the Energy Agency.

Apart from the fact that the sulphur tax helps to reduce sulphur emissions, it will also reduce the amount of CO_2 emission. This is due to the fact that the sulphur-rich fuels will become more expensive. This in itself will lead to a tendency to reduce energy consumption, and thereby CO_2 emission. As the sulphur-rich fuels also typically contain relatively large amounts of CO_2, the reduction in energy consumption will lead to a relatively large reduction in CO_2 emissions. By replacing coal by fuel oil, the CO_2 emissions will be reduced by about 20 percent. If the coal is replaced by natural gas, emissions will be reduced by almost 50%.

The sulphur tax therefore has a greater effect on CO_2 emissions than a similar CO_2 tax with the same burden on trade and industry. If a CO_2 tax were to give the same incentive to change from coal to natural gas, the CO_2 coal tax would have to be twice as great as the SO_2 coal tax calculated according to energy content. The SO_2 gas tax is zero.

The sulphur tax has had a significant effect on the sulphur content of fuels. The sulphur content of light fuel oil has been reduced from 0.2 percent to 0.05 percent.

The sulphur content of heavy fuel oil will be reduced from almost 1 percent to about 0.5 percent. The sulphur content of coal has been reduced by about 1/3.

The number of sulphur purification plants has grown. Not only are there more plants, but also the efficiency of existing plants has been improved.

The very sulphur-rich fuels have, in a number of cases, been replaced by other fuels which do not contain as much sulphur.

Appendix 1: The Green Tax Burden - Revenue from Green Taxes, 1980-1998 (mill. Danish Kroner)											
Tax/duty	1980	1985	1990	1991	1992	1993	1994	1995	1996	1997 (1)	1998 (1)
Duty on energy products	**6,557**	**8,043**	**14,150**	**14,222**	**14,192**	**14,703**	**15,843**	**17,932**	**20,006**	**20,905**	**23,475**
Coal.	-	198	851	892	797	738	592	602	650	703	750
Electricity	1,213	1,984	4,380	4,336	3,938	3,562	4,139	4,482	5,167	5,726	7,525
Gas	63	45	39	41	15	43	47	50	45	44	0
Natural gas	-	-	-	-	-	-	-	-	28	37	525
Oil	1,591	1,369	3,136	3,507	3,791	4,749	4,945	5,411	5,897	5,854	5,900
Petrol	3,690	4,447	5,744	5,446	5,651	5,611	6,121	7,387	8,219	8,541	8,775
Weight duty	**2,888**	**3,203**	**4,363**	**4,547**	**4,213**	**4,225**	**4,268**	**4,404**	**4,918**	**5,172**	**5,650**
Registration duty	**3,049**	**10,972**	**8,007**	**8,256**	**8,532**	**7,998**	**13,312**	**14,967**	**15,363**	**16,366**	**17,800**
Duty on third part liability insurance	**476**	**602**	**933**	**894**	**855**	**856**	**894**	**944**	**1,068**	**1,336**	**1,350**
Road toll							227	289	262	270	286
Eco taxes	**122**	**262**	**1,093**	**1,196**	**2,605**	**4,264**	**4,860**	**5,236**	**6,589**	**7,599**	**9,356**
CO_2	-	-	-	-	1,401	3,177	3,318	3,245	3,693	3,930	4,550
SO_2	-	-	-	-	-	-	-	-	296	396	400
Disposable tableware	-	25	74	79	73	69	66	72	59	56	55
Certain retail containers..........	100	198	399	433	462	305	439	479	516	513	900
CFC	-	-	27	13	22	12	5	2	0	0	1
Waste	-	-	404	473	454	529	571	619	601	867	1,000
Extraction and import of raw materials.......	16	16	129	141	140	120	122	136	135	145	150
Piped water	-	-	-	-	-	-	295	652	970	1,279	1,600
NiCd batteries	-	-	-	-	-	-	-	-	34	35	35
Chlorinated solvents	-	-	-	-	-	-	-	-	3	3	5
Pesticides	6	23	60	57	54	52	44	31	282	235	300
Waste water	-	-	-	-	-	-	-	-	-	140	325
Antibiotics	-	-	-	-	-	-	-	-	-	-	35
Total	**13,091**	**23,081**	**28,546**	**29,115**	**30,397**	**32,046**	**39,404**	**43,772**	**48,206**	**51,648**	**57,917**
% Share of GDP	**3.50**	**3.75**	**3.46**	**3.39**	**3.42**	**3.54**	**4.10**	**4.33**	**4.52**	**4.58**	**4.87**
Share of total tax revenues	**7.68**	**7.64**	**7.09**	**6.93**	**6.94**	**7.04**	**8.23**	**8.83**	**9.19**	**9.34**	**10.03**

NB: (1) Estimates from BO 4 - 1997.

Appendix 2: Energy Taxes 1995-2002

Product	1995	1996	1997	1998	1999	2000	2001	2002
				---Tax rate---				
Electricity for other purposes than heating oere/kWh[1]	33	36	40	46	52	52	52	52
Electricity for heating oere/kWh[1]	29,5	32,5	36,5	39,5	41	42,5	44	45,5
Gas and diesel oil, used as motor fuel oere/l	200	202	212	212	212	212	212	212
Gas and diesel oil for other purposes than motor fuel oere/l	149	149	149	170	170	173	178	183
Light diesel oil oere/l	190	192	202	202	202	202	202	202
Fuel oil oere/kg	166	166	166	191	191	195	200	206
Fuel tar oere/kg	150	150	150	173	173	176	181	186
Kerosine, used as motor fuel oere/l	200	202	212	212	212	212	212	212
Kerosine for other purposes than motor fuel oere/l	149	149	149	170	170	173	178	183
Leaded petrol oere/l	367	392	397	402	442	452	462	472
Unleaded petrol oere/l	302	327	332	337	377	387	397	407
Leaded petrol w/ "return of petrol vapour" oere/l	364	389	394	399	439	449	459	469
Unleaded petrol w/ "return of petrol vapour" oere/l	299	324	329	334	374	384	394	404
Carburetter liquid oere/l				337	377	387	397	407
Autogas (LPG) oere/l	134	136	143	143	143	143	143	143
Bottled gas and other gas (LPG) oere/kg	200	200	200	218	218	222	228	235
Natural gas oere/Nm3	0	0	1	135	147	150	155	161
Lubricants, hydraulic oils etc. oere/kg	178	178	178	201	201	204	209	214
Coal kr./GJ	30,6	34,1	37,7	41,3	45	47	49	51
Pet coke kr./GJ	29,9	31,4	36,8	41,3	45	47	49	51
Lignite kr./GJ	31,1	34,7	38,3	41,3	45	47	49	51
Heating from incineration of waste kr./GJ					**4,9**	**7,6**	**10,2**	**12,9**

Where tax rates has been changed more than once during a year the rate at the end of the year is stated.

1) The rate on electricity is increased by 0.6 oere per kWh from 1st January 1997 and this increase is earmarked to a pool for electricity saving measures.

285

Table 1: CO2-Tax Rates for Different Energy Products and Reductions, 1996

Product/Reduced rate in %	Full rate 100%	Light process 50 %	Light process w/agreement 50 %	Heavy process 5 %	Heavy process w/agreement 3 %
---------- Effective CO_2 - tax rates ------------					
Gas[1] and diesel oil oere/l	27	13.5	13.5	1.35	0.81
Fuel oil[1] oere/kg	32	16	16	1.6	0.96
Fuel tar oere/kg	28	14	14	1.4	0.84
Kerosine oere/l	27	13.5	13.5	1.35	0.81
Coal kr/t	242	121	121	12.1	7.26
Pet coke kr/t	323	161.5	161.5	16.15	9.69
Lignite kr/t	178	89	89	8.9	5.34
Electricity oere/kWh..................	10	5	5	0.5	0.3
Autogas (LPG) oere/l	16	8	8	0.8	0.48
Bottled gas (LPG) oere/kg.........	30	15	15	1.5	0.9
Gas other than LPG oere/kg	29	14.5	14.5	1.45	0.87
Natural gas oere/Nm[3]	22	11	11	1.1	0.66

[1]: For purposes outside agriculture and certain other sectors fuel oil must at least be taxed at 11 oere/kg and gas oil at 5 oere/l. The sulphur tax can be included in calculating the tax on fuel oil.

Table 2: CO₂-Tax Rates for Different Energy Products and Reductions, 1997

Product/Reduced rate in %	Full rate 100%	Light process 60 %	Light process w/agreement 50 %	Heavy process 10 %	Heavy process w/agreement 3 %
---------- Effective CO_2 - tax rates ------------					
Gas[1] and diesel oil oere/l........	27	16.2	13.5	2.7	0.81
Fuel oil[1] oere/kg	32	19.2	16	3.2	0.96
Fuel tar oere/kg	28	16.8	14	2.8	0.84
Kerosine oere/l	27	16.2	13.5	2.7	0.81
Coal kr/t	242	145.2	121	24.2	7.26
Pet coke kr/t	323	193.8	161.5	32.3	9.69
Lignite kr/t	178	106.8	89	17.8	5.34
Electricity oere/kWh	10	6	5	1	0.3
Autogas (LPG) oere/l.............	16	9.6	8	1.6	0.48
Bottled gas (LPG) oere/kg	30	18	15	3	0.9
Gas other than LPG oere/kg...	29	17.4	14.5	2.9	0.87
Natural gas oere/Nm[3]	22	13.2	11	2.2	0.66

[1]: For purposes outside agriculture and certain other sectors fuel oil must at least be taxed at 11 oere/kg and gas oil at 5 oere/l. The sulphur tax can be included in calculating the tax on fuel oil.

Table 3: CO$_2$-Tax Rates for Different Energy Products and Reductions, 1998

Product/Reduced rate in %	Full rate 100%	Light process 70 %	Light process w/agreement 50 %	Heavy process 15 %	Heavy process w/agreement 3 %
	---------- Effective CO$_2$ - tax rates ------------				
Gas[1] and diesel oil oere/l....	27	18.9	13.5	4.05	0.81
Fuel oil[1] oere/kg	32	22.4	16	4.8	0.96
Fuel tar oere/kg	28	19.6	14	4.2	0.84
Kerosine oere/l	27	18.9	13.5	4.05	0.81
Coal kr/t	242	169.4	121	36.3	7.26
Pet coke kr/t	323	226.1	161.5	48.45	9.69
Lignite kr/t	178	124.6	89	26.7	5.34
Electricity oere/kWh...........	10	7	5	1.5	0.3
Autogas (LPG) oere/l	16	11.2	8	2.4	0.48
Bottled gas (LPG) oere/kg..	30	21	15	4.5	0.9
Gas other than LPG oere/kg	29	20.3	14.5	4.35	0.87
Natural gas oere/Nm^3..........	22	15.4	11	3.3	0.66

[1]: For purposes outside agriculture and certain other sectors fuel oil must at least be taxed at 11 oere/kg and gas oil at 5 oere/l. The sulphur tax can be included in calculating the tax on fuel oil.

Table 4: CO$_2$-Tax Rates for Different Energy Products and Reductions, 1999

Product/Reduced rate in %	Full rate 100%	Light process 80 %	Light process w/agreement 58 %	Heavy process 20 %	Heavy process w/agreement 3 %
	---------- Effective CO$_2$ - tax rates ------------				
Gas[1] and diesel oil oere/l.....	27	21.6	15.66	5.4	0.81
Fuel oil[1] oere/kg	32	25.6	18.56	6.4	0.96
Fuel tar oere/kg	28	22.4	16.24	5.6	0.84
Kerosine oere/l	27	21.6	15.66	5.4	0.81
Coal kr/t	242	193.6	140.36	48.4	7.26
Pet coke kr/t	323	258.4	187.34	64.6	9.69
Lignite kr/t	178	142.4	103.24	35.6	5.34
Electricity oere/kWh	10	8	5.8	2	0.3
Autogas (LPG) oere/l	16	12.8	9.28	3.2	0.48
Bottled gas (LPG) oere/kg ..	30	24	17.4	6	0.9
Gas other than LPG oere/kg	29	23.2	16.82	5.8	0.87
Natural gas oere/Nm^3	22	17.6	12.76	4.4	0.66

[1]: For purposes outside agriculture and certain other sectors fuel oil must at least be taxed at 11 oere/kg and gas oil at 5 oere/l. The sulphur tax can be included in calculating the tax on fuel oil.

Table 5: CO$_2$-Tax Rates for Different Energy Products and Reductions 2000

Product/Reduced rate in %	Full rate 100%	Light process 90 %	Light process w/agreement 68 %	Heavy process 25 %	Heavy process w/agreement 3 %
---------- Effective CO$_2$ - tax rates ------------					
Gas[1] and diesel oil oere/l	27	24.3	18.36	6.75	0.81
Fuel oil[1] oere/kg	32	28.8	21.76	8	0.96
Fuel tar oere/kg	28	25.2	19.04	7	0.84
Kerosine oere/l	27	24.3	18.36	6.75	0.81
Coal kr/t	242	217.8	164.56	60.5	7.26
Pet coke kr/t	323	290.7	219.64	80.75	9.69
Lignite kr/t	178	160.2	121.04	44.5	5.34
Electricity oere/kWh............	10	9	6.8	2.5	0.3
Autogas (LPG) oere/l...........	16	14.4	10.88	4	0.48
Bottled gas (LPG) oere/kg ...	30	27	20.4	7.5	0.9
Gas other than LPG oere/kg.	29	26.1	19.72	7.25	0.87
Natural gas oere/Nm^3..........	22	19.8	14.96	5.5	0.66

[1]: For purposes outside agriculture and certain other sectors fuel oil must at least be taxed at 11 oere/kg and gas oil at 5 oere/l. The sulphur tax can be included in calculating the tax on fuel oil.

Appendix 4: Sulphur Tax in 1996-2000 - Effective Rates for Typical Sulphur Content (sulphur tax is 20 kr per kg sulphur emitted)

Product	Typical sulphur content (%)	1996	1997	1998	1999	2000
Gas and diesel oil, kr./1000 l	0.1	8.4	8.4	8.4	8.4	16.8
Fuel oil, kr./t	0.5	20	40	60	80	100
Fuel tar, kr./t	0.5	28	46	64	82	100
Kerosine, kr./1000 l	0.1	8.4	10.5	12.6	14.7	16.8
Coal, kr./t	0.6	57.6	70.2	82.8	95.4	108
Pet coke, kr./t	1	127.8	142.85	157.9	172.95	188
Lignite, kr./t	0.6	72	81	90	99	108
Leaded petrol, oere/l..........	0.001	0	0	0	0	0
Unleaded petrol, oere/l	0.001	0	0	0	0	0
Electricity, oere/kWh..........	-	0.9	0.9	0.9	1.3	1.3
Autogas, (LPG) oere/l..........	0	0	0	0	0	0
Bottled gas and other gas (LPG), oere/kg..........	0	0	0	0	0	0
Gas (except LPG) oere/kg..........	0	0	0	0	0	0
Natural gas, oere/Nm^3	0	0	0	0	0	0
Wood, straw etc., kr./t..........	0.0951	0	4.75	9.5	14.25	19
Waste, kr./t	0.0451	0	2.25	4.5	6.75	9

289

Appendix 5: Theoretical Considerations Concerning the Danish CO2 Tax

Denmark is a small, open economy where a large proportion of the agricultural sector and industry have competition from abroad. There is a limit as to how much Danish companies are able to raise prices without losing their market share.

Denmark is also one of the countries which has the highest taxation on energy, including a CO_2 taxation.

A unilateral tax on energy can have a significant effect on the competitiveness of Danish companies concerned. The competitiveness of the business sector could be maintained by a system where the tax burden is reimbursed on export, whilst imports are taxed in the same way as normal excise duty. This means that the companies which have been taxed would be able to shift the tax in higher prices without losing their market share to foreign companies. This kind of system would give an incentive both to companies to undertake energy savings and to consumers to reduce their consumption of CO_2 -rich goods.

In accordance with the various trade arrangements concluded in, *inter alia*, the WTO, EU, OECD, this indirect tax burden on the production of various goods cannot be rebatted on exports, and it is not possible to tax imported goods the equivalent of the average charge on nationally-produced goods.

For this reason, taxation of the business sector's energy consumption only affects CO_2 emission from Danish territory, and exempts CO_2 emission arising from the foreign production of goods which are imported into Denmark.

This tax base for a CO_2 tax thereby deviates from the ideal tax base, because imports are not taxable but also environmentally harmful, and it is therefore not possible directly to transfer orthodox recommendations which use the same rate of levy on all sectors. The problem will be facilitated if international agreements are entered into about CO2 taxation

The general effect of the taxation on competitiveness can be neutralised by recycling the yield from the taxation to the business sector. With a complete recycling of the revenue, the net increase in costs will consist solely of the substitution costs resulting from industry changing its factor composition away from raw materials, which emit CO_2 and towards more expensive raw materials, which do not emit so much CO_2 and more manpower etc.

If the CO_2 tax burden is distributed amongst the various companies and branches in the same way as it is transferred back, it will be possible to charge different companies the same rate of levy without affecting the business structure or employment, and to achieve an economically optimal reduction of CO_2 emissions.

However, different companies use very different quantities of energy in their production. In Denmark, 20 per cent of the CO_2 emission from the business sector is caused by the most energy-intensive companies, which contribute 1 per cent of the total value added of the VAT registered private business (excl. power plants, district heating stations etc.). Forty per cent of the CO_2 emission comes from companies which contribute 5 per cent of value added, and 50 per cent of the CO_2 emission comes from those contributing 10 per cent.

If CO_2 taxes equivalent to 1 per cent of the business sector's total value added were introduced, and the yield were transferred back in proportion to the value added, the 15-20 per cent most energy-intensive companies would have a net charge of between 0-25 per cent of their value added, whilst the remaining 80-85 per cent of companies would have a return of between 0 and 1 per cent of their value added. The large numbers of non-energy-intensive companies would experience some increase in production and employment, whilst the energy-intensive companies would experience a significant worsening of their situation.

Figure 1 shows the effect of a tax on CO_2 in two dimensions - the quantity of finished goods and the emission of CO_2. At a given tax the costs of production of the finished goods will increase, if the production implies emission of CO_2. At given world market prices there will be no possibility to shift the cost increase on to the consumer prices. The result is then that the supply of finished goods is reduced and the producers will suffer a loss of profit corresponding to the hatching in the lower part of the figure. In other words Denmark will see a loss of competitiveness. As to the environmental aspect there will be a "national" environmental gain as explained above as a consequence of the lower direct Danish CO_2 emission.

With a relatively high uniform taxation, the most energy-intensive companies would stop production in Denmark. CO_2 emission from Danish territory would then be reduced, but CO_2 emission from abroad could be expected to increase correspondingly. There would not, therefore, be any welfare gains from a reduction in pollution, but rather a loss of efficiency, because production would be located in areas other than where the costs (without taxation) are lowest.

Figure 1: Effects on Quantity of End Products and CO2 Emissions

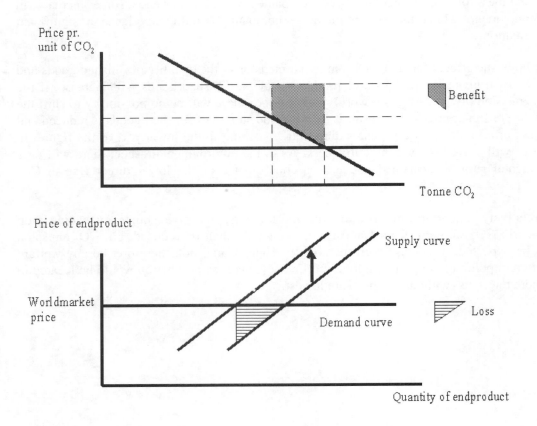

If, on the other hand, taxes were differentiated so that the charge on the value added was the same for all branches, the loss of income would be avoided by a non-optimal localisation of production, but the reduction in CO_2 emission would not be economically optimal, as the less energy-intensive companies would use significantly more resources per tonne CO_2 to reduce CO_2 emission by factor substitution than the energy-intensive companies.

The reduction in CO_2 emission as a result of a different factor composition (the substitution effect) is therefore beneficial, whilst the Danish CO_2 reduction arising from a changed production composition (the income effect) is unwanted.

A balance can be found between these two effects, namely by using differentiated rates where the tax burden per unit produced increases less than proportionally with the companies' energy intensity.

Appendix 5A shows that the optimal rate for an industry branch is approximately the same as the marginal external effect multiplied by the share of the total CO_2 reduction which would occur as a result of a production line with less CO_2 emission per unit produced. In other words, the optimal rate is the factor

292

substitution effect's share of the total price effect of higher factor prices, including the income or competitive effect multiplied by the external expense[1].

One ought, therefore, to use a levy rate of 50 percent of the marginal negative external effect in a branch N, if one half of the CO_2 reduction is due to factor substitution and the other half to a reduction in production[2].

A simple, but also incorrect solution, would be to allow the rate of levy in the taxation laws to decrease automatically with increasing energy intensity as indicated in Figure 2.

On average, the right tax burden will be achieved, but the marginal taxation will be less than the average.

Until 31st December 1995, Denmark had a system with rates of taxation which declined as a function of the energy intensity of the company. Apart from the theoretical problem, however, there were also practical problems in the form of companies splitting the energy-intensive parts out of the overall company. It is easier for a boiler to be energy-intensive than for a whole factory. The tax burden on production was therefore not independent of the company's organisation.

---

[1]   See Appendix 2 SA for a calculation of the tax rate.

[2]   The ideal tax can also be approximated by:

$$t'_n = \frac{\alpha_n}{\alpha_n + \beta_n \times (I_n - g)} \times E$$

where t'_n is the optimal rate of levy for industry branch n, α_n is the elasticity of substitution of CO_2, E is the marginal external effect, β_n is the elasticity of supply, I_n is the intensity of CO_2, and g is the average tax burden on production in all branches which is transferred back to the business sector according to the value added.

Figure 2: An Illustration of an Optimal Indirect Tax Structure

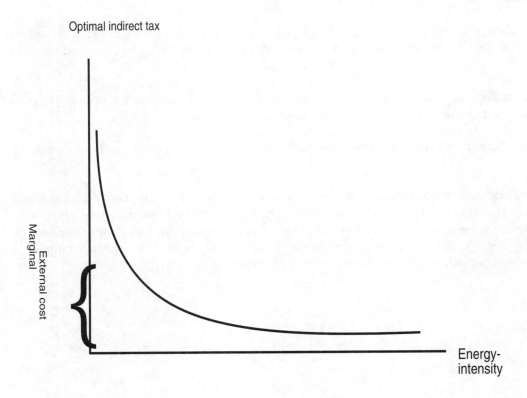

We have tried to solve this problem in Denmark by fixing different rates for different processes, applications or productions directly by law. The lowest rates are used on the most energy-intensive companies, but such that the tax burden per unit produced still increases with the energy intensity. This principle is illustrated in Figure 3. The general theory says that a uniform rate should be applied in all enterprises. When the general theory is adjusted to the Danish conditions, the theoretic solution is a gliding tax rate which is depending on the energy-intensity. In the practical implementation of the Danish CO2 tax this theoretic solution is approached with different rates for groups of processing with the same energy-intensity. In practise groups of processing with nearly the same energy-intensity will be within a band where the marginal tax is the same but where the average tax burden and the energy-intensity varies a little.

In this way, internal competitive distortion is avoided. The tax burden is independent of the organisation and the marginal taxes will not be lower than the average taxes. The consumption of energy within the same branch will be charged the same, so that a company using twice as much energy to produce a specific product will also be taxed twice as much.

These more theoretical considerations form the foundation for establishing the new Danish CO_2 tax, although various corrections have had to be made in practice.

Figure 3: Different Rates for Different Uses

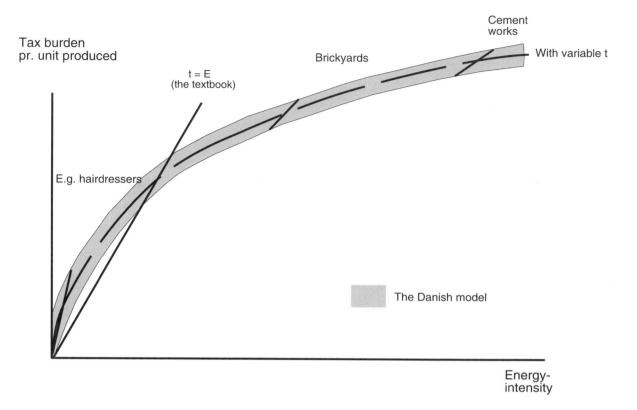

It is not claimed that the Danish system is optimal even though the above mentioned theoretical considerations have been made. A wide range of other political priorities have contributed to this.

Figures 4 and 5 show the net tax burden and ordinary and special reductions in CO_2 tax in 1996 and 2000.

Figure 4: CO$_2$ Tax Rates and Tax Base in 1996: VAT Registered Sectors

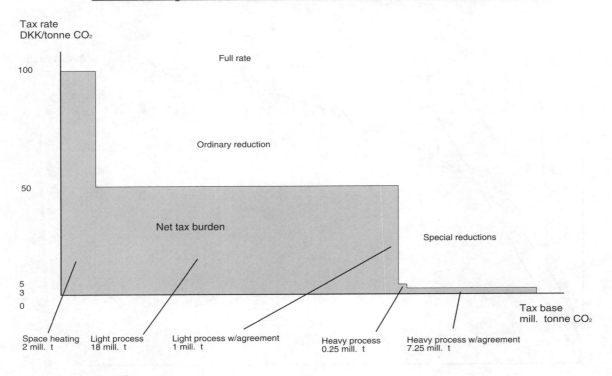

Figure 5: Projected CO$_2$ Tax Rates and Tax Base in the Year 2000: VAT Registered Sectors

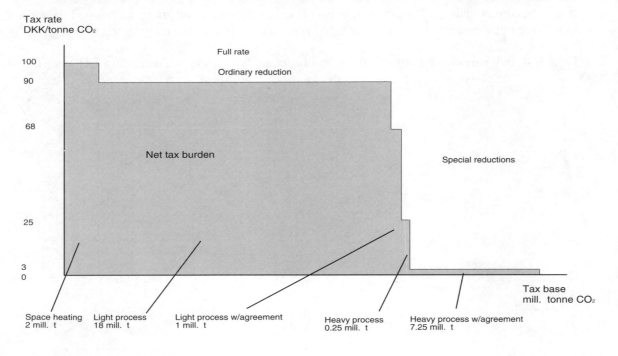

Appendix 5A: Calculation of the tax rate

Net benefit:

$$\pi = E \times (\Delta Q - \Delta Q^*) - \frac{1}{2} \times t \times \Delta Q$$

$$\underset{\text{benefit}}{\uparrow} \qquad \underset{\text{cost}}{\uparrow}$$

$$\pi' = E \times \varepsilon^B \times Q - E \times \varepsilon^C \times Q - t \times \varepsilon^B \times Q$$

$$\pi' = E \times \varepsilon^B \times Q - E \times \varepsilon^C \times Q - t \times \varepsilon^B \times Q$$

Optimum tax rate:

$$t = \frac{(\varepsilon^B - \varepsilon^C) \times E}{\varepsilon^B} = \frac{\varepsilon^S}{\varepsilon^S + \varepsilon^C} \times E$$

where:

ΔQ = total CO_2 reduction,

ΔQ^* = indirect change in supply,

ε^B = total elasticity,

ε^S = elasticity of substitution,

$\varepsilon^C = \varepsilon^B - \varepsilon^S$ = elasticity of income/competitiveness,

and

E = marginal external effect.

Appendix 6: List of Applications for Taxable Goods Covered by Special Repayments

1. Used for heating greenhouses in market gardens with a covered area of at least 200 m², but not for greenhouses from which there are retail sales.

2. Used directly for the dehydration and drying of sodium chloride dissolved in water.

3. Used directly for the pasteurisation, sterilisation, dehydration, homogenisation, concentration and drying of milk and milk-based products, with the intention of producing milk-based products with a solids content of at least 90 percent. The electricity used directly for heating and drying, and for the operation of special equipment involving concentration in the form of ultra-filtration, for example, as part of the manufacturing process, is also included. Concentration with a view to production of the milk-based products named is covered, regardless of whether it is carried out in the company which manufactures these products, or in other companies.

4. Used directly in the production of feed-stock, feed additives, including feed phosphate and feed mixes, and the drying and dehydration of vinasse, spent grains, root pellets and similar products intended for animal fodder. This does not, however, apply to consumption for the drying of corn or seeds.

5. Used directly for the production of meal, powder and pellets of meat or offal unsuitable for human consumption, found under position 2301.10 in the EU's combined nomenclature, apart from greaves suitable for human consumption.

6. Used directly for the production of vegetable meal, vegetable pellets and other artificially-dried vegetables.

7. Used directly for the production of pectins, pectinates and pectates, and for mucilage and gelatinisation agents, including modified agents extracted from vegetable products found under position 1302.20 up to and including position 1302.39 in the EU's combined nomenclature, for modified starch found under position 3505 in the EU's combined nomenclature, and that used directly for the production of emulsifiers intended for the production of foodstuffs or for technical use, made from vegetable or animal fat and oil products.

8. Used directly for the distillation of alcohol and, in combination with this, for the production of yeast, including the subsequent drying of yeast.

9. Used directly for the drying or dehydration of paper and cardboard pulp, or other goods or products dissolved in or mixed with water with a solids content of a maximum of 40 percent before drying, and a solids content of at least 90 percent after drying.

10. Used directly for the manufacture of glass.

11. Used directly for the production of

    a) slag wool, rock wool and similar mineral wool, expanded vermiculite, expanded clay, scum slags and similar expanded mineral matters, mixtures and products made from heat insulating, sound insulating or sound absorbing mineral matters found under position 6806 in the EU's combined nomenclature;

b) fibreglass, including glass wool, found under position 7019 in the EU's combined nomenclature;

c) chipboard, fibreboard and plywood, etc., found under positions 4410, 4411 and 4412 in the EU's combined nomenclature, and pressed corkboard; or

d) sheets or blocks of expanded polystyrene.

Electricity used for the manufacture of products named under paragraphs a, b, c and d is also covered, if the electricity is used solely for heating these products and intermediate products in the manufacturing process, and for keeping them hot, or if it is used for the ventilation of rooms in which these processes are carried out.

12. Used directly for ceramic firing and for the prior drying of products intended for this.

13. Used directly for the heating, dehydration, drying or burning of lime, chalk, limestone, marble and other calcium carbonate products, plaster, moler, bentonite and other types of clay, iron sulphate, copper sulphate and calcium oxide, as well as for fertilisers with a solids content of at least 90 percent, of which at least 5 percent is phosphate after drying. The electricity used directly for the production of calcium carbonate products, but only in the form of heating and drying, and for the operation of special equipment which concentrates the calcium carbonate products and taxable products as part of the manufacturing process, apart from electricity used for heating plaster board hardening rooms, is, however, also included.

14. Used directly for the production of vegetable oils, carbohydrates and proteins made from oil-bearing seeds, nuts and fruits. The further processing of vegetable oil for technical or chemical use is also covered. The consumption of electricity for the extraction or pressing of oil from fruit and nuts, etc., and for the extraction of proteins from oil-free cake, is also covered.

15. Used directly for the production of potassium sorbate.

16. Used directly for the production of fish oil and fish meal found under position 2301.20 in the EU's combined nomenclature, made from fish and crustaceans, molluscs or other invertebrate aquatic animals, and waste thereof. This does not, however, apply to the consumption of electricity for the production of fish meal once the fish oil and salt water have been separated from the oilcake, or once the fish oil has been separated from the solubles in the production process. Nor does this apply to the consumption of electricity for the further refinement of the fish oil once it has been separated from the solubles.

17. Used directly for the production of cane and beet sugar found under position 17.01 in the EU's combined nomenclature, made from sugar beets and sugar cane.

18. Used directly for the production of starch found under position 11.08 in the EU's combined nomenclature, if there is a minimum solids content of 80 percent.

19. Used directly for the drying and distilling of malt.

20. Used directly for the freezing of water to ice found under position 22.01 in the EU's combined nomenclature. This is conditional on at least 75 percent of the ice produced being sold to independent customers. Independent customers are companies other than those linked to the company in question

by having the same owner directly or indirectly owning 90 percent or more of the capital in each company, or directly or indirectly being in possession of 90 percent or more of any voting right in each company. Owners as named in section 19 a, subsection 3, of the Personal Tax Act shall be considered to be one and the same person.

21. Used directly for the production of paper and cardboard from recycled and waste paper, cardboard or pulp thereof, or cellulose, and that which is used for milling calcium carbonate products to powder with a maximum diameter of 3 my, if the powder is intended for use in the production of paper. This does not, however, apply to taxable goods which are used for the finishing of paper or cardboard, including the subsequent production of paper and cardboard or other paper and cardboard products made from ready-made paper, apart from coating or calendering. Electricity used for the production of paper and cardboard in forms other than rolls or sheets is not covered, however, if the paper or cardboard is in the form of anything other than egg cartons. Taxable goods used directly in the production of egg cartons made from other materials are also covered.

22. Used directly for the production of cellulose or pulp from recycled or waste paper and cardboard.

23. Used directly for the production of hydrogen, argon, inert gases, nitrogen, di-nitrogen monoxide, ozone and oxygen, including the filling of such gases in pressure containers, if the gases are used in the company's production instead of purchased gases, or instead of the gases being sold.

24. Used directly for the production of mineral or chemical fertilisers found in chapter 31 in the EU's nomenclature, and that which is used directly for the production of potassium nitrate and magnesium sulphate found under positions 28.34.21 and 28.33.21 in the EU's combined nomenclature respectively, in addition to that used directly for the production of nitric acid, sulphuric acid and phosphoric acid, regardless of whether or not these are used in the manufacture of fertiliser.

25. Used directly for the production of vitamins found under position 29.36 in the EU's combined nomenclature.

26. Used directly for the production of enzymes found under position 35.07 in the EU's combined nomenclature.

27. Used directly for the production of hormones, and other steroids primarily used as hormones, found under position 29.37 in the EU's combined nomenclature.

28. Used directly for refining and distilling mineral oil products, coal tar and other mineral tars, and products extracted from these.

29. Used directly for the production of cement.

30. Used directly for the smelting of metals and glass and for keeping smelted metals and glass hot. That used directly for the production of rolled or continually formed slabs and shafts, as well as that used for the further processing of slabs and shafts by hot rolling into sheets, wire, rods and similar products of iron and steel not further processed by sand blasting, etc., for metal heat processing equipment and for the ventilation of rooms where smelted metal and glass are processed. It is only the heating of glass to over 300 degrees, and keeping the glass hot once it has been heated above this temperature in the manufacturing process, which is considered to be the smelting of glass and keeping smelted glass hot.

31. Used directly for the production of chemical matters and products, when at least 75 percent is used for the manufacture of products found under position 38.08 in the EU's combined nomenclature.

32. Used directly for the production of recycled plastic in the form of pellets, powder or granulate from plastic waste, etc., or that used directly for the production of rubber powder from used tyres (rubber waste).

33. Electricity used for manufacturing the products named under points 1-16 above, if the electricity is used in dehydration plants where at least 40 percent of the liquid is evaporated at a temperature of less than 90 percent of the liquid's boiling point at normal pressure, although with a maximum 4 kWh per tonne of evaporated liquid.

34. Used directly for mixing various types of rubber with the intention of manufacturing unwrought sheets, belts or batches of non-vulcanised rubber mixes, and that used for the production of calendered rubber conveyor belts made from this, which have not passed the vulcanisation stage in their processing.

35. Used directly for the production of synthetic organic pigments and the production of preparations connected with this.

(ENVIRONMENTAL) ENERGY TAXES: THE EXPERIENCE OF FINLAND

Gustav Teir
Ministry of Finance, Finland

H𝜕3
φ28

1.0   Background

High energy consumption is a typical feature of Finnish industrial production. This applies to export production in particular, although the exports of sophisticated and high technology products continue to increase. In its energy use the key export sector, forestry, does, however, to a significant extent resort to the use of biomass. The efficient use of energy has increased considerably during the past few years. Energy consumption of industry in relation to the value-added has been reduced by one third.

Due to the country's northern location, one of Finland's special characteristics is the great need for heating. In addition, long transport distances owing to the fact that the country is sparsely populated hamper economic activity. The main markets for export industries are also located far away.

Over 30 per cent of Finland's electricity is generated by combined production with that of heat, either in district heating or backpressure power plants. This proportion ranks as one of the highest in the world. In these plants 80-90 per cent of the fuel's energy is recovered, whereas in condensing power plants the efficiency is some 40 %.

The structure of energy consumption in Finland has remained almost unchanged over the past decade. Table 1 shows the consumption of the different primary energy sources in 1996. Although CO_2 emissions have been important in considerations about the energy tax system, it is important to note that Finland is responsible for a mere 0.3 % of the world's carbon dioxide emissions.

Table 1: Consumption of Primary Energy, 1996

Energy Source	Share of primary energy
Natural gas	9%
Nuclear power	15%
Oil	28%
Imported electricity	3%
Coal	13%
Peat	6%
Hydro power	9%
Wood, etc.	17%

2.0   Introduction of Environmental Energy Taxation

Environmental energy taxation was introduced in Finland in 1990, when taxes based on the carbon content of fuels were adopted to supplement conventional fuel taxes.

From 1990 to 1992, environmental energy taxes were levied solely on primary energy sources containing carbon; that is, on coal, natural gas, fuel oils and milled peat. There was virtually no change in environmental taxation during this period. In 1993, however, the tax rate was almost doubled and a new electricity tax based on energy content was adopted.

The environmental and other energy taxes comprised fuel taxes and an electricity tax. The fuel tax consisted of a basic rate and an additional tax. The basic rate was a fiscal tax assessed on oil products. The additional tax was an environmental tax linked partly to the carbon content of fuel. Compared with other fuels, however, the additional taxes on gasoline and diesel oil were significantly higher than their carbon content justified.

The additional fuel tax was loosely linked to the carbon content of fuels. The same applied to the electricity tax introduced at the beginning of 1993. Environmental energy taxation was mainly determined by the revenue need for each budget year. There was no long-range plan. The impact of the tax on energy investment was minor, as investors knew neither the composition nor the size of the tax even for the immediate future.

From 1990 to 1992, taxation was based, at least in principle, on the carbon content of fuels. In 1993, a new electricity tax based on energy was introduced, shifting the emphasis in taxation from emissions to energy content. At the same time, an additional tax was imposed on liquid transport fuels on grounds other than carbon content.

The lack of any clearly defined linkage between the electricity tax and the additional fuel taxes led to uncertainty about the aims of future taxation.

The tax introduced in 1994 was a combined CO_2/energy tax in which 75 % was determined on the basis of CO_2 and 25 % on the basis of energy content. After its introduction in 1994, there have been frequent changes and increases in the tax level.

3.0   A Brief Review of Environment-related Energy Taxation in Finland

3.1   Context

There was a clear need to establish an environment-related energy tax strategy. In February 1992 the Environmental Economics Committee set up a group to investigate the application of economic instruments to the energy industry.

The group sought to establish what kind of environmental taxation would be justified in terms of environment, energy and economic considerations. The aim was to propose a scheme that could be adopted promptly and which also could provide a foundation for the long-term development of environmental taxation, while also taking international trends into account.

3.2   Alternatives Examined

To achieve efficient emission control, energy taxation should meet a number of criteria:

- the scheme and the considerations on which it is based should be determined consistently according to the main objective, i.e. the curbing of emissions.

- producers and consumers of energy should be able to act in such a way as to reduce both the environmental damages caused and the tax to be paid.

- taxation must be developed on a long-term basis to make it predictable.

- the tax system must be clear and administratively efficient.

- to strengthen its impact, the tax should form a part of a broader environmental energy policy strategy.

Of the energy tax schemes examined, the most viable appeared to be a tax based on carbon content (CO_2 emissions) and a dual tax scaled on the basis of energy and carbon content. The inclusion of taxes based on emissions of sulphur dioxide (SO_2) and nitrogen oxides (NO_x), however, would not add significant benefits over and above those of the CO_2 tax. Applying a higher turnover tax or value-added tax to energy did not appear to be an efficient form of environmental control, nor would it conform to the relevant European Commission directive.

The Energy Group selected a pure CO_2 tax and a combined energy/CO_2 tax for closer examination.

The CO_2 tax appeared somewhat more effective in terms of impact on emissions than the "EC tax", as it steers the energy production sector more forcefully towards lower emissions. Thus, greater reductions in emissions of CO_2, SO_2 and NO_x could be achieved with a carbon dioxide tax than with a composite tax.

The CO_2 tax also encourages energy savings. The inclusion of an energy component would not increase savings; quite the contrary. This is mainly because the pure CO_2 model would also increase the efficiency of energy production, whereas the energy component in the relevant European Commission draft directive would mainly affect the final stage of the energy cycle, i.e. consumption.

The calculations made by the group showed that even a very large increase in energy taxation would have a minor impact on emissions in the short run. The calculation showed quite clearly that the introduction of an unilateral energy tax would have negative consequences for the economy.

4.0   Problems Encountered

4.1.   Competitiveness Concerns of Industry

Until 1997 Finland was the only country that did not grant reductions in energy taxation to industry. Thus, compared to the other Nordic countries the energy taxation of industry was much higher and provoked concern among Finnish industry about the economic impact on their operations vis-à-vis that of their international competitors.

4.2.   Competition in the Electricity Market

Competition in the electricity market is in practice determined by electricity produced by coal. Thus the taxation of coal is critical. The high tax on coal, used in Finland for electricity production, dramatically reduced the competitiveness of Finnish energy production.

4.3.   Compatibility with the Treaty of Rome

As noted above, the electricity market in practice focuses on electricity produced by coal. In order not to make competition too unfair, there was a need to tax imported electricity. A starting point could have been to tax imported electricity in the same way as electricity produced by coal was taxed domestically. The Finnish system, however, taxed imported electricity at a very low rate. The tax was based on the average of taxes paid on electricity produced domestically. Thus, the tax on imported electricity was 2.2 pennies/kWh whereas for electricity produced by coal it was 4.3 pennies/kWh.

Clearly, it is not possible to tax imported electricity on the basis of how it is produced. The system adopted by Finland met legal opposition. It was argued that a tax on imported electricity is incompatible with, for example, Articles 12, 13 and 95 of the Treaty of Rome (this Treaty applies to member states of the European Union). According to some experts this argument had merit. If a tax on electricity importation, at a level of 51 % of the tax on a domestically produced product is considered to be an infringement of Article 95 of the Treaty, it is clear that electricity production domestically can only be taxed on the basis of a product tax. As there was no electricity tax on electricity produced domestically (only a tax on inputs) it was possible to argue that there could be no electricity tax on imported electricity. If this was the case there was no possibility to retain taxation on electricity production on the basis of the carbon content of inputs used.

The Court of Justice of the European Communities finally settled the question of taxation on imported electricity. According to the judgement of the court handed down on 2 April 1998 "The first paragraph of Article 95 of the EC Treaty precludes an excise duty which forms part of a national system of taxation on sources of energy from being levied on electricity of domestic origin at rates which vary according to its method of production while levied on imported electricity, whatever its method of production, at a flat rate which, although lower than the highest rate applicable to electricity of domestic origin, leads, if only in certain cases, to higher taxation being imposed on imported electricity."

On 21 December 1995 the Finnish government took a decision in principle concerning energy policy. Because of the difficulties involved with energy taxation, the government decided that taxation of electricity should be reformed in the direction of taxing the end product, i.e. electricity. This change came into force at the beginning of 1997. At the same time due to the increase in the tax level, two different categories of electricity tax were introduced. The category II tax, which is lower, applies when the electricity is used for manufacturing or professional glasshouse cultivation. For all other activities the higher category I electricity tax applies.

5.0   The Present Energy Tax System

The excise duty is divided into two parts:

- a basic duty, which is the fiscal part; and

- an additional duty, which is the environmental part.

From the beginning of 1997 the additional duty is calculated solely on carbon content. The tax on a ton CO_2 is 102 Finnish mark (equal to 17 ECU). For the "main" energy sources the excise duties have already been increased twice in 1998. The rates from 1 September 1998 are shown in Table 2.

Table 2: Energy Taxes in Finland from 1 September, 1998

Energy Source	Rate of Basic Duty	Rate of Additional Duty
Coal, lignite	-	246.0 marks/tonne
Peat	-	9.0 marks/MWh
Natural gas	-	10.3 pennies/nm^3
Electricity: Category I	-	4.1 pennies/kWh
Category II	-	2.5 pennies/kWh
Heavy fuel oil	-	32.1 pennies/kg
Light fuel oil	10.9 pennies/l	27.0 pennies/l
Diesel oil	166.6 pennies/l	26.9 pennies/l
Petrol	326.9 pennies/l	23.9 pennies/l

Electricity produced by wood or wood-based material are refunded on the basis of category I of the tax on electricity. In addition, energy intensive industries have the right to a partial refund of their energy taxes. Tax paid on electricity produced by wind power is also refundable on the basis of the higher electricity tax.

The level of energy taxation in Finland can be compared to the proposal by the European Commission for a framework tax on energy products (COM(97) 30). This comparison is shown in Table 3.

Table 3: Comparison of Energy Taxes in Finland with the European Commission Proposal (Unit = EURO)[1]

Energy Source		Energy Tax in Finland	EC Proposal for 1998	Energy Tax in Finland as per cent of EC Proposal
Coal	EURO/ton	41.3	5.17	800
Peat	EURO/MWh	1.51	0.67	226
Natural gas	EURO/nm3	0.017	0.007	250
Electricity: Category I	EURO/MWh	6.89	1	689
	Category II	4.20	1	420
Heavy fuel oil	EURO/kg	0.054	0.022	247
Light fuel oil	EURO/l	0.064	0.022	291
Diesel oil	EURO/l	0.325	0.310	105
Petrol	EURO/l	0.590	0.417	141

As can be seen from this table, energy taxes in Finland are very high. In addition, it should be noted that the exemptions and reductions in the Finnish tax system are both smaller in number and magnitude than those presented in the proposal by the European Commission.

6.0   Summary of Experience

- Due to the high tax rate on energy sources, a number of exemptions are needed.

- The lack of an international framework for energy taxes makes the future difficult to predict.

- Institutional factors such as international commitments and a liberalised electricity market have a significant influence on the tax system.

- Energy taxes have to be integrated within the overall tax system and be administered accordingly.

- Frequent changes to the energy tax system reduce its "environmental effect".

- The use of coal has been reduced in Finland as a result of introducing taxes on CO_2 emissions and the carbon content of fuels. Investment in multifuel boilers has increased, which provides opportunities to react rapidly to price changes among different fuels.

- During public discussion of an energy tax, a large number of its intended objectives are often "forgotten".

- Due to the relatively small number of taxpayers and the considerable amount of revenue involved, the present design of the energy tax system is appropriate.

---

[1]   1 EURO = 5.95 Finnish Marks.

ENVIRONMENTAL TAXATION OF TRANSPORT

Stephen Perkins
European Conference of Ministers of Transport

1.0   Introduction[1]

The purpose of this paper is to provide the basis for a discussion of possible directions for the development of transport taxes and charges in China drawing from recent developments in Europe. It first examines the **structure of existing charges** in Europe. Road freight is taken as an example as road haulage is likely to grow rapidly in China over the next decade. Road freight charges are examined in detail in four countries and **subsidies** are evaluated.

Proposals for the **internalisation** of transport's environmental and other social costs in ECMT countries are then presented with a view to informing debate on the issue in China. Finally there are some remarks on the need for a comprehensive approach to environmental protection, particularly in the urban context, based on integrated land use, transport, environmental and health planning together with regulatory and fiscal policy towards the transport sector.

2.0   The Structure of Transport Charges

Environmental taxes on transport fall into two categories: small charges designed to provide funds for environmental programmes or institutions; and rather more significant charges designed to produce incentives for economic actors to behave in ways that reduce damage to the environment. The second category is the subject of this paper. They operate not in a vacuum but in relation to the other costs faced by transport users and transport service providers. Their relationship to the existing structure of taxation is therefore crucial. In order to review the use of environmental taxes in Europe it is therefore important first to have some information on the structure of transport charges in general.

---

[1].   The views expressed in this paper are those of the author and do not necessarily reflect the views of the European Conference of Ministers of Transport (ECMT) or its Member countries.

Table 1 categorises the types of charges and taxes levied on heavy goods transport in 9 European countries. The exercise is more complicated than might at first appear because the purpose of taxes and the amount and destination of the money that they raise changes over time. Hence taxes with similar titles in different countries may operate in very different ways providing very different incentives. Table 1 categorises taxes and charges according to the following sets of criteria, enabling like to be compared with like and separating real from apparent differences in the way taxes are structured:

- point of application
  - vehicle
  - fuel
  - toll
- type of charge
  - fiscal
  - charge related to use
  - environmental charges
- other features
  - geographical relation - territoriality versus nationality
  - destination of revenues - general budget or earmarked
  - exemptions, discounts, etc.

Some of the resulting categories of charge are applied in all countries, for example diesel excise duty. Others exist only in some of the countries studied.

Table 1: Comparison of the Structure of Taxes and Charges on Road Freight Transport

	France	Italy	Austria	Germany	Switzerland	Spain	Sweden	United Kingdom	Netherlands
Registration charges	Charge by formula including engine displacement	IET and APIET	Administration fee	Administration fee	Registration fee	Exemption for HGVs	Tax based on environ-mental criteria	Registration fee	Administration fee
Vehicle tax (national)	Vignette uses above formula but varies by municipality	Auto-radio tax	None	None	Cantonal tax on vehicles	Vehicle tax; trucking tax	None	None	Vehicle tax
Vehicle tax (territorial)	Axle tax	Vehicle tax; surcharge on diesel vehicles	Registration tax	Registration tax differentiated by emissions and noise	None	None	Vehicle tax	Road tax	None
Diesel taxes	TIPP	Excise tax	Diesel tax	Diesel tax	Fuel tax	Fuel tax	Energy tax; CO$_2$ tax	Excise duty	Excise duty; Environmental fuel tax
Earmarked diesel charges	Several funds	-	None	None	Several funds	None	None	None	Stockpiling tax
Road use charges	Motorway tolls	Motorway tolls	StraBA (vignette); tolls on some motorways	Eurovignette	RPL (HGV tax)	Motorway tolls	None	None	Eurovignette
Earmarked charges on road tolls	Policing fund	Central guarantee fund	None	None	None	None	-	-	None
Tunnel / bridge tolls	Tunnels	Tunnels	Tunnels	None	Tunnels	Tunnels	None	Tunnels and bridges	None
VAT on:									
vehicles	20.6%	19%	20%	15%	6.5%	16%	25%	17.5%	17.5%
diesel	20.6%	19%	20%	15%	6.5%	16%	25%	17.5%	17.5%
road charges	5.5-8%	19%	20%	None	None	16%	-	-	-
tunnel / bridge tolls	France-Italy links exempt	Italy-France links exempt	20%	-	None	16%	-	None	-

Source: Federal Swiss Transport Studies Service report - Redevances sur le trafic Routier Lourd en Europe: Comparabilité et Possibilités d'Harmonisation, SET, Federal Department for Transport, Communications, Energy and Environment, Berne, 1998.

Four of these countries are now examined in more detail. Table 2 gives an overview of comparative rates of the major categories of taxation in the four countries, giving a qualitative indication of rates relative to each other.

Table 2: Summary of National Differences in the Structure of Taxation of Road Freight Transport

	Taxes on diesel	Taxes on vehicles	Tolls and use charges	Coverage of expenditure on infrastructure	Tax on capital	Tax on labour
Switzerland	High	Low	Average	Small under-coverage	High	Average
France	Average +	High	High	Balanced	Low	Average
Germany	Average	Average	Average	Over-coverage	Average	High
Netherlands	Average	Average	Average	Large over-coverage	Average	Low

Figure 1 shows the weight of different categories of tax on road freight transport according to revenues generated. The categories range from the most purely fiscal (on vehicle ownership) to the more economic instruments (related to road use). The figure illustrates that excise duties on diesel are the largest source of revenue in all countries. It should be noted that, though the smallest proportion of revenues accounted for by tax on diesel is recorded for France, France has the second highest rate of diesel excise duty among the four countries examined (see Figure 2).

Figure 1 also indicates the much greater significance of tolls in France compared to the other countries and in comparison to the European Union average. This is reflected as a fiscal distortion between the countries. The 28t limit on trucks in Switzerland also introduces a distortion. (Both distortions are apparent in Figure 3).

**Figure 1: Proportion of Revenues Generated
by Different Categories of Tax on Road Freight Transport**

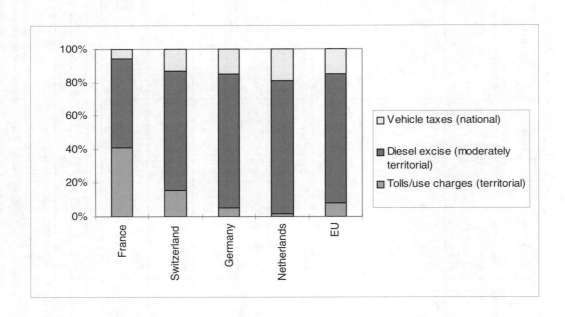

Figure 2: Diesel Excise Duties 1 February, 1998 (ECU / 1000 litre)

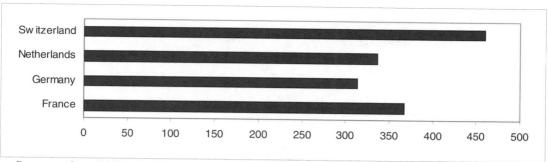

Source: Comité Professionnel de Pétrol, Paris.

2.1 Net Transport Taxes and Subsidies

In order to look at the effects of subsidies on transport, and to evaluate the impact of changes in taxation, e.g. through the introduction of environmental charges, it is useful to calculate the marginal rate of net taxation (taxes and charges minus exemptions and discounts related to marginal costs). This can be calculated by netting the charges paid by typical trucks using a typical international itinerary. This information was compiled in 1998 for the ECMT from the data base of a consultant[2] (in France a 50:50 mix of tolled motorways and un-tolled highways was taken to represent a rough average for the country as a whole). To compare net transport taxes with the other costs of haulage they need to be related to the price of an input to road freight transport. The pre-tax price of diesel was taken as the most suitable input factor. The result of converting net taxation per tkm into an *ad valorem* rate on fuel prices is shown in Figure 3.

---

[2] Professor Pillet of ECOSYS and Geneva Fribourg University, author of the report referenced in Table 1.

Figure 3: Net Taxation in Relation to Pre-Tax Diesel Prices

Country	Net taxes ECU	Pre-tax diesel price ECU	Net effective rates *ad valorem* (%)
Switzerland (28 t)	76.82	0.571	223.75
France	102.92	0.558	306.67
Germany	60.25	0.6632	151.07
Netherlands	58.16	0.655	127

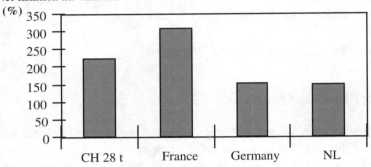

NB: In Figures 3-8, the abbreviations "CH" refers to Switzerland and "NL" refers to the Netherlands

The next step consists of taking the net transport charges, integrated above as a hypothetical tax on diesel, and combining them with net taxes on the other main inputs to road haulage - labour and capital - to derive an effective rate of net tax on the marginal cost of service. The results are shown in figure 4. Note that net transport charges (Figure 3) are highest in France, where they are 100% higher than in Germany and the Netherlands. Factoring in labour and capital charges reverses the trend with the highest marginal effective taxation rate in Germany, 15% higher than France and 25% higher than in the Netherlands.

Figure 4: Marginal Effective Tax Rates

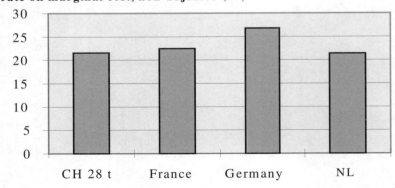

Taxes on transport, labour and capital were combined using a Cobb-Douglas type production function[3] to derive a marginal effective rate of taxation (METR). Data on input shares and on the rates of net taxation of labour and capital in the sector were obtained from studies undertaken by industry associations and government, and from academic comparative taxation studies.

2.2 The Impact on Marginal Effective Taxation of Increasing Excise Duty or Changing Other Taxes

The net effective taxation framework can be used to test the impact of changes in levels of specific taxes (e.g. for the purpose of internalising environmental costs) on overall marginal costs, and therefore profitability. The effects of a 10% and 20% increase in diesel excise duty are given in table 4. Table 5 shows the result for changes in labour taxes.

Table 4: Impact on Current Marginal Effective Taxation of Changes in Fuel Excise Duty

	10% increase in excise duty	20% increase in excise duty
Switzerland	1.7 %	4.0 %
France	1.2 %	3.0 %
Germany	1.7 %	4.0 %
Netherlands	2.5 %	6.0 %

Table 5: Impact on Current Marginal Effective Taxation of Changes in Labour Tax

	10% decrease	20% decrease
Switzerland	- 4.0 %	- 8.0 %
France	- 3.8 %	- 7.6 %
Germany	- 5.0 %	- 10.1 %
Netherlands	- 2.9 %	- 5.7 %

Though the revenues generated by labour taxes in the transport sector are smaller than those from diesel taxes, their specific impact on marginal effective taxation is larger. These results suggest that there is some scope for off-setting possible fuel tax increases, e.g. for the purpose of internalising external costs, with reductions in marginal rates of taxes on labour.

2.3 Intermodal Comparisons

The marginal effective taxation rate framework has also been applied to intermodal comparison of freight transport in a study for the Environment Directorate of the OECD (ENV/EPOC/GEEI/SUBS(98)5). The results are summarised in Figure 5.

---

[3] $METR = (1+\text{rate of tax on capital})^{\text{input share of capital}} \times (1+\text{labour tax})^{\text{input share}} \times (1+\text{diesel tax})^{\text{input share}} - 1$

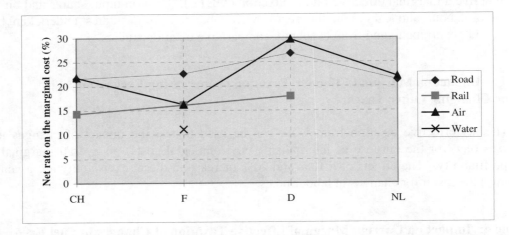

The results suggest significant intermodal distortions of competition in freight markets, with rail and probably inland waterways subject to much lower marginal effective taxation than road and air freight transport. A large national variation in rates of taxation of air freight transport is also apparent. Differences in the coverage of infrastructure costs are likely to exacerbate these differences in taxation significantly. ECMT will examine marginal effective taxation rates for passenger transport in 1998/99.

2.4   Subsidies

It is not only taxes that influence marginal costs. Public expenditure on infrastructure also has very large effects (Figure 6). It is therefore necessary to find some way to factor the level of expenditure into the calculations. A first approximation could be an expression of the difference between transport tax revenues and infrastructure expenditure in terms of marginal costs. Transfers of resources into or out of the sector as a result of under or over-coverage of the costs of providing infrastructure are first compared with net taxation rates as calculated above, and then factored into the marginal effective taxation function through an adjustment to the rate of tax on capital. An adjustment to the rate of capital taxation was preferred to an adjustment of the net taxes on diesel, as infrastructure provision affects the long-run marginal costs of production (as does the cost of capital) more than short-run marginal costs (where the cost of diesel figures prominently).

Figure 6: Rates of Infrastructure Cost Coverage

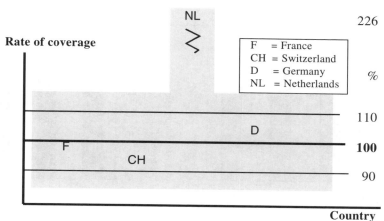

Figure 7 compares the present level of net transport charges and taxes (left hand side) with the level of net taxation that would result in a precise balance between costs and revenues.

Figure 7: Net Transport Taxes as a % of Pre-Tax Diesel Prices with and without Correction for Transfers

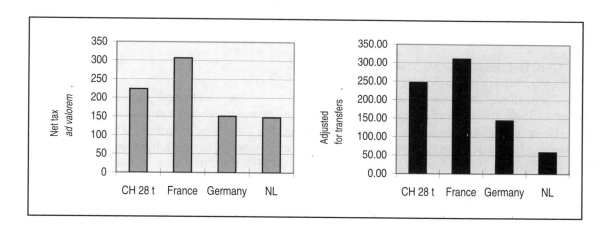

Figure 8 compares current levels of net effective taxation (left hand side) with levels that would result from an adjustment to capital taxation to compensate for existing over and under-coverage of costs.

Figure 8: Marginal Effective Tax Rate Adjusted to Compensate for Existing Transfers

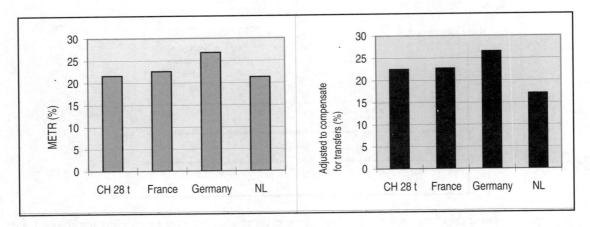

Of the four countries examined the effect of transfers is only really significant in the Netherlands, where a 226% coverage of infrastructure costs translates into a 20% change in marginal effective taxation (in the other countries the over/under-coverage of costs is only around ±5% and the effect on marginal effective taxation negligible). It should be noted that calculations of cost coverage are sensitive to the methodology used in calculating costs and highly sensitive to cost allocation practice (between trucks, passenger cars and other road users). Closer examination of road accounts would be desirable to confirm the differences recorded here for cost coverage.

2.5   Conclusions on the Structure of Taxation

To evaluate the impact on transport sector activities of changes in rates of taxation, it is misleading to look at transport charges in isolation from taxes on labour and capital (compare Figures 3 and 4). The range of difference in net taxation between the countries examined is roughly double when only transport charges are considered. It is reduced to 25% when taxes on labour and capital are factored in. More significantly the ranking of countries from low to high rates of taxation changes greatly.

Fuel taxation is far from the whole picture. A 10% increase in average diesel excise tax results only in increases in marginal effective taxation rates from 1.2 to 2.5%. A 10% change in taxes on labour changes overall taxation 2.9 to 5%. This implies that the real impact of increases in fuel taxes on the marginal costs of road haulage is less than might be expected and that profitability in the road haulage industry of these countries is more sensitive to rates of taxation on labour than to changes in the rate of diesel excise duty.

Introducing charges for the internalisation of transport's external costs in the range indicated by the ECMT Task Force on the Social Costs of Transport (see below) would increase the marginal effective tax rate for road transport by roughly 13% in France, 17% in Switzerland and Germany and 25% in the Netherlands. These changes would probably be large enough to influence behaviour, but are not as large as the existing gap in tax rates between road and rail transport. This confirms the conclusion of the Task Force that the introduction of charges for internalisation can be expected to attenuate growth in road freight transport but not alter modal preferences.

318

3.0   Internalisation Policy

Internalisation is *not,* as so often assumed, a synonym for pricing policy. In theory, setting correct prices might generate the desired result, but the practice is less simple for two main reasons. First, only if the market mechanism is perfect are prices "ideal" instruments; as this is seldom the case, other policy instruments might be preferred. Second, the "perfect" price instrument is often not available in practice; so second- and third-best instruments are used. Moreover, undesired side-effects may need to be corrected with supplementary policy instruments, which usually are not price incentives. For these reasons, all types of policy instruments -- communication, voluntary agreements, regulations, economic instruments -- should be considered for internalisation policy.

In 1998, the ECMT published a report, *Efficient Transport for Europe*, summarising the results of three years of investigation into the external costs of transport by a group of transport economists. The report covers the following ground:

- it discusses the theory of internalisation;

- assesses infrastructure costs;

- examines methodologies for estimating the external costs of accidents and environmental impacts;

- reviews recent estimates of external costs;

- examines instruments that can be used for internalisation;

- and makes recommendations on policies for internalisation in ECMT member countries.

The main policy conclusions of the group are described in the following section.

3.1   Conclusions of ECMT Work on Internalisation

Effective internalisation policies will be based on a mix of regulatory and pricing instruments. Existing regulations could be better enforced, tightened, and combined with incentives that are designed to encourage attainment of stricter second-stage standards. Existing charges and taxes should be differentiated to link them more closely to external costs. Higher use-charges for transport may be appropriate in many cases. Some promising instruments -- electronic km-charges and, most particularly, road pricing -- will take time to develop. Therefore, some priority should be assigned to developing them.

Internalisation has implications for both the structure and the level of prices. For some transport services with high external costs, internalisation is likely to lead to price increases. However, internalisation will primarily involve structuring prices more efficiently, rather than increasing prices overall.

The tax systems of many countries already internalise some external costs, either as a result of overt policy or as an implicit by-product of revenue-raising through taxes specific to transport. Though full internalisation will include higher overall transport charges in many countries, the change for some groups, including many car users, will be small. Very rough estimates suggest that transport costs might increase on average by 15-30% in Europe as a result of full internalisation of the main externalities.

Internalisation does not necessarily result in increased overall taxation. It simply redirects certain financial flows to make economies more efficient, and in the long run more competitive. Revenues arising from internalisation will provide resources for governments to use as they see fit, creating opportunities, *inter alia*, to reduce general taxes or to provide incentives for improved environmental performance.

To be effective, economic instruments require functioning markets. Measures aimed at internalisation will therefore necessitate co-ordination with financing arrangements and subsidies in the transport sector. This should be addressed in a coherent policy for reducing distortions in transport markets.

Internalisation should treat all transport modes and economic sectors equally. For example, charges for CO_2 emissions should be levied at the same unit rate regardless of whether they arise from road, rail, air or waterborne traffic, or indeed from industry or power generation.

Initiatives to internalise social costs should be implemented in ways that minimise disruption to the users and providers of transport services. This is most likely to be achieved if changes in prices are introduced gradually on a clearly defined schedule. Abrupt changes, especially in monetary charges, must be avoided to minimise stress on economic agents. The need for gradual change implies that action to tackle existing and growing distortions must be taken early.

Internalisation instruments should be dynamic; that is, they should take account of expected changes in technology and respond to changes in estimates of external costs. (This implies, for example, that where agreed schedules for tightening emissions standards exist, such as those for passenger cars in the EU, charges should be based on the new standards rather than existing emissions rates.) Changes in levels of external costs over time, together with progress in monitoring and measuring technologies, can also be accommodated in a step-wise internalisation process.

Box 1: Instruments and Approaches for Implementing Cost Internalisation

1. Continued development of dynamic regulatory standards for vehicles and fuels; in particular this entails raising emissions standards for light duty goods vehicles (vans) to the levels for passenger cars.

2. Strengthening of laws related to road safety, and their enforcement, and development of preventive measures based on education and policing.

3. Development of vehicle insurance systems or surcharges to increase a) the variabilisation of premiums, b) their relationship to driver safety records and c) cost coverage.

4. Increases in fuel charges to address a substantial part of external costs until general road pricing becomes available.

5. Differentiation of annual vehicle taxes to accord more closely with air and noise emissions factors.

6. Introduction of congestion charging, especially where tolls already exist, to improve traffic flows on trunk roads.

7. *Ex ante* negotiation and contracting of public service obligations, linking them to services rather than modes.

8. Phased increases in charges for the use of rail infrastructure (except in the relatively rare cases where this has already been done).

9. Phasing out of distortions to competition arising from mode-specific tax advantages (e.g. in air transport where ticket sales are exempt from Value Added Tax).

10. Development of more differentiated use-charge systems employing electronic km-charges[4] (axle weight/distance charges) for heavy goods vehicles and the gradual introduction of road pricing systems in metropolitan areas and on national/international networks. Experience from pilot cities should indicate which instruments road pricing can replace to best advantage.

---

[4] Assuming technological development and testing of electronic tolling systems continues to progress.

In timing the introduction of internalisation instruments there should be some linkage with productivity increases in rail services. The relationship is twofold. Internalisation could spur urgently needed productivity improvements, but implementation should be co-ordinated to avoid modal split changes that would be uneconomic in the long term. Under-coverage of costs on the railways is significant and the increase in charges to cover deficits[5] will have a greater impact on railways than the increase in charges to cover environmental and accident externalities will have on road use. This will be compounded by labour and other rigidities that make adjustments through increases in productivity slower in the railways.

Independent of the implementation of new internalisation instruments, emphasis should be placed on enforcement of existing legislation, especially in regard to road safety and road freight transport measures (maximum driving hours, health and safety regulations, etc.). It does not make much sense to add legislation if more could be achieved by improving enforcement of existing laws.

To recapitulate the twin elements of the fiscal part of internalisation policies are:

- variabilisation of charges, i.e. putting an emphasis on charges related to use (fuel taxes, tolls, electronic distance charges or road pricing);

- and differentiation of fixed charges.

4.0   Relevance for China

These conclusions point not only to the direction for change in the structure of taxation in transport but also underline the relationship between new measures and existing charges and regulations. As far as taxation is concerned the basic objectives are the introduction of incentives to reduce environmental and accident externalities and reduction of inter-modal distortions. This is in addition to the target set for the coverage of infrastructure costs. The last two objectives are fundamental because, if existing distortions are large, adjustments to taxation at the margin (in the interests of environmental protection) are likely to be inadequate to alter behaviour.

4.1   Infrastructure Costs

The paper in this volume entitled *"Taxation and the Environment in China: Practice and Perspectives"* suggests that although a vehicle use tax exists in China, the revenues it raises are insignificant when compared to the cost of road infrastructure provision. It also reports significant railway deficits. This suggests that the first step in developing an efficient transport tax system that also provides incentives to protect the environment in China is to ensure a closer coverage of infrastructure costs through the charging system. This is not to say that in specific cases modest tax incentives can not be effective, e.g. in influencing the choice of fuel or vehicle purchased under present conditions, they can. But for encouraging an efficient development of the transport sector overall, a closer relationship between costs and charges will be important. Historically, earmarked road funds have been an important source of financing for major expansions of European road systems.

---

[5]   Efficient pricing should be based on marginal social costs, which in railways will normally not result in full cost coverage given the declining costs that characterise railways. In practice, however, full or partial cost recovery targets are likely to be imposed on railways as they compete with other public sectors (health, education, etc.) for public finance, making it difficult for governments to cover the entire deficit.

In designing new infrastructure charges a number of factors should be considered. From a policy point of view, short-term marginal costs are of interest as they represent the lower limit of the infrastructure costs which should be covered by variable charges (e.g. through taxes on fuel, or on ticket sales for rail). It is important to distinguish between infrastructure with congestion problems and infrastructure with spare capacity. Efficient pricing implies that long-term marginal social costs — including future discounted capacity costs — should be charged for users of fully utilised or congested infrastructure. But when capacity is far from fully utilised and capacity costs are zero, only short-term marginal costs (including renewal) should be charged.

On average, roughly half of infrastructure costs relate directly to actual use of the road in uncongested circumstances. The other half of infrastructure costs can be considered fixed and not dependent on road use (levied for example through an annual road tax). The interest on invested capital, for instance, has to be paid whether the road is used or not. It is not efficient to make road users pay for fixed costs via use-charges. To achieve full coverage of infrastructure costs it is better to use fixed charges or a lump sum charge such as a vehicle tax. A fixed charge can be regarded as a ticket to enter the road network. (In uncongested circumstances marginal costs will be lower than average costs, and the fixed charge will be required to ensure that costs are covered).

Thus, in general, a combination of use-charges and fixed charges is needed to achieve both economic efficiency and a fair allocation of costs. In most countries the split between use-charges and fixed charges does not reflect the ratio between the two types of costs. The level of use-charges generally is too low and does not cover marginal infrastructure costs. Conversely, the level of fixed charges is often too high, at least where road traffic pays fully for infrastructure costs. A shift away from fixed charges towards use-charges is generally required. Such a shift, often called "variabilisation", will increase the efficiency of use of the available road infrastructure.

Projects for new infrastructure to open up isolated regions pose the problem of how much to charge for their use, for example in the case of a new toll road or section of railway. To make the project economic, charges might have to be set at such a high level that usage would be severely curtailed. In a large network, cross-subsidies can be used to keep down the level of charges on the new route, with the implicit assumption that the overall benefits in terms of regional development for the area served by the new route outweigh the increase in charge levels across the network needed to pay for the project. Where possibilities of cross-subsidy from tolls or fees for infrastructure use do not exist, governments must provide a direct subsidy for expansion of infrastructure. However, the cost of the subsidy can be passed on to transport users as a whole, for example through an increase in fuel tax or annual road tax (this is not ideal in terms of relating costs to use but at least ensures overall cost overage). The cost-benefit appraisal of the project should then include the socio-economic dimension, and weigh the economic benefits, including in terms of regional development, with the costs of the project including environmental impacts.

The variable part of infrastructure charges can be levied through tolls or fuel charges. Tolls can provide clearer signals to users on costs but have the disadvantage of being more costly to operate and difficult to apply to networks other than trunk roads, bridges and tunnels. Public acceptance is problematic when tolls are introduced on existing roads, but much less of a problem when the public perceive they are getting something new (e.g. a new motorway) so long as the original financing of the project is not perceived to have come from some other levy, such as local municipal taxes. Tolls also have the disadvantage of discouraging use of the road when alternative routes exist. This can divert traffic on to crowded and more dangerous by-roads. In European countries where tolled motorway networks are extensive, regulations to prevent trucks using alternative lower grade routes are enforced -- one of the objectives of providing the high grade motorways is to reduce traffic accidents. In China equity issues will be important -- only a small proportion of the population may be able to afford tolls. At the same time only a small proportion of population can afford cars. There may be an opportunity to introduce tolls as a standard system before car ownership becomes more generalised. Separating different classes of user - trucks, agricultural vehicles, cars, motorcycles, cycles, pedestrians - in the interests of safety will be a more important issue in China. Tolls have the advantage of being able to be varied by time of day/season to manage congestion.

For both tolls and annual fees it is important to relate them closely to the different costs that different types of vehicles impose in terms of wear and tear. In many, but not all European countries, heavy lorries have been undercharged relative to passenger cars.

Using tax on fuels to cover infrastructure costs is a possibility China might consider. Diesel has been taxed at lower rates in most European countries than gasoline as a way to assist hauliers and other commercial vehicle users. Once introduced this distortion is difficult to remove, although the United Kingdom has recently succeeded in eliminating the difference. The analysis in the first part of this paper suggests that preferential tax treatment in other areas (labour or capital) would be a more effective way to provide support to parts of the transport sector when deemed desirable, whilst avoiding distortion in fuel pricing. (This argument also applies to increasing the level of annual road fees or introducing tolls where public authorities may be inclined to avoid introducing charges that hauliers will pass on, resulting in pressure on inflation, unless they receive some form of compensation). The conclusion is that less inefficiency and less environmental impact is likely to result from subsidies to vehicle purchases or to labour costs than subsidies to the use of vehicles.

4.2   Environmental Costs

Many environmental externalities are also reasonably closely related to fuel use, and the ECMT work concluded that in the short term fuel taxes were the main fiscal approach to internalisation in view of the simplicity and relatively low cost of application. CO_2 emissions are directly related to fuel consumption, making fuel tax an ideal instrument for responding to climate change concerns.

Fuel quality standards and vehicle emissions standards constitute the main policy instrument to reduce air pollution from road traffic. This type of direct government regulation, which forced the introduction of catalytic converters on gasoline cars, has been very effective in Europe. Specific emissions have been reduced by around 80% and the amount of air pollution per vehicle-kilometre will likely be further sharply reduced in the coming decade. An even further reduction is technically feasible, but would require stricter emissions standards than those currently foreseen in the EU. Challenging standards form an effective way to force technical improvements. Standards for vehicle emissions and fuel quality also constitute an effective internalisation instrument. They make vehicle owners and fuel users pay for their cleaner fuels and vehicles, and reduce the environmental damage caused to others. The economic value of the remaining emissions will be rather low.

Distance driven, which at least in part corresponds to fuel consumption, is a factor in NOx, CO, VOC, Benzene and Particulate emissions (and in accident rates) so it is appropriate to include an element in fuel charges for internalisation of their residual costs. Differentiation of fixed charges (purchase taxes or annual vehicle or road fees) should be used as a complement to fuel charges to account for differences in specific emissions according to vehicle type, fuel used, engine size, presence of catalytic exhaust controls etc.

Several forms of direct government intervention can reduce noise nuisance. One is setting proper vehicle emissions standards. Measures affecting roads can also be taken, such as "quiet" road surfacing and noise screens. Traffic management can reduce noise nuisance, too: constant traffic flow and lower speeds both result in lower noise levels. Another option is to create bypasses around noise-sensitive areas. These options, however, will not reduce noise nuisance to the optimum and therefore will not result in full internalisation. Price incentives will need to be used as well, although none of the available or potential economic instruments can generate incentives corresponding to all of the various factors that influence noise. Fuel charges and a differentiated vehicle tax could be applied to cars, vans and trucks. For motorbikes effective enforcement of exhaust noise regulations is paramount.

4.3   Size of Environmental Charges

Because no markets exist for pollution or accidents, no market prices have been established for their social costs and shadow prices have to be estimated as a basis for designing internalisation policies. The core of the exercise is to establish what the price would be if a market existed. There is a large body of economic literature on theoretical and empirical approaches to estimating shadow prices. Most external costs are location-specific. Their valuation also depends on factors such as levels of income and cultural aspirations. Valuations of external costs are not easy to transfer between widely different countries and require at the very least a recalculation to account for purchasing power parities. Estimates for China therefore need to be established on the basis of Chinese data (not available to the author).

Table 6 compares estimates of average use charges for Europe corresponding to anticipated marginal costs with current average fuel charges. This assumes that the non-pricing elements of the ten-point strategy outlined earlier in Box 1 are also implemented. This table is presented only to give readers a notion of the magnitude of tax adjustments under consideration in Europe. They are in no way indicative of the level of charges that might be appropriate in China.

Table 6: Estimates of Average Use-Charges* Corresponding to Expected Future Marginal Costs (Excluding Congestion)
ECU/v-km

Cost component	Passenger car			Freight (truck, van)
	Gasoline	Diesel	LPG	Diesel
Infrastructure	0.023	0.023	0.023	0.041
Congestion	-	-	-	-
Accidents	0.028	0.028	0.028	0.028
Climate change	0.009	0.009	0.008	0.025
Air pollution	0.002	0.004	0.002	0.024
Noise nuisance	0.005	0.005	0.005	0.023
Total	**0.066**	**0.067**	**0.065**	**0.142**
Average fuel charge in EU countries, January 1996	0.041	0.022	n.a.	0.067

* Assuming the non-pricing instruments described in Box 1 are also implemented.
Source: ECMT.

5.0 Policy Instruments for Urban Areas and Subsidies for Public Transport

It is important to note that urban air and noise emissions have a greater impact on human health than do the same emissions in rural areas. First, more people are exposed in cities; second, the concentration of pollutants in the air is higher in urban areas, and the impact often rises more than proportionately to the concentration of emissions. Hence, the values attached to some pollutants ought to be higher in urban areas than in rural ones. Accordingly, the "price" per kilogram of (for instance) NO_x emitted in cities estimated by the ECMT is ECU 8, or twice the level in rural areas. Furthermore, for particulates only an urban price was estimated: ECU 70/kg (in rural areas the price is assumed to be zero).

Specifically urban forms of air pollution can be internalised only through urban policy instruments. Urban road pricing is one possibility. Cities might also be allowed to set emissions standards that are stricter than the general standards, requiring (for instance) use of so-called "city diesel"; another option is allowing only cleaner vehicles in the city centre. Another possibility is to tighten general emissions standards for vehicles driven mainly in urban areas, such as vans. Fuel taxes, the main economic instrument available for internalisation in the immediate future, is particularly unsuited to addressing the urban problem -- the very place where environmental impacts are highest.

In urban areas transport demand has to be carefully managed to avoid detriment to the environment, quality of life and public finances. Adequate access to opportunities for work, housing shopping, entertainment etc. are fundamental to economic growth and social welfare. Motorised transport can significantly expand these opportunities, but an optimal mix of non-motorised, public and private transport can result in much better performance than unmanaged growth of private transport. The fundamental factor is the integration of land use planning with transport planning and ensuring adequate environmental and public health impact assessment of these plans. The pattern of urban development that results from zoning laws-granting of permits to construct certain types of buildings in certain areas - has enormous impacts on the transport requirements of urban and suburban areas (for example a shopping development to be opened on the outskirts of Manchester, England in 1998 will generate an estimated 6 billion car and bus trips a year). Similarly the planning of transport systems has a major impact on the value of land and property. Planning one without the other usually results in large wastage of resources and problems of congestion, intrusion, community separation and environmental damage.

Few public mass transport systems have been developed without government financial intervention. Seeking to eliminate subsidies to public transport (as appears from the background conference papers to be one of the objectives of current transport policy in China) would probably be counter-productive. Control of costs, by putting pressure on the operators of public transport systems to reduce costs (and avoid simply passing on subsidies in the form of higher than average wages or larger than necessary workforces or general inefficiency), is essential. But without subsidy almost all mass-transit systems in Europe would not exist (private networks that make profits without subsidy do exist, but the profitable part of the business is in property development along rail lines rather than in transport alone). Of course, if tariffs for urban rail systems are set too low they may contribute to promoting inefficient patterns of urban sprawl.

In regulating public transport systems, including the national railways, the key to controlling finance is transparency. The public service functions required of railways, bus services, etc., must be identified and paid for by the state under a contractual arrangement that makes clear the services purchased and the compensation to be paid. Similarly, infrastructure investments assessed as beneficial by government but uncommercial by public transport operators should be funded with public money. Beyond these contracted public services, operators should be required to run their business on a commercial basis in the interests of economic efficiency. Making public service requirements transparent in this way should prevent the accumulation of uncovered deficits which tend to accumulate as a result of political objectives being imposed on public services without corresponding compensation (this has characterised most European railways in the past). Elimination of deficit financing, rather than elimination of subsidies, is the appropriate objective for public transport services in China.

OECD PUBLICATIONS, 2, rue André-Pascal, 75775 PARIS CEDEX 16
PRINTED IN FRANCE
(97 99 07 1 P) ISBN 92-64-17092-8 – No. 50747 1999